The Acquisition of German Modal Particles

Linguistic Insights

Studies in Language and Communication

Edited by Maurizio Gotti,
University of Bergamo

Volume 10

PETER LANG
Bern · Berlin · Bruxelles · Frankfurt am Main · New York · Oxford · Wien

Martina Möllering

The Acquisition of German Modal Particles

A Corpus-Based Approach

PETER LANG
Bern · Berlin · Bruxelles · Frankfurt am Main · New York · Oxford · Wien

Bibliographic information published by Die Deutsche Bibliothek
Die Deutsche Bibliothek lists this publication in the Deutsche Nationalbibliografie; detailed bibliographic data is available on the Internet at ‹http://dnb.ddb.de›.

British Library and Library of Congress Cataloguing-in-Publication Data:
A catalogue record for this book is available from *The British Library,* Great Britain, and from *The Library of Congress,* USA

ISSN 1424-8689
ISBN 3-03910-043-2
US-ISBN 0-8204-6273-X

Hochfeldstrasse 32, Postfach 746, CH-3000 Bern 9, Switzerland
info@peterlang.com, www.peterlang.com, www.peterlang.net

Printed in Germany

Table of Contents

Acknowledgements

I wish to thank Professor Christopher N. Candlin, who kindled my interest in pragmatics when I was a student in the Masters in Applied Linguistics program at Macquarie University, Sydney, and who has been an inspiring and invaluable mentor throughout the process of research and writing.

I am also indebted to my former colleague in German Studies at Macquarie University, Dr Nic Witton, who first introduced me to corpus linguistics and thus provided the seeding ground for the work presented in this study, and to Dr Claudia Benholz at the University of Essen, who was an unfailing source of hard-to-get copies of German publications on modal particles.

In addition, my thanks go to colleagues at the 'Institut für deutsche Sprache' in Mannheim for providing me with access to their databases and comprehensive library facilities and for many fruitful discussions in the early stages of my research.

1. Introduction

> *[...] the analysis of discourse is, necessarily, the analysis of language in use. As such, it cannot be restricted to the description of linguistic forms independent of the purposes or functions which these forms are designed to serve in human affairs.*
>
> *(Brown & Yule 1983: 1)*

Discourse particles occur in a variety of languages, a fact well documented for example in a special issue of *Multilingua* (Abraham 1991), and they have been analysed in great detail for the English language by Schiffrin (1987). German modal particles, which are occasionally discussed under the general heading of discourse particles (see e.g. Abraham 1991), have attracted a particularly strong research interest (see e.g. the compilations of scholarly articles in Weydt 1977, 1979, 1983 and 1989) and have been considered within different theoretical frameworks. In the past decade, a number of monographs following a contrastive approach (Beerboom 1991: German/ Spanish, Liedke 1994: German/Modern Greek, Masi 1996: German/Italian, Nekula 1996: German/Czech, Feyrer 1998: German/ French, May 2000: German/Spanish) have extended the body of research in this area as have studies, which look at modal particles in the context of grammaticalization (e.g. Diewald 1997, Molnar 2002). Modal particles are increasingly being considered in the field of teaching German as a second/foreign language (see e.g. compilation of articles in Weydt 1981; Rösler 1982, 1983; Busse 1992; Luchtenberg 1987, 1989; Jiang 1993; May 2000) and the present study aims at contributing to this area of research by suggesting an approach to the analysis and teaching of modal particles which draws on a number of theoretical frameworks and uses corpus linguistics as a methodology. The introduction briefly outlines the topic and scope of the study.

In her dissertation on German modal particles as a teaching and learning problem in the context of Chinese learners of German, Jiang writes in 1993: 101:

> Im Bereich der Modalpartikeln z.B., die man immer mehr in den neuen Lehrwerken vorfinden kann, funktioniert ihre bisherige Lernmethode [die Lernmethode chinesischer Deutschlerner] so gut wie überhaupt nicht. Die Studenten können diese nirgendwo als Lerngegenstand einorden weder in der Form von Vokabeln noch als grammatische Elemente. Weil in den meisten Lehrwerken gezielte Übungen fehlen, die diese schwer vermittelbare Wortklasse als Lernziel berücksichtigen, und weil die Lerner mit den Modalpartikeln weder mit Hilfe eines Wörterbuchs noch eines Grammatikbuchs etwas anfangen können, wenden sie sich bestenfalls dann an ihren Lehrer, der ihnen meist keine zufriedenstellenden Antworten geben kann.

She identifies a number of contributing factors which render the learning of German modal particles difficult in a GFL (German as a foreign language) context:

- Students are used to learning grammar and vocabulary; modal particles seem to fall into neither one of those categories.
- Most GFL textbooks do not provide exercises which target modal particles as learning objectives[1].
- Modal particles form a word class which is difficult to teach; students find help neither in dictionaries nor in grammars.
- Teachers do not provide satisfying explanations either.

Taking the difficulties outlined in Jiang's (1993) assessment as a starting point, this study explores the challenges German modal particles present to learners of German[2] (Chapter two), evaluates learning and teaching approaches to modal particles as reported in the relevant literature (Chapter three) and develops a corpus-based approach to teaching modal particles (Chapters four and five).

1 Jiang (1993: 100) lists the texts "Stufen", "Sprachbrücke" and "Sprachkurs Deutsch" as exceptions.

2 The distinction between German as foreign language and German as a second language will only be mentioned when differences in those types of acquisition are being addressed.

In order to discuss the challenges modal particles provide to learners of German, the complexity of those particles needs to be addressed.

In this study, I discuss the complexity on a number of levels. The distinction of modal particles as a word class, as it has been considered in the relevant literature, is reviewed critically in order to establish the difficulties which the analyst as well as the learner is faced with when approaching the words which are commonly referred to as modal particles. The fact that modal particles have at least one homonym in another function class (for a discussion see Chapter 2) makes them difficult to analyse and arguably even harder to learn. As many particles occur in a variety of functions, criteria such as position within the sentence play a role in determining whether a particle occurs as modal particle, as connective, adverb of time etc. The meaning of modal particles is dependent on context and co-text, and features of both need to be taken into account to interpret meaning. When considering the meaning of modal particles in context a number of function aspects are at play: as well as semantic and syntactic aspects, pragmatic and discursive aspects need to be taken into account. I explore the syntactic, pragmatic and discursive aspects of German modal particles – based on the existing literature on particles (Chapter 2) and based on corpus data (examples in Chapter 2, Chapter 5) – as well as their acquisition by non-native speakers (Chapter 3).

The analysis presented here shows that German modal particles fulfill pragmatic functions in that they reveal the speaker's attitudes about the context and/or seek to affect the listener's perspective of it but that they also perform discursive functions in that they help to create coherence (e.g. Schiffrin 1987) in a text. Modal particles may connect an utterance with its context of conversation and argumentation and thus they can influence the course of a conversation indicating that they not only relate to a particular speech act but also to the succession of moves in a conversation. For a discussion of the pragmatic and discursive functions modal particles perform, the terminology used in this study is derived from functionally oriented approaches to linguistics, such as pragmatics (e.g. Leech 1983, Levinson 1983, Mey 1993) and discourse analysis (e.g. Brown & Yule 1983, Coulthard 1985, Schiffrin 1994, McCarthy

& Carter 1994) as well as the systemic functional approach to grammar (Halliday 1985, 1994).

The prolific research into modal particles has led to an increased interest in modal particles as part of the acquisition process. In Chapter 3, a rationale for the teaching of modal particles is outlined on the basis of research into cross-cultural communication and interlanguage pragmatics (e.g. Rose & Kasper 2001, Kasper 2001). Studies on the acquisition of modal particles in instructed and uninstructed environments are critically evaluated and related to an assessment of selected teaching materials on modal particles.

In this study, the learning and teaching of modal particles is considered in the context of communicative competence, i.e. "what a speaker needs to know about how a language is used in particular situations for effective and appropriate communication" (McCarthy & Carter 1994: 172), which "entails a variety of abilities concerned with the use and interpretation of language in contexts. [...] It includes listener's ability to get past the language and understand the speaker's real intentions, especially when these intentions are not directly conveyed in the forms." (Bialystok 1993: 43). German modal particles have an important role to play in effective and appropriate communication and they may serve to convey the speaker's real intentions. The ability to understand their meaning in context therefore indicates a level of pragmatic competence on the part of the learner.

Based on the premise that 'consciousness-raising' (e.g. Rutherford 1987), which relates to the refinement of learners' metacommunicative awareness, could be an effective approach to teaching modal particles (see Chapter 3 for a discussion) I present corpus-based analyses of selected modal particles and examples of how these analyses might be utilised for the creation of teaching materials. The analyses of individual modal particles and the teaching materials based on these analyses are derived from concordances, a procedure of organising text for analysis in the field of corpus linguistics which is increasingly applied in language teaching (e.g. Tribble & Jones 1990, Thurstun & Candlin 1997, Wichmann *et al.* 1997, Rüschoff & Wolff 1999).

The main body of the study then deals with a corpus-based approach to German modal particles. In Chapter 4, the principles and methodologies of corpus-based research are outlined to provide a basis for discussion of a quantitative analysis of particle frequency in corpora of German. Based on the premise that modal particles appear with greater frequency in spoken rather than in written German (Rudolph 1991; for a discussion see Chapter 2.6), the analysis is limited to four corpora of spoken German:

- Freiburger Korpus (FKO)
- Dialogstrukturenkorpus (DSK)
- PFEFFER-Korpus (PFE)
- a collection of telephone conversations published by Brons-Albert (1984) (BRO)

FKO, DSK and PFE are held by the Institut für deutsche Sprache (IDS) in Mannheim (http://www.ids-mannheim.de, 2001). All three corpora can be accessed via a data retrieval system – COSMAS – developed at the IDS[3]. For the purpose of this study, the printed texts of the BRO data were scanned into computer-readable files to make them accessible for concordancing procedures. The first step in the process of data analysis was to establish the frequency of particles which could potentially function as modal particles in the four corpora. In the present study, particle frequency is addressed in two steps: first, the overall frequency of particles in the corpora of spoken German is established in order to determine how salient each particle would be for a learner of German (see discussion of grading criteria in Chapter 3). A subset of the occurrences of a select group of particles (EBEN, NUR, DENN, SCHON, DOCH, MAL, ABER, AUCH, JA) is then analysed qualitatively on the basis of the BRO data. The qualitative analysis provides a distinction between frequency of occurrences in modal particle function and other functions.

Chapter 5 presents the corpus-based analyses of modal particles selected on the basis of the quantitative analysis and provides examples of teaching materials based on these analyses.
The qualitative analysis shows that each particle has to be understood in relation to syntactic and semantic, as well as pragmatic and

3 For the analysis presented here, COSMAS version R.1.3-1 was used (al-Wadi 1994).

discursive aspects, but that one or more perspectives are more highlighted in different situations; for example, the discursive aspect of the particle JA is particularly salient in the data because of the specific nature of telephone conversations (for a detailed discussion see Chapter 5.10). Not all particles appear in the same contexts and co-texts and the collocation of one particle with another (e.g. JA AUCH, SCHON MAL; see Chapter 5) impact on the meaning of both.

This complex interplay of co-text, context and particle meaning is difficult to grasp for learners of German and they therefore need tasks which make them aware of the difficulties at hand and provide them with knowledge about possible decodings. The limited ranges of speech events which learners are exposed to in classroom discourse do not provide enough input on modal particles to lead to an understanding of their meaning. An important factor in teaching modal particles is therefore the exposure of learners to particles in various contexts and the focussing of learners' attention on their meaning in those contexts. It is the contention of this study, that corpus examples are effective in doing so as they expose learners to the type of language they will encounter in real communicative situations (McEnery & Wilson 1996: 120). Collocations, involving both grammar and lexis, have an important place in language pedagogy as they can be identified empirically by the methodologies developed in corpus analysis (Kennedy 1998: 289). The analysis of real-language data unveiled structures, patterns and predictable features relating to the various usages of particles and formed the basis for sample worksheets for learners of German.. Their possible application is discussed critically (see Chapter 5.11) and it is hoped that they will provide a useful extension to the existing teaching materials on modal particles.

2. Identifying modal particles in German

There is a general principle in language, that the easier a thing is to recognize, the more trivial it is likely to be; the outward sign of a semantically significant category is usually not clear-cut, and many factors may have to be taken into consideration in identifying it.
(Halliday 1994: xxxiii)

2.1 Introduction

Particles of the modal particle type (see discussion below), which were typical for Classical Greek (von der Gabelentz 1891 in Coseriu 1980: 199), are prevalent in West-Germanic languages: in Dutch, Frisian and German (e.g. de Vriendt *et al.* 1991, for a comparison between German and Dutch see e.g. Westheide 1991, Abraham 1991a for the 'middle-field' (see pages 17 & 22) link between German, Frisian and Dutch). Research interest in German modal particles arose in the late 1960's with the advent of a more pragmatically oriented approach to linguistics. They started to shed their image as superfluous, stylistically dubious "fillers" [Füllwörter; Flickwörter] that had to be avoided in "proper German" (cf. Busse 1992) and since Kriwonossow's (1963, first published in 1977) and Weydt's (1969) seminal studies on German modal particles, a large body of work on the subject has emerged. In those publications, different terms are used to name the words that are here described as 'modal particles'. Thus, we find, for example: "flavouring words" [Würzwörter] (cf. Paneth 1981), "intentional particles" [Intentionale Partikeln] (Rall 1981), "pragmatic particles" (Held 1983), "discourse particles" (Abraham 1991b) and "toning particles" [Abtönungspartikeln] (cf.

Weydt 1981, Helbig 1994), the term which together with the German "Modalpartikel" (cf. Weinrich 1993) is most commonly used[4].
In a number of publications (cf. Dalmas 1990, 1992; Rudolph 1991), however, the term 'particle' (German: Partikel) is used without further specification.

2.2 Modal particles as a category

Although these different labels might seem arbitrary at a first glance, they are each motivated by the particular underlying theoretical approach to studying the words they subsume. Their common denominator, the term 'particle', stems from a structural approach to categorising the various parts of speech into word classes where the category first appears in the writings of early Greek linguists (Weydt & Ehlers 1987). The classical distinction of 'word classes' is based on inflexional properties of words (cf. Halliday 1994: 28) and according to this morphological criterion for classification the term 'particle' is often used to refer to 'non-declinables', i.e. in German the large group of words that cannot be considered as part of the word classes noun, adjective, verb, article or pronoun. In this sense, 'particles' may be adverbs, conjunctions, prepositions, interjections (Helbig 1994) sentence adverbs ("Satzadverbien", "Modalwörter" in Thurmair 1989) and 'particles in a narrower sense'. It is here where the first problem with this type of categorisation appears, as the same label is used on different levels of description as the following diagram shows:

4 See Thurmair 1989: 3 for further terminology.

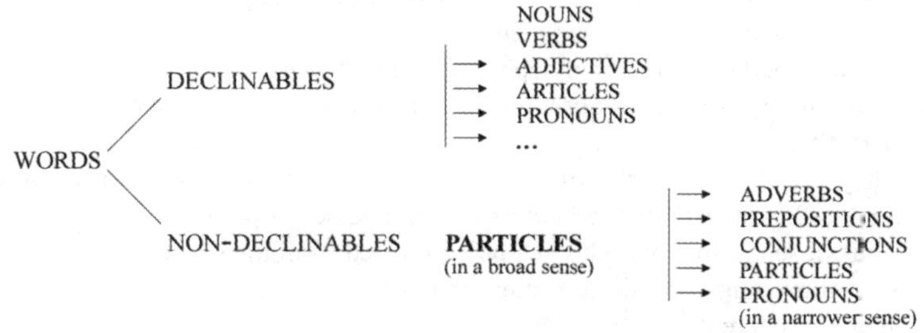

Figure 1

Whereas the criterion 'declinability' for the broadest definition of particles as non-declinables is evident, the narrower definition is not quite so distinctly outlined. 'Particles in the narrower sense' seem to be defined mainly by what they are not, that is to say prepositions, conjunctions, adverbs etc. (see also the criticism in Thurmair 1989: 8). It is here that the second major problem with a word class approach to particles occurs. A word like ABER, for example, which is a particle in the broader sense as it cannot be inflected, can be categorised as a member of the word class 'conjunction' as well as of the class 'particles in a narrower sense', specifically as modal particle (e.g. Bublitz 1977) depending on the linguistic context it occurs in (see more detailed discussion below). Thus, in a word class definition, the words considered as modal particles all have at least one homonym in another class or subclass, depending on the model of categorisation.[5]

Not surprisingly, the categorisation of particles into one or more word classes as described above has been discussed critically (e.g. Helbig 1989). In the literature on the topic under discussion the term 'particle' is commonly used in its narrower sense, excluding the other groups of non-declinables. Helbig (1994: 21ff) argues that there are certain characteristics which enable a distinction between the word class particles (in the narrower sense, see Figure 1) and other word classes of non-declinables. He describes these as follows:

5 See, however, Meibauer (1994) and Autenrieth (2002) who use the concept of 'Heterosemie' in their approach to classifying modal particles.

1) Particles cannot be independent sentence elements.
2) Because particles are not independent sentence elements they can usually not occupy first position, i.e. they cannot occupy the position in front of the finite verb in a German main clause.[6]
3) Because particles are not independent sentence elements they cannot stand alone in answering a question (but compare further below: answering particles).
4) They do not change the truth value of statements but add information of another kind which differs between the subclasses of particles.
5) Thus, it seems that particles can be eliminated from the sentences they occur in without rendering those sentences ungrammatical syntactically or losing semantic content.
6) Nevertheless, particles do modify (for a discussion see further below) an utterance partly semantically, partly pragmatically. How they do this and which parts of the sentence they modify (parts of it or the sentence as a whole) differs between the various subclasses of particles.

The word class 'particle' in the narrower sense is then seen to include subcategories, 'modal particles' being one of them. The following subcategories have been described (Helbig 1994: 31):

PARTICLES (in a narrower sense)	→ MODAL PARTICLES	(Abtönungspartikel)
	→ SCALAR/FOCUS PARTICLES	(Gradpartikel)
	→ COMPARATIVE PARTICLES	(Steigerungspartikeln)
	→ ANSWERING PARTICLES	(Antwortpartikeln)
	→ NEGATION PARTICLES	(Negationspartikeln)
	→ INFINITIVE PARTICLES	(Infinitivpartikeln)

Figure 2

Thurmair (1989: 9) presents the notion of 'function' as underlying her use of the term 'modal particle':

> Die Partikeln im gesamten sind als Wortart zu sehen; die einzelnen Subklassen dagegen nicht als Wortarten, sondern als Funktionen, in denen bestimmte Partikeln auftreten können. Damit ist auch leichter zu erklären, daß viele Partikeln polyfunktional sind, d.h. in mehreren Funktionen auftreten können... Wenn im folgenden also von bestimmten Partikelgruppen die Rede ist, so soll damit immer eine bestimmte Funktion gemeint sein, die eine bestimmte Gruppe

6 For a more detailed discussion of German sentence structure and different positions ('fields') within the sentence see further below.

> von Partikeln übernehmen kann. Wenn also z.B. von der Modalpartikel doch die Rede ist, soll immer die Partikel doch in Modalpartikel-Funktion (im Unterschied z.B. zur Partikel doch in Konjunktions-Funktion) gemeint sein.

She identifies particles as being 'polyfunctional' and describes their 'occurrence in different functions', providing as an example the use of the particle DOCH as modal particle and as conjunction. However, the use of the word 'function' in this context needs to be clarified and in order to do so it is necessary to examine the characteristics of her use of the term 'modal particle function'.

The starting point for Thurmair's (ibid.) definition is the broad description of particles as 'non-declinables' as outlined above (Figure 1). The term 'function' as used here in "Modalpartikel-Funktion" goes back to another more traditional twofold division of words into 'content words' and 'function words', as outlined for example by Richards *et al.* (1985: 61):

> Words can be divided into two classes: content words and function words. Content words are words which refer to a thing, quality, state or action and which have meaning (lexical meaning) when the words are used alone. Content words are mainly nouns, verbs, adjectives and adverbs, eg book, run, musical, quickly. Function words are words which have little meaning on their own, but which show grammatical relationships in and between sentences (grammatical meaning). Conjunctions, prepositions, articles, eg and, to, the are function words.

or Bußmann (1990: 260):

> Funktionswort:
>
> 1) Bezeichnung für sprachliche Elemente, die primär grammatische (anstelle von lexikalischer) Bedeutung tragen und vor allem syntaktisch-strukturelle Funktionen erfüllen, wie → Artikel, Pronomen, Präposition, Konjunktion
> 2) Partikel

Whereas the definition given by Richards *et al.* (1985) names grammatical function only, the definition by Bußmann (1990) indicates that there are function words, namely particles[7], which cannot be subsumed under the heading of syntactical-structural (→ grammatical) function[8]. Although no further explication is provided, as to what other type of function might be inherent to particles, the subdivision between particles and other function words in the German definition is interesting to note. The underlying rationale will become more evident as an interpretation of 'modal particle function' unfolds. Modal particles have long been described in terms of grammatical function, e.g. Weydt 1977: 218:

> *Abtönungspartikel* bezeichnet eine Funktionsklasse (Weydt (1969: 51). Alle Lautkörper – dieser Ausdruck wird hier gebraucht, um zu unterstreichen, daß es fraglich ist, ob es sich hier um identische Zeichen handelt – gehören außerdem noch anderen Funktionsklassen an: Konjunktion, Adverb, [...]. Es gibt keine Partikel, die nur Abtönungspartikel ist (nur abtönende Funktion hat).

The inconsistencies in the literature in the use of the term 'modal particle' as a function category as well as a word class category have been criticised (Thurmair 1989)[9]. She proposes formal criteria – syntactical and distributional patterns – to distinguish 'modal particle function' from other 'particle functions', e.g. 'conjunction'. Thurmair (ibid.) discusses ABER, AUCH, BLOSS, DENN, DOCH, EBEN, EIGENTLICH, EINFACH, ETWA, HALT, JA, MAL, NUR, RUHIG, SCHON, VIELLEICHT und WOHL as particles which may occur in 'modal particle function'. BLOSS, EBEN, EIGENTLICH, EINFACH and RUHIG, however, cannot be classified as particles in the sense of non-declinables – they may occur in inflected forms as adjectives, e.g. "die eigentlich*e* Frage", "das einfach*e* Leben", "ein ruhig*er* Moment", but

7 She is using a 'narrower' definition of particles (see Figure1), (see also Bußmann 1990: 562).

8 In Halliday's view (e.g. 1994: xix) there is no clear line between semantics and grammar; rather, he sees meanings on a cline between between lexicality and grammaticality.

9 Thurmair (1989: 9): "Die Modalpartikel-Forschung verfährt in dieser Hinsicht zum Teil recht inkonsequent: zum Teil wird das Modalpartikel-Vorkommen als Funktion bezeichnet (Weydt 1969: 51), wird von einer Wortart Modal- bzw. Abtönungspartikel gesprochen, deren Elemente Homonyme in anderen Wortarten haben (Weydt/Hentschel 1983: 4f., Hentschel 1986: 3f; vgl. dazu auch Thurmair 1989: 176)."

they are commonly referred to as modal particles (cf. Helbig 1994, Weinrich 1993, Macheiner 1991) – another issue that might be seen as problematic with a 'word class approach' to modal particles.[10]

2.3 Modal particle function: syntactic aspects

The following features have been described as criteria which – for the main part formally – distinguish 'modal particle function' from other particle functions (Thurmair 1989: 37):

- modal particles are not inflected
- they are not stressed, i.e. cannot be stressed
- they are optional elements
- they cannot answer a question
- their scope is the sentence
- they cannot be negated
- they only occur in the middle field[11]
- they mostly occur before rheme
- they are dependent on the mode of the sentende: different modal particles occur in different types of sentences
- they can be combined with one another (certain restrictions apply)
- they can modify the illocutionary force of a sentences

These features are only seen as a basic pattern of distribution,[12] however, because not all features are present in all instances of modal particle function. In the following paragraphs, I investigate the characteristics ascribed to 'modal particle function' in more detail.

10 ETWA could be seen to belong to this group as well, as in combination with the suffix '-ig' it can be inflected as an adjective, e.g. 'etwa*ige* Fragen'

11 For a discussion of the position of particles within a German sentence see further below.

12 Thurmair (1989: 37): "Alle Abweichungen von diesem Grundmuster, bei denen keine deutlichen semantischen Veränderungen festzustellen sind, sollen als Idiosynkrasien der einzelnen Modalpartikeln angesehen werden."

Modal particles are not inflected

If only those words that belong to the morphologically defined class of particles as non-declinables were to be used as modal particles, this descriptor would be obsolete. But as discussed before, BLOSS, EBEN, EIGENTLICH, EINFACH, RUHIG and ETWA are commonly seen to belong to the modal particle group as well. Thus, the formal criterion of identifying the use of a word in its inflected or non-inflected form helps to distinguish between its use as an adjective or modal particle.

Adjective:	`...` **einfache** Landschaften gemalt wurden: paar -- paar Bäume am Wasser, also keine theatralischen, pathetischen Landschaften. [... **simple** landscapes were painted: (a) few -- (a) few trees down by the water, that is no theatrical, dramatic landscapes.] (PFE/BRD.gj022, Passau)
Modal Particle:	...ich finde sie **einfach** dumm ... [...I find her **simply** stupid → I **simply** find her stupid] (DSK/DAM.00000)

However, inflection alone is not a sufficient indicator, as there are non-inflected forms of those words in applications different from that of modal particle.

Prepositional Adjective:	...so ganz **einfach** is es natürlich nich, das is klar.. [...naturally, it's not that **simple**, that's obvious...] (DSK/DBR.00000)

Descriptors other than inflection are necessary to identify modal particle usage.

Modal particles are not stressed, i.e. cannot be stressed

The attempt to classify certain words as a distinct group of 'modal particles' has led to some divergence in opinion as to whether they can be stressed or not. One position is that modal particles cannot be stressed (Thurmair 1989, referring back to Weydt 1969, Bublitz 1978), if stressed the word is said to be used in other than modal particle function. The only exceptions to this rule which Thurmair (ibid.) accepts are JA, BLOSS, NUR in certain uses, mainly in imperatives (1989: 22-23 and also 35). She argues that in these particular cases the particle is not carrying the main accent as there is always another element stressed as well. She posits that in these cases the stress is likely to be "emphatic". According to her, modal particles in general cannot be stressed by accent or change of position.
Helbig (1994), as one representative of the contrary position, argues that modal particles can, in fact, have to be stressed in particular contexts. As examples he names the use of JA in imperatives, which Thurmair sees as "emphatic", and the use of DENN in particular types of questions (see also Weydt 1986), for example (Helbig 1994: 25):

> Wie heißt du **dénn** (, wenn du nicht Peter heißt)?
> [What is your name then (, if it is not Peter)?]

DENN here implies that the speaker expected the interlocutor to be called Peter. It stresses the contrast between this expectation and the need to establish differing information.
Thurmair (1991a: 377) argues convincingly that in this type of question, which is said to be always in response to a negation, DENN is not used in modal particle function. As proof she names the fact that in such instances it can be replaced by DANN, which is an adverb, and the fact that it can be combined with DENN in modal particle function. The following two excerpts exemplify the distinction:

A: Tag, B, hier is A. Hör mal, ich wollt dich fragen, mußt du **denn** nich zum Flughafen gebracht werden und abgeholt werden?
[Hi, B. A here. Listen, I wanted to ask you, don't you **denn** need a lift to and from the airport?]

→ [...I was wondering, don't you need a lift ...]

B: Eh, nein, diesmal nicht, weil ich ja nicht wieder zum Flughafen zurückkomme.
[Ah, not this time, because I'm not returning to the airport.]

A: Ah so.
[I see.]

(BRO 1 Bd 1/9)

B: Oh!

A: Sind das Flöhe?
[Are they fleas?]

B: Nein!
[No!]

A: Was **dénn**?
[What **then**?]

B: Wanzen!
[Bugs]

(BRO 1 Bd 1/9)

Modal particles are optional elements

As Thurmair (1989) rightly states, modal particles are syntactically optional elements (see also cf. Franck 1980, Helbig 1994). In the following example:

A: Ich hab jedes Jahr so zwei drei Reisen mitgemacht.
[I went on a trip two or three times a year]

B: Das is **doch** herrlich.
[That is **doch** wonderful]

(DSK/DAG.00000)

B2: Das is herrlich.
[that is wonderful]

Sentence B2 is as syntactically correct as B. In terms of meaning, however, there is a difference between the two, as will be discussed below.[13]

Modal particles cannot answer a question

This descriptor refers to a distinction between words like JA, DOCH and EBEN as “Antwortpartikeln” and as modal particles. Because modal particles are seen as lacking the status of an independent sentence element, they cannot occur as independent elements in answer to a question. If these words do occur in such a context – as in the following example – it is argued that they are not being used in modal particle function:

A: ....und na ja sie war verstockt, wie's eben so ist bei jungen Menschen, nicht ?
[...and, well, she was stubborn, as young people are, aren't they?]

B: **Ja.**[14]
[Yes.]

(DSK/DAC.00000)

The scope of modal particles is the sentence

Modal particles do not refer to individual sentence elements but to the predicate of the sentence (cf. Kriwonossow 1977b) and thus to the sentence as a whole. This fact finds expression in the term “Satzpartikeln” which has been used by some scholars to refer to this group (cf. Asbach-Schnitker 1977, Hartmann 1977; for a criticism of the use of this term see Weydt 1977: 219). They cannot be assigned to particular sentence elements – neither semantically nor syntactically.

13 Thurmair (1989: 24) also describes a number of exceptional cases where modalparticles seem to be obligatory: DOCH in sentences where the finite verb is in first position and DOCH/BLOSS/NUR in sentences expressing a wish.

14 For a more detailed discussion of JA, see Chapter 5.10.

Modal particles cannot be negated

As their scope is the whole sentence, modal particles cannot be negated and have to be placed before the negator ("nicht", "kein...")

```
...dem kannst du bringen, was du willst, der
kapierts ja doch nicht ...
```

(DSK/DBP.00000)

```
[... he won't ja doch understand it][15]
[... he won't understand it, anyhow]
```

Modal particles only occur in the Middle Field

Modal particles are said to occur only in the middle field of a sentence (e.g. Abraham 1991a, Weinrich 1993, Thurmair 1989):

```
Die können doch gar nicht besser        sein.
        |            middle field               |
        ----------------------------------------
                   sentence bracket
         (They can doch not be better.)
```

(PFE/BRD.az005)

Thurmair (1989: 26-7) discusses possible exceptions, i.e. instances where modal particles do occur or seem to occur in initial field. She comes to the conclusion that the position of modal particles is restricted to middle field (see also Abraham 1991a), the only exception being the rarely occurring combination with a question word/interrogative pronoun (Thurmair 1989: 26):

```
Was nur findet sie an ihm?
[What nur does she see in him?]
```

15 See below for combinations of modal particles.

Modal particles mostly occur before the rheme

Although the meaning of the terms 'theme' and 'rheme' varies between different grammatical models (for a critical discussion of German grammars see Schneider 1996, for a discussion from a functional point of view see Halliday 1994: 37ff) a minimal definition describes as theme that which is less salient/prominent – in most instances given, known information – and rheme that which is more salient/prominent – new, unknown information. Within the middle field, there is a tendency to present thematic information at the beginning and rhematic information at its end (cf. Weinrich 1993).[16]
In most cases modal particles are said to appear before rheme, a major exception to this rule being those instances where the finite form of the verb (in second position within the sentence and thus before the middle field) is part of rheme (cf. Thurmair 1989: 29ff).

The use of modal particles depends on the sentence type

Different modal particles occur in different types of sentences. The word DENN for example, one of the frequently used modal particles, occurs only in questions as a modal particle:

```
Wie alt ist denn ihr Mann?
[How old is your husband, then?]
```
[17]

(DSK/DAG.00000)

Nevertheless, it occurs very frequently in statements as a conjunction:

16 Weinrich (1993: 25): "THEMATISCH wird das jeweils weniger Auffällige, RHEMATISCH das jeweils Auffälligere genannt. In einem gegebenen Text kann häufig (jedoch nicht immer) die ältere und bekannte Information thematisch, die neuere und unbekannte Information rhematisch genannt werden." Weinrich (1993: 81): "Für die Anordnung und Abfolge der Sprachzeichen im Mittelfeld gilt grundsätzlich die bereits erwähnte Regel, daß am Anfang des Mittelfeldes eher die unauffälligere (thematische), an seinem Ende eher die auffälligere (rhematische) Information untergebracht wird."

17 For a more detailed discussion see subsection on DENN in Chapter 5.4.

...mein Vater sich in dieser Beziehung überhaupt gar keine Sorgen machen konnte, **denn** das Geld gehörte einzig und allein meiner Mutter
[... **because** the money belonged solely to my mother]

(DSK/DAH.00000)

Modal particles can be combined with one another (certain restrictions apply)

Thurmair (1991b) describes certain regularities for combinations of modal particles: they must be acceptable in the same sentence type, they must be compatible with regard to their meaning and they occur in a fixed linear order. She posits that the more specific a particle is, the further to the right it will stand in a combination and that the second or last particle seems to be more important. Helbig refers back to Engel (1968: 91ff in Helbig 1994: 75-6) to describe a possible order of combinations:

(a) denn, doch (unbetont); eigentlich, etwa, ja
(b) aber, eben, halt, vielleicht, wohl
(c) doch (betont)
(d) auch, mal
(f) noch

Normalerweise gilt die Reihenfolge: (a) - (b) - (c) - (d) - (e) - (f)

Modal particles in group (a) would usually precede those in group (b) which precede the ones in group (c) and so on as the following example shows:

B: Ja. Also, wenn ihr dann da trotzdem in Ruhe essen könnt, und könnt euch dann absetzen
[Yes. Well, if you can then eat there in peace and quiet all the same, and then you can take off]

A: Ja, Mensch, anderthalb Stunden, das reicht **doch wohl**!
[Yes, sure, one and a half hours, that **should** be enough, **shouldn't it**?] (BRO 11 Bd 2/6)

The data analysis in Chapter 5 provides more detailed information about actually occurring combinations but it seems plausible that the distribution of particular modal particles in certain sentence types and their specific meanings restrict possible combinations.

Modal particles can modify the illocutionary force of a sentence

Whereas the characteristics of modal particles described so far mainly describe structural and distributional aspects, this descriptor is closely related to the meaning aspect. The function of modal particles is not to be found with regard to the proposition, but with regard to the illocution. In very general terms, they indicate the speaker's attitude towards the utterance as well as the intended perception on the part of the hearer (cf. Helbig 1977, Weydt 1979, Bublitz 1978, Thurmair 1989). For example:

> Das wird schon wieder heilen.
> [That will (schon) again heal]
> Don't worry, that'll heal! (Bublitz 1978: 226)

> Sie bleiben doch noch?
> [You stay (doch) a little longer]
> You are staying a little longer, (aren't you?) (König & Requardt 1991: 71)

There is general agreement on the fact that the lexical meaning of modal particles is "blurred" (Abraham 1991a), "bleached" (Vorderwülbecke 1981), that they have "little denotative" meaning (Helbig 1977). Helbig (ibid.) described them as "illocutive indicators", a position that has been revised and elaborated upon (cf. Jacobs 1986, Abraham 1991 a & b, Thurmair 1989). Thurmair (1989) posits that modal particles do not create, but modify illocutionary force which is created by an interplay between the modal particle and the sentence type it occurs in (see also Abraham 1991a). They are said to be able to point to the interlocutors' common knowledge, to the speaker's or listener's suppositions and expectations, to create cohesion with previous utterances or to mark the speaker's evaluation of the importance of the utterance. The investigation of pragmatic and

discursive aspects of the use of modal particles in Chapter 2.4 will specify these different capacities in more detail.
To conclude this subchapter on modal particles as a category, I would like to refer to a distinction proposed by Halliday (1994). He suggests that there are two principles according to which the constituents of a grammatical structure can be labelled: by class and by function. Halliday (1994: 27):

> Class labels are, so to speak, part of the dictionary; they indicate the potential that the word, or other item, has in the grammar of the language. Function labels are an interpretation of the text; they indicate the part that the item is playing in the particular structure under consideration.

As the discussion above has shown, the term 'particle' can be seen as referring to class. To use the example of the word DOCH again: DOCH is a particle that "plays different parts" in different structures. As outlined before, in a word class definition the words considered as modal particles all have at least one homonym in another class or subclass: "playing a different part" is seen as becoming member of a different word class. Using the Hallidayan approach, it is possible to overcome the problem of class labelling and the attached questions of homonymy/heterosemy. It is important to note that there is no one-to-one relationship between class and function, as Halliday (1994: 26) exemplifies with the class label 'noun' and the function labels 'Subject' and 'Object' (1994: 29):

> The label 'noun' thus indicates in a general way the grammatical potential of a linguistic item; but it does not indicate what part the item is playing in any actual structure. It is part of its entry in a dictionary. In order to interpret the meaning of the item in a given instance, we use a label which specifies not the class but the function. [...] The purpose of functional labelling is to provide a means of interpreting grammatical structure, in such a way as to relate any given instance to the system of the language as a whole.

In much the same way the discussion of modal particles as a category may be summarised. Adopting Halliday's distinction the term 'particle' is used as a class label whereas 'modal particle' is used as a function label. At this stage, modal particle function has mainly been described as a syntactical/grammatical function, but there are discursive and pragmatic functions that need to be taken into account as well. To approach the meaning of a word like DOCH in a particular context its grammatical, pragmatic and discursive functions have to be analysed. The following subchapter is a step in that direction.

2.4 Modal particle function: pragmatic and discursive aspects

A plethora of publications within different theoretical frameworks have dealt with pragmatic and discursive functions fulfilled by modal particles. They are described, for example, in terms of the management of interaction (Franck 1979), as constituting consensus (Lütten 1979), as a guidance for the hearer/listener (Rehbein 1979), as a 'means of expression regulating attitudes' (Wolski 1989) and as playing a part in establishing text coherence (Rudolph 1989).

Several diverse und complex 'functions' which modal particles fulfill have been described (Helbig 1994: 55ff). A general description goes back to Weydt (1969 in Helbig 1994): Modal particles serve to express the position of the speaker on what is being said and to inform the listener as to how s/he has to perceive the information. Helbig (ibid.) posits that a more specified and differentiated description is called for as different research orientations have accentuated different functions which, in his view, complement one another. He lists the following six main functions which I describe in the subsequent paragraphs:

- Modal particles serve to express the interlocutors' attitude
- Modal particles help to define a communicative situation (more clearly)
- Modal particles indicate and/or modify an illocution
- Modal particles help to direct a conversation
- Modal particles have strategic functions within an interaction
- Modal particles work as connectives within a text

Modal particles serve to express the interlocutors' attitudes

As briefly outlined before, modal particles can serve to express the interlocutors' attitudes towards the proposition. Referring back to Bublitz (1978: 9), Helbig (1994: 55-56) describes those attitudes as modal ones[18]:

> Sprechereinstellungen sind solche modalen Einstellungen des Sprechers, die sich auf seine Ansichten, Haltungen, Erwartungen, Annahmen, Emotionen sowie auf die seines Hörers sowie auf die jeweilige Rollenverteilung beziehen.

Doherty (1985 in Helbig 1994) uses the expression "lexikalische Ausdrucksmittel für Einstellungen" which Wolski (1989) criticises as too vague because in his opinion modal particles do not express those attitudes. In his view, attitudes are indicated by other means of expression, for example sentence mode (declarative, interrogative, imperative) on the syntactic level which is interpreted as a particular attitude on the semantic level. Modal particles are said to provide additional information about the interplay of attitudes.

The following sample of natural language data, which is an excerpt from a discussion between secondary students and a well known German author, will illustrate the point. It provides an example of particles in use in authentic spoken German[19]. Amongst others, the particle ABER occurs frequently:

A: Ich nehm' Ihnen das ehrlich gesagt gar nich' ab. Ich hab' den Verdacht, ich meine, natürlich wird' ich mich wahrscheinlich sogar irren, **aber**(1) daß Sie die Sache so geschrieben haben, daß Sie eben sagen "na schön", dann haben Sie sich das überlegt, und dann haben Sie die Stelle gelesen und haben sich gesagt "na Donnerwetter, das wird **aber**(2) ziehen, die werden **aber**(3) staunen, was ich mich so, was ich mir so alles traue..."

18 See discussion of modality in Chapter 2.5.

19 Freiburger Korpus: Schulklassengespräch mit Günter Grass (FKO/XAM.00000). The transcription has been modified to facilitate reading comprehension.

In (1) and (4) ABER is used as a conjunction. It connects the clause it appears in to the preceding one and thus creates cohesion (cf. Halliday & Hasan 1976) on the textual level of the text. This function can be realised in English by using the conjunction "but".

```
aber 1    aber daß Sie die Sache so geschrieben haben....
          [but that you've written it in that particular
          way...]

aber 4    aber daß Sie den lieben Gott für so leicht zu
          beleidigen halten...
          [but that you think our Lord could be insulted
          as easily as that...]
```

As a conjunction ABER occurs mainly at the beginning of a clause. Its reference is anaphoric; it expresses contrast in its immediate context, i.e. to the preceding proposition or propositions. Incidentally, in its two occurrences in the text sample under discussion it is accompanied by another conjunction "daß".[20]
In (2) and (3) ABER appears in modal particle function. Here, it is not as easily translated into English:

```
aber 2    ... das wird aber ziehen...
          [that will (aber) be a success]

aber 3    ...die werden aber staunen...
          [they will (aber) be surprised]
```

ABER expresses surprise and an approximation would be the following translations:

```
aber 2    ... das wird aber ziehen...
          [boy, what a success that is going to be]

aber 3    ...die werden aber staunen...
          [they're going to be surprised, I can tell
          you][21]
```

20 The qualitative analysis in Ch. 5 provides more detail on particle combinations.
21 See Bublitz (1978) for a comparison on expressing surprise in English and German.

In the excerpt under discussion, both occurrences of ABER in modal particle function are part of what I would like to call here 'projected direct speech': speaker A, a student partaking in a discussion with a very well known German author suggests what the author might have thought when he wrote a particular passage (Sie haben sich gesagt ... – 'you said to yourself' ...). Within his speech turn he creates a second "voice" (Bakhtin 1986), namely that of the author, and his use of modal particles helps to create the impression of direct speech. The student implies that the author writes on provocative topics for the effect of it and he uses the two clauses comprising ABER to paint a picture of that effect. Both clauses serve as exclamations and ABER further emphasises the aspect of 'surprise' that is part of the illocutionary force of an exclamation. 'Surprise' may refer to the extent of divergence from what is expected (as in these examples) or it may refer to the fact that there is divergence from expectations at all.[22] Thus, ABER links the actual speech event with a wider context – with 'what is expected'; shared knowledge – and serves to enhance the element 'surprise' in an utterance with the illocutionary force 'exclamation'. It can thus be said that 'modal particle function' in this instance comprises a syntactic function, a pragmatic function, in that it reinforces the illocutionary force of the utterance (see also below) and a discursive function, as it places the speech event in a wider context.

The discursive function is, in a sense, twofold: 'textimmanent' and 'textextern'. On the one hand, a word in modal particle function can point to part of the discourse. As such it is part of the 'discourse deixis' which Levinson (1983: 85) describes as "the use of expressions within some utterance to refer to some portion of the discourse that contains that utterance". By means of either anaphoric or cataphoric reference (Halliday & Hasan 1976) the modal particle activates part of the running discourse for the hearer/listener. On the other hand, the discursive function can be seen with regard to the intertextual character of discourse. In its discursive function a modal particle may point to texts outside the speech event at hand – to what I have called the wider context with regard to the example above.

22 For a detailed discussion of ABER see the analysis in Ch. 5.8.

In this instance one may again speak of deixis – here exophoric reference – if Levinson's (1983: 54) definition is accepted:

> [...] deixis concerns the ways in which languages encode or grammaticalise features of the context of utterance or speech event and thus also concerns ways in which the interpretation of utterances depends on the analysis of that context of utterance.

Modal particles help to define a communicative situation

Not only are modal particles said to generally express and/or regulate attitudes but they also provide information as to how the actual speech event is to be perceived and evaluated in the context of a larger communicative situation. The capacity to create this connection between the speech event and a wider cultural/social context is crucial to the modal particle function as a discursive function. In modal particle function a word serves to 'bring to bear' the cultural/social context of the interlocutors, to make it salient for the particular speech event as the example above has shown.

Modal particles indicate and/or modify an illocution

As outlined before, the occurrence of specific modal particles is restricted to particular sentence types. Thus, there is a strong connection between the modal particle and the illocutionary force of a proposition. According to Helbig (1994), they may function as "illocutive indicators and/or modifiers" which can disambiguate an utterance.[23]

a) `Schildern Sie` **`doch mal`** `den Hergang...`
`[`**`Why don't you`**` describe what happened...]`
`(PFE/BRD.ai002,Lübeck)`

23 Helbig (1994: 58): "Die Abtönungspartikeln gehören zu den illokutiven Indikatoren, d.h. zu den in der Sprache ausgebildeten Mitteln, die die Äußerung auch relativ unabhängig vom Handlungskontext eindeutig oder wenigstens eindeutiger machen."

b) Schildern Sie den Hergang...
[Describe what happened...]

In version a) an interviewer is encouraging an interviewee to provide more details with regard to a particular description. Although syntactically the clause is an imperative, the addition of the two modal particles DOCH and MAL turns it into an invitation or suggestion to keep talking rather than a demand. Version b) – the imperative clause without modal particle(s) – indicates a very different setting, namely that of an unequal encounter. The connotation is e.g. a police officer formally interviewing a witness or accused. The illocutionary force here is that of a command. In this instance, one could argue for either modification or indication of illocutionary force:

Modification: The illocutionary force of the utterance (b) is that of a command. By adding the modal particles DOCH and MAL the command is "downtoned" (cf. Faerch/ Kasper 1989) to a suggestion or polite request.

Indication: The combination of imperative and modal particle(s) DOCH and/or MAL may be seen as formulaic; the combination always expressing a suggestion.[24]

In both cases – be it indication or modification of illocutionary force – the modal particle is used in a pragmatic function, clarifying the force of a speech act to the interlocutor.[25]

Modal particles help to direct/control a conversation

Although Helbig (1994) emphasises the force of modal particles with regard to illocutionary force, he also stresses their ability to connect an utterance with its context of conversation and argumentation – what I have labelled earlier as the particle's discursive function. Modal particles can influence the course of a conversation which indicates

24 The English translation 'why don't you' which is equally formulaic seems to support this argument.

25 For a further discussion of modification, see also Thurmair 1989, Abraham 1991b, König in Weydt (ed.) 1977: 117.

that they not only relate to a particular speech act but also to the succession of 'moves'[26] in a conversation.[27]

```
B:    Aber ringsum kann sich natürlich dann durch die
      Allergie was anderes jebildet haben. ( ) Wie sollt
      ihr denn an Wanzen kommen?
      [But all around it, of course, something else may
      have developed then because of the allergy. ( ) How
      are you [denn] supposed to have caught bedbugs?]
A:    Ja, das weiß ich eben auch nich!
      [Well, that's exactly what I don't understand]
B:    Meistens sitzen die ja im Bett, nich, oder in der
      Wand.
      [They mostly live in the bedding, don't they, or in
      walls]
```

(BRO 1 Bd 1/9)

DENN in speaker B's move connects the question to previous utterances. The use of DENN indicates that the question is motivated by the actual speech event (cf. Thurmair 1991a). Thus, B's utterance could not be an initial turn, DENN indicates that there must be preceding information. The combination EBEN AUCH is a confirmation of the previous speaker's stance. B has expressed astonishment by using the modal verb 'sollen'. Speaker A takes up B's attitude with EBEN AUCH. The use of JA continues this theme: both speakers wonder where speaker A got bedbugs. Both do not have an explanation, so B refers to 'common knowledge' by using JA.

26 The term 'move' refers to the substructure of a stretch of discourse and is derived from the theoretical premises of conversation analysis (e.g. Sacks et al 1974). We distinguish for example 'opening moves', 'answering moves' and 'follow-up moves'.

27 Helbig (1994: 61): "Die Abtönungspartikeln steuern die Konversation im Sinne der Sprecher. Sie nehmen Einfluß auf die Weiterentwicklung der Kommunikation, besonders auf die Fortsetzungskonstellation für den folgenden Sprecher."

Modal particles have strategic functions within an interaction

What Helbig (1994: 61f) summarises under this heading has partly been mentioned with regard to some of the previous headings – what is important here, though, is the discursive function of expressing a preference for an interlocutor's answer.[28]

A: Herr Vetter, Sie und manche ihrer Kollegen haben in der letzten Zeit in Reden wieder zusehends härtere Kritik an den Herrschaften, herrschenden gesellschaftspolitischen Zuständen geübt.
[Mr. Vetter, you and your colleagues have recently been criticising in your speeches more and more strongly the [] ruling sociopolitical conditions]
Ist dies **etwa** notwendig, um die wachsende Unruhe in den Gewerkschaften etwas zu dämpfen?
[*Do you* **really** *think* this is necessary to soothe the unions' growing uneasiness?]

B: Nein. Wir kommen gerade vom Bereich des Lohns und da muß ich sagen...
[No. We are just coming from the area of wages and I have to say...]

(FKO/XDU.00000)

The use of ETWA in this example indicates preference for a negative answer. Speaker A is not simply asking for information but is at the same time expressing an opinion. His opinion (or the one that he officially represents as a reporter for a particular institution) is that the proposition expressed in his first move and referred to by 'dies' is not necessary and by using ETWA in his question he prompts his illocutor to answer in the negative.

28 Helbig (1994: 62): "Sie drücken auch Annahmen, Bewertungen oder Erwartungen im Hinblick auf die Reaktion des Gesprächspartners, im Hinblick auf die Antwort aus: [...]".

Modal particles work as connectives within a text

In describing the discursive function modal particles fulfil I have previously outlined their ability to work as connectives within a text. Helbig refers back to Kemme to point out how this aspect of their discursive function resembles the role played by conjunctions and provides the following example (1979 in Helbig 1994: 63):

> Ich gehe nicht schwimmen, weil das Wasser noch viel zu kalt ist.
> Ich gehe nicht schwimmen. Das Wasser ist ja noch viel zu kalt.
>
> [I won't go swimming, because the water is still much too cold.
> I won't go swimming. The water is still much too cold, as you know.]

Importantly, however, he also points out that conjunctions always connect explicit utterances, which does not hold true for modal particles who may connect what is implicit (Grice 1968, also Levinson 1983 on presupposition and implicature) to a more or less explicit utterance. Thus, modal particles do contribute to the texture (e.g. Fairclough 1995, Halliday and Hasan 1976) of a text in much more complex ways than conjunctions. They also create cohesion in Schiffrin's sense: "Cohesive devices do not themselves create meaning; they are clues used by speakers and hearers to find the meaning which underlie surface utterances." (Schiffrin 1987: 9). Rather than "local coherence between adjacent units in discourse" (ibid.) the reference framework may be beyond the text[29] and we may therefore speak of exophoric reference. Whereas conjunctions operate on the textual level of text, modal particles are part of the interpersonal structure of an exchange and therefore linked to the mood structure. This will be discussed in more detail in the following subsection.

29 See also discussion on "kommunikative/metakommunikative Deixis" in Hentschel (1986) and Zifonun *et al.* (1997: 1216): "Abtönungspartikeln operieren über dem Satz als kommunikativer Einheit. Ihre Funktion besteht darin, den Stellenwert der kommunikativen Einheit in einem größeren Textzusammenhang zu verdeutlichen".

2.5 The 'modal' aspect of modal particles

In a more functionally oriented view of language, 'modality' encompasses much more than expression of subjectiveness through modal verbs or through the different modes of a verb. Mc Carthy and Carter (1994: 104) summarise this position:

> Various studies (Hermerén 1978, Holmes 1983, Stubbs 1986b) have encouraged us to make a broader sweep in the kinds of items that we include under the general umbrella of modality: lexical modals such as the various forms of words such as possible, probable, likely, certain and so on, along with certain discourse markers (sort of, like, etc) should take their place alongside the modal verbs in performing the functions of modality.

In agreement with this view and with Palmer (1986: 16):

> Modality in language is, [...], concerned with subjective characteristics of an utterance, and it could even be further argued that subjectivity is an essential criterion for modality. Modality could, that is to say, be defined as the grammaticalization of speakers' (subjective) attitudes and opinions.

and Butt *et al.* (1995: 77):

> We use the term *modality* to refer to all signs of the speaker's opinion in a text [...]

modal particles constitute an important part of the modality system of the German language.

A modal particle helps to express the modality of an utterance in that it reveals the speaker's attitudes about the context and/or seeks to affect the listener's perspective of it. House and Kasper (1981) describe some modal particles as 'modality markers' namely as 'downtoners' that may be used to lessen the impact an utterance may have on a hearer.[30]

As outlined above, modal particles contribute to the expression of speakers' attitudes in a variety of – sometimes rather subtle – ways.

30 They follow Leech's (1983) definition of politeness as indirectness; more details on this study in Chapter 3.

For example, a reference to common knowledge, which is achieved by using the modal particle JA, as shown in the following excerpt, is not immediately recognisable as a subjective attitude.

B: is **ja** albern
[that's ridiculous][31]

A: im Übrigen ist es **ja** so, und sie selbst sind unter den Leuten gewesen, die versucht haben aus der Verfassung von Weimar, aus ihren vielleicht vorhandenen Mängeln zu lernen ...
[by the way, **it is a well-known fact**, and you yourself were one of the people who tried to learn from the Weimar constitution, from the shortcomings it possibly had...]

(DSK/DAA.00000)

The tone of the exchange seems rather aggressive and so speaker A does not confront speaker B with opposing him on a personal basis but refers to common knowledge to introduce his next argument. He thus tries to establish some common ground, a pretense of consensus. In other words, the use of the modal particle provides a hedge.[32] Although speaker A's attitude is subjective, the reference to common knowledge is supposed to disguise this fact. Halliday (1985: 340) describes this type of mechanism as follows:

> The importance of modal features in the grammar of interpersonal exchanges lies in an apparent paradox on which the entire system rests – the fact that we only say we are certain when we are not [...]. Hence whereas the subjective metaphors, which state clearly 'this is how I see it', take on all values (I'm sure, I think, I don't believe, I doubt, etc) most of the objectifying metaphors express a 'high' value probability or obligation – that is, they are different ways of

31 Underlining indicates that the word is stressed.

32 In the sense suggested by House & Kasper (1981: 167): by means of hedging the speaker "avoids a precise propositional specification thus circumventing the potential provocation such a specification might entail".

claiming objective certainty or necessity for something that is in fact a matter of opinion.[33]

According to Weinrich (1993) the speaker uses modal particles to indicate to the listener how to 'modalise' the truth value of a proposition, i.e. how to 'match' proposition and context.[34] Halliday's (1985: 1994) systemic functional view of language seems to provide a framework for analysing how this 'match' comes about (see 2.7).

2.6 Modal particles in different text types

Modal particles are generally said to occur more frequently in spoken than in written texts.[35] Rudolph (1991) classified text types according to the supposed dichotomies of oral/written and fictional/non-fictional. She then investigated the text types 'everyday conversations' (oral/non-fictional), 'newspaper articles' (written/non-fictional) and (sections from) 'narrative texts' (written/fictional) for the occurrence of particles in the narrower sense of the term and conjunctions and conjunction-like particles. For each text type she analysed a corpus of 15,000 words and found that "in Conversation words from the category of particle/conjunction are used almost three times as frequently as in Press and Literature" (Rudolph 1991: 208-9) but there is no specific analysis of words in modal particle function as her definition of particles is a very wide one.

The approach to a distinction between spoken and written texts as dichotomies has been criticised. Biber (1988), for example, posits that

33 For a more detailed discussion of modal particles as grammatical metaphors see further down.

34 Weinrich (1993: 841): "Durch Modalpartikeln gibt der Sprecher seinem Hörer insbesondere zu verstehen, wie die Geltung einer Feststellung 'modalisiert', das heißt, flexibel in den Kontext oder in die Situation eingebunden werden kann."

35 Following the definition that a text is "either spoken or written discourse, so that for example the words used in a conversation (or their written transcription) constitute a text" (Fairclough 1995: 4).

there is no such dichotomy of dimensions across texts, no clear cut distinction between spoken and written texts but multidimensional distinctions. McCarthy (1993) uses the terminology "spoken and written medium" but like Biber (1988) describes complexities and mixing. He proposes as a useful distinction the terminology of 'medium' which "is concerned with how the message is transmitted to its receivers" and 'mode' which "is concerned with how it is composed stylistically, that is, with reference to sociolinguistically grounded norms of archetypical speech and archetypical writing. These norms are norms of appropriacy, culturally conditioned on a cline of 'writtenness' and 'spokenness'." (McCarthy 1993: 171). He also points out that many texts written to be read use 'markers' to create an image of spoken text. He concedes, however, that "[...] it does seem that some markers are almost uniquely associated with speech, or as Biber (1988: 241) says, are 'rare outside of the conversational genres'. Ones which spring to mind in English are *mind you, you know,* and *oh.*" (Mc Carthy 1993: 173). He analyses the use of 'well' which is well documented for the spoken mode (e.g. Schiffrin 1987) in the written medium.

Biber *et al.* (1999), in their corpus-based grammar of spoken and written English, investigate the grammatical features which are particularly characteristic of conversational language. They describe English discourse particles (e.g. 'well', 'right') as non-clausal units playing an important part in the construction of spoken grammar (1999: 1086):

> Discourse markers [...] are inserts which tend to occur at the beginning of a turn or utterance, and to combine two roles: (a) to signal a transition in the evolving process of the conversation, and (b) to signal an interactive relationship between hearer, speaker and message.

With regard to German, Macheiner (1991) provides an interesting example for the use of modal particles in the written medium:

> "Ich weiß nicht", rief ich ohne Klang, "ich weiß ja nicht. Wenn niemand kommt, dann kommt eben niemand. Ich habe niemandem etwas Böses getan, niemand hat mir etwas Böses getan, niemand aber will mir helfen. Lauter niemand. Aber so ist es doch nicht. Nur daß mir niemand hilft –, sonst wäre lauter Niemand hübsch. Ich würde ganz gern – warum denn nicht – einen Ausflug mit einer

Gesellschaft von lauter Niemand machen. Natürlich ins Gebirge – wohin denn sonst?"

(Kafka, Der Ausflug ins Gebirge in Macheiner 1991: 303, my emphasis)

The use of modal particles in this excerpt constitutes 'otherness' (cf. 'voices', dialogic interaction, Bakhtin 1986), it invokes the impression that there is an illocutor to be addressed. Thus, the text seems to be a dialogue rather than a monologue.

Hentschel (1986) investigated the level of privacy of a speech event and its influence on the frequency of use of modal particles. As determining factors for the level of privacy she analysed:

- level of familiarity of interlocutors
- level of familiarity with the situation
- investment/ interest in the topic
- differences in social status between interlocutors
- familiarity with topos and medium of interaction
- liveliness of interaction
- type of communication (descriptive/argumentative/associative)

Following the analysis of a corpus of about 20,000 words she came to the conclusion that the frequency of occurrence of modal particles rises proportionate to the communication being informal, personal, associative and with a high level of familiarity.[36]

We can thus assume, that particles in modal particle function occur with a high frequency in spoken German, particularly in text types that reflect an informal style and a high level of familiarity between speakers.

36 Hentschel (1986: 243): "Es ist mir damit gelungen, wenn nicht zu beweisen, so doch mit sehr hoher Wahrscheinlicheit zu belegen, daß die Häufigkeit, mit der Abtönungspartikeln gebraucht werden, in dem Maße steigt, wie das Gespräch einen informellen, persönlichen, vertrauten und assoziativen Charakter annimmt."

2.7 Modal particles from a Systemic Functional perspective

As shown in 2.3 and 2.4, words used in modal particle function have a syntactic as well as a pragmatic and a discursive aspect to them. In order to analyse modal particle function, a grammatical model which accommodates those different aspects is necessary. Systemic Functional grammar offers such a model as it provides a multi-level analysis of text, as will be outlined below.

Looking at the linguistic system from the viewpoint of Systemic Functional grammar, the focus is on meaning and how language operates to express meaning: "[...] the exchange of meanings is a creative process in which language is one symbolic resource – perhaps the principal one we have [...]" (Halliday 1978: 4). Language is seen as a semiotic system (ibid.) where meaning is created through choice. Eggins (1994: 2) summarises the position as follows:

> [...] leads systemic linguists to advance four main theoretical claims about language: that language use is functional; that its function is to make meanings; that these meanings are influenced by the social and cultural context in which they are exchanged; and that the process of using language is a semiotic process, a process of making meanings by choosing.

For a meaning to be understood there has to be a certain extent of agreement about it – an anticipation of meaning, so to speak – between the parties participating in an act of communication. On the highest level of organisation the social system (in Malinowski's (1923: 46) terminology the 'context of culture') provides a framework for agreement on meaning. The social system through the validation and activation of the semiotic systems thus creates a meaning potential available to its members: "Language is the ability to 'mean' in the situation types, or social contexts that are generated by the culture." (Halliday 1978: 34). The actualisation of this meaning potential is what Halliday (1978: 2) defines as text: "Language does not consist of sentences; it consists of text, or discourse – the exchange of meanings in interpersonal contexts of one kind or another."

Which fraction of the potential of possible meanings is actually chosen for actualisation is determined by the context of situation and its interpretation by the speakers and listeners participating in the interaction.

The social system as such is too complex to be analysed in every particular situation in order to determine meaning. Such an analysis would have to deal with too much information that is redundant for a situation which only reflects a tiny portion of the social system realised in an instance of communication. It seems therefore sufficient to concentrate on the 'portion' in question and to explore how it can be described and in which way it determines the particular meaning which is at stake in a particular instance of communication. These 'parts' of the social system which are most important in respect to the definition of meaning for the participants of an act of communication are what Halliday refers to as the 'context of situation'. In developing Malinowski's concept of context of situation, which was based on an anthropological point of view and which intricately described the non-verbal goings-on of single situations, Halliday (cf. 1985, 1994) has arrived at a concept which describes the context of situation as the interface between the environment and the text.

He describes the semiotic structure of the context of situation as 'register' and considers three different aspects:

- type of social action: 'What is going on?' (Field)
- role relationships: 'Who is taking part?' (Tenor)
- symbolic organisation: 'Which role is assigned to language?' (Mode)

According to the systemic functional view of grammar the semiotic structure of the context of situation as described above is realised within the grammar of the text. The register variables field, tenor and mode are actualised through three 'metafunctions' of language or, to use Halliday's own words: "[...] experiential meanings are activated by features of the field, interpersonal meanings by features of the tenor, and textual meanings by features of the mode." (Halliday & Hasan 1985: 29)

Halliday (cf. 1985, 1994) describes the three metafunctions of language which cooperate in transmitting meaning as:

1) the ideational metafunction, subdivided into logical and experiential,
2) the interpersonal metafunction
3) the textual metafunction

In every text all three are said to be at work to construe the social exchange of meanings, e.g. Fairclough (1995: 6):

> [...] language in texts always simultaneously functions ideationally in the representation of experience and the world, interpersonally in constituting social interaction between participants in discourse, and textually in tying parts of a text together into a coherent whole (a text, precisely) and tying texts to situational contexts (e.g. through situational deixis).

It has been shown before (see Chapter 2.5) that modal particles form a notable part of the modality system of German. The systemic functional approach discusses modality as a feature of the interpersonal metafunction under the system of 'Mood', which is seen as "the grammatical resource for realizing an interactive move in dialogue" (Martin *et al.* 1997). A Mood analysis of text looks at how clauses are structured to express different speech functions such as a challenge, a contradiction, an assertion etc. 'Modality' in this grammatical model refers to the the sub-systems of 'modalization' and 'modulation' whereby "language allows us to temper the exchange by expressing degrees of either probability/usuality or obligation/ inclination." (Eggins 1994: 192), or, in Halliday's words (1994: 356): "Modality refers to the area of meaning that lies between yes and no – the intermediate ground between positive and negative polarity. What this implies more specifically will depend on the underlying speech function of a clause." As has been shown before, it is in this domain that modal particle function operates. Modal particles share at least a number of features with 'Mood Adjuncts' in the systemic functional model which Butt et al. (1995: 82) describe as devices to modify the argument of a proposition by the speaker's opinion. Mood Adjuncts are said to "encode speakers' opinions about the probability, obligation, usuality, presumption, inclination, degree and intensity or even time of the activity in the clause"(ibid.)[37].

37 See also Aijmer 1997: "I think – an English modal particle".

In analysing modal particles, it is of interest to take into account another feature which the systemic functional approach describes: grammatical metaphor. In a more general description of metaphor, a word is used for something that resembles that which it commonly stands for (Halliday 1985: 321):

> [...] the assumption is that to any metaphorical expression corresponds another, or perhaps more than one, that is 'literal' – or, as we shall prefer to call it, congruent. In other words, for any given semantic configuration there is (at least) one congruent realization in the lexicogrammar. There may then be others that are in some respect transferred, or metaphorical.

Halliday (ibid.) describes two types of grammatical metaphor: metaphors of transitivity and metaphors of mood. It is the latter that is of interest in an analysis of modal particles. Butt et al. describe as examples of "modal grammatical metaphor" (1995: 82) (later "interpersonal grammatical metaphor" (2000: 116)) clauses like 'I think' for 'probably' or 'I believe' for 'almost certainly'. 'Probably' and 'almost certainly' – Mood adjuncts in a systemic functional analysis – are seen as the congruent form. Choosing the clauses 'I think' and 'I believe' instead is seen as using the grammar metaphorically (see also Aijmer 1997). Eggins (1994: 67) discusses the concept of grammatical metaphor at the clause level by stating that "clauses which package requests indirectly, using structures other than imperatives, are examples of grammatical metaphor."

The detailed analysis of individual modal particles in Chapter 5 attempts to employ this concept of grammatical metaphor where it is seen as helpful in conveying the meaning of modal particle function in a particular utterance to a meaning in the English translation of that utterance.

2.8 Summary

The preceding subsections have provided an overview of the characteristics of words used in modal particle function. The description of modal particles as a category has shown the complexity of a word class approach to the group of words commonly labeled as modal particles. I have distinguished between a syntactic function, a pragmatic function and a discursive function. In its syntactic function, a modal particle creates meaning through contrast with other possible applications of the word. In its pragmatic function, a modal particle indicates or modifies an illocution and serves to express the interlocutor's attitude. In its discursive function, a modal particle contributes to the texture of a text. Modal particles form an essential component of the modality system of German as they indicate to the hearer how to modalise the truth value of a proposition and how to match proposition and context. The complexity of modal particle functions makes them a difficult item to learn in second/foreign language acquisition. The following chapter will outline those difficulties in detail and report on research on the acquisition of modal particles by learners of German as a second/foreign language. It will also critically discuss some existing teaching materials on modal particles.

Frequency analyses on particles in general (Rudolph 1991) and on modal particles in particular (Hentschel 1986) have shown that modal particles are most likely to occur in spoken German, in particular in texts which show a high level of informality and familiarity between speakers. The data chosen for analysis in this study are therefore based on a number of corpora of spoken German. In Chapter 4, I will describe and critically discuss the choice of those corpora which form the basis for the data analysis in this study.

3. Modal particles in second language acquisition

[...] what are the effects of various approaches to instruction in pragmatics? Given the wide range of instructional contexts, there is not likely to be one approach which is to be preferred over all others in every context.

(Kasper & Rose 2001:8)

3.1 Introduction

Due to their complexity, which has been explored in the previous chapter, modal particles pose numerous problems for learners of German as a second/foreign language (e.g. Jiang 1993, Götze 1993, Busse 1992, Zimmermann 1981). In Chapter 2, discursive and pragmatic functions of modal particles have been described. On the one hand modal particles can contribute to directing a conversation, have strategic functions within an interaction and may work as connectives within a text. On the other hand they can express an interlocutor's attitude, define a communicative situation more clearly and indicate or modify the illocutionary force of an utterance. Whether second language learners understand and use German modal particles appropriately is therefore a question that falls into the broader field of enquiry of interlanguage pragmatics, which in turn builds on the study of cross-cultural communication. Hence, findings in cross-cultural communication and interlanguage pragmatics are considered here in developing a rationale for the importance of teaching German modal particles.

In order to discuss what should be taught when and how, it is necessary to establish what awareness of modal particles second language learners bring into the learning/teaching process. Hence, in this chapter studies on second language learners' perception of, and knowledge about, modal particles are explored before the instruction of modal particles is addressed. In a further step, findings from studies on the instruction of modal particles and their acquisition in uninstructed contexts are evaluated so as to inform the approach to teaching which is proposed in the present study.

With the rise of a communicative approach to language teaching, specific teaching materials on modal particles have been published (e.g. Kemme 1979, Weydt et al. 1983, Kummer 1984, Helbig & Helbig 1995) and modal particles have found their way into textbooks for German as a second language (e.g. "Stufen" 1995, "Tangram" 1998, "em: Abschlusskurs" 1999). These materials are critically assessed and set in relation to the approach to teaching modal particles suggested in the present study.

In the final section of this chapter, a novel approach to teaching and learning modal particles is proposed. This proposal aims at the comprehension of modal particles by learners of German and is based on authentic dialogue data (Brons-Albert 1984), which have been compiled as a corpus and are accessed with the help of a concordancing program.

3.2 A rationale for teaching modal particles: cross-cultural and interlanguage pragmatics

Researchers working in the area of cross-cultural pragmatics (cf. Thomas 1983, 1984; Tannen 1984; Wierzbicka 1985 & 1991) have challenged the assumption that pragmalinguistic phenomena such as the realisation of politeness through indirectness (Brown & Levinson 1987) are universal. The cross-cultural approach to pragmatics proposes that the realisation of speech acts is language- and culture-specific. The recognition that speech acts might be realised differently in different cultures and subcultures has led to a large body of research which attempts to identify these differences (e.g. Blum-Kulka & Olshtain 1984; Blum-Kulka, House & Kasper 1989; Kasper & Blum-Kulka 1993).

Following the premise that speech plays a major role in the creation and affirmation of cultural identity, studies of speech acts are said to show how clashes between interactional styles can lead to cross-cultural miscommunication. The main focus in the cross-cultural study of speech acts has been on two areas: the value and function of politeness or deference in speech act realisation, and the universality of politeness phenomena across languages and cultures. In particular, the speech acts 'request' and 'apology' have been studied in great detail across a variety of cultures (Blum-Kulka, House & Kasper 1989). There is no one generalizable set of communication strategies across cultures and critical moments in cross-cultural communicative settings occur (Candlin 1987). Misunderstandings and misinterpretations in cross-cultural communication have been described and categorised as due to 'sociopragmatic' and 'pragmalinguistic' failure (Thomas 1983). With Tannen (1984), Thomas (1983, 1984) assumes that a second/foreign language learner applies pragmatic strategies in the L2 according to his/her L1. Sociopragmatic failure occurs when a learner is unaware of the speech act strategies of the L2 culture. As one example for sociopragmatic failure one might think of an L1 English learner of German using the informal form of address "du" in a communicative setting where the use of the formal form of address "Sie" would be the appropriate politeness strategy because of the relative power of or social distance to the interlocutor.

'Pragmalinguistic' failure occurs when "the pragmatic force mapped onto a linguistic token or structure is systematically different from that normally assigned to it by native speakers" (Thomas 1983). Thomas (ibid.) describes 'pragmalinguistic transfer' (the inappropriate transference of speech act strategies form L1 to L2) as a frequent cause for pragmalinguistic failure and cites using a direct speech act where a native speaker would use an indirect speech act or "off-record" politeness strategy (cf. Brown and Levinson 1987) as an example. In English, a request would frequently be realised as an indirect speech act by means of an interrogative construction, often in combination with a modal verb.[38] In German, requests are often

38 Thomas (1983: 101): "It can be shown for example, that native speakers fairly predictably assign certain pragmatic force to certain utterances. Thus *can you X?*

performed by imperatives in combination with a modal particle. The following text is an excerpt of a telephone conversation (Brons-Albert 1984). Speaker A, a student, is talking to B, an employee of the company for which she is translating a text:

A: Ja, gut. Da schreib ich einfach "querlaufendes System aus querlaufenden Wänden", ne. dann wird der Herr Z das verstehen.
[Yes, good. I'll just write "diagonal system of diagonally running walls", I suppose Mr Z will understand that then]

B: **Versuchen Sie doch mal** ., Frau, öh, öh, A, **versuchen Sie doch mal**, ne Parallele zum Schiffsbau zu ziehen. ..
[**Why don't you try** , Ms, eh, eh, A, **why don't you try** to draw a line parallel to shipbuilding...]

(BRO33 Bd 17/3)

The general social context of this exchange can be described as a formal and public rather than an informal and private setting.
The specific social context is problem solving in a professional context. The situation is not one of unequal encounter (cf. Thomas 1984), in the sense that one interlocutor is in a position of authority relative to the other, the role relationship between speaker A and speaker B is relatively equal.[39] The phrase "versuchen Sie" is an imperative form and translates literally into "try to ...", a direct request. Given the contextual features of the speech event outlined above, a direct request is not the expected speech act realisation strategy in this context and might be perceived as a threat to face (Scollon and Scollon 1981). The addition of the two modal particles DOCH and MAL, however, modifies the illocutionary force of 'direct request' into an indirect request, which may be interpreted as suggestion or advice, as the English translation indicates:

is a higly conventionalized politeness form in British English, likely to be interpreted by native speakers as *request* to do X, rather than a question as to one's *ability* to do X."

39 The description of contextual factors presented here draws on Kasper 1984.

versuchen Sie doch mal ...
[why don't you...]

If a non-native speaker does not perceive the force of those two particles s/he will gravely misjudge the tone of the exchange between the two interlocutors. 'Requests' may be coded in an interrogative or interrogative-cum-conditional form, but are in a variety of speech events performed by imperatives in combination with a modal particle and the German equivalent of 'please' (see House 1989).

Færch and Kasper (1989) in a discussion of requests in interlanguage, refer to two distinct forms of downgrading a request, namely syntactic downgrading as opposed to lexical or phrasal downgrading. Syntactic downgraders would include, amongst others, the use of interrogative or conditional structures. Applied to the above example a modification involving syntactic downgraders would yield downgraded requests as in:

Haben Sie versucht eine Parallele zum Schiffbau zu ziehen?
or: Sie könnten eine Paralle zum Schiffbau ziehen.

As lexical downgraders Færch and Kasper (ibid.) list politeness markers (such as 'please'), consultative devices ('do you think') and downtoners, a category in which they include modal adverbs (such as 'perhaps', 'possibly') and modal particles. In their study of the interlanguage of English L1 learners of German they come to the conclusion that (ibid.: 233-4):

> The downtoner is underused in the learner data in all situations, compared to native speaker use [...]. There can be little doubt that using downtoners efficiently requires a higher pragmalinguistic competence than the use of the politeness marker. For one thing, the politeness marker can be placed extrasequentially and thus involves less psycholinguistic planning capacity on the syntactic level. For another thing, the semantics of the most frequent German downtoners, the modal particles, is intricate and still not sufficiently understood.

Instead of downtoners, in particular modal particles, the non-native speaker subjects of their study resorted to syntactic downgraders and politeness markers (ibid.: 244-5):

> The overall trend for learners with closely related native and target languages and cultures, and a linguistic proficiency level at an intermediate to advanced state, is that they approximate native speakers of the target culture both in the degree of face work involved in sociopragmatically different situations and in the activated request procedures. Their request behaviour has its most conspicuous interlanguage-specific features in the learners' use of more transparent, overcomplex, explicit and longer procedures of request modification, as is evident from their use of politeness markers, of syntactic downgraders [...] and most strikingly of supportive move.

One reason for the avoidance of German modal particles by non-native speakers seems to lie in their lack of understanding of the illocutionary force of those particles. In a study on Spanish L1 Mexican students (Rall 1981), students were reported to have enquired about the 'directness' of German speech acts such as 'asking' or 'uttering of opinion'. Non-native speakers might perceive directness by looking at the syntactic mode of the encoding of a particular speech act without perceiving the modifications brought about by the use of modal particles (see also House & Kasper 1981). The following example of 'uttering of opinion' illustrates this:

a) Es ist nicht einfach, dieses Problem zu lösen.
[It is not easy this problem to solve]
This problem is not easily solved.

b) Es ist **ja** nicht einfach, dieses Problem zu lösen.
[It is (**ja**) not easy this problem to solve]
This problem is not easily solved (**as you know**).

c) Es ist **doch** nicht einfach, dieses Problem zu lösen.
[It is (**doch**) not easy this problem to solve]
(**But you know that**) this problem is not easily solved.

Native speakers are likely to perceive a) as a turn in a discussion as quite abrupt, whereas b) and c) involve the illocutor's anticipated point of view. In b) shared knowledge is assumed, while c) expresses shared knowledge together with the wish to overcome a perceived difference of opinion. Modal particles can create what Schiffrin in her work on discourse markers in English (1987) calls “conversational cohesion”; specifically in the case of DOCH and JA with reference to shared knowledge. Schiffrin assigns a similar function to the discourse marker “y’know” in English, namely to refer to meta-knowledge about what speaker and hearer share and to meta-knowledge about what is generally known.

Luchtenberg (1989) refers to this type of meta-knowledge as ‘common-sense knowledge’ (her translation of “Alltagswissen” which I prefer to refer to as ‘common knowledge’) and classifies it as:

a) internal knowledge of families or other small groups
b) knowledge within a society or larger social group about everyday processes which are self-evident within the group and may therefore remain implici
c) knowledge within a society or larger social group about traditions, cultural experience etc.
d) specialist knowledge of a particular group
e) linguistic knowledge comprised of routine formulae, idiomatic expressions, choice of style and register

Not every native speaker would share all types of knowledge listed above, as an example for type a) knowledge in Luchtenberg’s framework shows. The following text is an excerpt from a telephone conversation between two friends (Brons-Albert 1984):

A: Un die Arbeit macht ihr zwar im Augenblick noch keinen Spaß
[at the moment she is not enjoying work very much yet]
B: hm
A: aber vielleicht kommd’s noch, so, vor allen Dingen will sie **ja** promovieren jetz, un dann brauch se eh schon ma zwei Jahre, un auch zwei Jahre Ruhe zu.
[but that might change, most of all she wants to do her PhD now (**as you know**), and then she needs a good two years anyhow and two tranquil years, too]

(BRO 21 Bd 11/1)

Speaker A assumes that speaker B is familiar with the plans which the third person they are talking about has for her future. He indicates this assumption through the use of JA. Luchtenberg (1989) provides the following example for type b) knowledge (ibid.: 662):

A: Ich will morgen mal zum Arzt.
[I'll go to the doctor's tomorrow.]

B: Morgen ist **doch** Mittwoch.
[(But) tomorrow is Wednesday]

DOCH here refers to common knowledge about the fact that surgeries in Germany are normally closed on Wednesday afternoons.

In the following example, reference is made to type d) knowledge, the specialist group in this case being linguists.

Seit Saussure ist **ja** der Systemcharakter der Sprache..... (ibid.: 667)
[Since Saussure the character of language as a system is (**ja**)...]
[Since Saussure the character of language as a system is, **as we all know**,...]

Amending a proposition in an academic text with a modal particle such as JA or DOCH evaluates the proposition as common knowledge and therefore indisputable, but there is a difference in tone between the use of JA or DOCH. If DOCH were used in the example given above there would be a more critical undertone:

Seit Saussure ist **doch** der Systemcharakter der Sprache...
[**After all**, since Saussure the character of language as a system is...]

Luchtenberg (ibid.) indicates that the acquisition of modal particles which refer to common knowledge can be difficult because non-native speakers might not be familiar with the sociocultural context that forms the basis for common knowledge. Therefore pragmalinguistic as well as sociopragmatic failure might occur (Thomas 1983).

Although non-native speakers might not have access to the types of knowledge categorised as a)–d) in Luchtenberg's (1989) model, increased linguistic knowledge as described in type e) might help to expand an awareness of how the sociocultural context is brought to bearing in a particular speech event. With regard to the present study,

I would like to argue that the force of modal particles needs to be made salient to non-native speakers to show how they, by means of exophoric reference, can point to the wider sociocultural context in the speech event. The example chosen by Luchtenberg (1989: 662) lends itself to such a demonstration. If the modal particle DOCH is not understood the exchange is nonsensical, B's response does not seem to be related to A's statement:

A: Ich will morgen mal zum Arzt.
[I'll go to the doctor's tomorrow.]

B: Morgen ist (doch) Mittwoch.
[Tomorrow is (doch) Wednesday.]

Even though a learner of German might not know that surgeries are commonly closed on Wednesdays, an understanding of the force of DOCH as pointing to shared knowledge and involving a degree of criticism[40] will indicate to the learner that there is implicit information which needs to be taken into account. It is therefore crucial that learners of German understand the impetus of modal particles so that they are able to consider all contributing factors in a speech event.

The non-native speaker should be enabled to access the context of a speech event in a similar way to a native speaker. S/he should be enabled to refer to the same context of experience and evaluation and to express this reference linguistically. Steinmüller (1981) points out the significance of modal particles for expressing attitudes which are evaluated as positive such as courtesy, group membership, and the willingness to modify personal opinions and actions to contribute to intra-group agreement. In presenting an impressionistic view of the productions of mainly Turkish L1 learners of German, he posits that modal particles are not at all or rarely used, pointing out DOCH and MAL as the most frequent ones. The interlanguage productions he analysed did not provide any evidence of a relationship between grammatical development and frequency of use of modal particles.

40 For a detailed analysis of DOCH see chapter 5.6.

A more detailed description of the use of modal particles by non-native speakers of German is given by Husso (1981). She investigated four different groups of subjects:

1) native speakers of German (n=78), aged 20-40
2) students of the German school in Helsinki with Finnish L1, aged 16-18, who had at least one parent who spoke German, had been taught German since pre-school and who were then taught in German in most school subjects, supposedly having integrative motivation (n=65)
3) students of a Finnish high school, aged 16-18, who started learning German in an instructed context at the age of 14-15 and who had no contact to native speakers of German, supposedly having instrumental motivation (n=44)
4) university students with different L1s, attending a preparatory class for a language examination in order to achieve admission to the University of Berlin, aged 19-30, supposedly having integrative motivation (n=71).Most of these studens had attended private language classes for three to six months prior to the preparatory course

Husso's hypotheses were that a) subjects with a higher degree of contact with competent speakers of German would prove more competent in the use of modal particles, b) subjects with an integrative motivation would prove more competent than subjects with an instrumental motivation (cf. Gardner & Lambert 1972), c) native speakers would often use more than one particle per situation, d) native speakers would use combinations of particles, e) non-native speakers would use few combinations of particles. She used questionnaires based on situations taken from everyday life and provided background information on the wider context and the speakers' roles and emotions to ensure that interpretation would be as uniform as possible. The subjects were presented with sentences containing gaps that had to be filled with modal particles out of a given choice. She analysed the data by counting the particles per situation and calculating their frequency in percentages. Her results show that native speakers provide relatively homogenous judgements about which particles fit into which context. Non-native speakers considered more particles as fitting for a situation and showed a more or less higher scattering than native speakers in the use of different particles. Group 2 proved to be most competent in the correct suppliance of modal particles followed by 3 and 4, thus verifying part of her hypotheses. She found the particles AUCH, DENN, DOCH to be employed most frequently, but very often incorrectly. BLOSS, EBEN, ETWA, HALT were used more frequently by the group of university students than by the other groups. ABER, MAL, JA were the particles which were most often used correctly, which Husso ascribes to their frequent appearance as part of formulae. Her hypotheses concerning particle combinations were verified. The fact that – contrary to her hypothesis – the Finnish high school students proved more competent than the group of university students living in Germany is discussed with a view to possible interference of L1, as Finnish contains a number of modal particles as well.

Husso limits the validity of her study by pointing to the elicitation method chosen, as a different picture might emerge when learners are not presented with a choice of particles which obliges them to use one or the other. Trying to overcome this limitation, Weydt (1981a) conducted a pilot study on oral communication. He videotaped short situations consisting of four to six turns which he describes as rather emotional and therefore highly interactive. Two native speakers acted out the situations as a model. Subjects were presented with the model once or twice and then asked to act out the situations. They were taped and the dialogues transcribed. He analysed the data for occurrences of modal particles as well as other particles and calculated the average production frequency per 1000 words per speaker:

Table 1: Production frequency of particles by NS and NNS
(Weydt 1981a)

	Modal particles	Non-modal particles	Total
Native speakers	87,3	34,9	122.2
Non-native speakers	30,9	21,6	52,5

Because of the considerable differences, he regards his findings as reliable, although the number of subjects he investigated is quite small (non-native speakers: n=12, native speakers: n=?). The hypotheses he tried to prove beyond those expressed by Husso were a) that staying in Germany would correlate positively with competence in the use of particles and b) that receiving instruction in German would not prove significant. In criticising the reliability and validity of his study, however, he reports the length of instruction as not adequately described, not enough information on the intensity of contact with native speakers provided, and not enough consideration given to the subjects' L1. Furthermore, he points to the small number of subjects and the fact that no distinction was made between correct and incorrect particle use. He thus states a falsification of his first hypothesis as a tendency. He concludes that modal particles are not learned 'automatically' – at least not in the early stages of language acquisition where lexical and grammatical difficulties might preoccupy the learner – and argues that therefore instruction on modal particles is necessary.

Research findings (Husso 1981, Steinmüller 1981, Weydt 1981a) provide an ambiguous picture of the relationship between language acquisition in general and the acquisition of modal particles. There is agreement on a much lower frequency of use by non-native speakers which is hypothesised to be due to either lack of understanding of the important functions of modal particles because they do not occur in the learner's first language, lack of contact with native speakers, lack of instruction, or a combination of those factors. The issues and research questions put forth in studying the acquisition of modal particles are to be seen in the context of the broader field of enquiry commonly labelled as interlanguage pragmatics (e.g. Kasper & Blum-Kulka 1993, Kasper 1981, Blum-Kulka, House & Kasper 1989). While interlanguage pragmatics is modelled on cross-cultural pragmatics and has therefore emphasized the differences between native and non-native speakers in speech act performance and politeness strategies, recent discussions and studies in this area have focussed more on developmental issues (Kasper and Schmidt 1996, House 1996, Rose 2000, Kasper 2000/2001) and the correlation between pragmatic development of learners' interlanguage and second language acquisition in general (Kasper 1996, Kasper and Rose 1999, Rose and Kasper 2001).

Weydt's (1981a) conclusion that instruction on modal particles is necessary because they are not learned automatically is affirmed by research findings in interlanguage pragmatics in general. There is evidence that instruction can improve learners' sociolinguistic competence. Wildner-Bassett (1984) studied the use of gambits – conversational strategy signals, which indicate how a stretch of utterance is to be understood – by adult L1 German learners of English. Analysing videotaped data of interactional tasks conducted as role-plays, she found that as far as ratios of gambit quality and gambit quantity were concerned (among other variables she tested for) instruction had a positive effect. Billmyer (1990) reports that the production of, and reply to compliments by learners of American English was influenced positively by formal instruction. She compared the productions of learners in social interaction with native speakers outside the classroom and found that the subjects who had received instruction performed significantly better than a control group on measures of frequency of norm-appropriate compliments, level of spontaneity, repertoire of adjectives used and appropriateness of reply. Bouton (1994) investigated conversational implicature, the means of expressing a message indirectly, in the context of second language learning. His subjects were international college students in the United States. The longitudinal study shows that it takes non-native speakers of English a long time to interpret implicatures in a way that is not significantly different from native speakers' interpretations if there is no systematic teaching of implicature. House (1996) studied the effects of explicit and implicit instruction aimed at developing conversational fluency (use of speech acts, discourse strategies, gambits) over a period of fourteen weeks. Her subjects were 32 very advanced learners of English at a German university. Data included pre- and post-instruction interviews, audiotaped conversations and three role plays at equal intervals throughout the instruction phase. The results of the study showed that both groups benefitted from instruction and that metapragmatic information provided via explicit instruction is essential to avoid negative pragmatic transfer.

In their evaluation of studies on the teachability of pragmatic information and the most effective approaches to instruction in L2 pragmatics, Kasper & Rose (1999: 96-97) conclude:

> Results are encouraging, suggesting that most pragmatic features are indeed teachable. Instruction in pragmatic information is generally facilitative and necessary when input is lacking or less salient (e.g., for some types of implicature, Bouton 1994). Explicit instruction yields better results than implicit teaching; however, while explicit teaching is helpful for consciousness raising, it may be less effective for some aspects of skill development.

An even stronger penchant for explicit instruction is expressed by Kasper (2000: 21):

> A strong general trend emerging from these studies is a distinct advantage for explicit pragmatic instruction, irrespective of such factors as the specific pragmalinguistic or sociopragmatic learning objective, L2, learners' L2 proficiency level, their L1 background, or length of instruction.

The evidence for the positive effects of instruction on pragmatic features of language provides a strong rationale for the teaching of modal particles. In particular, consciousness raising through explicit instruction has been proven to be a successful approach which will be discussed with regard to the present study later in this chapter.

3.3 Acquisition of modal particles in instructed and uninstructed environments

The fact that the theoretical explication has not yet reached a comprehensive and thus satisfactory level is one of the reasons why the teaching of German modal particles is considered problematic (cf. Jiang 1993, Götze 1993; Busse 1992). Different methodological approaches have been suggested. In this subchapter different proposals for the teaching of modal particles are discussed and related to the acquisition of those particles in uninstructed contexts.

What do second language learners know about modal particles?

A lack of understanding of the important functions of modal particles in German has been advanced as one possible reason for a lower frequency of use by non-native speakers. In an empirical study involving L1 English learners of German, Harden and Rösler (1981) investigated the perception of the use of modal particles. Listening to dialogues and comparing those speakers using modal particles to those who did not, learners are reported to have recognised that modal particles play an important part in the expression of emotions. The learners did not, however, judge the use of modal particles as an important indicator of a good command of German. The detailed results of the study are as follows (ibid.: 73):

- The listeners' language competence is significant for their evaluation of the use of particles.
- The relationship between the use of particles and the expression of emotions seems to have been recognised.
- The speaker's accent influences the assessment of his/her command of German more than the use of particles.
- Learners who received instruction in German as a foreign language do not seem to perceive the communicative value of particles as very high.

Learners' (L1: English) listening comprehension data on differences between two dialogue versions (Möllering and Nunan 1995) corroborate the finding that learners who receive instruction in German as a foreign language have difficulties in evaluating the communicative value of particles correctly.

Which particles should be taught and when should they be taught?

The timing and the progression of instruction on modal particles have been considered in a number of publications.

Vorderwülbecke (1981) suggests teaching groups of modal particles following these criteria for progression:

- frequency of the particle
- restrictions of the particle's use regarding sentence types
- modal particle's function in expressing intentions

(Are they adequate to learner's roles and general language competence?[41])

Applying these criteria, he suggests that the particles DENN, EBEN, MAL, VIELLEICHT should be introduced in the first stage, ABER, AUCH, DOCH, EIGENTLICH in the second stage and the remaining modal particles at a more advanced level. He favours an early introduction of modal particles in order for learners to achieve communicative competence and pragmatic adequacy. With regard to teaching methodology, he proposes focussing on the meaning of modal particles in context, an explanation of their illocutionary force within a dialogue and paraphrasing as a method of describing their meaning. Vorderwülbecke's (1981) proposals have been realised in part in the introductory level German textbook "Stufen International I" (Vorderwülbecke & Vorderwülbecke 1995) which is discussed in subsequent parts of this chapter.

Following a very thorough evaluation of the literature on modal particles and the difficulties of teaching them to learners of German as a foreign language, Busse (1992: 55) develops an eight-point catalogue, which addresses (amongst others) the questions: a) which particles should be taught and b) when they should be taught. The following is a summary of his proposals:

1) It is essential to teach the most frequent modal particles because of their important communicative functions in German. Particles should be taught and practised in authentic communicative situations.
2) If the instruction takes place in German exclusively (i.e. not in the learners' L1), instruction on modal particles should not start before learners have reached an intermediate level of proficiency[42], in earlier stages ad-hoc explanations should be given.

41 The concept of 'general language competence' is not elaborated on.

42 Busse (1992: 55): "[...] können sie im einsprachigen Unterricht erst ab der Mittelstufe behandelt werden [...]". No further criteria for measuring proficiency are provided.

3) In homogenous groups of learners, modal particles should be contrasted with those linguistic means which are used in L1 to express the same/a similar meaning.
4) Examples of modal particles should be given in context rather than at a sentence level, so that learners can take the linguistic context, the situational context and the wider social context (e.g. presuppositions) into account.
5) Some modal particles should be learned as part of idiomatic phrases.
6) Learners should practise the relationship between particle meaning, sentence type and intonation.
7) It is crucial that learners are able to distinguish modal particles from their homonyms.
8) To simplify comprehension of a modal particle's meaning 'quasi-psychological descriptions' of the particle's force should be given (such as 'expression of surprise', 'expression of astonishment' etc).

This catalogue seems particularly valuable when considering the comprehension aspect of the acquisition of modal particles and I will refer to it again when outlining my own proposal in more detail.

In contrast to such externally motivated catalogues of grading criteria, Rösler (1983) advises a more student-centred approach. He argues that the situations where communication is relevant for the learner can only be determined in view of the actual group of learners under consideration and cannot be deduced from a given progression of speech events; an argument which is also put forward by Tarone and Yule (1989) in a more general consideration of sociolinguistic competence in second language acquisition.

One possible way of reconciling a content-based grading approach with a student-centred approach to teaching modal particles could be a modular one. Teaching materials on specific modal particles could be made available in accordance with learners' enquiries, i.e. when they are confronted with those particles in context.

Reports on instruction of modal particles

A number of qualitative studies – belonging to the category of classroom-research studies (cf. Nunan 1989, 1991, 1992) – report on instruction in the area of German modal particles. Paneth (1981) describes instruction of German modal particles to English L1 university students which draws on audio-lingual as well as translation methods. Students were presented with German texts on tape containing modal particles and their English translations. They were also provided with a list of functions for each particle under discussion, which – together with the tapes – they used to group occurrences of particles according to appropriate translation into English. They then provided their own translations of the given and additional texts. Paneth (ibid.: 108) observed that "in general the subjects find it easier to specify the meaning of a modal particle by translating rather than by choosing between alternatives or paraphrasing".

Rall (1981) reports on a teaching and learning project with Mexican university students after six semesters of instruction in German. Instruction started with a presentation of material in Spanish on modal particles in general and the problem of homonymy in particular followed by a detailed description of 25 particles in their modal and non-modal occurrences with examples. The explanations were illustrated by using audiotaped and written texts. Exercises included reading tasks aiming at correct intonation; drills, if they appeared necessary in the classroom context; paraphrasing, which is reported to have caused difficulties; gap exercises and open-ended role play as well as authentic communication with visiting native speakers of German. Production data showed that 15 of the 25 modal particles students had received instruction on were used with varying degrees of naturalness and appropriateness. Rall (ibid.) reported a number of avoidance strategies in the use of modal particles and concluded that interaction in German was crucial to the learning process.

Möllering and Nunan (1995) examined the influence of instruction on the acquisition of modal particles with a group of 23 Australian undergraduate students of German. The students had varying backgrounds in learning the language, some having commenced the program at beginners' level, others having studied German in high school. A number of students within this group had lived in a German speaking country for varying amounts of time. All of the students were enrolled in a second year language course. In the course of their studies, students had been exposed to a large number of spoken dialogues (tape program and classroom input) with a relatively high frequency of modal particles. A number of modal particles had been taken up for metalinguistic discussion.

In this study, instruction was operationalised as a three-step process of awareness-raising, explanation and practice. Acquisition was seen as a twofold process of perception/comprehension and production (for a discussion, see Nunan, 1995).
The subjects' competence regarding modal particles before the onset of instruction was assessed. Competence was operationalised as

- the ability to perceive the illocutionary and emotive force of modal particles
- the ability to use modal particles in context
- metalinguistic knowledge about modal particles.

Also assessed were the input on modal particles prior to instruction (the texts students had studied were compiled as a computer-readable corpus and concordanced for modal particles) as well as the subjects' motivation regarding the acquisition of modal particles.

Before instruction, the group of students under study showed poor comprehension of the force of modal particles. Their metalinguistic knowledge was restricted to a vague notion of the functions modal particles fulfil and they reported having had little or no input on the topic in their course of studies. Input in form of occurrences of modal particles in context (see concordance data) without focus on the particles seems to have had no influence on the subjects. Self-report data indicated that students used only a small number of modal particles with DENN, JA, DOCH and EIGENTLICH being mentioned by at least a third of the students. Their use of modal particles in a given context deviated from native speaker expectations, especially with regard to the particle DOCH. Production data revealed an under-representation of DOCH although it had occurred in modal particle function more often than any other particle in the texts the students had read, as the concordance data showed. Thus, DOCH was chosen as the focus of instruction.

Materials for instruction consisted of a handout with detailed explanation of DOCH. It introduced different occurrences of DOCH in functions other than as modal particle as well as its overall modal particle function. This was further elaborated upon by specifying the illocutionary force it carries in different sentence types. Throughout the explanations, examples were provided which had been drawn from the corpus of texts used for the concordance so that it was possible to keep the examples short without having to lose situational context as the students had read the texts and were familiar with the context of situation as well as with the wider context. In cases where the concordance did not provide appropriate examples they were created to fit in with the students' experiential knowledge. In a next step, the students were asked to go back to a dialogue text they had read and discussed in class some weeks earlier. The text reflected a debate between a father and his son and showed ample use of DOCH. Students were asked to discuss in pairs the occurrences of DOCH and to classify them according to the explanation they had been given earlier. Most of the students had considerable difficulty in doing so and in the ensuing class discussion they stated that they found the explanation very complex and needed more time to go over it again. The last stage required students to use DOCH in the context of drill exercises which were amended by further explanation of the issues of word order and intonation. Opportunities for additional questions were given and error feedback provided. Following the instruction phase, the subjects were presented with a questionnaire consisting of four sections:

Section 1 described three situations, the subject might be in. S/he was asked to respond to the situations, which provide an optional context for the use of modal particles.

Section 2 consisted of two authentic examples of the modal particle in question in a context the subjects were familiar with. In the form of an open-ended question, they were asked to explain the meaning with respect to the context.

Section 3 again tested for suppliance of the particle, but this time in an obligatory context. The subjects were presented with short gap exercises in the form of dialogues, where they were required to fill the gaps with appropriate modal particles out of a given number of choices including the one instruction was focused upon. The exercises, published in Weydt et al. (1983) are based on native speaker intuitions about the correct use of modal particles in these contexts.

Section 4 consisted of a closed questionnaire, where the students were asked to give ratings on their progress and their perceptions on the value of different aspects of the instructional process.

DOCH was used with considerably more frequency after the instruction phase, though in what might be called "semi-obligatory" contexts rather than optional ones. Less than half of the students were able to explain or translate DOCH in a way which showed that they fully understood its illocutionary force. Thus, an improved understanding could not be posited for the group as a whole but could be seen as a tendency.

The students showed great interest in the acquisition of modal particles and they perceived the instruction as having had a positive effect. They found the detailed explanations and the accompanying examples the most effective means of instruction but remarked that they needed more time to grasp the distribution of meaning of DOCH according to function and sentence type. The suppliance of DOCH varied considerably according to context. This confirms the observation of Kasper and Dahl (1991) in an analysis of elicitation methods. Husso (1981) also pointed out the limited validity of her findings with regard to elicitation, which was - as is the case in this study - a gap exercise. DOCH was not frequently employed in optional contexts, which might be due to avoidance strategies (cf. Færch and Kasper 1983) or to the ambiguity of the situation described. The provision of DOCH as incorrect choice after instruction had taken place might be seen as overgeneralisation of the possible contexts of use, similar to the effects Lightbown (1983), Pica (1985) and Brindley (1987) observed in their studies on the acquisition of morphosyntactic features of language. As DOCH had been the particle focussed upon it was the most likely one to be supplied when in doubt.

The frequent use of the modal particle DENN reported by Husso (1981) was confirmed by this study. Vorderwülbecke's (1981) progression criteria provide a plausible explanation. DENN belongs to the group of most frequently used modal particles and it is bound to the sentence type 'question' which considerably limits the contexts of its use and thus renders it less complex to learn than DOCH.

The study can be seen as providing evidence for the beneficial effects of instruction on the acquisition of modal particles although DOCH was not fully acquired in all its complexity.

Modal particles and uninstructed language acquisition

In addition to reports on the instruction of modal particles, acquisition has been investigated in uninstructed contexts. In a longitudinal case study over a period of three and a half years, Kutsch (1985) examined the acquisition of German particles[43] by a Turkish girl, aged 11 when data collection was completed. Her language data, transcriptions of everyday interactions (games, visit to the zoo, swimming pool etc.), were compared to those of a native speaker child of the same age. A quantitative and qualitative evaluation of the data showed that after six years of learning German in uninstructed contexts, the child had only acquired half of the communicative types of particles[44] and their functions and that the non-native speaker used particles less frequently than the native speaker.

Kutsch (ibid.: 249f) arrived, amongst others, at the following conclusions which are pertinent for the present investigation:

- The fact that each particle is used in a variety of functions influences the use of particles by non-native speakers and the acquisition process.
- The acquisition of communicative particles seems to be completed earlier than the acquisition of semantic particles, which is in keeping with the assumption that in second language acquisition pragmatic elements are needed earlier than semantic elements. The variety of functions of communicative particles leads to discontinuity in the acquisition of those particles.
- Particles are learned in an additive manner and then their communicative and semantic functions are modified. When the use of a particle has stabilised, it starts appearing in combinations with other particles.

The fact that a particle is first learned in one of its functions concurs with findings on the acquisition of morphological language features (cf. Pica 1985), where a one-to-one relationship between form and function has been stated as one reason for an item to be learned early on. Kutsch (ibid.: 241) elaborates on the point as follows:

43 Following a broad definition of the term 'particle'.

44 Kutsch distinguishes between 'communicative' and 'semantic' particles. The group he refers to as communicative particles includes modal particles like DOCH, JA, ABER, DENN, SCHON, MAL.

> Offensichtlich erwirbt die L2-Lernerin zunächst die Form (Partikel) in Verbindung mit ausschließlich einer Funktion, ablesbar an der Partikel *doch* mit der Funktion Konsensherstellung. Auch *ja*, *so*, *aber* und *schon* bestätigen diese Annahme, wodurch die These an Bedeutung gewinnt, daß zunächst Formen gebunden an eine Funktion erworben werden. Der Erwerb dieser Formen vollzieht sich additiv, zu t3 [zum Zeitpunkt t3] sind *doch*, *ja* und *so* erworben, später kommen *schon*, *aber* und *zwar* hinzu.

The learner Kutsch reports on first acquired the particle DOCH in its function of creating consensus. Similarly, JA, SO, ABER and SCHON were acquired, giving weight to the hypothesis that these forms are first learned in only one function. More forms were added over time; DOCH, JA and SO were acquired first, SCHON, ABER and ZWAR were added at a later stage.

Cheon-Kostrzewa & Kostrzewa (1997a & 1997b) report on the acquisition of the particles ABER and DOCH by a Polish L1 learner of German in uninstructed contexts. At the onset of data collection, which spanned a period of two and a half years, the subject had been living in Germany for a year. Data were collected monthly in different types of discourse which are described as open/free conversation, narratives and reports, stating of opinion, instruction and problem solving. Throughout the data, only three ocurrences of ABER in modal particle function (once in month 10, twice in month 28) were found, which limits potential statements about acquisition patterns. The researchers assume that the non-frequent use of ABER can be attributed to the fact that it is restricted semantically to contexts where surprise is expressed (cf. the example of ABER as modal particle in chapter 2.4). DOCH in modal particle function is reported to appear 35 times in the data, starting with a phrase that occurs so frequently in native speaker use that it may be seen as formulaic ("das ist DOCH egal"), followed by the use of DOCH in declaratives. Only in much later stages of her language acquisition (month 24) does the subject begin to use the modal particle DOCH in exclamatives, imperatives and interrogatives. Cheon-Kostrzewa & Kostrzewa's (1997b) findings are therefore in agreement with Kutsch (1985), who stated that a particle is first learned in one function with a differentiation of further functions taking place at a later stage. Their findings are also congruent with Kutsch's with regard to the acquisition of pragmatic function versus semantic function[45], as they report the acquisition of DOCH as modal particle to preceed the acquisition of DOCH as adverb.

The tendencies of the research findings on the acquisition of modal particles can be summarised as follows: In uninstructed acquisition contexts, modal particles are acquired relatively slowly (c.f Bouton 1984 on the acquisition of implicature). The input learners receive seems to play an important role in the acquisition process as modal particles used frequently in routine formulae in native speaker speech are first reproduced by learners. The difficulty for the learner of having to analyse multiple particle functions seems to be overcome by the frequency in the input.[46] Modal particles are acquired in an accumulative manner: a particle which occurs with high frequency in the input is first produced in only one of its functions before the learner begins to distinguish others. A modification of semantic and communicative functions does not take place before the particles already acquired have been stabilised and differentiated as part of the lexicon (Kutsch 1985: 243):

> Die Modifikation semantischer und kommunikativer Funktionen erfolgt offensichtlich erst, nachdem eine Stabilisierung und Differenzierung der erworbenen Partikeln im Bereich des Lexikons stattgefunden hat.

Instruction on modal particles seems to have a positive effect, although none of the studies discussed above can show that instruction can lead to the acquisition of modal particles in all their complexity. The productions of non-native speakers after instruction took place reflect a tendency for overgeneralisation of the particles the instruction was focussed upon. This is in keeping with findings on the instruction of morphosyntactic language features (e.g. Lightbown 1983, Pica 1985, Brindley 1987). The type of instruction discussed above and the elicitation methods used lead to suppliance of modal

45 They use the term 'semantic' to refer to DOCH as answering particle and adverb.

46 Kutsch (1985: 242): "Die bemerkenswerte Stabilität im Sprachgebrauch dieser Funktionswörter ist ein Anzeichen dafür, daß das Analyseproblem des L2-Lerners zumindest bei den kommunikativen Partikeln durch die Häufigkeit ihres Auftretens in spontan gesprochener Sprache weniger stark ist, als zunächst angenommen wurde."

particles in obligatory contexts, but avoidance strategies can be observed in non-obligatory contexts.

3.4 Teaching materials on modal particles

The research findings on modal particles and on their acquisition by non-native speakers and the prevalence of those particles in spoken German – considered in a more communicative approach to language teaching – have resulted in the publication of teaching materials on modal particles. One of the early publications (Kemme 1979) is directed at teachers of German as a foreign language. Following a brief introduction which addresses the categorisation of modal particles, their restrictions of occurrence with regard to sentence type and speech act type as well as aspects of their discursive and interpersonal functions, explanations and exercises are provided for specific groups of modal particles. Kemme (ibid.) distinguishes four broad groups of modal particles

- JA, BLOSS, NUR as emphatic particles in requests
- modal particles in a discursive function as anaphora in a text[47]
- modal particles in a discursive function pointing to the wider context of the speech event [48]
- modal particles pointing to common knowledge

After a short explanation of the respective modal particles in the functions outlined above, exercises are presented in the form of pattern drills and gap exercises where the learner is asked to supply individual modal particles (ibid.: 35):

47 here: textimmanent, see my distinction on p. 33.

48 here: textextern, see my distinction on p. 33.

> Übung 14 – WOHL
>
> Erklärung:
> Die Modalpartikel wohl kann eine Äußerung als Annahme kennzeichnen, die aus einer Voräußerung abgeleitet ist.
>
> Anleitung:
> Reagieren Sie auf die folgenden Sätze mit Annahmen (Vermutungen) mit WOHL!
>
> Beispiel:
> A: Hans macht Urlaub auf den Seychellen.
> Sie: Der hat wohl im Lotto gewonnen.
>
> Aufgabe:
> Die Lieselotte ist ganz braungebrannt. [Gebirge]
> Ich hab' den Erwin eben im dunklen Anzug getroffen. [Examensfeier] …

or select a particle from a given choice (ibid.: 31):

> Übung 8
>
> Setzen Sie entweder JA oder DOCH in die Lücken ein. In einigen Fällen ist beides möglich, jedoch beachten Sie, daß JA eher in zustimmenden oder übereinstimmenden, DOCH eher in widersprechenden Feststellungen steht.
>
> Heute morgen habe ich Manfred gesehen.
> Wieso der ist .... in Paris!
> Wirklich? Da muß ich mich getäuscht haben. Aber das ist .... auch egal! Im Grunde wollte ich Dir etwas anderes erzählen: In unserem Büro arbeitet........ ein Portugiese!

In view of the research results on the acquisition of modal particles by non-native speakers it might be argued that the type of pattern drill exercise proposed by Kemme (1979) is likely to enforce patterns of overgeneralisation, as has been observed for instructed acquisition.[49] More promising seems Kemme's proposal to focus the learner's attention on modal particles in short dialogues (1979: 79ff):

> Dialog 1 (Rückbezug im Text)
>
> A: Morgen kommt Fritz nach München.
> B: Was will der denn (1) hier? Der hat (2) jetzt gar keinen Urlaub.
> A: Er kommt ja (3) nur fürs Wochenende.
> B: Lohnt sich denn (4) das bei der langen Reise? Er muß doch (5) mindestens sechs Stunden fahren. Was macht der denn (6), wenn wir wieder Glatteis kriegen?
> A: Dann muß er eben (7) einen Tag blau machen.
>
> Nachsprechen! Lesen mit verteilten Rollen!
>
> Erklärungen
> Modalpartikeln können sich auf vorangegangene Äußerungen beziehen.
> 1.) DENN verlangt eine Erklärung der Voräußerung (Begründung der Möglichkeit, Vernünftigkeit o.ä. dessen, was sie ausdrückt). Es kennzeichnet den Fragesatz, in dem es steht, als Fragehandlung. Es wird eine Handlung erwartet.
> 2.) DOCH kennzeichnet die Äußerung, in der es steht, als eine Gegenfeststellung, die sich auf den Inhalt oder das Implikat der Voräußerung bezieht.
> 3.) JA kennzeichnet die Äußerung, in der es steht, als Bestätigung oder Rechtfertigung einer vorangehenden Äußerung oder ihres Implikats.
> 4.) = 1
> 5.) = 2
> 6.) = 1
> 7.) EBEN gibt der Äußerung in der es steht, den Charakter einer abschließenden Folgerung aus Voräußerungen.

It seems questionable, however, whether repeating the dialogue and reading it out aloud are suitable learning strategies. This type of

49 It would also be of interest to examine native speaker suppliance of JA and DOCH in this particular exercise. It seems to me that especially in the sentence "In unserem Büro arbeitet ... ein Portugiese" there might be variation in native speakers' suppliance of JA and DOCH.

learner activity does not seem congruent with the language level the learner must have achieved to benefit from the rather complex explanations of modal particles in context. The activities proposed in Kemme (1979) are very much focussed on teacher input and repetition and pattern drills on the part of the learner. His proposal for teachers to create texts which include the "right mix" of modal particle and exclude occurrences of homonyms is not in keeping with an approach to teaching which promotes the use of authentic materials and places the learner at the centre of the learning process.

Weydt, Harden, Hentschel & Rösler (1983) published teaching materials (text/exercise book and audiocassette) on modal particles which introduce speech acts with the particles that may be used to modify their illocutionary force. The particles and the modification their use indicates are exemplified in short dialogues accompanied by a description of the situational context. Explanations are followed by drill exercises and gap exercises where learners are required to choose between different particles. There is also a very brief description of the position of modal particles within a sentence and a register for the 26 particles discussed, which describes their homonyms, the speech acts they occur in, syntactic features and an attempt at specifying a comprehensive meaning inherent to all homonyms. These materials are designed to be used as supplements to a text book after at least one year of instruction in German. Modal particles are introduced and practised around twelve speech acts, such as expressing astonishment, assumption, objection, warning or threat etc. In relation to these materials, Muhr (1989) criticised the order in which the speech acts are presented, indicating that a potentially face-threatening act such as 'warning' and 'threatening' would not be of great importance to a second language learner. Apart from the slightly patronizing attitude towards non-native speakers this criticism reveals, it does not seem valid as Weydt et al. (1983) explicitly state the flexible order in which the speech acts are presented. The materials present a variety of exercises primarily aimed at production and place great emphasis on intonation patterns accompanying the use of modal particles. Kummer (1984) focuses on the particles DENN, DOCH, EBEN, EIGENTLICH,

ETWA, JA in a program which aims at teaching knowledge about and skills in using modal particles.[50]

The first part is mainly directed at teachers and advanced learners. Titled 'Syntax, semantics and pragmatics of modal particles', it provides a brief introduction followed by a second part with more detailed explanations and exercises. Weydt et al. (1983) assemble modal particles around certain speech act types and offer exercises which practise those particles in relation to those, as well as exercises which help the learner to distinguish between particles which can be used in the same speech act types (e.g JA and DOCH). Unfortunately, no such ordering pattern is discernible in Kummer (1984). A large part of the exercises presented here are based on listening comprehension segments where learners practise to supply modal particles or to interpret the meaning of modal particles. The listening comprehension component is a valuable part of the program, but the related exercises, especially the ones focussing on production, do not seem instrumental in distinguishing between different particle usages.

Based on a very comprehensive dictionary of German particles (Helbig 1988, 1994), Helbig & Helbig (1995) published an exercise book on particles in the broader sense. It is arranged into three chapters one of which deals with modal particles. Here, each particle is listed in its different grammatical functions. The word AUCH, for example is described under the following headings (ibid.: 21ff):

AUCH
- as adverb
- as scalar particle
- as part of a coordinating conjunction
- as part of a subordinating function
- as modal particle:
  1. in statements
  2. in yes/no questions
  3. in wh-questions
  4. in imperatives
  5. in exclamatives
  6. in free subordinate clauses[51]

50 Kummer (1984: 5): "Das vorliegende Modul ist ein Programm zur Vertiefung, Erweiterung und zum Neuerwerb von Kenntnissen und Fertigkeiten im Gebrauch der Modalpartikeln."

Examples and explanations are given for each category, followed by exercises which concentrate on distinguishing between the different particle categories and on practising the particle in its different functions, mostly in the form of drill exercises. At the end of the chapter on modal particles, mixed exercises on groups of modal particles (according to sentence types) are presented in the form of gap exercises or pattern drills, similar to the ones discussed for Kemme (1979). While this exercise book provides the most comprehensive collection of exercises on particles in general, its focus on pattern drill exercises to teach production might – as has been discussed for the types of exercises in Kemme (1979) – enforce patterns of overgeneralisations, as has been reported for instructed acquisition.

Modal particles are now also being discussed in a number of textbooks for German as a second language. The examples discussed below are taken from three recently published textbooks of German and they exemplify different approaches ("Stufen" 1995, "Tangram" 1998, "em Abschlusskurs" 1999).

"Tangram" (Dallapiazza et al. 1998), aimed at learners at beginners level, contains a grammar section in the form of an overview in the learner's textbook. Amongst shorter sections on sentence structure, morphology and textgrammar, the main part of this grammatical overview consists of a section on different word classes. The explanation of modal particles follows the common model of categorisation as outlined in chapter 2.2: modal particles are described as a subcategory to particles in the broader sense.

Surprising is the list of 'modal particles' which is given on the contents page (ibid. G1):

> §21 Die Modalpartikeln: etwa, mal, denn, fast, sehr, doch, wirklich, etwas, ziemlich, ganz.

which includes a number of scalar particles which cannot occur in modal particle function ('fast', 'sehr', 'etwas', 'ziemlich', 'ganz') and the adjective 'wirklich' which does not belong into the broad category

51 (Helbig & Helbig 1995: 22) "[...] in selbständigen mit daß eingeleiteten Nebensätzen ohne übergeordneten Hauptsatz."

of particles. More confusion awaits the prospective learner when s/he is then presented with the "explanations" (ibid.: G18):

§21 Die Modalpartikeln

Modalpartikeln setzen subjektive Akzente. Sie modifizieren den Satz oder einzelne Satzteile. Modalpartikeln dekliniert man nicht. Vergleichen Sie:

*Die Wohnung ist **sehr** schön!*	+++
Die Wohnung ist schön.	++
*Die Wohnung ist **ganz** schön.*	+
Der Kühlschrank ist günstig. Oh, der ist aber günstig.	zeigt Überraschung
*Wie alt sind **denn** Ihre Kinder?*	zeigt Interesse
*Hast du **vielleicht** auch Tee?* *Gebt ihr mir **mal** eine Schachtel Zigaretten?*	machen Fragen freundlich
*Helft mir **doch mal**!* *Kommen Sie **bitte** mit.*	machen Aufforderungen freundlich
*Schau mal, das Sofa ist **doch** toll.*	*„Findest du nicht auch?"*
*Das ist **doch** altmodisch.*	*„Nein, ich finde es nicht toll."*
*Ich finde das Sofa nicht **so** schön.*	höflich für *„nicht schön"*
*Das ist **zu** teuer.*	*„Soviel Geld möchte ich nicht bezahlen."*
*Sie ist **schon** 8 Monate in Deutschland.*	*„Ich finde, das ist eine lange Zeit."*
*Sie ist **erst** 8 Monate in Deutschland.*	*„Ich finde, das ist nicht lange."*
*Ich spreche **etwas** Deutsch.* *Kann ich auch **etwas** später kommen?*	≈ nicht viel, ein bisschen
*Roman möchte **noch** ein Cola.*	≈ das zweite, dritte, ... Cola
*Lesen Sie den Text **noch** einmal.*	≈ das zweite, dritte, ... Mal
In Deutschland haben...	*„Ich weiß es nicht ganz genau."*
*... **fast** alle Haushalte eine Waschmaschine.*	< 100% (≈ 95-99%)
*... **über** die Hälfte der Haushalte einen Videorekorder.*	> 50% (≈51-55%)
*... **etwa** die Hälfte der Haushalte eine Mikrowelle.*	< > 50% (≈45-55%)
*Ich komme **so** um zehn.*	< > 10 Uhr (9.45-10.15 Uhr)
*Haben Sie auch andere Teppiche? **So** für 500 Mark?*	< > 500 DM (450-550 DM)
*Die Vorstellung war **ganz** fantastisch.* *	macht die Aussage „fantastisch" stärker
*Wir haben gleich **sehr** nette Leute kennen gelernt.*	macht die Aussage „nett" stärker
*Die Tempel waren **wirklich** schön.* *Ich war **wirklich** sauer auf Ralf.*	betont „schön" und „sauer"
*Der Flug war **ganz** schön lang.* *Die Snacks waren **ziemlich** teuer.*	macht die Aussagen „lang" und „teuer" etwas stärker
*Der lange Flug war **etwas** langweilig.* *Ich war auch **ein bisschen** müde.*	macht die Aussagen „langweilig" und „müde" etwas schwächer

▶ Die Partikeln sehr, ganz schön, ein bisschen, ziemlich, etwas kann man nicht mit den positiven Attributen fantastisch und super kombinieren.

* Die (betonte) Partikel ganz kann man nicht mit den negativen Adjektiven teuer und anstrengend kombinieren.

The main function of modal particles is being described as "adding subjectiveness", their main grammatical feature as being non-declinable. The authors state that modal particles modify the sentence or part thereof – very much in disagreement with the research on modal particles (see discussion in Chapter 2), which concludes that the scope of modal particles is always the whole sentence. The authors arrive at this explanation because they group together modal particles and scalar particles; the scope of scalar particles may be the sentence or part thereof. Out of the whole list of examples on "modal particles" given, only the examples on DENN, MAL, DOCH and ABER represent modal particle function, and the explanation of their meaning seems wanting.

The function of modal particles is summarised under the heading "subjective emphasis" (Subjektiver Akzent). For DENN the explanation given is that it "expresses interest", there is no hint as to the restrictions of its use in interrogatives only, no explanation of its discursive function with regard to text coherence (for a detailed discussion of DENN see Chapter 5.4). The modal particle MAL is grouped together with VIELLEICHT; the explanation being that both "make questions sound more friendly". One example of MAL in an interrogative is provided; its formulaic use in imperative constructions (see Chapter 5.7) is represented in combination with DOCH. DOCH is represented with three examples. The first one is grouped together with an example for BITTE; both are said to "make a request sound more friendly". DOCH occurs in collocation with MAL in an imperative construction ("Helft mir DOCH MAL!"); there is no explanation whether it is DOCH or MAL or the combination of those two which brings about the 'friendliness' of the request. For the other two examples with DOCH, no explanatory comment is provided, but paraphrases are given. As it is not at all clear whether the two examples and their paraphrases constitute a sequence in a dialogue, the explanatory force of the paraphrases is likely to be lost on the learner. ABER is represented by the example: "Der Kühlschrank ist günstig. Oh, der ist ABER günstig." Again, it is not all clear what the relationship between the two clauses is. Is the second one meant to be a response to the first, or is it meant to be an expansion of the first by the same speaker? As learners would find it difficult to develop a clear picture of the speech event at hand, the explanation that ABER expresses surprise might be lost on them. While it is a very positive move, indeed, to include modal particles in textbooks for German as a second language, it can only be hoped that the results of the prolific research on modal particles which has been published over the past three decades will be taken into account when creating those teaching materials.

A more detailed and context-oriented approach to incorporating material on modal particles into a beginners' level textbook can be found in "Stufen International 1" (Vorderwülbecke & Vorderwülbecke 1995), which introduces the modal particles DENN (Lesson 2), DOCH and MAL (Lesson 6). The particles have occurred in short dialogues (textbook and audiocassette) and are then taken up in the grammar section of the textbook and accompanying audiocassette (ibid.: 27 & 88):

3. Partikeln - *denn*

> *denn* als Partikel steht nur in Fragesätzen.
> *denn* macht Fragen oft freundlich und persönlich.
> *denn* steht nicht am Satzanfang und hat nie Satzakzent.

a) Position von *denn* - suchen Sie Fragen mit denn in 4. b) S. 21.

Wie	*heißt*	______	*denn*	*das* ?
______	______	______	*denn*	______ ?
______	______	______	*denn*	______ ?
______	______	______	*denn*	______ ?

b) Hören Sie, und markieren Sie die Position von *denn* mit ✓.

Beispiel: Wie heißt du ✓? Wie heißt du denn?

1. Wie ist dein Vorname? 2. Woher kommt deine Familie?
3. Wo ist das? 4. Wo wohnst du?

c) Hören Sie noch einmal, und sprechen Sie nach.

d) Wiederholen Sie die Übung in der *Sie*-Form.

Partikeln

7. *Doch* und *mal*

doch	*mal*
in Imperativsätzen: Aufforderung, Ratschlag (hier: freundlich)	in Imperativsätzen: Bitte (informell) (intensiviert durch *bitte mal / mal bitte / doch mal bitte*)

a) Hören Sie, und markieren Sie die Position von *doch* und *mal*.

doch

1. Gehen Sie in die Stadt!
2. Fragen Sie den Taxifahrer!
3. Fragen Sie die Auskunft!
4. Versuchen Sie es später noch einmal!
5. Schreiben Sie bitte Ihre Adresse auf den Zettel hier!

mal

6. Zeigen Sie bitte!
7. Kommen Sie bitte!
8. Warte einen Augenblick!
9. Kommt bitte!
10. Seid leise!

b) Hören Sie noch einmal, und sprechen Sie nach.

c) Ergänzen Sie *denn, doch, mal*.

1. Was kostet ein Brief nach Kanada? 2. Sieh im Gebührenheft nach! 3. Wo ist es? 4. Ich weiß es nicht. Frag Linda! 5. Wo ist sie?

In keeping with the progression criteria proposed by Vorderwülbecke (1981), the introduction of these three modal particles takes into account the interrelation between the modal particle and the sentence type it occurs in and the learners' attention is focussed on its position within the sentence.

Whereas the first two examples are excerpts from textbooks for learners at beginners level, the following is taken from a text for upper intermediate learners of German. "em Abschlusskurs" (Perlmann-Balme et al. 2000) consists of a texbook, workbook and audiocassette program. Modal particles are discussed in the grammar section of the textbook in the form of a brief overview and exercise material is presented in the corresponding workbook chapter. The overview provides general information about modal particles (e.g.: "they occur mainly in spoken German, they express an intention or emotion with regard to the utterance"), lists examples of the particle in context (sentence level), states which sentence type they occur in and then provides a gloss for their “meaning” (e.g. ‘surprise’, ‘friendly request’).

8 Modalpartikeln

Besonders in der gesprochenen Sprache: Ausdruck einer bestimmten Absicht oder emotionalen Färbung des Gesagten.

Modalpartikel	Beispiel	Satzart	Bedeutung
aber	*Das ist aber praktisch!*	Aussagesatz	Überraschung
eben	*Das ist eben so!* *Dann versuchen wir es eben noch einmal.*	Aussagesatz	logische Schlussfolgerung, oft mit resignativem Unterton
einfach	*Sie geben mir einfach eine genaue Beschreibung.*	Aussagesatz	Lösungsvorschlag
ja	*Das sind ja dann auch 400,- DM.* *Erzähl ihr ja nichts davon!*	Aussagesatz	unbetont: Hinweis auf etwas Bekanntes; betont: Warnung, Drohung
ruhig	*Sie können dann ruhig noch einmal darüber nachdenken*	Aussagesatz	niemand hat etwas dagegen oder ist gestört, freundliche Aufforderung
vielleicht	*Könnten Sie mir vielleicht eine Infobroschüre schicken?* *Die Verkäufer hier sind vielleicht unfreundlich!*	Ja/Nein-Frage Ausrufesatz	hat den Charakter einer Aufforderung; drückt Verärgerung oder Erstaunen aus
mal	*Kannst du mal helfen?* *Komm doch mal her!*	Frage oder Aufforderung	verbindlich-höfliche Aufforderung
eigentlich	*Wer ist das eigentlich?* *Das ist eigentlich eine tolle Idee!*	Fragesatz Aussagesatz	großes Interesse Überraschung, Bestätigung
denn	*Gibt es denn einen Mindestbetrag beim Einkauf?* *Bist du denn wahnsinnig?*	Fragesatz	bekundet Interesse oder Vorwurf
doch	*Gehen wir doch hinein!* *Das hättest du mir doch sagen können!* *Das ist doch eine gute Idee, oder?*	Aufforderung Ausrufesatz Fragesatz	freundliche Aufforderung Vorwurf Erwartung einer positiven Antwort

In the exercise section, learners are being asked to use modal particles from a given selection in three separate exercises. In the first one, learners are to produce only interrogatives with modal particles (DENN, DOCH, EIGENTLICH, VIELLEICHT, MAL), so restrictions of use regarding sentence type are being taken into account.

6 Modalpartikeln in Fragesätzen → **GRAMMATIK**

Setzen Sie in die Fragen jeweils an der passenden Stelle eine Modalpartikel ein: *denn - doch - eigentlich - vielleicht - mal.* Manchmal gibt es mehrere Lösungen.

Beispiel: Wie heißt du? Jetzt unterhalten wir uns schon seit zwei Stunden miteinander und ich weiß deinen Namen gar nicht.
Wie heißt du eigentlich?

a Würden Sie mir helfen, den Kinderwagen hochzutragen? Hier gibt es keine Rolltreppe.
b Du hast ihm nichts von meiner neuen Stelle erzählt, oder?
c Weiß Petra genau, wie die Couch aussieht und was sie kostet?
d Hättest du auch noch so einen Katalog für mich?
e Haben wir das Auto schon ganz abbezahlt oder ist da noch was offen?
f Herr Meining, hätten Sie einen Moment Zeit für mich?
g Wäre es möglich, gemeinsam eine Lösung für das Problem zu finden?
h Warum hat er allen davon erzählt, dass er Schwierigkeiten mit seinem Vermieter hat?
i Das hat er hoffentlich nicht unüberlegt getan, oder?

The second exercise aims at practising modal particles in statements and requests (ABER, EBEN, DOCH, JA), by prompting the learner to respond by making use of given vocabulary. In this exercise the information the learner receives about the speech event at hand includes a brief description of speaker roles (e.g. "student talking to professor") as well as the opening of a speech event as introduced by one of the interlocutors. The learner is supposed to role-play the second speaker.

7 Modalpartikeln in Aussage- und Aufforderungssätzen ⟶ GRAMMATIK

Reagieren Sie auf die Aussagen der Personen und verwenden Sie dabei eine der Modalpartikeln *aber* - *eben* - *doch* oder *ja*.

Beispiel: Maria sagt zu Hans: „Martin holt seine Freundin jeden Tag von der Arbeit ab." (Auto haben)
Hans entgegnet: „Der hat ja auch ein Auto!"

a Eine Studentin sagt zu ihrem Professor: „Ich konnte das Referat leider nicht bis heute vorbereiten." (früher sagen sollen)

b Eine Mutter zu ihrem 14-jährigen Sohn: „Stimmt das, dass du am Wochenende bei Peter übernachtest?" (schon vor einer Woche darüber gesprochen)

c Die Wohnungssuchende zur Mitarbeiterin in der Mitwohnzentrale: „Es ist wirklich ärgerlich, dass die Wohnung, die Sie mir gestern angeboten haben, schon weg ist." (sich früher entscheiden müssen)

d Sekretärin zu einer Kollegin: „Jetzt muss ich alles noch mal schreiben, weil der Computer schon wieder abgestürzt ist." (Dateien speichern müssen)

e Eine Frau klagt bei ihrer Freundin: „Mein Mann lässt mich die ganze Hausarbeit machen und wirft mir noch dazu vor, dass ich schlampig sei." (nicht besonders nett sein)

f Eine Frau spricht mit ihrer Bekannten über ihre Gewichtsprobleme: „Ich muss jetzt endlich mal ein paar Kilo abnehmen." (schon letztes Jahr vergeblich versucht)

In the third exercise, the learner is supposed to fill gaps by using modal particles. The exercise includes a glossary which is supposed to provide the learners with hints as to which particle they should use.

8 Bedeutung der Modalpartikeln ⟶ GRAMMATIK

Setzen Sie in den Dialog passende Partikeln ein. Berücksichtigen Sie die angegebene Bedeutung. Nehmen Sie, wenn nötig, dazu die Grammatikübersicht im Kursbuch Seite 44 zu Hilfe.

aber - denn - eben - eigentlich - einfach - ja - mal - ruhig - vielleicht

A Sag (0) ...., weißt du (1).........., wo man preiswerte Möbel findet?	(0) höfliche Aufforderung (1) Aufforderung in Ja/Nein-Frage
B Nein, das weiß ich leider nicht. Aber du könntest dir (2) .... mal Kataloge von Möbelhäusern zuschicken lassen. Da gibt es oft sehr interessante Angebote.	(2) Hinweis auf etwas schon Bekanntes
A Das ist (3) .... keine schlechte Idee.	(3) Überraschung, Bestätigung
B Lass dir (4) .... verschiedene Angebote zuschicken. Dann hast du bessere Vergleichsmöglichkeiten. Und wenn du etwas Passendes gefunden hast, siehst du dir die Möbel vor Ort an.	(4) niemand hat etwas dagegen oder ist gestört
A Würdest du mich (5) .... beraten, ich bin etwas unsicher bei den Farben.	(5) Interesse oder Aufforderung
B Natürlich gern. An deiner Stelle würde ich (6) .... Stoffreste in verschiedenen Mustern besorgen und in das entsprechende Zimmer legen.	(6) Lösungsvorschlag
A Du hast wirklich geniale Vorschläge! Man merkt (7) ...., dass du ein eigenes Geschäft hast und immer kreativ sein musst.	(7) logische Schlussfolgerung
B Das ist (8) .... ein nettes Kompliment. Vielen Dank.	(8) Überraschung

Of the three German text books discussed here, "em" presents the most comprehensive approach. In its approach to modal particles "em" makes use of exercise types which build on those presented in earlier materials published specifically for the teaching of modal particles (e.g. Kemme 1979, Weydt et al. 1983, Kummer 1984, Helbig & Helbig 1995), but rather than using pattern drills on one particular particle, the exercises focus on choosing between a number of particles in a given sentence type. As the answers are not always unambiguous – multiple answers are possible in number of examples – some form of feedback, e.g. in the form of class discussion, would be necessary for disambiguating different particle choices. I am not certain that the examples chosen for the exercises always match the explanations and examples given in the introductory section. In exercise 7, example a), my native speaker intuition would lead me to use ABER as the particle of choice for a response:

> Eine Studentin sagt zu Ihrem Professor:
> "Ich konnte das Referat leider nicht bis heute vorbereiten."
>
> Antwort:
> "Das hätten Sie mir ABER früher sagen sollen."

In my opinion, ABER is here not used to express surprise but rather as a slight rebuke, or in more general terms: a difference of opinion (for a detailed discussion of ABER see Chapter 5.8). The last exercise (8) is the most comprehensive one, as learners are asked to choose the right particle for different sentence types. A very positive aspect of this exercise is the fact that it represents a running dialogue between two speakers, rather than isolated example sentences.

3.5 Summary with regard to present study

In the teaching materials discussed above, the production of modal particles by learners of German plays a major part. Although the learner's comprehension of modal particles is addressed – mostly by a short explanation of the 'meaning' of the individual particle – for the main part the materials practise the use of modal particles by the learner. Studies on the acquisition of modal particles in instructed contexts have shown that drill exercises on one particular particle have led particularly to overgeneralisations in learners' usage of this particle. On the other hand, studies have shown that modal particles are significantly underrepresented in non-native speaker productions of German, a fact which is likely to be due to their complexity and learners' uncertainty about their meanings.[52]

In order to interpret all contributing factors in a speech event adequately and to take into account implicit information, learners of German need to understand the meaning of modal particles. Research findings on the acquisition of modal particles in uninstructed contexts (Kutsch 1985, Cheon-Kostrzewa and Kostrzewa 1997a, 1997b) have shown that the acquisition process is influenced by the fact that each particle is used in a variety of functions. The acquisition of communicative particles seems to be completed earlier than the acquisition of semantic particles and the diversity of functions of communicative particles leads to discontinuity in the acquisition of those particles. The input learners receive is considered important as modal particles used frequently in routine formulae in native speaker speech are first reproduced by learners.

52 cf. Willing's (1992: 62) description of the use of routine formulae by non-native speakers in problem-solving. It is also possible, however, that learners consciously choose not to use modal particles, cf. Kasper and Rose (1999: 97): "There is mounting evidence that divergence from native norms does not always stem from pragmatic or linguistic incompetence but may be a more or less deliberate choice on the part of the learner not to participate in target practices."

Learners who received instruction in German as a foreign language do not perceive the communicative value of particles as very high. The limited range of speech events learners are exposed to in classroom discourse and the fact that a range of emotions are rarely expressed in this setting[53] are contributing factors to this lack of understanding. One component factor in teaching modal particles is therefore to expose learners of German to modal particles in various contexts and to focus learners' attention on their meanings in those contexts. Zimmermann (1981: 117) distinguishes the following components in the overall aim of learning modal particles:

> [...] dann bedeutet 'eine Fremdsprache lernen' (hier besonders 'die Modalpartikeln des Deutschen lernen') den ganzen Hintergrund des sozialen Alltagswissens lernen. Unter diesem Aspekt muß man analytisch mehrere Teilschritte des Lernziels 'Modalpartikeln' unterscheiden:
>
> 1) Die Einsicht, daß in einer Sprache X bestimmte Kommunikations-relevante Beziehungen, wie z.B. Unterstellungen, Erwartungen, interpersonale Beziehungen in der Art der Sprachäußerung zum Ausdruck kommen. Im Deutschen u.a. durch die Modalpartikeln.
> 2) Die Einsicht, daß Partikeln benutzt werden müssen (d.h. im Konkreten, daß der Schüler weiß
>   a. daß im Deutschen diese Partikeln im Gegensatz zu seiner Muttersprache eine Rolle spielen,
>   b. welche Rolle sie spielen und
>   c. daß man durch sie etwas Bestimmtes ausdrücken kann.
> 3) Die Fertigkeit, die Partikeln in formaler und intentionaler Hinsicht richtig zu gebrauchen.

In the present study, the main objective is to be found under Zimmermann's step 2, the learner should discover:

53 Harden and Rösler (1981: 75): "Wir meinen allerdings, daß es bei einer Einführung von Partikelnauf einer rein technischen Ebene nicht belassen werden sollte, denn eigentlich ist im herkömmlichen Fremdsprachenunterricht gar kein Platz für derartige Entitäten. Die formale Kommunikationsform des Unterrichts, die man durchaus als 'Zwangskommunikation' bezeichnen kann, läßt Gefühlsäußerungen wie Erstaunen, Mißfallen, Resignation usw. normalerweise nicht zu. Mit anderen Worten, selbst wenn Partikeln über irgendeineTechnik eingeführt werden, ergäben sich im Unterricht selbst wenig Situationen für ihre Verwendung."

a. that German modal particles convey meanings which might be expressed otherwise in the learner's L1 (here: English)
b. which role modal particles play within a dialogue
c. that very particular nuances can be expressed by the use of modal particles

In addition to those aims, I consider the distinction between modal particles and their homonyms a major teaching objective (cf. Busse 1992). As the findings on modal particle acquisition in uninstructed contexts have shown, particle functions are acquired in an accumulative manner over a long period of time. Research findings on the instruction of pragmatic language features in general (Kasper 2000) have provided promising results which allow for the hypothesis that explicit instruction of different particle functions could accelerate and enhance the acquisition process.

The approach to teaching modal particles I would like to propose here is less concerned with learners' production of modal particles than with their comprehension of modal particle meanings in context. Research findings in interlanguage pragmatics have shown that the instruction of pragmatic features of language is facilitative and necessary when input is lacking or less salient and that explicit instruction is particularly effective in the area of consciousness raising (Kasper and Rose 1999: 96-97). The concept of 'consciousness-raising' (e.g. Rutherford 1987) refers to the refinement of learners' metacommunicative awareness, i.e. their ability to judge the relationship between a form and its meaning in context. It is this type of awareness that needs to be honed for a learner to comprehend the intricacies of modal particle meanings. With McCarthy and Carter (1994), I would like to argue that language awareness is not necessarily best taught by direct input language teaching (1994: 68):

> That is to say the normal *presentation-practise-production* cycles should not be seen as binding for all features of discourse, and in the case of [discourse] markers, these would seem to be a feature best handled by other types of activity; language-observation activities, problem-solving, perhaps cross-linguistic comparisons.

The approach I propose is based on authentic language data[54] as collected in a number of corpora of spoken German (for details see Chapter 4). Rather than providing the learner with a list of grammatical particle functions supplemented by examples on sentence level, as shown for the example AUCH (Helbig & Helbig 1995; discussed on page 83), an analysis of such corpora yields examples of particles in context (cf. Busse 1992). With the use of concordancing procedures (see Chapter 4) patterns of collocation can be established, for example the use of modal particles in idiomatic phrases (cf. Busse 1992) or the relationship between particle function and sentence type (cf. Busse 1992, Vorderwülbecke 1981). An application of the principles and methods of corpus linguistics (see Chapter 4) also permits us to establish the frequency of modal particles, which has been advanced as one grading criterion (cf. Vorderwülbecke 1981, Busse 1992). A detailed analysis of modal particle occurrences in context (see Chapter 5) allows for an approach that combines contrasting modal particles with the linguistic means which are used in English to express a similar or the same meaning, and describing the force of modal particles (such as "expression of surprise") to simplify comprehension (cf. Busse 1992).

54 cf. Harden and Rösler (1981: 79): "Für das Erlernen von Partikeln mag daher die Erstellung eines partikelfreundlichen Klimas im Unterricht ebenso wichtig sein, wie das Material, das diese überhaupt erst zugänglich macht."

4. A corpus-based perspective on modal particles

For the learner, there are no extra challenges beyond the perennial problems of language idiosyncrasy and complexity. Corpora will clarify, give priorities, reduce exceptions and liberate the creative spirit.

(Sinclair 1997: 38)

4.1 Introduction

In this and the following chapter, the actual use of words which may function as modal particles is investigated. The aim of the analysis was to identify main patterns of use which could form the basis for developing an effective approach to teaching the use of modal particles to non-native speakers of German. In order to do so, I analysed naturally occurring language following a corpus-based approach. In the course of Chapter 4, I briefly outline how the principles and methodologies of corpus linguistics have been applied in this study for a quantitative and qualitative analysis of particles in spoken German. The corpora of spoken German which formed the basis of my analysis are then described. The quantitative analysis of the corpus data constitutes the main body of this chapter, whereas a qualitative analysis of particular particles and its application in the creation of teaching materials will be outlined in Chapter 5.

4.2 Principles and methodologies of corpus-based research

Over the past decade, corpus-based research has had an increasing influence on language teaching pedagogy, with regard to linguistic content as well as to teaching methodology. Kennedy (1998: 281-2) outlines the potential influence of a corpus-based approach on language teaching as follows:

> For those concerned with the teaching and learning of second or foreign languages in particular, information on the distribution of the elements and processes of a language can influence pedagogy in a number of ways. First it can influence the content of language teaching by affecting selection of what to teach, the sequencing of pedagogy, and the weight given to items or parts of the language being taught, thus contributing directly to the content of instruction. Secondly, through the consciousness raising of teachers about language and language use, it can show that likelihood of occurrence, or frequency of use, is an important measure of usefulness. Corpus studies can also contribute to language teaching methodology by influencing the approach to instruction and making available techniques and procedures which encourage self-access and individualized instruction through interaction with authentic, analyzed text from a corpus database.

In this study, a corpus-based approach is proposed with regard to the content as well as with regard to the methodology aspect of language teaching as described by Kennedy above. Before referring in detail to the corpus analysis carried out for the present study, the principles and methodologies of a corpus-based approach are briefly discussed.

Corpus linguistics (e.g. Aarts & Meijs 1984; Aijmer & Altenberg 1991; Biber, Conrad & Reppen 1998; Kennedy 1998; McEnery & Wilson 2001; Sinclair 1991; Svartvik 1992; Thomas & Short 1996) as a method of enquiry in linguistics is of an empirical nature, as it is based on the analysis of external data (for a discussion of the empirical-rational distinction in linguistics see McEnery & Wilson 2001, Chapter 1). In very simple terms, it can be described as the study of language based on examples of language use in real life. Advances in computing technology have made it possible to store large amounts of language data referred to as corpora.

A corpus is a principled collection of texts, i.e. when compiling a corpus a number of considerations are taken into account. We distinguish, for instance, between general corpora and specialised corpora (e.g. dialect corpora, non-standard corpora, learners' corpora). A general corpus is usually assembled to form a base for unspecified linguistic research. To be considered representative of the language it exemplifies, such a corpus is typically balanced, i.e. it contains texts from different domains and genres, including spoken and written, private and public language, etc. Balanced or general corpora are sometimes named core corpora (cf. Kennedy 1998: 20) and can be used as a basis for comparative study in contrast with specialised corpora. How representative a corpus is depends in part on the way it has been sampled and in part on its size. A general corpus attempts to capture the scope of linguistic variation which is present in a language. This requires a stratified approach (Biber et al. 1998), which catalogues the different categories of texts in a language and samples each of them. An important question is how the categorisation criteria have been arrived at, i.e. which situational characteristics were used to define registers (for a more detailed discussion of sampling see McEnery & Wilson 2001: 77ff).

As there are important differences in the use of grammatical, lexical and discourse features across different varieties of language, a general corpus needs to represent this diversity (Biber et al. 1998: 248):

> Several areas are important to consider for diversity. Prime among them is register variation. Register variation is central to language: all speakers of a language control many registers, and every time people speak or write, they must choose a register to use […]. A well-designed corpus must therefore represent the different registers of the language.

As previously established (see Chapter 2), modal particles occur more frequently in spoken than in written German and so the database chosen for the analysis in the present study are specialised corpora in the sense that they represent only spoken German.

The size of a corpus is often ascribed in terms of finite size as represented by a total number of words (e.g. 100,000,000 words for the British National Corpus, McEnery & Wilson 2001). Such a corpus may be referred to as a static corpus (cf. Kennedy 1998), which is compiled up to a certain size or date and then not amended any further[55]. An unofficial standard for electronic corpora (of the general kind as described above) used to be around the one million word mark until the early 1990s. Nowadays, much larger corpora, like the Bank of English with 400,000,000 words (McEnery & Wilson 2001) are becoming available. Although the spoken language is the more common mode of use, most corpus-based studies of language so far have been carried out on written language, as the amount of time and effort necessary to create a sizeable corpus of spoken language is far greater than for the written language. Transcriptions of spoken language data are time-consuming, especially when phonetic and prosodic features are included.

The majority of corpus-based studies have so far been carried out on the English language, as a large body of sizeable corpora is available for different varieties of English[56], but more and more languages are being researched with the help of corpora (McEnery & Wilson 2001: 188):

> [In 1996], work had begun on corpora of western and eastern European languages. It seemed that corpus linguistics was expanding to cover Europe [...] and English speaking countries [...] but no further. In an amazingly short period of time – in essence the 1990s – corpus linguistics has spread to cover a large number of world languages.

Corpus-based research has investigated the use of language features in areas such as lexicography, grammar, lexico-grammar and discourse characteristics as well as characteristics of language varieties. Thus, the focus is either on the use of a linguistic feature, lexical and/or grammatical, or on the characteristics of texts or varieties. Corpus-based analyses explore associations of the feature under investigation as summarised by Biber et al. (1998: 6) in the following overview:

55 In contrast to static corpora, dynamic (Kennedy 1998) or monitor corpora (Sinclair 1991) are constantly added to, not necessarily in the balanced way described above.

56 McEnery & Wilson provide an up-to-date description of corpora (2001: 201ff).

A. Investigating the use of a linguistic feature (lexical or grammatical)
  (i) Linguistic associations of the feature
    - lexical associations (associations with particular words)
    - grammatical associations (associations with particular grammatical constructions)
  (ii) Non-linguistic associations of the feature
    - distribution across registers
    - distributions across dialects
    - distribution across time periods

B. Investigating varieties or texts (e.g. registers, dialects, historical periods)
  (i) Linguistic association patterns
    - individual linguistic features or classes of features
    - co-occurrence patterns of linguistic features

The association patterns which were of particular interest in the present investigation are linguistic features in terms of lexical and grammatical associations. Non-linguistic associations like the distribution of modal particles across registers have been dealt with to some degree through the selection of corpora for the analysis, while distribution across dialects or across time periods was not examined.

The analysis of corpora is usually carried out as an interaction between human processing, computer processing and corpus data. Leech (1991: 14) describes this interaction in the following way:

> There are a number of ways in which human, software and corpus resources can interact, according to how far the human analyst delegates to the computer the responsibility for analysis. At one end of the scale, the computer program (e.g. concordance program) is used simply as a tool for sorting and counting data, while all the serious analysis is performed by the human investigator. … At the other extreme, the human analyst provides no linguistic insight, just programming ability; the machine discovers its own categories of analysis, in effect implementing a 'discovery procedure'.

Between these two ends of the scale lie a number of procedures which result from the interaction between human analysis and computer analysis. In order to facilitate the analysis of large machine-readable corpora, these are commonly annotated. Annotation criteria are in a first step developed on the basis of human analysis, then fed back into computer programmes, so that the annotation can be carried out automatically by the machine. Annotation, the enhancement of a corpus with various types of linguistic information, makes explicit what is implicit information in the language forms represented in the corpus. Typical forms of annotation include lemmatisation, tagging and parsing[57].

Lemmatisation refers to a process by which a "lemma", the headword form that one would look for if looking up a word in a dictionary, is ascribed throughout the corpus. For instance, the word-form 'ate' belongs to the lemma 'eat'. A corpus which is lemmatised recognises the word-form 'ate' as an occurrence of the lemma 'eat'. As particles in general are not inflected in any way, lemmatisation procedures are not relevant for a corpus-based analysis of modal particles as undertaken in the present study.

Tagging concerns attaching a code to words in a text. This code may represent some feature or set of features relating to those words. A corpus may, for instance, be tagged for word classes or part-of-speech. Parsing, then, refers to the process of annotating a corpus with syntactic information, e.g. a phrase structure type. The corpora on which the present study is based are not tagged for modal particle function and manual disambiguation procedures, undertaken on a subset of the total number of occurrences, were necessary to establish in which instances a particle was used in its modal particle function.

Common procedures used in corpus analysis include the compilation of word lists, frequency counts and concordances. Concordancing software typically produces KWIC (key word in context) files or concordances, in which the key word appears in the centre of the line, with its co-text to the left and right. The co-text contains immediate and less immediate collocates so that collocation

57 For a detailed description of annotation procedures see McEnery & Wilson (2001: 32ff).

can be studied with the help of the concordancing software. The file can be sorted in various ways, e.g. alphabetically by the first or second word to the right or left, so that recurring patterns can be illuminated. The frequency of a key word or collocate can be established and, for instance, be used for comparisons between text types or – as e.g. Kennedy (1998) proposed – to establish how salient a linguistic feature is for the language learner.

While the majority of studies reporting on corpus-based teaching approaches refer to English (e.g. Fligelstone 1993; Biber, Conrad & Reppen 1994; Wichmann et al. 1997; Conrad 2000) a number of studies have discussed German[58]. Dodd (1997) reports on exploiting a corpus of written German for advanced language learning, using the 'Bonner Zeitungskorpus' (Bonn Newspaper Corpus), which is held by the 'Institut für Deutsche Sprache' (IDS) in Mannheim and has just over 3 million words of running text. Students access the corpus using MicroConcord (Scott and Johns 1993) through the university's computer network. Dodd (ibid.) discusses three ways of exploiting unedited data: as an informal resource for students to browse through, as a resource for formulating explicit grammatical knowledge and as a resource for student-led projects on grammatical or sociolinguistic topics. Jones (1997) compiled a corpus of spoken German of about 600,000 words, which he uses with students of German at Brigham Young University. Students can access the corpus through the college network and work on a given assignment, which, in a first step, is usually a single word. They analyse the word, as it occurs in the corpus, then compare the analysis with a German-English dictionary, a standard German reference grammar and with a beginning and intermediate textbook for learning German. Jones (1997: 154) reports that students have found grammatical functions of words which are sometimes not explained in reference grammars.[59] Jones (ibid.) points out that it is useful for students to learn the relative frequency of various functions of a word. He observes the high frequency of

58 A collection of essays on corpus-based research on German can also be found in Dodd (2000); there is, however, no focus on teaching.

59 See also Conrad (2000: 552) for a discussion of register dependent grammar: "The implication of corpus research for pedagogy is that grammatical study needs to take place within the context of a register or by comparing registers."

particles in the corpus he compiled and comments on the teaching of particles as follows (Jones 1997: 155):

> As was mentioned earlier, colloquial spoken German contains a high number of modal particles, e.g. *denn*, *doch*, *eben*, *eigentlich*, *halt*, *mal*, *wohl*, *zwar*, etc. It is very difficult to give a translation for these words, and most reference grammars only begin to discuss their complicated use in the language. By analysing a spoken corpus, however, students are able to develop a better feel for their function in the language and how to use them correctly. Students have learned that in most cases these particles may be left out without altering the basic meaning of the sentence. However, their use definitely does carry some meaning, eventhough it cannot be translated easily. They are sometimes referred to as 'flavouring particles', suggesting that without them the language is a bit less savoury.

It is the contention of the present study, that learners may be aided in the comprehension of German modal particles by a corpus-based approach which unveils structures, patterns and predictable features regarding a particle's different usages. The exploitation of language corpora is proposed here in order to arrive at authentic teaching materials which facilitate the comprehension of German modal particles. The approach is twofold: in a first step, the frequency of those word forms which may function as modal particles was established. In the second step, concordance data of the more frequently occurring particles were analysed qualitatively and teaching materials based on this analysis were developed (see Chapter 5). Leech (1997) distinguishes between the direct use of corpora in teaching and the use of corpora indirectly applied to teaching. Teaching about corpora, teaching the exploitation of corpora and exploiting corpora to teach are said to represent a direct use of corpora, whereas reference publishing, materials development and language testing are indirect applications (Leech 1997: 6-7). Thus, the approach proposed here is direct in that it exploits the corpora of spoken German described below to arrive at relevant data. The approach is indirect, though, in the sense that the concordance data are not compiled by the language learners themselves but presented as work sheets that confront the learner with the task of distinguishing particle meanings in context (see Chapter 5).

4.3 Corpora of spoken German

The largest and most varied selection of corpora of German is held by the Institut für deutsche Sprache (IDS) with a total of 1080 million words (http://www.ids-mannheim.de, 2001). Large parts of these corpora (a total of about 653,000,000 words) are publicly accessible, but only a relatively small proportion of the corpora represent spoken German. The quantitative analysis is based on three corpora of spoken German held at the IDS in Mannheim, namely the 'Freiburger Korpus (FKO)', 'Dialogstrukturenkorpus (DSK)' and 'PFEFFER-Korpus (PFE)', and a collection of telephone conversations published by Brons-Albert (1984).

Freiburger Korpus (FKO)

The corpus consists of 224 texts with a total of 700,000 words. It was compiled mainly between 1966 and 1972 as part of a project at the IDS that aimed at describing grammatical and stylistic features of spoken German. Audiorecordings from radio and television broadcasts as well as other recordings of private and public speech events were collected. Speakers were either not aware of being recorded or recording was a natural part of the speech event (as in the radio and television broadcasts) and they did not know that their productions were to be linguistically analysed. The recordings have been transcribed and categorised into the following: discussions, interviews, talks, reports and narrations.
(http://www.idsmannheim.de/ldv/cosmas/corpora-fko.htm, 1996)

Dialogstrukturenkorpus (DSK)

This corpus contains 72 texts with about 200,000 words. It was compiled by a group of researchers of the German department at Freiburg University in conjunction with the IDS in the periods from 1968-1972 and 1974-1977 in order to further analyse the organisation

of natural conversation (see FKO). It consists mainly of interviews (radio and television broadcasts) and discussions.
(http://www.ids-mannheim.de/ldv/cosmas/corpora-dsk.html, 1996)

Pfeffer-Korpus (PFE)

Compiled by A. Pfeffer and W. Lohnes at Stanford University, USA, in the early 1960's, the corpus comprises 398 texts with a total of 650,000 words. Recordings were made in 56 different areas of Germany, Austria and Switzerland with a total of 400 different speakers. Each recording is about 12 minutes in length (about 1500 words) on one of 25 topics. The subjects (with a spread of age, sex, education and profession following a statistical analysis) were interviewed on those topics in 397 of the texts; text 398 is a group discussion between four speakers. An update of the PFEFFER-Korpus (Jones, 1997) was not yet accessible (personal communication with Jones) at the time of data analysis.
(http://www.ids-mannheim.de/ldv/cosmas/corpora-pfe.html, 1996)

All three corpora can be accessed via a data retrieval system – COSMAS – developed at the IDS[60]. It allows an analysis of the data through frequency counts and concordancing procedures which makes it possible to search all three corpora of transcribed spoken German – with a total of about 1.5 million words – for occurrences of particles in context.

Telephone conversations (Brons-Albert, 1984: BRO)

This collection is made up of 35 texts and includes a total of about 44,000 words. The data were arrived at by recording telephone conversations which the researcher, Brons-Albert, had on her private phone over a period of 10 months. Callers were unaware of being

60 For the analysis presented here, COSMAS version R.1.3-1 was used (al-Wadi 1994).

recorded. With permission of the individual speakers, a selection of conversations were transcribed and published. For each dialogue, information on the speakers' age, profession and/or education, dialect and the relationship between the speakers is provided. For the purpose of the present study, the printed texts were scanned into computer-readable files to make them accessible for concordancing.

The existing corpora of spoken German are relatively small in comparison to the corpora available for spoken English, e.g. the 'British National Corpus' with a spoken component of about 10 million words (see e.g. Berglund 1999). The composition of the different corpora indicates that although they can be broadly classified as "spoken German", there are significant differences with regard to "mode" (McCarthy 1993). German modal particles have been found to occur most frequently in texts which are informal, personal, associative and with a high level of familiarity (Hentschel 1986). In particular the level of informality and familiarity of speakers with one another varies considerably between the four corpora. The predefined corpus text categories provided in the description of the corpora held at the IDS are rather broad. Although all the corpora comprise dialogues, the nature of these dialogues in FKO and DSK is rarely personal. The dialogues in PFE are determined by the method of data collection: an interviewer talking to a person s/he is not familiar with. The ensuing dialogues are in fact largely monologic as the interviewer's brief questions prompt long stretches of narrative on the part of the person interviewed. The highest level of informality and familiarity between speakers can be found in the compilation of texts by Brons-Albert (1984) which, for this study, led to the decision to concentrate on those texts in the qualitative analysis of the data (for a discussion of text categories with regard to formality see e.g. Sigley 1997).

4.4 Particle frequency: a quantitative analysis

The first step in the process of data analysis was to establish the frequency of particles which could potentially function as modal particles[61] in the four corpora. Frequency of occurrence has been advanced as one grading criterion (cf. Vorderwülbecke 1981; Busse 1992) for the teaching of modal particles. Taking into account the multifunctionality of particles and learners' difficulties with distinguishing different particle functions, the term "particle frequency" can be seen as ambivalent. The term "frequency" might on the one hand refer to the occurrence of a word in modal particle function or it might refer to all occurrences of a word, of which only some might be occurrences in modal particle function. In the present study particle frequency is addressed in two steps: first, the overall frequency of particles in the corpora of spoken German is established in order to determine how salient each particle would be for a learner of German. A subset of the occurrences of the most frequent particles was then analysed qualitatively (see Chapter 5). The qualitative analysis provides a distinction between frequency of occurrences in modal particle function and other functions. Concordancing software used in analysing corpus data lists the occurrences of the word under investigation in context, but it is not able to distinguish between different functions of the word in question. The corpora used in this study do not have annotations regarding particle functions (cf. Jones 1997: 152) and a qualitative analysis was necessary to distinguish between modal particle function and others. The three corpora held at the IDS (DSK, FKO, PFE) were searched with the help of COSMAS, the fourth corpus (BRO) was searched using Microconcord (Scott & Johns 1993). The number of total occurrences of each word in each of the corpora was established.[62]

61 The list represents the core particles considered to occur in modal particle function and is based on an evaluation of a substantial part of the literature on modal particles (Weydt 1979, 1981, 1983, 1989; Helbig 1994; Thurmair 1989).

62 See Appendix V for a detailed account.

As the different corpora vary considerably in size, raw counts of frequency were normed to make counts comparable. Frequency per 1000 words of text was chosen as a basis of comparison.[63] The following table provides an overview as to how frequent particular particles are in all four corpora, i.e. over a total of nearly 1,600,000 words:

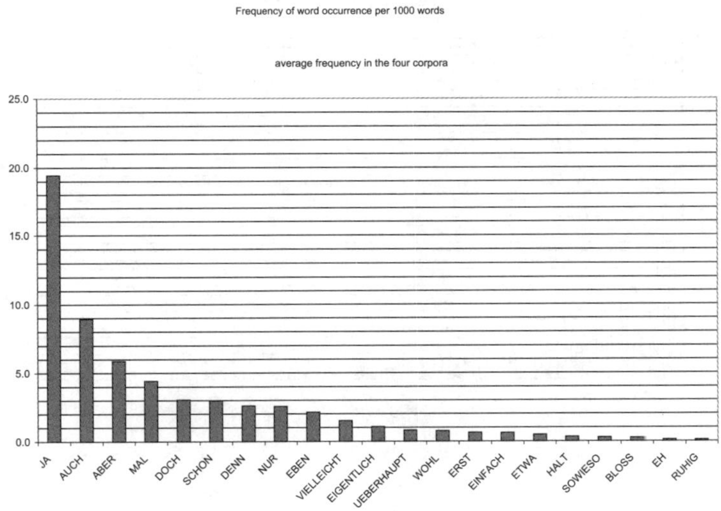

Table 2

Most striking is the frequency of JA with 19.5 occurrences per 1000 words overall, which is more than double the frequency of the next word in line AUCH with 8.9 occurrences, followed by ABER with 5.9 occurrences per 1000 words. MAL with 4.4 occurrences down to EBEN with 2.1 follow. More than half the words analysed occur with an average frequency of less than 2 (VIELLEICHT 1.5 down to EH and

63

DSK:	200,000 words	70 texts	average length of text	2857 words
FKO:	700,000 words	220 texts	average length of text	3182 words
PFE:	650,000 words	386 texts	average length of text	1684 words
BRO:	44,000 words	35 texts	average length of text	1257words

RUHIG with 0.1). I decided to focus on the group of more frequently occurring words (JA down to EBEN) in the qualitative analyis as these are the words with a potential for modal particle function learners of German are most likely to encounter. The following table presents the frequency of occurrence per 1000 words in the four different corpora:

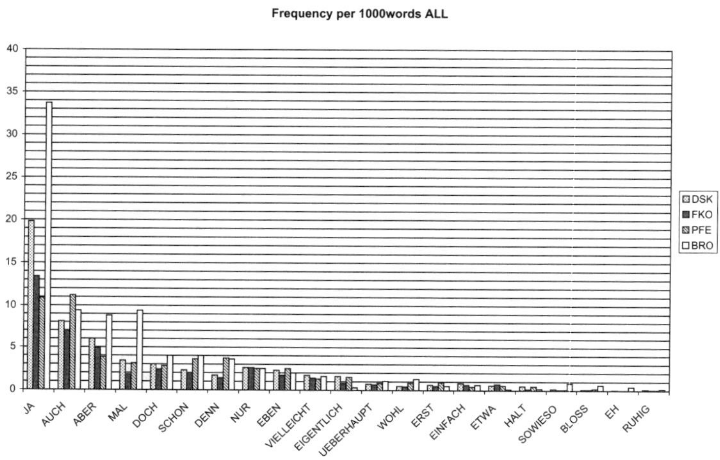

Table 3

Again JA provides the most striking pattern with an enormous variation of frequency between the four corpora. It is most frequent in the BRO corpus with 33.7 occurrences per 1000 words, followed by 19.8 in DSK, 13.4 in FKO and 10.9 in PFE. The qualitative analysis illuminates how the high frequency in BRO can be explained and how it relates to the type of spoken language which makes up this specific corpus. The most frequently occurring words which might be used in modal particle function (JA down to DENN) occur with a particularly high frequency in BRO. The high frequency of DENN in PFE can be explained by its strong collocation with questions and the frequency of interviewer's questions in the corpus.

Both tables show clearly that JA, AUCH and ABER are the most salient words which may occur in modal particle function, followed by a second group made up of MAL, DOCH, SCHON, DENN, NUR and EBEN.

The qualitative analysis in Chapter 5 investigates the occurrences of each of those words in the BRO corpus in detail.

4.5 Summary

At the beginning of this chapter, a corpus-based approach was proposed to inform the content of language teaching (Kennedy 1998) by establishing how salient a linguistic feature is for a language learner. Applying this approach to the teaching of German modal particles, a quantitative analysis of particle frequency was carried out on four corpora of spoken German with a total of over 1,500,000 words. The particles JA, AUCH, ABER, MAL, DOCH, SCHON, DENN, NUR and EBEN were identified as those occurring most frequently across the four corpora analysed, with an average frequency of above 2 per 1000 words. Although the quantitative analysis does not distinguish between different particle functions, it can be said that these particles are the most salient for a learner of German. Learners are likely to encounter them in interaction with native speakers of German and would be required to comprehend their meaning in context. In the next phase of analysis outlined in Chapter 5, a subset of particle occurrences – namely the occurrences in the BRO corpus – are analysed qualitatively. A manual disambiguation of particle functions is carried out to reveal patterns of lexical and grammatical collocations which might help the language learner to comprehend the complex meanings of those particles.

5. Teaching modal particles: A corpus-based approach

> *[...] the task of understanding does not basically amount to recognizing the form used, but rather to understanding it in a particular, concrete context, to understanding its meaning in a particular utterance [...]. In other words the understander, belonging to the same language community, also is attuned to the linguistic form not as a fixed, self-identical sign, but as a changeable and adaptable sign. (Vološinov 1929/1973 in Morris 1994:33)*

5.1 Introduction

In this chapter, I present detailed analyses of the particles EBEN, NUR, DENN, SCHON, DOCH, MAL, ABER, AUCH and JA. In a first step, the analyses distinguish between the use of the word in question in modal particle function and in other functions, as I have identified this distinction as a major teaching objective earlier on (cf. Chapter 3). Assuming that learners of German may be aided in the comprehension of German modal particles by a corpus-based approach which unveils structures, patterns and predictable features regarding a particle's different usages, I outline those in detail and summarise the findings at the end of the section on each particle. For each particle, the summaries are followed by a sample worksheet which gives an example as to how the results of the corpus-based analysis might be used in teaching. The materials are created to facilitate comprehension, they do not aim at the production of modal particles by learners of German (cf. Chapter 5.11).

The results of the corpus-based analyses can be used for language teaching by using the concordance output to create teaching materials (see e.g. Thurstun & Candlin 1997). One popular way of putting concordance data to use is having the learner deduce the meaning of words in context (Tribble & Johns 1990: 35). It will obviously depend on the learners' proficiency, learning styles, etc. how those teaching materials will be structured and what type of activities they will encourage but the sample worksheets presented here illustrate how the topic could be approached (cf. Chapter 5.11).

As outlined in Chapter 4 (4.3), the qualitative analysis has been limited to data from the BRO corpus. Particles were investigated in context in order to establish patterns of collocation in terms of lexical co-occurrence as well as co-occurrence with certain grammatical choices (Sinclair 1991). To this end, KWIC concordances were compiled of the BRO data using the concordancing software package MicroConcord (Scott & Johns 1993). The BRO corpus was searched for the word in question and the ensuing concordances were categorised by making use of the program's classification feature. Moving the cursor to the concordance line and entering a number allows subsequent sorting of lines according to categories. The categorisation of occurrences was in the first instance based on native speaker intuition. It had to be carried out in many instances by looking at larger stretches of the text, as the information provided in the KWIC concordances was often not sufficient to distinguish between different usages of the word under investigation. In order to distinguish use in modal particle function from other possible functions of the words in question, it was necessary to manually disambiguate each occurrence of the word to establish patterns which language learners could be made aware of to assist them in distinguishing modal particle functions from others and to comprehend their meaning in context.

5.2 EBEN

The word EBEN occurs 88 times in 20 different texts in BRO. The qualitative analysis, which I outline below, has shown these occurrences to belong to several function categories. In addition to modal particle function, EBEN was found to occur in a confirming function as an answering particle and as an adverb of time[64].

Answering Particle

As an answering particle (27 occurrences) EBEN is easily recognised within the concordance data, as it can be found in the initial position of an utterance. In some instances its representation is capitalised, as an utterance on its own:

1 höne Bücher, die man lesen kann. A: **Eben**! B: und so viele schöne Sachen, di
2 . kann man so nie wissen. B: (lacht) **Eben**! C: Ja, aber hättsde das direkt ge
3 sen müssen, was wer noch kaufen. A: **Eben**. B: Würd ich sagen, dann geh ich d

or as the opening of an utterance where it is separate from the following proposition:

4 Doppelte als die ganze Zeit, ne. B: **Eben**. Is auch schön. A: Undie Arbeit ma
5 ja nichts Schlimmes! A: Ja, ne? B: **Eben**. Solang se sich dabei wohlfühlt, si
6 alles, wozu man jetz nich kommt! B: **Eben**. Du, meine Mutter, die hatte ne gan
7 n die elf Kilo abgenommen hätte! D: **Eben**, ich denk, die is doch gar ni mehr
8 er Frau auch Frau Doktor Sounso. B: **Eben**, dann bisde ooch Herr Dokta! A: Ri
9 ort "werden" nich, anscheinend . B: **Eben**, siehsde, un, stimmt auch wirklich,

It also occurs in combination with a second answering particle JA, NEIN (here pronounced 'nee') or HM, where it lends emphasis to the polarity expressed by JA or NEIN:

11 , ich helf ihr, soweit's geht B: ja, **eben** A: und son bißchen Telefongespräch
12 uns ja nun wieder auch nich B: Nee, **eben** ( ) Hast du mal deinen Pullover aus
13 m Telefon merkt es ja keiner. B: Ja, **eben**! A: Und dann kriegt der hinterher
14   Hauptsache, es klappt! B: Och ja, **eben**, wenn et so janz jut weiterläuft, s
15 ann alles, wenn ich will, ne. D: Ja, **eben**, eben. Versteh ich. B: Naja! Zwei
16 h kann Sie nur beglückwünschen. Nee, **eben**, das war, wie C, ich war der Meinun
17 tung, das Rauchen einstellen! D: Ja, **eben**, nee / B: Das versucht manch einer

64 These categories are based on an evaluation of the literature on EBEN in different function categories (Hartmann 1979; Lütten 1979; Trömel-Plötz 1979; Hentschel 1986; Thurmair 1989; Helbig 1994).

18 der Effekt ja oh ni mehr da! A: Ja, **eben**, genau! Vor allen Dingen, es geht j
19 eder mal die Eßbremse ziehen. D: Ja, **eben**, kann ich verstehn, dat kann ich ve
20 alle 8 Tage da . losjehn, ne. A: Ja, **eben**. B: Das geht nich. Könn Se noch ma
21 einer allein schuld is, ne. B: Ja, **eben**. A: Irgendwie en ganz kleinen Grun
22 irekt am 31. feiern, abends. B: Ja, **eben**. dass ja wirklich Klasse! A: Hm. J
23 les, wenn ich will, ne. D: Ja, eben, **eben**. Versteh ich. B: Naja! Zwei Kilo n
24 jetz niet, wann se kommt. A: Jaja, **eben**. So lange dauert die Fahrt ja nich.
25 esigen Vertrag beim Notar ab. B: Hm, **eben**.. Nee, ganz davon abgesehen, nem. I
26 , ne? A: Jo, is ja ejal, ne. B: Ja, **eben**. (lacht) A: (lacht) B: Bis ja noc
27 uern zu sparen, zu heiraten. B: Jo, **eben**.. klar, und außerdem ist das total
28 wann un wie oft er Lust hat, ne? A: **Eben**, ja. B: Paar Würste dazu oder irge

In all these occurrences it serves to reconfirm the interlocutor's previous contribution, but it also hints at the potential for different evaluation. The following instance exemplifies this:

Line 21

A: Ja, ich mein, man kennt die Hintergründe nich, ne, um da irgendwie was sagen zu können jetz.
[Yes, I mean, you/we don't know the background to that, in order to somehow say something now]

B: Naja, er is ausjezogen, weil sie en andern hat.
[Well, he has moved out, because she has got somebody else]

A: Ah so.. Ja, aber meistens isses doch so, daß . nich nur einer allein schuld is, ne.
[I see... Yes, but in most cases it's not only one person's fault,is it?]

B: Ja, **eben**.
[Yes, **exactly**]

(BRO 22 Bd 15/15)

Adverb of time

In its occurrences as adverb of time (13), EBEN is a short form of SOEBEN ('just, a moment ago'). In this particular use it is harder to distinguish from modal particle function as its position within the clause is similar to that of modal particle.

1 ja B: Telefon so anders. Em, ich hab **eben** mit der Frau X von der Verwaltung
2 C: C A: Guten Tag, Herr C, ich hab **eben** mit einem Kollegen von Ihnen gespr
3 Ja, hörma, wat sachsde dazu, was ich **eben** . der A erzählt hab? B: Nee, was

4 n dann? . Meine Mutter hat dich zwar **eben** schon den ganzen Quark gefragt, abe
5 u, ich wollt dir nur sagen, der Z war **eben** hier, die Schreibmaschine is also
6 a, ich hab der A eben gesacht, daß se **eben** vorbeigebracht wurde B: Ach so! C:
7 . den Abend ruhig gestalten, die war **eben** einkaufen und mußte sich danach hi
8 onsequent wär, ich war zwar sachtich **eben** noch zu C, ich bin jetz noch stolz,
9 hen das über'n DeAEs, und der meinte **eben**, ja, ich solle auf jeden Fall nen
10 ppelt belegt hat, ich seh nämlich da **eben**, Fenelon, Lettres a l'Academie hab
11 erzählt hab? B: Nee, was hasde denn **eben**, ich . hab das nich / C: Ja, von w
12 a, der X hat sich gewundert, weil ihr **eben**, als ihr ihn aus demAuto ließt, g
13 acht? Mit der A? C: Ja, ich hab der A **eben** gesacht, daß se eben vorbeigebracht

A contextual clue, however, is the collocation with one of the German tenses expressing reference to the past: Simple Past, Present Perfect, Past Perfect. Investigating a larger stretch of the dialogue reveals that this is the case in nearly all occurrences with the exception of line 10:

line 1	hab...gesprochen	(present perfect "hab" = habe)
line 2	hab...gesprochen	(present perfect)
line 3	hab...erzählt	(present perfect)
line 4	hat...gefragt	(present perfect)
line 5	war	(simple past)
line 6	wurde...vorbeigebracht	(simple past, passive voice)
line 7	war (einkaufen)	(simple past)
line 8	sachtich	(sagte ich, simple past)
line 9	meinte	(simple past)
line 11	hasde...?	(present perfect: hast du ...ellipsis of past participle)[65]
line 12	habt gesagt	(present perfect)
line 13	hab...gesacht	(habe gesagt; present perfect)

Line 10 is a rather particular case, as B's utterance is not in response to A's, but indicates a completely new subject. The immediacy of the new topic might have motivated speaker B to use the present tense, to distract from the fact that she was changing the topic, but of course this can only be speculation.[66]

A: Verbrecherphotos sammeln, oh, ich hab dem Schul-
kollegium ein Photo von mir geschickt, das war das

64 In this instance the past participle has been ellipsed, the clause is grammatically incomplete. A look at a larger stretch of dialogue confirms this. B's utterance is a question for clarification, referring back to C's "hab...erzählt"
C: Ja, hörma, wat sachsde dazu, was ich eben . der A erzählt hab?
B: Nee, was hasde denn eben, ich . hab das nich /

66 When presenting an example in the context of a larger stretch of dialogue the particle in question is emphasised in bold print.

letzte, was ich auftreiben konnte, irgendwo / das hatte ich nie gewagt, irgendwo hinzugeben, son ganz mißglücktes Photomaton- Bild, aus som Automat, ne? ja, da sah ich also / wie sone Hexe aus, so unheimlich giftig guck ich da rein, naja
[collect photos of criminals, oh, I sent a photo of myself to the school, it was the last one I could find anywhere. I had never dared sending that anywhere, it was a Photomaton-photo gone very wrong, out of one of those automats. well, I looked, like a witch, with a really poisonous look, well]

B: Wie is es eigentlich, wenn man son Seminar mal doppelt
belegt hat, ich seh nämlich da **eben**, Fenelon, Lettres a l'Academie hab ich mal bei der Y un jetz auch bei der Z mal be
[[Do you know] What happens if you enrol for a seminar twice, I **just** see there [I've just seen there] Fenelon, Lettres a l'Academie, I've done once with Y and now again with]

A: Das is doch egal, das heißt doch nur, daß du dich mit dem Thema sehr beschäftigt has
[That doesn't matter, it only means, that you got very involved with the topic]

(BRO 3 Bd1/3)

What can be established from the evidence, though, is a tendency for EBEN in its function as SOEBEN ('just, a moment ago') to collocate with verb forms expressing the past. For a native speaker familiar with all the functions of EBEN this is quite obvious but for a learner of German this collocational pattern might be of help in distinguishing the different meanings of the word.

A particular meaning of EBEN in its temporal function comes about when it collocates with MA(L) (12 occurrences):

```
1 eben / B: Ja, Augenblick, ich hör ma eben, Frau A:  Hm. B: Ja?  ((Stimme im Hin
2onntag oder bis Montag, Momentchen ma eben, ja? ((20s))  Ne, das is bis zum 9. A
3 rade, das könnt nich sein, Moment ma eben! (lacht) Ich gebn dir ma. D:  Ja, Mom
4r Messe! A:  Ah! 69 B:  Da müßtich ma eben nachgucken, das is entweder nur bis
5ame) C:  (Straßenname)? Da muß ich ma eben nachguggen, nech. A:  ja. ((59s)) C:
6her ein Bier getrunken/ B:  Moment ma eben! (zu ihrer Mutter) Ja, ich komm gleic
7          Ich mein, wenn der schon mal eben . dieses Knöllchen da  ausgestellt ha
8  kommen? B:  Ja, kommen Se morgen mal eben, ja? A:  Is gut. Hm, danke. B:  Ne? B
9 llt mir  grade ein, kannst du mir mal eben mit kurzen Worten sagen,  wie man ein
```

10 orz. B: Warte mal, kann ich noch **mal eben** sehen? Das is Porz, ja achthundertzw
11 Sie vielleicht freundlicherweise **mal eben** so durchrufen, wann der Herr U da Fr
12 ng an / einschalten, daß er dann **mal eben** so tickt, das hat ja nicht zu sagen,

In these instances, EBEN does not refer to a point in the past but together with MA(L) functions to point to the short duration of an event[67]. This is particularly apparent in lines 2, 3 and 6:

2onntag oder bis Montag, **Momentchen ma eben**, ja? ((20s)) Ne, das is bis zum 9. A
3erade, das könnt nich sein, **Moment ma eben**! (lacht) Ich gebn dir ma. D: Ja, Mom
6her ein Bier getrunken/ B: **Moment ma eben**! (zu ihrer Mutter) Ja, ich komm gleic

where the collocation with 'Moment' and especially with its diminutive form 'Momentchen' stresses the temporal aspect as well as the short duration of the wait.

In a number of instances there is a further aspect to the combination of MAL EBEN:

1 eben / B: Ja, Augenblick, ich hör **ma eben**, Frau A: Hm. B: Ja? ((Stimme im Hin
4 r Messe! A: Ah! 69 B: Da müßtich **ma eben** nachgucken, das is entweder nur bis
5 ame) C: (Straßenname)? Da muß ich **ma eben** nachguggen, nech. A: ja. ((59s)) C:
8 kommen? B: Ja, kommen Se morgen **mal eben**, ja? A: Is gut. Hm, danke. B: Ne? B
9 llt mir grade ein, kannst du mir **mal eben** mit kurzen Worten sagen, wie man ein
10 orz. B: Warte mal, kann ich noch **mal eben** sehen? Das is Porz, ja achthundertzw
11 Sie vielleicht freundlicherweise **mal eben** so durchrufen, wann der Herr U da Fr

Here, the temporal aspect 'it doesn't take long' has also a pragmatic function: if something does not take long to do, then it is not much of an imposition to ask for it being done. This is to do with our cultural concept of time as being a precious asset, as Lakoff and Johnson (1980: 8) point out in their study on metaphors in everyday life:

> Time in our culture is a valuable commodity. It is a limited resource that we use to accomplish our goals. [...] Corresponding to the fact that we act as if time is a valuable commodity – a limited resource, even money – we conceive of time that way. Thus we understand and experience time as the kind of thing that can be spent, wasted, budgeted, invested wisely or poorly, saved, or squandered.

In this sense, the time value attached to carrying out a particular action belongs into the category of 'goods' – the faster an action is carried out the less imposition it poses on the actor.

67 The English phrases 'just a moment', 'wait a minute', 'hang on a bit' correspond to its meaning here.

In lines 1, 4 and 5 the speaker wants to assure his/her interlocutor that what is being done for him/her is not too much of an inconvenience [68]:

```
ich hör ma eben, Frau
[I'll quickly find out]

Da müßt ich ma eben nachgucken
[I would have to have a quick look]

Da muß  ich ma eben nachguggen
[I have to have a quick look]
```

In 8, 9, 10 and 11 the interlocutor is being assured that the imposition posed on him/her is minor:

```
8     kommen Se morgen mal eben, ja
      [why don't you quickly come by tomorrow]
9     kannst du mir mal eben mit kurzen Worten sagen
      [could you quickly tell me in a few words]
10    kann ich noch mal eben sehen?
      I quickly have another look]
11    (könnten)Sie  vielleicht  freundlicherweise  mal
      eben so durchrufen
      [would you be so kind to give us a quick call]
```

There is one instance where EBEN can be found in the function of minimising imposition on its own, although the addition of "ne" at the end turns the declarative sentence, in which EBEN occurs, into an interrogative, thus adding to the indirectness of the request and lessening the imposition further:

```
rufsde aber so/wenns geht so mittags an, eben, ne?
[but you'll call if it's possible round noon, quickly, won't
you]
```

68 For a more detailed discussion see the qualitative analysis of MAL.

Modal particle

In the following 32 occurrences EBEN functions as modal particle:

1	agst, wie das gewesen wär, du hättest	**eben**	damals die Bankgeschichte nich wei
2	ich. Und . da muß ich jetz am Montag	**eben**	. meinen Widerspruch begründen. A:
3	ne, bloß / bloß B: ah! A: muß sie	**eben**	für die Doktorarbeit muß sie das Ga
4	und so weiter un alles dafür. Und da	**eben**	möglichst, öh, viel von, ne, damit
5	zwanzig, jo. A: Aber montags geht	**eben**	/ B: Ja, Augenblick, ich hör ma ebe
6	ch schicken will, dann schicke ik se	**eben**	nich. A: Doch, schick sie ruhig! I
7	dagegen Widerspruch eingelegt und muß	**eben**	jetz vor's Amtsgericht. A: Ja, un
8	A: Ich mein, sie hat	**eben**	bloß bessere Changsen, da weiterzu
9	möglichst, öh, viel von, ne, damit se	**eben**	auch sagen kann, das sind nich blo
10	jetz von der Schule bringen, weil er	**eben**	zu autoritär is, ne, auf der Schule
11	Verrücktheit und so. Aber das Eine is	**eben**	doch ne Geschichte, die e
12	albe Stelle abtreten und inoffiziell	**eben**	nur ne Viertel. B: nur ne Viertel!
13	r du tust Milch und Zucker rein, mußt	**eben**	auch wieder Süßstoff nehmen und au
14	ht möglich sein, ja, weil 8.000 Mark	**eben**	viel Geld sind, dann, em, müßten w
15	n auch zu uns kommen, A. Ihr könnt .	**eben**	. einfach ma nur so vorbei / brauch
16	st nie damit gerechnet, daß die Bank	**eben**	so'n Mist macht oder die . entsprec
17	machen. A: Jaja, klar. B: Das is ja	**eben**	dat Doofe. ((Räuspern)) A: Sicher.
18	en, mit/mit Ananas drin, so un/ mußt	**eben**	Süßstoff nehmen, darfs kein/ keine
19	Wanzen kommen? A: Ja, das weiß ich	**eben**	auch nich! B: Meistens sitzen die
20	es aus B: mal alles aus, weil wer ja	**eben**	wissen müssen, was wer noch kaufen
21	ißig Parteien A: hmhm B: un wenn da	**eben**	größere, öh, Reparaturen notwendig
22	besichtigt, und so, ne. Bloß, es is	**eben**	/ du kanns schlecht en Fenster aufm
23	? A: An un für sich, ja, bloß, es is	**eben**,	. daß ich doch son bißchen / also
24	B: un Schulen, und, em, na, Bücherei	**eben**,	die Ärzte befinden sich alle in d
25	viduelle . Vergütung und ä, das wird	**eben**	dadurch erleichtert, daß es nur hal
26	ätten wer hinterher aufgegeben, weil	**eben**,	öh, sie mit ihrem Bekannten dann.
27	Ah so! B: da is eine Kiesgrube und	**eben**,	öh, A: ja B: sons nix, re.. Un b
28	Na, ich ja im Grunde auch. Da ham wer	**eben**/	C: Ja, ich hab da bestimmt en unh
29	n, ich hatte aber . grad zu der Zeit	**eben**	keine Zeit, öh, "lernschwache Milli
30	Vielleicht wollt ich mir auch selbst	**eben**	bloß beweisen, ich kann alles, wen
31	das nur sagen. B: Hm C: Die wurde mir	**eben**	als etwas . unterkühlt vorbeigebrac
32	, verzichten müssen. Nein, ich hatte	**eben**	gedacht, ö, daß . er . offiziell .

In the vast majority of occurrences in modal particle function (26: 32), EBEN collocates with a verb in present tense, as can be seen from the concordance data provided here[69]. In two instances, line 1 and line 5, a subjunctive form can be found and only in four instances (lines 29 to 32) EBEN in its modal particle function collocates with a verb form indicating past. The concordance data show that EBEN as modal particle occurs in more complex sentences (e.g. lines 9, 10, 14, 16, 20, 21, 26) as well as in simple ones (e.g. 15, 17, 19). All of these are statements, there are no occurrences in interrogatives or imperatives. This is in line with its meaning in modal particle function, which is that of 'unchangeability', 'unavoidability' of 'undeniable fact' as a detailed analysis of the following instances will show.

69 The verb forms which are not included in the concordance lines shown here have been established by investigating larger stretches of the respective dialogue and are as follows: [line 4 – braucht]; [line 12 – würde]; [line 21 – sind].

The most obvious examples of stating a 'given fact' are those where EBEN appears as part of an existential clause[70], i. e. where the main verb is 'sein' ('to be'):

```
22  besichtigt, und so, ne. Bloß, es is  eben / du kanns schlecht en Fenster aufm
23 ? A:  An un für sich, ja, bloß, es is eben, . daß ich doch son bißchen  / also
```

Line 22

es	is	eben	du kanns schlecht en Fenster aufmachen
Subject	Process: Existential		Existent: Event
	Finite/ Predicator	Interpersonal Adjunct Modality: implicit	Adjunct/ Complement

Line 23

es	is	eben	daß ich doch son bißchen also ...
Subject	Process: Existential		Existent: Event
	Finite/ Predicator	Interpersonal Adjunct Modality: implicit	Adjunct/ Complement

EBEN functions interpersonally, expressing that a fact – the Existent – is evident and undeniable.[71]

There are two instances of relational clauses with SEIN occuring as dependent clauses introduced by WEIL, where EBEN can be seen in an emphatic function:

```
10 jetz von der Schule  bringen, weil er eben zu autoritär is, ne, auf der Schule
14 ht  möglich sein, ja, weil 8.000 Mark eben viel Geld sind, dann,  em, müßten w
```

70 'existential' is here used as a systemic functional term as coined by Halliday (e.g. 1994: 143). In this model, existential processes with the verb 'be' function to set up sole participants.

71 Compare Lütten 1979: 33.

Line 10

weil er	eben	zu autoritär	is
Carrier	Attribute		Process: relational intensive: attributive
Subject	Interpersonal Adjunct Modality: implicit	Adjunct/ Complement	Finite/ Predicator

Line 14

weil 8000 Mark	eben	viel Geld	sind
Carrier	Attribute		Process: relational intensive: attributive
Subject	Interpersonal Adjunct Modality: implicit	Adjunct/ Complement	Finite/ Predicator

Here, EBEN works together with WEIL to create the impression of uttering an undeniable fact. EBEN points to the relationship between *carrier* and *attribute* as undeniable, and so the relational clause is posited as a valid argument introduced by 'weil'. The following excerpts exemplify this in the context of larger chunks of text:

Line 10

B: ..., un wenn se frech waren, oder irgendwie was nich richtig gemacht ham, mußten die vor die Klasse, oder aus der Klasse un in der Ecke stehn, un so, under muß so ungefähr, öh, der hatte also sein erstes Referendarjahr, alson ganz junger noch, ne.

[...and when they were cheeky or somehow didn't do something right, they had to stand in front of the class, or leave the classroom and stand in a corner, and the like, and he must roughly. , er, he was doing his first year of teaching, so a really young one, you know.]

A: Das gibt's gar nich!
[You don't say!]

B: Hm, und . da . ham sich aber die ganzen, öh, öh, Eltern wahnsinnig beschwert, un wollen den jetz von der Schule bringen, weil er **eben** zu autoritär is, ne, auf der Schule jedenfalls.
[Hm, and . then . all the, er, er, parents complained madly,and now they want to get him out of the school, because he is **simply** too authoritarian, you know, at school at least]

A: Ah so!
[I see!]

B: Das is also völlig unnormal, daß sich da einer so benehmen würde, erzählte die Y mir/
[It's really abnormal that somebody should behave like that, Y told me]

(BRO 31 Bd 8/13)

In this excerpt, by using EBEN speaker B stresses the unavoidability of the parents' actions: they had to act like they did, because the teacher's behaviour lies outside of what is considered normal behaviour, an argument which is expressed again explicitly in B's next move.

Line 14

B: Ja, die Garage hat uns damals 8.000 Mark extra gekostet und sehr viel drunter wollten wer se auch nich verkaufen, ne.
[Yes, the garage cost us an extra 8000 Mark then and we don't want to sell it for much less, you know]

A: Ja. Is ja unverschämt, was die für Einstellplätze nehmen!
[Yes. It's outrageous how much they charge for car spaces]

B: Ja, leider. Aber wir warn damals laut Vertrag an den . Kauf der Garage gebunden und müssen auch laut Vertrag die Garage auch mit verkaufen, wenn wer die Wohnung verkaufen. Ich mein, sollte das um alles in der Welt nicht möglich sein, ja, weil 8.000 Mark **eben** viel Geld sind, dann, em, müßten wer uns versuchen, da ne andere Lösung einfallen zu lassen. [Yes, unfortunately. But according to the contract we were b bound to buy the garage then and according to the contract we also have to sell it when we sell the appartement. I mean, if that's not at all possible, yes, because 8000 Marks simply ARE a lot of money, then, er, we would have to try to find some other solution]

(BRO 28 Bd 5/2)

Using EBEN, speaker B posits that the proposition "because 8000 Marks simply are a lot of money" is an undeniable fact, common knowledge that is generally agreed upon. Within the larger argument "the garage may be difficult to sell" the phrase containing EBEN is a supportive move, EBEN providing the necessary emphasis.

In a fairly large proportion of occurrences as modal particle, EBEN collocates with modal verbs, namely 'müssen' ['have to'] (lines 1-5), 'können' ['be able to'] (lines 6-7) and 'wollen' ['want to'] (lines 8-9):

1	ich. Und . da **muß** ich jetz am Montag	**eben**	. meinen Widerspruch begründen. A:
2	ne, bloß / bloß B: ah! A: **muß** sie	**eben**	für die Doktorarbeit muß sie das Ga
3	dagegen Widerspruch eingelegt und **muß**	**eben**	jetz vor's Amtsgericht. A: Ja, un
4r	du tust Milch und Zucker rein, **mußt**	**eben**	auch wieder Süßstoff nehmen und au
5	en, mit/mit Ananas drin, so un/ mußt	**eben**	Süßstoff nehmen, darfs kein/ keine
6	möglichst, öh, viel von, ne, damit se	**eben**	auch sagen **kann**, das sind nich blo
7	n auch zu uns kommen, A. Ihr **könnt** .	**eben**	. einfach ma nur so vorbei / brauch
8	ätten wer hinterher aufgegeben, weil	**eben**,	öh, sie mit ihrem Bekannten dann.[72]
9	Vielleicht **wollt** ich mir auch selbst	**eben**	bloß beweisen, ich kann alles, wen

In collocation with a form of 'müssen', EBEN functions as part of the Mood structure[73] to lend emphasis to the obligation of carrying out a particular act, as the following analysis of the Mood structure of one example sentence shows:

72 The text continues as follows: "[...] schon auf die Bekanntgabe der Ergebnisse warten wollte."

73 "Mood structure" is here used as a systemic functional term (e.g. Halliday 1994).

Line 1

muß	ich	jetz am Montag	**eben**	meinen Widerspruch	begründen
Finite	Subject	Adjunct	Interpersonal Adjunct: Modality: implicit	Complement	Predicator
Mood		Resi-	Mood	due	

The types of processes expressed in lines 1-5 vary, there are mental processes (Line 1: 'begründen', Line 2: 'ausweiten') as well as material processes (Line 3: 'gehen' ellipsed, Line 4-5: 'nehmen').In these types of clauses, EBEN serves to express the unavoidability of the obligation as the following example shows in more detail.

Line 3

A: Gut, wenn das dann alles ma fertig ist, les ich's dir ma vor! Wie sich das anhört. Die schreibt nämlich auch Dialekt un sowas genau wortwörtlich ab, da.
[Right, when it's all ready at some stage, I'll read it to you. The way it sounds. You know, she writes down the dialect and all that word for word.]

B: Ja?
[Does she?]

A: Ja, in ihrer Examensarbeit hatte se sowas ähnliches gemacht, ne, bloß / bloß
[Yes, in her [Staatsexamen]thesis she did something similar, you know, but]

B: ah!

A: **muß** sie **eben** für die Doktorarbeit muß sie das Ganze en bißchen ausweiten, noch
[for her doctoral thesis **she'll simply have to expand** the whole thing a bit, still]

B: un noch / noch mehr bringen, ne.
[and still, still provide some more, you know. ....]Hmhm

(BRO 21 Bd 11/1)

The English 'simply' could here be expressed metaphorically as 'it's as simple as that', i.e. no discussion about it is necessary.

In lines 6, 7 and 9 EBEN not only collocates with a modal verb but also with other words in modal particle function:

```
6   möglichst, öh, viel von, ne, damit se eben auch sagen kann,  das sind nich blo
7   n auch zu uns kommen, A. Ihr könnt  . eben . einfach ma nur so vorbei / brauch
9    Vielleicht wollt ich mir auch selbst eben bloß beweisen, ich  kann alles, wen
```

Therefore the Mood structure of those clauses is rather complex as the following analyses demonstrate:

Line 6

damit se **eben** **auch** sagen **kann**

<table>
<tr><td>Adjunct</td><td>Subject</td><td>Interpersonal Adjunct:
Modality: implicit</td><td>Predicator</td><td>Finite</td></tr>
<tr><td colspan="2">Resi-</td><td>Mood</td><td>due</td><td>Mood</td></tr>
</table>

Line 7

Ihr könnt **eben** **einfach** **ma** **nur** so vorbei **(kommen)**

<table>
<tr><td>Adjunct</td><td>Subject</td><td>Interpersonal Adjunct:
Modality: implicit</td><td>Predicator</td><td>Finite</td></tr>
<tr><td colspan="3">Mood</td><td colspan="2">Residue</td></tr>
</table>

The above example would provide a language learner with a number of decoding difficulties, as s/he would have to identify for each particle in which of several possible functions it operates and how it relates to the preceding and following particles. It might be helpful to look at such an example and its translation into English step by step:

A Ihr könnt so vorbei kommen
[you can just come over] (i.e. without notice)

B Ihr könnt **eben** so vorbei kommen
[you can simply just come over]

C Ihr könnt **eben einfach** so vorbei kommen
[* you can simply just simply come over]

D Ihr könnt **eben einfach ma(l)** so vorbei kommen
[*why don't you simply just simply come over]

E Ihr könnt **eben einfach mal nur** so vorbei kommen
[*why don't you simply just simply just come over]

As the step-by-step translation quite clearly shows, this accumulation of modal particles as part of the Mood structure is an exercise in downtoning (to the point of almost "wheedling" as in version E) which cannot necessarily be translated into English in a similar manner, as the deviant constructions in C, D and E show.[74]

The KWIC concordances also showed collocations of EBEN in modal particle function with AUCH, BLOSS, DOCH and JA in modal particle function, but none of the collocations occurred with significant frequency. There were three occurrences of EBEN in the data which could not be analysed with a sufficient degree of certainty as they seem to represent a highly idiosyncratic use of EBEN and an analysis even on the basis of larger stretches of context would be purely speculative. The results of the qualitative analysis carried out on EBEN can be summarised as follows:

Summary of results: EBEN

Position in clause	Grammatical co-occurence	Lexical collocation	Category	Meaning
inital			answering particle	'exactly'
	indication of past		adverb of time	'just' / 'a moment ago'
medial/ final		MAL	adverb of time	'quickly'
medial/ final	tendency for present tense	form of 'sein'	modal particle	'simply' (undeniable fact)
medial/ final		form of 'müssen'	modal particle	'simply' (unavoidability of action)

74 More discussions of particle collocations will follow later in the text.

Sample Work Sheet: EBEN

1.) The word EBEN has different meanings which depend on the context of use. Can you find out by looking at the following groups of examples which of the translations given below best reflects the meaning of EBEN in each group?

a moment ago/just	**simply**	**exactly**	**quickly**

Group 1 ____________________

Group 2 ____________________

Group 3 ____________________

Group 4 ____________________

Group 1

1 schöneBücher, die man lesen kann. A: **Eben**! B: und so viele schöne Sachen, di
2 doppelte als die ganze Zeit, ne. B: **Eben**. Is auch schön. A: Undie Arbeit ma
3 alles, wozu man jetz nich kommt! B: **Eben**. Du, meine Mutter, die hatte ne gan
4 n die elf Kilo abgenommen hätte! D: **Eben**, ich denk, die is doch gar ni mehr
5 er Frau auch Frau Doktor Sounso. B: **Eben**, dann bisde ooch Herr Dokta! A: Ri
6 ort "werden" nich, anscheinend . B: **Eben**, siehsde, un, stimmt auch wirklich,
7 der Effekt ja oh ni mehr da! A: Ja, **eben**, genau! Vor allen Dingen, es geht j
8 , ich helf ihr, soweit's geht B: ja, **eben** A: und son bißchen Telefongespräch
9 uns ja nun wieder auch nich B: Nee, **eben** ( ) Hast du mal deinen Pullover aus
10 h kann Sie nur beglückwünschen. Nee, **eben**, das war, wie C, ich war der Meinun

Group 2

1 Ja, hörma, wat sachsde dazu, was ich **eben** . der A erzählt hab? B: Nee, was

2 n dann? . Meine Mutter hat dich zwar **eben** schon den ganzen Quark gefragt, abe

3 u, ich wollt dir nur sagen, der Z war **eben** hier, die Schreibmaschine is also

4 a, ich hab der A eben gesacht, daß se **eben** vorbeigebracht wurde B: Ach so! C:

5 . den Abend ruhig gestalten, die war **eben** einkaufen und mußte sich danach hi

6 onsequent wär, ich war zwar sachtich **eben** noch zu C, ich bin jetz noch stolz,

7 hen das über'n DeAEs, und der meinte **eben**, ja, ich solle auf jeden Fall nen

8 a, der X hat sich gewundert, weil ihr **eben**, als ihr ihn aus dem Auto ließt, g

9 acht? Mit der A? C: Ja, ich hab der A **eben** gesacht, daß se eben vorbeigebracht

Group 3

1 eben / B: Ja, Augenblick, ich hör **ma** **eben**, Frau A: Hm. B: Ja? ((Stimme im Hin

2 onntag oder bis Montag, Momentchen **ma** **eben**, ja? ((20s)) Ne, das is bis zum 9. A

3 rade, das könnt nich sein, Moment **ma** **eben**! (lacht) Ich gebn dir ma. D: Ja, Mom

4 r Messe! A: Ah! B: Da müßtich **ma** **eben** nachgucken, das is entweder nur bis

5 ame) C: (Straßenname)? Da muß ich **ma** **eben** nachguggen, nech. A: ja. ((59s)) C:

6 her ein Bier getrunken/ B: Moment **ma** **eben**! (zu ihrer Mutter) Ja, ich komm gleic

7 Ich mein, wenn der schon **mal** **eben**. dieses Knöllchen da ausgestellt ha

8 kommen? B: Ja, kommen Se morgen **mal** **eben**, ja? A: Is gut. Hm, danke. B: Ne? B

9 llt mir grade ein, kannst du mir **mal** **eben** mit kurzen Worten sagen, wie man ein

10 orz. B: Warte mal, kann ich noch **mal** **eben** sehen? Das is Porz, ja achthundertzw

11 Sie vielleicht freundlicherweise **mal** **eben** so durchrufen, wann der Herr U da Fr

12 ng an / einschalten, daß er dann **mal** **eben** so tickt, das hat ja nicht zu sagen,

Group 4

1 besichtigt, und so, ne. Bloß, es is **eben** / du kanns schlecht en Fenster aufm

2 A: An un für sich, ja, bloß, es is **eben**, . daß ich doch son bißchen / also

3jetz von der Schule bringen, weil er **eben** zu autoritär is, ne, auf der Schule

4h: möglich sein, ja, weil 8.000 Mark **eben** viel Geld sind, dann, em, müßten w

5ich. Und . da muß ich jetz am Montag **eben** . meinen Widerspruch begründen. A:

6 ne, bloß / bloß B: ah! A: muß sie **eben** für die Doktorarbeit muß sie das Ga

7dagegen Widerspruch eingelegt und muß **eben** jetz vor's Amtsgericht. A: Ja, un

8 du tust Milch und Zucker rein, mußt **eben** auch wieder Süßstoff nehmen und au

9en, mit/mit Ananas drin, so un/ mußt **eben** Süßstoff nehmen, darfs kein/ keine

2.) Where is the position of EBEN in the clause? Please circle the correct answer.

Group 1	initial position	middle/end position
Group 2	initial position	middle/end position
Group 3	initial position	middle/end position
Group 4	initial position	middle/end position

3.) Now look at Group 2 again and identify the verb forms in the clauses with EBEN
Write down the verb forms and their reference to time.

Line 1 _erzählt hab; Past_ Line 2 ____________
Line 3 ____________ Line 4 ____________
Line 5 ____________ Line 6 ____________
Line 7 ____________ Line 8 ____________
Line 9 ____________

4.) Which word appears in front of EBEN in Group 3?
____

5.) Examine Group 4 again. Write down the verb forms in each clause.

Line 1 ______________ Line 2 ______________
Line 3 ______________ Line 4 ______________
Line 5 ______________ Line 6 ______________
Line 7 ______________ Line 8 ______________
Line 9 ______________

Which two verbs do you find in these clauses?

Verb 1 ________________

Verb 2 ________________

Which tense is used in these clauses?

____

6.) Please supply the appropriate translation for EBEN.

Position in clause	Grammatical co-occurence	Lexical Collocation	Category	Meaning
inital	---	---	answering particle	
---	indication of past	---	adverb of time	
medial/ final	---	MAL	adverb of time	
medial/ final	tendency for present tense	form of 'sein'	modal particle	
medial/ final	---	form of 'müssen'	modal particle	

5.3 NUR

The word NUR occurs 109 times in 27 different texts in BRO. In the majority of occurrences by far, NUR functions as restrictive particle.[75] In the discussion of NUR in its restrictive function different categorisations have been proposed. König & Stark (1987) discuss NUR as a focus particle and consider focus particles as a subclass of adverbs. Weydt and Hentschel (1983: 15) use the term focus particle ("Gradpartikel") parallel with the term "adverb". Weydt, Harden, Hentschel & Rösler (1983: 168) use the term "restrictive adverb", whereas Helbig distinguishes between focus particle (1994: 192), adverb and conjunction (1994: 194).

In the current analysis, the main focus was to isolate modal particle function from other functions of NUR. The principal functional aspect of NUR in other than modal particle function is "restrictive". Taking into account syntactic distinctions, occurrences of NUR in its restrictive function have been grouped into two grammatical categories: conjunction and focus particle.

Conjunction

There are 17 occurrences of NUR as a conjunction. As a conjunction NUR can be found in initial position within a clause:

```
1 ja, dann wirders ja auch verlängern . nur, du mußt  dir das wirklich überlegen
2 r. Ich weiß o noch nich, was los is,  nur, eh, um  neunzehn Uhr dreißig is doc
3 an Einkäufer, ne an . wie sacht ma? . nur  immer mehrere Mengen, ja . größere
4 as  Wasser, das lief herrlich ab, du. Nur leider alles in die Küche  (lacht) A
5 igentlich ne ganze Menge Millionäre,  nur lernt man die nich kennen, ne ((lach
```

In instances 1-5 NUR can be translated into English by the phrase 'it's just/only that', as the following example shows:

Line 1

A: Jaja. Vom Dekanat . oder so hinge das nur für den
Fall ab, daß ich irgendwie . was klauen, oder .

75 See e.g. Helbig 1977: 38, Hentschel & Weydt 1989: 11ff.

weiß der Teufel, irgendwelche schwere Dienstvergehen bege/ den Studenten erzähle, was in der Prüfung kommt, oder so
[yes, yes. It would only be up to the dean's office in case I should . nick something or . I don't know, act against the official regulations/tell the students what's in the exams, or something]
(lacht) [laughs]

B: Naja, so . ja, dann wirders ja auch verlängern . **nur**, du mußt dir das wirklich überlegen, ob das wirklich günstig is, je nach dem, wie so die Lehrerausbildung hinterher aussieht, in drei Jahrn
[Well, then . yes, then he'll renew it . **it's just/only that** you really have to think about it, whether it's really best, depending on what the teacher training is going to be like later on, in three years time]

(BRO 10 Bd 2/1)

NUR as conjunction collocates with the conjunction 'wenn':

6 en? Ein Haus kaufen? A: ja, das kann **nur** gefördert werden, **wenn** das nicht in
7 ung / Mehraufwand für Verpflegung is **nur**, glaubich, möglich, **wenn** man mehr a
8 eres is, dann / also, **wenn**s wirklich **nur** sehr, sehr dringend, dann könnwer Se
9 chotten-Systemen" ja, genau! B: darf **nur**/"darf auf einen statischen Nachweis[76]
10Haus gern kaufen, aber, äh, das kann **nur** C: Kaufen? Ein Haus kaufen? A: ja,[77]

In occurrences 6-10, NUR can be translated as 'only (if)'. The following example demonstrates this:

Line 6

A: Guten Tag, Herr C, ich hab eben mit einem Kollegen von Ihnen gesprochen /
[Hello, Mr C, I just spoke to one of your colleagues/]

C: Ja . der hat weidergegeben.
[yes. he passed that on]

76 WENN occurs in the continuation of the clause, as an analysis of a larger section of the text shows.

77 WENN occurs in the continuation of the clause, as an analysis of a larger section of the text shows.

A: ja, der, e, sagte mir, em, ich / ich wollte'n bestimmtes Haus gern kaufen, aber, öh, das kann nur
[yes he, eh,told me, em I / I would have liked to buy a certain house, but, eh, that can only]

C: Kaufen? Ein Haus kaufen?
[Buy? Buy a house?]

A: ja, das kann **nur** gefördert werden, **wenn** das nicht in der Lärmzo / zone liegt /
[yes, that can **only** be subsidised, **if** its not within the area with high noise levels]

C: ja, ja. [yes.yes]

(BRO 16 Bd 4/4)

NUR as conjunction also collocates with the conjunction 'dass':

```
11 ber offiziell aussieht  wie ne halbe, nur daß ers mit Ihnen intern verrechnen
121e? A:  Hm. Ja. Oder zwei Tage vorher, nur daß ich noch ma mim T  spreche/ B:
13 ßt, weißt du nich? A:  Nein. Ich weiß nur, daß es mehr / etwas mehr psychologi
14 b ik nie en Programm, also,  ich weeß nur, daß ik am Sonnabend zum Jeburtstag
15  A:  Das is doch egal, das heißt doch nur, daß du dich mit dem  Thema sehr bes
16  mir das widder  passiert is, das läg nur daran, daß ich zu oberfläch_ich wäre
17 worden ., aber die könn auf dem  Foto nur erkennen, daß en Mann den Wagen gefa
```

A uniform translation for all occurrences 11-17 is not possible. There is a slight difference in meaning between occurrences 11-12 and occurrences 13-17, which might not be immediately obvious to a learner of German. The position of the comma in the transcription indicates a prosodic break which helps to distinguish between different nuances of meaning.

NUR in 11 and 12 appears in initial position of the clause. It is in fact separated from the preceding as well as from the following clause. It might be seen as an ellipsed form of the full clause: "es ist nur" and can therefore be translated in the same way as NUR as a conjunction on its own (see occurrences 1-5 above):

- aber offiziell aussieht wie ne halbe, **nur daß** ers mit Ihnen intern verrechnen
  [but officially it looks like a half (position), **it's just that** he (can) work it out internally with you]
- A: Hm. Ja. Oder zwei Tage vorher, **nur daß** ich noch ma mim T spreche/
  [hm. yes. Or two days before, **it's just that** I (can) talk to him again]

In occurrences 13-17, NUR is part of the pair NUR...'dass' and can be translated quite literally as 'only/just ... that'.

- Das is doch egal, das heißt doch **nur, daß** du dich mit dem Thema sehr beschäftigt has
  [that doesn't matter, that **just/only** means **that** you have looked into this topic very thoroughly]

Focus Particle

In 90 occurrences I have classified NUR as restrictive focus particle. The scope of the restriction can be a noun phrase as in the following selection of examples, where the noun phrase which NUR refers to has been underlined. In these instances the noun phrase carries the main stress:

1	gossen? B Die hab ich auch ganz/ich will\	**nur**	Mineralwasser trinken, da krie
2	aufen, ja verkaufen, ach so, **nur** an,	**nur**	an Einkäufer, ne an . wie sacht ma?
3	macht, B und A kennen sich praktisch	**nur**	aus solchen Anrufen. A: A. B: Fra
4	A: Französisch! B: …h / A: Ich hab	**nur**	Deutsch und Französisch als Fach. B:
5	h telefonisch erreichen, ich hab hier	**nur**	die Adresse! A: Ja, sons wei§ ich
6	ssen Krankheit sich abzeichnete, hat	**nur**	diesen Unterricht bekommen, obwohl
7	B: Ja, ich weiB es nich, das war ja	**nur**	ne Frage, ne. Freitag, was is Freit
8	auch nur. Dann sin das also insgesamt	**nur**	acht Stunden. A: Hm, ja. B: Insgesa
9	dann die weiße Hochzeit, da hat ich	**nur**	drei verwackelt davon, weil's so wa
10	bei der VHS gewesen. Aber da bin ich	**nur**	drei oder vier mal hingegangen, du.
11	irjentwann reinkommen, dat dauert ja	**nur**	fünf Minuten, is et widder / müssen
12	er Stelle übernimmt, inoffiziell aber	**nur**	ein Viertel und Ihnen die Differenz
13	ravemünde, das is was Neues und fährt	**nur**	eine Nacht, oder einen Tag, ich we
14	er meistens isses doch so, da§ . nich	**nur**	einer allein schuld is, ne. B: Ja,
15	ch. Wenn wir verheiratet sinn, kricht	**nur**	einer die Pension, und wenn wir ges
16	g zu werden! B: Nee, Neenee, es wird	**nur**	einer, das steht definitiv fest! A:
17	kann man / A: (lacht) B: a, es gibt	**nur**	einige Worte, aber, na, die gebrauch
18	gelung. B: Ja. Also das geht sowieso	**nur**	bis 31. März, nich, diese Regelung.
19	h ma eben nachgucken, das is entweder	**nur**	bis Sonntag oder bis Montag, Moment
20	se wieder arbeiten, aber dat sin ja	**nur**	noch 4 Wochen, glaubich. . Dann hat
21	aja, sicher. A: Ja, dat is ja Grunde	**nur**	noch so ne Fortführung der Prüfung

In all of those examples NUR can be translated as 'only', although there are slight differences in meaning.[78] In line 1-7 the underlying meaning of 'only' is 'nothing but/else':

1 [I only drink mineral water] → *and nothing else*
2 [they only sell to retailers] → *and to nobody else*
3 [they know each other only from phone calls] → *and from nowhere else*

78 For a more detailed discussion of quantifying versus scaling aspects of NUR see e.g. Foolen 1983.

4 [I only have German and French as subjects] → *and no others*
5 [I only have the address here] → *and nothing else*
6 [only had these classes] → *and no others*
7 [it was only a question] → *and nothing else*

In lines 8-17 NUR is followed by a numeral, the underlying meaning of 'only' is 'not more than', as the following examples show:

8 [so all up it's only eight hours] → *not more than eight hours*
9 [I only ruined three (photos)] → *not more than three*
10 [I went there only three or four times] → *not more often than that*
11 [it only takes five minutes] → *not more than five minutes*
12 [but inofficially only a quarter] → *not more than a quarter*
13 [it drives only one night or day] → *not longer than that*
14 [it's not only one person's fault] → *more than one person's fault* [79]
15 [only one will get superannuation] → *not more than one*
16 [it's going to be one only] → *not more than one*
17 there are only some words] → *and not more than some*

NUR as focus particle was found to collocate with prepositions (e.g. bis in line 18-19) and other focus particles (e.g. NOCH in line 20-21), which help to further specify the restriction expressed by nur:

18 [it's on only up until 31 March]
19 [it's only up until Sunday]
20 [but that's only four weeks left] → *not more than four weeks*
21 [that's basically nothing but an extension of the exam]

In many instances the scope of NUR is the whole clause, as shown in the following selection of examples:

1 später anrufen. A: Neenee, ich stell **nur** ab. B: Gut. ((11s)) A: Ich wollt m
2 ich, ich hab, öh, mich an un für sich **nur** an 1000 Kalorien am Tach gehalten,
3 eenee, neenee, neinnein, die krabbeln **nur**. Die sitzen im allgemeinen hintern
4 also die ersten 3 Stunden hab ich da **nur** jammernd im Auto gesessen und mir m
5 h! 43 B: Die ham die ganze Zeit also **nur** rumgemeckert, e... Das war also wir
6 e auch, sie hätte sons immer morgens **nur** rumgesessen, son bißchen Zeitung ge
7 die war/ die war nich sauer, die hat **nur** so getan, ne... Und er wurde immer
8 cht) B: "Bis du sicher, daß die sich **nur** verlobt haben, oder ham die viellei
9 doch nich so'n Quatsch, die ham sich **nur** verlobt!" A: Ja, wozu braucht man d
10in Monat hasde Schonfrist, brauchsde **nur** zu hospitieren und so, ne. A: Hm B:
11 also, weiß nicht / B: Ja, ich meine **nur**, müßten Se also könn, ne / A: Ja so
12bt's also kaum noch. B: Ja. Ich weiß **nur** von Ws nebenan, da is also'n Lehrer,
13e Menqe wert. Un dann müßten wer uns **nur** überlegen, was wer noch dazuholen, f
14 klappt das hier alles. Jetz muß ich **nur** noch umräumen, hier alles . en besch
15 also wie gesagt, dann. Ich kann Sie **nur** beglückwünschen. Nee, eben, das war

79 Here the polarity is reversed because of the negation: "nicht ...nur".

16uch nen weiten We.g Ne, wir könn alle **nur** versuchen, obs klappt, klappt nich,
17 . A: A B: B. Ich wollt **nur** Bescheid sagen. Seid ihr sehr böse,
18nge. B: Ja? Isch wollte sie einlisch **nur** bitten, da§ sie am Montag statt zu
19 B: Ah, hallo A! A: Ich wollt mich **nur** für die Hefte bedanken! B: Ach! A:
20s will ich auch nicht, ich will Ihnen **nur** ganz klar sagen, wie die Situation
213s)) A: Ja, C? C: Du, ich wollt dir **nur** sagen, der Z war eben hier, die Sch
22so offiziell, jaja, das wollt ich ihr **nur** sagen, ich mein, es ändert im Grund
23 Buchforst fahren, ich wollte ihr das **nur** sagen. B: Hm C: Die wurde mir eben a

In these instances it can be translated with 'just' or 'only' in the sense of 'doing just/only this, nothing else', as the following excerpts exemplify:

Line 22

B: B.
C: Tag B, is die A da?
[Hello,B. Is A there?]
B: A, C für dich! ((3s))
[A, it's C for you]
A: Ja, C?
[yes, C?]
C: Du, ich wollt dir **nur** sagen, der Z war eben hier, die
Schreibmaschine is also bereits bei mir.
[Hi, I **just/only** wanted to tell you, Z was here a moment ago, so the type writer is already here at my place]

(BRO 30 Bd 5/5)

Line 16

B: Da sehn Sie denn das Gebäude, links un dann gehn Sie denn herein . spazieren un bleiben am besten vorne . in der Eingangshalle stehen.
[There you'll see the building, on the left, and then you'll walk in and it's best to wait in the entrance hall]
A: Ja, . gut
[yes, right]
B: Versuchen Sie, pünktlich zu sein. Das gilt für uns alle. Ich hab ja auch nen weiten We.g Ne, wir könn alle **nur** versuchen, obs klappt, klappt nich, aber manchmal / Un dann komm dazu die Herren S, der

```
kommt vleich etwas später und ein Herr K, das sind
zwei Romanisten.
[Try to be on time. We all should. I have to come a
long way myself. Well, we can **only** try, whether
it'll work out, but sometimes it doesn't/And then
Mr S will join us, he'll probably come a bit later
and Mr K, they are Romance scholars]
```

(BRO 32 Bd 10/7)

In this last example, 'only' seems to be the preferred option over 'just'. This is also true of line 15 "Ich kann Sie nur beglückwünschen" [I can only congratulate]. The preference for 'only' as translation of NUR seems to come about because of the collocation with a form of the modal verb 'können', but further occurrences would have to be analysed to prove this connection.

Modal Particle

The literature on NUR (e.g. Kriwonossow 1977a, Bublitz 1978, Held 1983, Weydt & Hentschel 1983, Helbig 1988) lists its appearance in modal particle function as limited to the clause types: wh-interrogatives, imperative clauses and conditional clauses expressing wishes. Only one example of NUR in modal particle function – in a wh-interrogative – occurred in the BRO data:

1 lernschwache,.. oh Gott. Wie kann man **nur** sowas in ne Anzeige reinschreiben?

In this occurrence, NUR marks a rhetorical question: no answer is expected; the clause expresses criticism, as a look at a larger stretch of the dialogue reveals:

```
A:   Ah, ich hatte ne schöne Anzeige im., öh, in der
     Rundschau oder im Stadt-Anzeiger gesehen, ich hatte
     aber . grad zu der Zeit eben keine Zeit, öh,
     "lernschwache Millionärs, öh, Tochter sucht
     Nachhilfe, öh, zur Vorbereitung auf das, öh,
     Abitur"
```

[Ah, I had seen [saw] a good advertisement in.,eh, in the "Rundschau" or in the "Stadt-Anzeiger", but at the time I simply didn't have the time, eh, "slow-learning daughter of a millionaire is looking for tutoring, eh, in preparation for the 'Abitur'"]

B: lernschwache,.. oh Gott. Wie kann man **nur** sowas in ne Anzeige reinschreiben? Auf das T (=Zeitungsname) bin ich ja unheimich sauer.
[slow-learning,...oh God. How **on earth** can you put something like that into an advertisement? I'm really angry with T (=name of a paper), you know.]

(BRO 34 Bd 18/3)

Summary of results: NUR

Position in clause	**Grammatical co-occurence**	**Lexical collocation**	**Category**	**Meaning**
inital			conjunction	'it's just that'
medial		'wenn'	conjunction	'only if'
medial		'dass'	conjunction	'only just/that'
medial			focus particle	'only/just' • nothing but/ else • not more than
medial/ final	wh- interrogative		modal particles	'(wh-) on earth'

Sample Work Sheet: NUR

Please study the two groups of examples of NUR carefully and then work with the questions which follow.

Group 1

1	ja, dann wirders ja auch verlängern .	**nur**,	du mußt dir das wirklich überlegen
2	r. Ich weiß o noch nich, was los is,	**nur**,	eh, um neunzehn Uhr dreißig is doc
3	an Einkäufer, ne an . wie sacht ma? .	**nur**	immer mehrere Mengen, ja . größere
4	as Wasser, das lief herrlich ab, du.	**Nur**	leider alles in die Küche (lacht) A
5	igentlich ne ganze Menge Millionäre,	**nur**	lernt man die nich kennen, ne ((lach
6	ber offiziell aussieht wie ne halbe,	**nur**	daß ers mit Ihnen intern verrechnen
7	e? A: Hm. Ja. Oder zwei Tage vorher,	**nur**	daß ich noch ma mim T spreche/ B:
8	ßt, weißt du nich? A: Nein. Ich weiß	**nur**,	daß es mehr / etwas mehr psychologi
9	b ik nie en Programm, also, ich weeß	**nur**,	daß ik am Sonnabend zum Jeburtstag
10	A: Das is doch egal, das heißt doch	**nur**,	daß du dich mit dem Thema sehr bes
11	mir das widder passiert is, das läg	**nur**	daran, daß ich zu oberflächlich wäre
12	worden ., aber die könn auf dem Foto	**nur**	erkennen, daß en Mann den Wagen gefa
13	en? Ein Haus kaufen? A: ja, das kann	**nur**	gefördert werden, wenn das nicht in
14	ung / Mehraufwand für Verpflegung is	**nur**,	glaubich, möglich, wenn man mehr a
15	eres is, dann / also, wenns wirklich	**nur**	sehr, sehr dringend, dann könnwer Se

Group 2

1	sen? B Die hab ich auch ganz/ich will\	**nur**	Mineralwasser trinken, da krie
2	aufen, ja verkaufen, ach so, nur an,	**nur**	an Einkäufer, ne an . wie sacht ma?
3	macht, B und A kennen sich praktisch	**nur**	aus solchen Anrufen. A: A. B: Fra
4	A: Französisch! B: …h / A: Ich hab	**nur**	Deutsch und Französisch als Fach. B:
5	h telefonisch erreichen, ich hab hier	**nur**	die Adresse! A: Ja, sons wei§ ich
6	ssen Krankheit sich abzeichnete, hat	**nur**	diesen Unterricht bekommen, obwohl
7	B: Ja, ich weiB es nich, das war ja	**nur**	ne Frage, ne. Freitag, was is Freit
8	auch nur. Dann sin das also insgesamt	**nur**	acht Stunden. A: Hm, ja. B: Insgesa
9	dann die weiße Hochzeit, da hat ich	**nur**	drei verwackelt davon, weil's so wa
10	bei der VHS gewesen. Aber da bin ich	**nur**	drei oder vier mal hingegangen, du.
11	irjentwann reinkommen, dat dauert ja	**nur**	fünf Minuten, is et widder / müssen
12	er Stelle übernimmt, inoffiziell aber	**nur**	ein Viertel und Ihnen die Differenz
13	ravemünde, das is was Neues und fährt	**nur**	eine Nacht, oder einen Tag, ich we
14	er meistens isses doch so, daß . nich	**nur**	einer allein schuld is, ne. B: Ja,
15	ch. Wenn wir verheiratet sinn, kricht	**nur**	einer die Pension, und wenn wir ges

1.) Can you give a word in English which generally translates NUR?

____

2.) Let's have a closer look at Group 2 now. Can you underline the word or group of words which NUR refers to?

3.) Which translation is most appropriate for the examples in group 2? Please circle the choice which you think is correct.

Lines 1-7	nothing but/nothing else not more than
Lines 8-15	nothing but/nothing else not more than

4.) Now have a look at the following example:

`lernschwache,.. oh Gott. Wie kann man` **`nur`** `sowas in ne Anzeige reinschreiben?`

5.) Can NUR here be translated in the same way as for the examples in group 1 and 2?
Below is an excerpt from the dialogue the example occurred in:

A: Ah, ich hatte 'ne schöne Anzeige in der Rundschau oder im Stadt-Anzeiger gesehen, ich hatte aber gerade zu der Zeit eben keine Zeit, "lernschwache Millionärs-, öh, Tochter sucht Nachhilfe, zur Vorbereitung auf das Abitur".

B: lernschwache,.. oh Gott. Wie kann man **nur** sowas in ne Anzeige reinschreiben?

6.) In your opinion, which translation makes best sense in the context of this dialogue? Please circle your choice:

	how can only one...
"wie kann man NUR..."	how can you only...
	how on earth can you...

5.4 DENN

The word DENN occurs 160 times in 27 different texts in BRO. The occurrences fall into the function categories of expressing causality as a conjunction, expressing sequence as an adverb of time and modal particle.

Conjunction

In its function as conjunction (20 occurrences) DENN appears in clause initial position.

1	werd ich das Thema noch erweitern /	**denn**	der is ja jetz ers mal weg bis zum
2	,ne. A: Ja, sicher. Is ja klar! B:	**Denn**	. allmählich ermüdet se doch . rela
3	ßte eigenlich dann der 31. frei sein.	**Denn**	das is doch en evangelischer Feier
4	noch ma Frau Y, nich. A: Ja, hm. B:	**Denn**	die kennt sich in solchen Sachen pr
5	örderungsfähig ist. A: Ach, eh / B:	**denn**	wenn es innerhalb der Lärmzone is,
6	h scheiden zu lassen, nem B: Hm A:	**denn**	. öh . die Scheidungskosten findich
6	Geldern - / ich sag das mal weiter,	**denn**	da müssen Se auf jeden Fall her, a
7	an, daß die da eingeweiht sin ( ).	**Denn**	sons / sons wär dat nich so prompt
8	mpons, die würde sie ja nich nehmen,	**denn**	da müßte man ja, em . seinen eigene
9	A: das war wohl zu viel auf einmal,	**denn**	die feiern schon . nächste Woche W
10	Joja. Neue kaufen hat ja keinen Sinn,	**denn**	irgendwann bin ich wahrscheinlich
11	öh, rechnet ma am besten nich damit,	**denn**	. es hat ja auch keinen Sinn, ne.
12	Ja? Sie soll zu mir nachhause kommen,	**denn**	meine Mutti hat Geburtstag, da hab
13	menraufen mußten, als es . jetz is .	**Denn**	jetz kennt man im Grunde den andern
14	mer auch / wär vielleicht au gut, ne.	**Denn**	. ich will ganz ehrlich sahn, mit
15	B: Das sind ja schlechte Aussichten!	**Denn**	ne eins machen, is glaubich nich g
16	ch ers vorstellen, wenn du komms....	**Denn**	sons machen wer die Tür nich auf,
17	n und Hosen enger machen. C: Hm. B:	**Denn**,	öh/ C: Un das kann die auch, das
18	machen. C: Dat wär ma was Besseres.	**Denn**,	immer Käse, ich mein, das wird ja
19	D: ach so ja, kann ich verstehn. B:	**Denn**,	öh, ich wollte, so also . nich meh
20	upt Geld kriegt! B: …m . doch! Doch,	**denn**,	ö, das einzige, was sich ändern wü

DENN as conjunction expresses causality and can be translated into English as 'because', as shown in the following example:

B:	Ja, das muß funktionieren, ich rechne es auch mal aus, und, ö, dann frag ich auch noch ma Frau Y, nich. [Yes, that should work out, I'll do the figures, too, and, er, then I'm also going to ask Ms Y, ok]
A:	Ja, hm. [yes, hm]
B:	**Denn** die kennt sich in solchen Sachen prima aus. [**Because** she really knows a lot about these things.]
A:	Gut! [Good]

B: Sprechen wer doch noch mal am Freitag drüber, nich?
[We'll talk about it again on Friday, won't we?]

(BRO 4 Bd 9/2)

Adverb of Time

In 24 occurences, DENN was analysed as a regional colloquial variant of DANN which is an adverb of time.[80]

1	l! B: Ja, da brichsde zusammen, wenn	**denn**	sowas hörst!.. Jaa, ich hab ja auc
2	daß dich ma wieder jemeldet has, und	**denn**	grüß ma dein Frauchen schön sach i
3	nur so vorbei / brauch ja nich lange	**denn**	sein! A: Ja. B: Weil ja / wenns m
4	chaft, hat ja Urlaub. A: Ach so, ja,	**denn**	/ denn wir gehn Steak essen, aber .
5	chen! Die sin doch bestimmt/ B: Na,	**denn**	. ach . da hör ma, dann werdik sŠmt
6	enwände A: drei . zwo B: dann steht	**denn**	"bei Ausfachungswänden von Fachwer
7	telstunde, daß ik später komme . und	**denn**	könn se ja meintwejen abfl_tzen ja
8	§ man dann mal sehn, ne. Das is halt	**denn**	auch/ So vierzig, fünfzig Mann werd
9	gramm! Schichtwechsel! . Ja, Mensch,	**denn**	grüß ma schoma den X, ne! Dann erho
10	en traurig (lacht). B: Naja.. Ja, un	**denn**	bin ich dann da hingefahren. A: Ah
11	n das Gebäude, links un dann gehn Sie	**denn**	herein . spazieren un bleiben am b
12	74 A: Hm, Parknischen B: Da sehn Sie	**denn**	das Gebäude, links un dann gehn Sie
13	haupt denn schwierig, ne. Der hat ja	**denn**	Angst, du könns ihm ürgendwie sein
14	e irsendwann mal sagen? Ihr könnt ja	**denn**	auch zu uns kommen, A. Ihr könnt .
15	B: Das is natürch / das is überhaupt	**denn**	schwierig, ne. Der hat ja denn Angst
16	nachhause, wenns dunkel wird kommse	**denn**	endlich nachhause. A: Freiwillig? B
17	komm die / schmeißen die ihre Mappe	**denn**	vor de Tür, undenn sindse erstma we
18	Laufen isses zu weit eintlich ., und	**denn**	treffen wer uns alle zuhause, manc
19	sind, was länger erzählen! B: Jaja,	**denn**,	okay, du rufs vorher an, und denn.
20	aja. B: aber die haun immer gleichab	**denn**.	A: Wie alt sind de denn jetz? B:
21	a, denn, okay, du rufs vorher an, und	**denn**.	A: jo! B: sehn wer ürgendwie zu,
22	meine Sorgen, wie de's kris, un so. Un	**denn**/	Ne, das is also schon mal ne qanz
23	B: Das is natürch das is überhaupt	**denn**	schwierig, ne. Der hat ja denn Ang!
24	chaft, hat ja Urlaub. A: Ach so, ja,	**denn**	/ denn wir gehn Steak essen, aber . w

In these instances DENN can be translated into English as 'then' as the following example shows:

B: bis zur ersten . Kreuzung, da is ein großes U, das is der U-Bahnhof E-Straße. Rechts rein, 500 m, **dann** können Sie, dasis für Sie einfacher, Ihr Auto rechts an den Straßenrand stellen, da sind Park . nischen.
[up to the next crossroads, there is a large "U", that's the subwaystation "E-Straße". Turn right, 500m, **then** you can, that's easier for you, leave your car on the right hand side of the road, there are parking lots there

80 cf. Thurmair 1989: 163; Helbig 1994: 110.

A: Hm, Parknischen
[hm, parking lots]

B: Da sehn Sie **denn** das Gebäude, links un **dann** gehn Sie **denn** herein . spazieren un bleiben am besten vorne . in der Eingangshalle stehen.
[There you'll see the building **then**, on the left, and **then** you'll walk in **then** and it's best if you wait in the front of the foyer.]

A: Ja, . gut
[Yes, .ok]

(BRO 32 Bd 10/7)

Modal Particle

In its function as Modal Particle (116 occurrences) DENN occurs in interrogatives (cf. König 1977, Hentschel & Weydt 1983, Kosaka 1989, Nehls 1989, Burkhardt 1989, Luchtenberg 1989). The concordance data yielded 29 occurrences in yes/no interrogatives and 87 occurrences in wh-interrogatives.

Occurrences in yes/no interrogatives

```
1   los? Is dir schlechtgeworden? Is das denn schlimm?  Komm, steh doch wieder au
2  ) B:  Wie sieht das denn aus, könnter denn heute abend auch  kommen? Wenn ihr
3  das geht da einfach so weiter. A:  Is denn sons/ diese Kraftfahrzeugverbände,
4  der Tür un ham gefragt: "Ja, klappt's denn jetz, oder klappt  es nich?" A:  (L
5  e . kämen. A:  Ach so. Ja, meinen Sie denn, sowas is machbar? B:  Ja, das weiß
6  e). Das is natürlich übel! A:  Habter denn morgen abend mehr Zeit? B:  Das is
7  fferenz auszahlt. A:  Ja. Und kann er denn dann vom 1.9.an, also vom 1.4., wen
8  gut! A:  Verflucht! 85 B:  Hatten Sie denn, öh, öh, als Sie dieser Tage mit ih
9  hen. A:  Ah so! Ehm, was is denn/ hat denn der Freund bestanden? B:  Der is ja
10 Ja, das is wahr... Hasde die Quittung denn noch davon? A:  Jaja.... B:  Sons r
11 perfekt angesehn A:  ja B:  Hatten Se denn dieser Tage, als Se drüber sprachen
12 rlich  verständlich is A:  Wissen die denn überhaupt Bescheid? C:  Uber überha
13 t? A:  Nee! B:  Ja sowas! Hab ich die denn so mißverstanden? A:  Nee, wahrsche
is     richtig schön saftig/ C:  Darfsde denn kein Ei, en hartgekochtes? B:  Doch
    mal, ich wollt dich fragen, mußt du  denn nich zum  Flughafen gebracht werden
    nachhaus gekommen.  Ja, haste, bisde denn sons nich irgendwie iner Stadt? A:
17 ehter jeden Sonntag an!" "ja, willsdu denn  nich ma bald heiraten?" - "Nee, wi
18 eiten. A:  Ja sicher. … . arbeitet se denn nich mehr? B:  Bidde? A:  Brauch se
19 ihr denn nich mal en Kind und wollter denn nich mal  zusammen en Haus bauen, w
20 n nich sehr lästig? B:  Bitte? A:  Is denn das nich lästig? B:  Nö - nö, das h
21 ngesprochen, ne B:  Hm A:  "wollt ihr denn nich mal en Kind und wollter denn n
22 treicherleben an! A: Ja, erzählen die denn nich hinterher, wo se gewesen sind?
23 usgeschriebenen? B:  Ja, weißt du dat denn nich mehr, fürs Staatsexamen, für d
24 zu tun, wer  weiß?  B: Hör ma, has du denn nich ma Zeit, en Cafe zu kommen? Ic
25 , das wär doch schön! ..  Könntet ihr denn, ach so, ihr könnt nich zu uns komm
26   Flughafenbus, der fährt/ A:  Is das denn nich sehr lästig? B:  Bitte? A:  Is
27  Ich hoffe ja. B:  Ja, hör mal, gibts denn da nichts Genaues? A:  Nö! B:  s ja
```

In yes/no interrogatives, DENN has the pragmatic function of expressing 'astonishment', 'surprise'[81] in the sense that the speaker had taken a particular fact as given, his/her preconception is challenged in the course of the exchange and the question containing DENN asks for clarification. Line 23 exemplifies this:

```
A:    Ja, steht drüber Lebenslauf, und ich weiß nich ich
      glaub für für/  Mußt de en tabellarischen machen,
      oder nen e, nen ausgeschriebenen?
      [Well, it says CV on top of it, and I don't know I
      think for/do you have to write it in tabular form
      or, er, a full version?]
B:    Ja, weißt du dat denn nich mehr, fürs Staatsexamen,
      für die Meldung jetz
      [Well, don't you remember that, for the exam, for
      the application now]
A:    Nee, da mußde nen ausgeschriebenen machen, ne, wenn
      de
      nen tabellarischen machen darfst, steht et dabei.
      Ja, un dann fängt das also an "Ich, B, geboren
      usw./
      [No, you'll have to write a full version, if it's
      ok do it in tabular form it says so. Yes, and so
      you start with " I, B, born ... and so forth]]
```

(BRO3 Bd 1/3)

B talks to A about writing up a curriculum vitae for an application to sit for a university exam, which A has done in the past. B expects A to be informed about the procedures involved and is surprised when she finds out that A herself is not too sure about them. In the English

80 cf. Bublitz (1978: 59): "Fragesätze mit DENN drücken gewöhnlich die Überraschung des Sprechers aus, die auf die Diskrepanz zwischen der Erwartung und einem aus der Situation oder der vorhergegangenen Äußerung des Gesprächspartners erschlossenen impliziten Satz zurückgeht." Weydt *et al.* (1983: 19): "In Fragen, auf die man mit *ja* oder *nein* antworten kann, also in Entscheidungsfragen, drückt *denn* Erstaunen aus."
Helbig (1994: 105f): "Im Sprechhandlungstyp Frage; kennzeichnet eine Einstellung des Sprechers, daß etwas in Frage steht, was er eigentlich als gegeben (oder nicht gegeben) vorausgesetzt hat; damit wird Erstaunen (und Überraschung) ausgedrückt, [...]"

translation, DENN can be represented by a pattern of intonation (see underlined) which serves to express astonishment.

In this example, DENN connects the question "Ja, weißt du dat DENN nich mehr?" with the preceding stretch of conversation; it helps to establish a cohesive tie (cf. Halliday & Hasan 1985:75ff) between the utterance and the preceding ones. DENN in collocation with the deictic "dat" (standard German "das") creates anaphoric reference (ibid.), i.e. it refers back to the content of the preceding utterances and thus fulfills a discursive function on the level of the text.

The combination of DENN with other deictic elements, and in particular with the definite article in a deictic function, occurs with a high frequency in the data (38 occurrences):

```
  Flughafenbus, der fährt/ A:  Is das denn nich sehr lästig? B:  Bitte? A:  Is d
 ner Party! (lacht) B:  Wie sieht das denn aus, könnter denn heute abend auch  k
  os? Is dir schlechtgeworden? Is das denn schlimm?  Komm, steh doch wieder auf,
hr  mich (dann mal / ) B: Wie war das denn mit der Schreibmaschine, was habder d
logen! B:  Was? A:  Hm B:  Wie is das denn gekommen? A:  Ich hab/ war nich autor
Tagen  dann fest. B:  Wann habter das denn vor? A:  Also, wahrscheinlich, äh, Fr
 uns vielleicht da! B:  Wann soll das denn sein, hat se schon was gesagt? A:  Ja
 mitgefahren! C: Ja, wie kann man das denn ma einrichten? Daß ihr ma  kommt. Hör
ktuell . werden, ne. . Ja, wie is das denn mit dir, willste  trotzdem noch weite
 die bekloppte Schule! B:  Was is das denn für ne Schule? Ich mein, sicher, ich
 al B:  (lacht) Seit wann has dir das denn vorgenommen? A:  Seit zwei Wochen. B:
 aa,Mensch, verflucht, wo hab ich das denn jetz stehen?..  Dieses . dieses Ding
 gesehen!" A:   Hm B:  "Ja, wieso das denn? Die ham dir doch nie was getan!" "Ja
 er Tennis als Kanonen"/ B: Wo is das denn? A: Ach, das war . im / . im ersten,
 anziehen?" - "Ja", sagich,"wieso das denn?  Ich hoffe,  die ziehter jeden Sonnt
 Da in der Kneipe:  "Ja B, wie is das denn? Wann könn mer denn unsere  Sonntagss
      B:Wieviel Quadratmeter warn das denn? A:  Achtzig, also 160.000 Mark wollt
 , und da hab ich mich/ B: Was is das denn? 186 A:  Och. Das is ein./eine genaue
 ma bald heiraten?" - "Nee, wieso das denn?" "Ja, das  macht man doch so!" 41 A:
en  das Wochenende!" "Naja, wieso das denn?" "Ja, Y hat sich  verlobt . und am S
(lacht) D:  Mensch. B. wie ham Se dat denn iemacht? 144 B:  Ja, ich wei§ es auch
usgeschriebenen? B:  Ja, weißt du dat denn nich mehr, fürs Staatsexamen, fŸr die
nzen! A:  Wanzen? Wie hab ich mir dat denn geholt? 2           B:  Jah, also, ich
tel von einem Viertel, wieviel is dat denn?  ein Achtel oder was? A:  Nee, ein V
 zählt hat, ich sach der B, wieso dat denn? B:  Jaja, ich hatt doch unheimlich w
ft  wohl nichts. B:  Wie lang hat der denn gebraucht? A:  Zwei Jahre. Zweienhalb
en A:  ja sicher B:  ma hörn, was der denn von der Wohnung sacht, vielleicht  wä
rlich  verständlich is A:  Wissen die denn überhaupt Bescheid? C:  Uber überhaup
aben. B:  Wieso? Bis wann muß man die denn abgegeben haben? A:  Nee, die muß man
  Nee... Ich weiß nich, wie sieht die denn aus? A:  Ich weiß nich, wie die aussi
t? A:  Nee! B:  Ja sowas! Hab ich die denn so mißverstanden? A:  Nee, wahrschein
treicherleben an! A: Ja, erzählen die denn nich hinterher, wo se gewesen sind? B
  für ne Zeitlang. B:  Wie heißen die denn sons, die Hefte, ham die auch nich oo
e  riechen etwas. A:  Wie riechen die denn? B:  Das riecht so etwas süßlich dann
auch gesacht!... Und?..  Was macht er denn jetz? (Stimme im Hintergrund)). Ja. J
fferenz auszahlt. A:  Ja. Und kann er denn dann vom 1.9.an, also vom 1.4., wenn
   B:  Genau, ne. Aber warum feierder denn an som ungünstigen  Termin? A:  Ja, d
ne! A:  Mach ich! B:  Wie lange hader denn noch Urlaub? A:  Bis Donnerstag! B:
```

These occurrences of DENN in collocation with other implicit devices for establishing anaphoric reference support the argument that one function of DENN in interrogatives is to establish cohesion between the utterance and the preceding ones.[82]

But DENN also serves to create cohesive ties of a different nature, as the following example shows:

Line 15

A:	Tag, B, hier is A. Hör mal, ich wollt dich fragen, mußt du **denn** nich zum Flughafen gebracht werden und abgeholt werden? [Hello, B, A here. Say, I wanted to ask you, don't you [**denn**] need a lift to the airport and a pick-up when you get back?]
B:	Eh, nein, diesmal nicht, weil ich ja nicht wieder zum Flughafen zurückkomme. [Er, no, not this time, because I don't come back to the airport, you know]

(BRO 1 Bd 1/9)

In this stretch of dialogue DENN appears in the opening move[83], there is no preceding utterance which Speaker A could refer to. The point of reference for DENN in this example is exophoric, the reference goes beyond the text, broadly speaking to the context of situation.

A's opening move and B's response in this particular context of situation enable us to draw the following conclusions:
Context of situation: A (female student, 24 years old) calls B (male professor, 56 years old, close relative of A) on the phone

A's utterance	"Mußt du denn nich zum Flughafen gebracht und wieder abgeholt werden?" → A expects B to need a lift to the airport, she might want to offer her help, she might be surprised that the topic has not been discussed yet

82 For a discussion of this argument see e.g. König 1977: 119, Weydt 1989a: 331.

83 König 1977: 120ff discusses the seeming impossibility of DENN occurring in opening moves and suggests verbal as well as non-verbal points of reference.

B's response: "Eh, nein, diesmal nicht..."

→ usually B would need a lift but this time the situation is different

In this sequence, the speaker's surprise – expressed by the use of DENN – is not in relation to a previous utterance but in relation to shared knowledge between the two illocutors. A's utterance is an attempt to clarify whether any corrections in regard to this shared knowledge (cf. Luchtenberg 1989: 663) are necessary[84]. Here, in addition to its pragmatic function of expressing 'surprise' on the part of the speaker, DENN fulfills a discursive function above text level: it connects the speech event with the wider context of situation.
In two instances, DENN occurs in reported yes/no interrogatives:

```
28 n wollte, da hab ich gefragt, ob sie denn jetz von mir wollte, daß ich mich v
29ne Mutter meinte auch neulich, ob ich denn  nich jetz endlich mal heiraten wol
```

Again, the function of DENN is to express 'surprise' or 'astonishment', not as experienced by the speaker in the present exchange, but rather as a reported sentiment. In (28) the speaker refers back to a communicative event in the past where she was surprised about the demands imposed on her:

da hab ich gefragt, ob sie **denn** von mir wollte, daß ...
[I asked whether she [**denn**] wanted me to ...]

In (29) the speaker reports on another speaker's interrogative utterance:

meine Mutter meinte neulich, ob ich **denn** jetz nich endlich mal heiraten wollte
[my mother remarked recently, whether I didn't **[denn]** finally want to get married]

In both cases, it is not only the request for clarification which is reported, but also the stance of the speaker who uttered the interrogative in the first place.

84 Her motivation to undertake this attempt cannot be clearly identified from this particular communicative event.

Wh-interrogatives

In more than half of the total occurrences in the BRO data, DENN functions as a modal particle in wh-interrogatives (87 occurrences), following the interrogative pronouns *was* (27), *wie* (25), *wieviel* (9), *wieso* (6), *warum* (4), *wo* (5), *wann* (9), *woran* (1) und *welche* (1).

1	B: Bei Y. A: Tag, B. Was macht ihr	**denn**	so? B: Ja, ich bin allein. Die Z un
2	Das is schlimm, du! B: Was machste	**denn**	mit dem? A: Der will französische
3	A: Was Zukünftijet? . Was machst de	**denn**	morgen? B: Du, also, da fürn nächs
4	aufregen! B: Ja. A: Was machen wir	**denn**	am Donnerstag? B: Ja, ich dachte,
5	Hilden! A: Ach, übrigens, e, was is	**denn**	nun mit Freitag abend, könnt ihr d
6	un auch nich. C: .. Hör ma, was is	**denn**	das für'n komisches Geräusch im Hi
7	un übernachten dann da. Nee, was is	**denn**	da? Feiert ihr vor Silvester noch
8	! C: 1000? Ja hör ma, was/was ißt du	**denn**	dann? . Meine Mutter hat dich zwar
9	, und da hab ich mich/ B: Was is das	**denn**?	186 A: Och. Das is ein./eine gena
10	? Komm, steh doch wieder auf, was is	**denn**	los?" A: (lacht) B: Die wurde ers
11	A: Sind das Flöhe? B: Nein! A: Was	**denn**?	B: Wanzen! A: Wanzen? Wie hab ic
12	auch gesacht!... Und?.. Was macht er	**denn**	jetz? (Stimme im Hintergrund)). Ja.
13	auch mit A: fein! Joa. Was machst du	**denn**	da? B: Ach so . em . Lederwarensac
14	auern. C: Nee, Moment ma, wat hammer	**denn**	überhaupt? Freitag. Ja, Freitag (
15	die bekloppte Schule! B: Was is das	**denn**	für ne Schule? Ich mein, sicher, ic
16	emesterferie. Schön, ne? A: Ja? Was	**denn**?	B: Hm. Auch als Technischer Zeich
17	en A: ja sicher B: ma hörn, was der	**denn**	von der Wohnung sacht, vielleicht
18	er A erzählt hab? B: Nee, was hasde	**denn**	eben, ich . hab das nich / C: Ja,
19	h möchlich! A: Ja, aber wat machemer	**denn**	da? B: Müssemer sehn, sons müssen
20	hnt habe ((lacht)). B: Was machs du	**denn**	jetz? A: Ich, öh, arbeite als Wiss
21	ich werd nich fertig! B: Was machsde	**denn**?	A: Ach, i / ich hatte für meine M
22	Kilo hat die auch weg! 146 D: Wat is	**denn**	da groß zu kochen? ja Moment, aber,
23	nsde dir nich vorstellen. "B, was is	**denn**	los? Is dir schlechtgeworden? Is da
24	ocht. D: So, ja,ja is ja klar, wat is	**denn**	da groß / B: So drei Kilo hat die
25	r auftauchen. A: Ah so! Ehm, was is	**denn**/	hat denn der Freund bestanden? B:
26	s Spaß macht! A: Ja, was verdient se	**denn**?	B: Dreihundert Mark im Monat. B:
27	serbriefen A: Was? B: Hm A: Was stand	**denn**	da drin? B: Die waren/ die waren wo
28	A: A. B: Hallo, A, wie geht's dir	**denn**?	A: Ja . Gut. Hör mal, mir brennt
29	Nee... Ich weiß nich, wie sieht die	**denn**	aus? A: Ich weiß nich, wie die aus
30	Da in der Kneipe: "Ja B, wie is das	**denn**?	Wann könn mer denn unsere Sonntag
31	für ne Zeitlang. B: Wie heißen die	**denn**	sons, die Hefte, ham die auch nich
32	gemerkt, ne. B: Ja, wie spät es es	**denn**?	A: Halb sieben. B: Halb sieben, j
33	mitgefahren! C: Ja, wie kann man das	**denn**	ma einrichten? Daß ihr ma kommt. H
34	ner Party! (lacht) B: Wie sieht das	**denn**	aus, könnter denn heute abend auch
35	wollt noch eins fragen: Wie lang ist	**denn**	der Kollege . vermutlich krank? B:
36	(lacht) D: Mensch. B. wie ham Se dat	**denn**	iemacht? 144 B: Ja, ich weiß es au
37	acht) B: sachtse "Ja, B, wie kommsde	**denn**	darauf?" "Ja", sachich, "weißde, i
38	at ja noch nich. A: ( ) Wie kann man	**denn**	sowas kriegen? B: Ja, also an sich
39	e riechen etwas. A: Wie riechen die	**denn**?	B: Das riecht so etwas süßlich da
40	eibt. B: Nee? A: Wie schreibt man's	**denn**?	B: Soll ich dir sagen? A: Ja? B:
41	er gleichab denn. A: Wie alt sind de	**denn**	jetz? B: Y ist acht und X is sechs
42	es jebildet haben. ( ) Wie sollt ihr	**denn**	an Wanzen kommen? A: Ja, das weiß
43	Fahrt ja nich. B: Wie lange fahrn Se	**denn**?	A: 25 bis 30 Minuten. 88 B: Och,
44	ft wohl nichts. B: Wie lang hat der	**denn**	gebraucht? A: Zwei Jahre. Zweienha
45	hr mich (dann mal /) B: Wie war das	**denn**	mit der Schreibmaschine, was habder
46	in Frage. A: Doch, doch. B: Wie war	**denn**	dein Jeburtstag? A: Oweia! Feucht.
47	ktuell . werden, ne. . Ja, wie is das	**denn**	mit dir, willste trotzdem noch wei
48	logen! B: Was? A: Hm B: Wie is das	**denn**	gekommen? A: Ich hab/ war nich aut
49	ne! A: Mach ich! B: Wie lange hader	**denn**	noch Urlaub? A: Bis Donnerstag! B:
50	nzen! A: Wanzen? Wie hab ich mir dat	**denn**	geholt? 2 B: Jah, also, ic
51	ö, wieso? C: Nö?.. Un wie geht's dir	**denn**	sons? B: Naja.. Zwei Kilo noch run
52	Tag, B, hier is A! B: Jo, wie geht's	**denn**	so? A: Naja, wir hatten also kein u
53	Bußgeldbescheid B: Ach je! Wieviel	**denn**?	A: Dreienzwanzig Mark 191 B: ((l
54	, 200 Mark. B: Wieviel Stelle has du	**denn**?	A: Ne ganze. B: Ach, ne ganze. I
55	134 B: Wieviel Quadratmeter warn das	**denn**?	A: Achtzig, also 160.000 Mark wol
56	Ach, ja. Mal sehn, wieviel Uhr is es	**denn**?	48 B: Ich hab zwei, viertel nach
57	cht Klasse! A: Ja. Wieviel Leute ham	**denn**	überhaupt Platz . bei dir? B: Also
58	es nich, um was / um wieviel Uhr habt	**denn**	ihr/ ihr ausgemacht? C: Ja, wenn

59 gut! B: Ja, um wieviel Uhr soll ich **denn** da sein, dann? A: Wann de willst!
60 n das machen. Wieviel Stunden sind es **denn** überhaupt? B: Es geht um Englisch
61 tel von einem Viertel, wieviel is dat **denn**? ein Achtel oder was? A: Nee, ein
62 gesehen!" A: Hm B: "Ja, wieso das **denn**? Die ham dir doch nie was getan!" "
63 em, "hör mal, wieso verlobst du dich **denn** einlich so schnell?" "Tja", hat de
64 anziehen?" - "Ja", sagich, "wieso das **denn**? Ich hoffe, die ziehter jeden Son
65 en das Wochenende!" "Naja, wieso das **denn**?" "Ja, Y hat sich verlobt . und am
66 ma bald heiraten?" - "Nee, wieso das **denn**?" "Ja, das macht man doch so!" 41
67 zählt hat, ich sach der B, wieso dat **denn**? B: Jaja, ich hatt doch unheimlich
68 Dezember. B: Dass ja passend! Warum **denn** nich am 25. Dezember? (lacht) A: (
69 . Soweit ich weiß. A: Warum ham se's **denn** dann . so . komisch datiert? B: Ka
70 68 B: Genau, ne. Aber warum feierder **denn** an som ungünstigen Termin? A: Ja,
71 iben. A: Warum? 27 B: Warum willsde **denn** hier bleiben, Y? Kanns do mitkommen
72 C: Geht dat so telefonisch? Wo liegt **denn** das? A: In Porz-Lind (Straßenname)
73 aa, Mensch, verflucht, wo hab ich das **denn** jetz stehen?.. Dieses . dieses Din
74 einlich gar nich in Köln B: Wo bisde **denn** da? Wieder unterwegs? A: Zu Hause
75 er Tennis als Kanonen"/ B: Wo is das **denn**? A: Ach, das war . im / . im ersten
76 hm B: nach Rheinbreitbach! A: Wo is **denn** das? B: Das is rechts . rheinisch,
77 schlecht. B: Ah so. C: Wann seider **denn** widder da aus Brüssel? B: Aus Brüs
78 uns vielleicht da! B: Wann soll das **denn** sein, hat se schon was gesagt? A:
79 "Ja B, wie is das denn? Wann könn mer **denn** unsere Sonntagsschuhe anziehen?" -
80 aben. B: Wieso? Bis wann muß man die **denn** abgegeben haben? A: Nee, die mu$ m
81 al. B: (lacht) Seit wann has dir das **denn** vorgenommen? A: Seit zwei Wochen.
82 ig kommen, blo$ e/ C: Wann kommen se **denn** Sonntag? B: Wann kämt ihr Sonntag,
83 n beim Essen. A: Ah so. B: Hm. Wann **denn**? A: Ja, wann ihr wollt! B: Nachm
84 prüfen können. A: Ja, wann könnt ich **denn** mal kommen? 90 B: Oder rufen Se ma
85 Tagen dann fest. B: Wann habter das **denn** vor? A: Also, wahrscheinlich, öh,
86 : so in dem Stil, ne. A: Woran lag's **denn**, daß die Spüle verstopft war, das w
87 euß die, aber gute / A: Welche sind **denn** das? B: Klettenberg würde uns auch

Wh-interrogatives with DENN ask for further specification of available information and presuppose that the interlocutor is able to provide this information.[85] In wh-interrogatives the main function of DENN is to establish cohesion. Thus, its main function is discursive on the level of text. DENN links the utterance it occurs in to preceding ones and thus creates anaphoric reference within the specific linguistic context. This type of reference is particularly salient in interrogatives with the interrogative pronouns *wieso* and *warum* which also create anaphoric reference:

62 gesehen!" A: Hm B: "Ja, wieso das **denn**? Die ham dir doch nie was getan!" "
63 em, "hör mal, wieso verlobst du dich **denn** einlich so schnell?" "Tja", hat de
64 anziehen?" - "Ja", sagich, "wieso das **denn**? Ich hoffe, die ziehter jeden Son
65 en das Wochenende!" "Naja, wieso das **denn**?" "Ja, Y hat sich verlobt . und am
66 ma bald heiraten?" - "Nee, wieso das **denn**?" "Ja, das macht man doch so!" 41
67 zählt hat, ich sach der B, wieso dat **denn**? B: Jaja, ich hatt doch unheimlich
68 Dezember. B: Dass ja passend! Warum **denn** nich am 25. Dezember? (lacht) A: (
69 . Soweit ich weiß. A: Warum ham se's **denn** dann . so . komisch datiert? B: Ka
70 68 B: Genau, ne. Aber warum feierder **denn** an som ungünstigen Termin? A: Ja,
71 iben. A: Warum? 27 B: Warum willsde **denn** hier bleiben, Y? Kanns do mitkommen

and in those instances where DENN collocates with another deictic device (see page 155-6). DENN in wh-interrogatives might be

85 cf. König 1977.

translated into English by ‘then’ or ‘so’[86], as the following excerpt exemplifies:

Line 71

B: Y sacht grad, mir sollden mit euch alleine fahrn, er wollt hierbleiben.
[Y just said, we should go with you alone, he wants to stay here]

A: Warum?
[Why?]

B: Warum willsde **denn** hier bleiben, Y?
[Why do you want to stay here, **then**, Y?]
or
[**So**, why do you want to stay here, Y?]

(BRO 7 Bd 3/4)

In some instances, DENN in wh-interrogatives can refer to the wider context of speech rather than to preceding utterances as for example in the following excerpt:

Line 1

B: Bei Y.
[Y.]

A: Tag, B. Was macht ihr **denn** so?
[**So**, what are you doing **then?**]

B: Ja, ich bin allein. Die Z und der Y sind drüben.
[Well, I’m alone. Y and Z are over at...]

(BRO 12 Bd 2/7)

The results of the qualitative analysis carried out on DENN can be summarised as follows:

86 cf. König *et al.* 1990.

Summary of results: DENN

Position in clause	**Grammatical co-occurence**	**Lexical collocation**	**Category**	**Meaning**
inital			conjunction	'because'
			adverb of time	'then'
medial/ final	yes/no interrogative		modal particle	'surprise' rendered in English by intonation pattern expressing surprise
medial/ final	interrogative	wh-interrogative pronoun	modal particle	'then'/ 'so'

Sample Work Sheet: DENN

1.) The word DENN can have different meanings depending on the context of use. Can you find out by looking at the following two groups of examples which of the translations given below best reflects the meaning of DENN in each group?

because	then/so

Group 1 ____________________

Group 2 ____________________

Group 1

1 A: Was Zukünftijet? . Was machst de **denn** morgen? B: Du, also, da fürn nächs
2 aufregen! B: Ja. A: Was machen wir **denn** am Donnerstag? B: Ja, ich dachte,
3 wollt noch eins fragen: Wie lang ist **denn** der Kollege . vermutlich krank? B:
4 eibt. B: Nee? A: Wie schreibt man's **denn**? B: Soll ich dir sagen? A: Ja? B:
5 ft wohl nichts. B: Wie lang hat der **denn** gebraucht? A: Zwei Jahre. Zweienha
6 134 B: Wieviel Quadratmeter warn das **denn**? A: Achtzig, also 160.000 Mark wol
7 cht Klasse! A: Ja. Wieviel Leute ham **denn** überhaupt Platz . bei dir? B: Also
8 gesehen!" A: Hm B: "Ja, wieso das **denn**? Die ham dir doch nie was getan!" "
9 en das Wochenende!" "Naja, wieso das **denn**?" "Ja, Y hat sich verlobt . und am
10 Dezember. B: Dass ja passend! Warum **denn** nich am 25. Dezember? (lacht) A: (
11 iben. A: Warum? 27 B: Warum willsde **denn** hier bleiben, Y? Kanns do mitkommen
12 C: Geht dat so telefonisch? Wo liegt **denn** das? A: In Porz-Lind (Straßenname)
13 er Tennis als Kanonen"/ B: Wo is das **denn**? A: Ach, das war . im / . im ersten
14 uns vielleicht da! B: Wann soll das **denn** sein, hat se schon was gesagt? A:
15 aben. B: Wieso? Bis wann muß man die **denn** abgegeben haben? A: Nee, die muß m
16 al. B: (lacht) Seit wann has dir das **denn** vorgenommen? A: Seit zwei Wochen.
17 prüfen können. A: Ja, wann könnt ich **denn** mal kommen? 90 B: Oder rufen Se ma
18 Tagen dann fest. B: Wann habter das **denn** vor? A: Also, wahrscheinlich, öh,
19 : so in dem Stil, ne. A: Woran lag's **denn**, daß die Spüle verstopft war, das w
20 euß die, aber gute / A: Welche sind **denn** das? B: Klettenberg würde uns auch

Group 2

1	werd ich das Thema noch erweitern /	**denn**	der is ja jetz ers mal weg bis zum
2	,ne. A: Ja, sicher. Is ja klar! B:	**Denn**	. allmählich ermüdet se doch . rela
3	ßte eigenlich dann der 31. frei sein.	**Denn**	das is doch en evangelischer Feier
4	noch ma Frau Y, nich. A: Ja, hm. B:	**Denn**	die kennt sich in solchen Sachen pr
5	örderungsfähig ist. A: Ach, eh / B:	**denn**	wenn es innerhalb der Lärmzone is,
6	h scheiden zu lassen, nem B: Hm A:	**denn**	. öh . die Scheidungskosten findich
6	Geldern - / ich sag das mal weiter,	**denn**	da müssen Se auf jeden Fall her, a
7	an, daß die da eingeweiht sin ( ).	**Denn**	sons / sons wär dat nich so prompt
8	mpons, die würde sie ja nich nehmen,	**denn**	da müßte man ja, em . seinen eigene
9	A: das war wohl zu viel auf einmal,	**denn**	die feiern schon . nächste Woche W
10	Joja. Neue kaufen hat ja keinen Sinn,	**denn**	irgendwann bin ich wahrscheinlich
11	öh, rechnet ma am besten nich damit,	**denn**	. es hat ja auch keinen Sinn, ne.
12	Ja? Sie soll zu mir nachhause kommen,	**denn**	meine Mutti hat Geburtstag, da hab
13	menraufen mußten, als es . jetz is .	**Denn**	jetz kennt man im Grunde den andern
14	mer auch / wär vielleicht au gut, ne.	**Denn**	. ich will ganz ehrlich sahn, mit
15	B: Das sind ja schlechte Aussichten!	**Denn**	ne eins machen, is glaubich nich g
16	ch ers vorstellen, wenn du komms....	**Denn**	sons machen wer die Tür nich auf,
17	n und Hosen enger machen. C: Hm. B:	**Denn**,	öh/ C: Un das kann die auch, das
18	machen. C: Dat wär ma was Besseres.	**Denn**,	immer Käse, ich mein, das wird ja
19	D: ach so ja, kann ich verstehn. B:	**Denn**,	öh, ich wollte, so also . nich meh

2.) Where is the position of DENN in the clause? Please circle the correct answer.

Group 1	initial position	middle/end position
Group 2	initial position	middle/end position

3.) Now let's look at group 1 again. In which type of clause does the word DENN occur?

____

4.) Please underline the clauses in which DENN appears in Group 1. Then list the words at the beginning of those clauses.

Line 1–2	____________	Line 12–13	____________
Line 3–5	____________	Line 14–18	____________
Line 6–7	____________	Line 19	____________
Line 8–9	____________	Line 20	____________
Line 10–11	____________		

5.) Now look at the use of DENN in the following excerpt of a telephone dialogue. In which type of question does DENN appear?

____

```
B:    Wie lang geht dein Vertrag?
A:    Bis zum 31.8.
B:    Ach so, und wird dann verlängert oder wie?
A:    Ich hoffe ja.
B:    Ja, hör mal, gibts denn da nichts Genaues?
A:    Nö!
```

Here, the use of DENN is emphatic: speaker B expresses her surprise. She assumes that speaker A's work contract will be renewed ("und er wird dann verlängert"). When speaker A cannot confirm this firmly ("ich hoffe ja"), she asks for clarification. In English, this function of DENN would be expressed by an emphatic intonation expressing surprise.

6.) Have a look at the following table and – based on the exercises and explanations above – try to give a translation for DENN into English.

Position in clause	**Grammatical co-occurence**	**Lexical Collocation**	**Category**	**Meaning**
inital	---	---	conjunction	
medial/ final	yes/no interrogative	---	modal particle	
medial/ final	interrogative	wh-interrogative pronoun	modal particle	

5.5 SCHON

The particle schon occurs 174 times in 27 different texts in BRO. In the majority of occurrences by far, namely 131 instances, SCHON appears in a temporal function, either as an adverb or as a focus particle. In 9 instances, SCHON acts as a focus particle without having a temporal function. There is one occurrence of SCHON in an answering function and 33 occurrences of SCHON as modal particle.[87]

Temporal Function[88]

The most frequently occurring functional aspect of SCHON is "temporal". In its temporal function the scope of SCHON is either the sentence on the whole, as for example in the following occurrences:

1	B: Mir ham se	**schon**	das Kindergeld abgezogen. A: Ja? B
2	. dann lag das genau daran, wie ich	**schon**	vermutet hatte, e, war nämig ein di
3	du auch garnich, da warst du nämlich	**schon**	weg. Du bis ja unheimlich früh die
4	Aber ich glaub, da die ganze Sache	**schon**	am Laufen war, äh, verjährt das gl
5	Promotion fertig is, ne. Un er hat	**schon**	gesacht, also . unter ner eins is
6	: Wie war's im Übrigen noch, ham Se	**schon**	den Kaufvertrag abgeschlossen? A:
7	B: Wann soll das denn sein, hat se	**schon**	was gesagt? A: Ja, sie denkt an de
8	(lacht) B: Wie lange fährt se jetz	**schon**	? A: Ich? B: Na, du fährs ja bald
9	t solles? A: (lacht) Hatteter euch	**schon**	dran gewöhnt? B: (lacht) A: Aber i
10	n von Holland zurück/ A: Hasde auch	**schon**	? B: Hab ich auch schon, sind auch

In this type of occurrences, SCHON could be replaced by the temporal adverb 'bereits' and it can be translated into English by 'already' in statements (occurrences 1-5) and 'yet' in questions (occurrences 6-10).

1 [They have ALREADY deducted my children's allowance. …]
2 […as I had ALREADY assumed.…]
3 […you had ALREADY left then..]
4 […, as the whole thing was ALREADY going on,..]

87 The categorisation of SCHON into grammatical and functional categories draws on Bublitz 1977, Franck 1980, Gornik-Gerhardt 1981, Borst 1985, Thurmair 1989, König *et al.* 1990, Helbig 1994. For detailed references see descriptions of categories.

88 A full list of occurrences is given in the appendix.

5 […and he ALREADY said,…]
6 […have you signed the contract of sale YET?]
7 […has she said anything YET?]
8 […how long has she been driving YET?]
9 […had you become used to it YET?…]
10 […have you (got) (them)YET?..]

In a number of occurrences, the focus of SCHON is a temporal phrase, as exemplified in the following instances:

11 an.   B: Ja, aber wenn die **schon** namittachs sacht, daß et ihr nich g
12 zu viel auf einmal, denn die feiern **schon** . nächste Woche Weihnachten, weil
13 , datihr euch da / A: Nee, wir gehn **schon** um halb sieben B: in Porz oder wie
14 ich! A: Ja, legen wir ganz bestimmt **schon** in den nächsten Tagen dann fest. B
15 Uni kann. B: Ja, ich trage Sie dann **schon** für 9 Uhr ein, ja? A: Ja   das wär

Here, the translation of SCHON into English might vary between 'already', 'as early as' and 'the very next'[89]

11 [yes, but if she **already** says in the afternoon, that…]
12 […, because they celebrate Christmas **as early as** next week,..]
13 [….No, we'll leave **as early as** half past six…]
14 [….Yes, we'll definitely decide this within **the very next** days]
15 […Yes, I'll put you down for **as early as** nine o'clock then, won't I?…]

In its temporal function SCHON collocates frequently with MA(L) (18: 131 occurrences):

16 nich A: hm B: Ich mein, wenn der **schon** mal eben . dieses Knöllchen da aus[90]
17 hab doch, weiß nich, ob ich dir das **schon** ma erzählt hab, ma für sen Lederty
18 Ja. Ja. B: (lacht) A: Ich hab mir **schon** mal überlegt, bin ich da eigenlich
19 ne B: ja A: un da bisde natürlich **schon** mal . en bißchen gehemmt und so, n
20 A: Also, auf jeden Fall gebrauchsde **schon** ma das Wort "werden" nich, anschei
21 A: hm B: aber so ab un zu kommt es **schon** mal A: ja klar! ... B: Samma, wan
22 den ganzen Scheiß, besorgen, undann **schon** ma sons bißchen was vorbereiten, d
23 e im Hintergrund)) Is das einer, der **schon** ma hier war?.. Wie heißt der? ((St
24 er nochen neues drauftun. Das kommt **schon** ma vor, daß die neuen auch ni mehr
25 hier is B. A: Tach B! B: Ich hatte **schon** ma angerufen, aber da war keiner da
26 is, un so. Un denn/ Ne, das is also **schon** mal ne qanze Menqe wert. Un dann m
27 n! B: Ja, Gut! Dann wer ich mir das **schon** ma merken! ((3s)) Bestell dem X ma
28 n, aber ich glaub, also, sie war ja **schon** ma vorher da, ne, an der Schule, d
29 nach mir, Geburtstag, da ham wir das **schon** ma zusammengelegt, ne. ob mer dat
30 ne. A: hmhm B: Klar, das wurd auch **schon** ma später. A: jaja B: wenn ich ir
31 romovieren jetz, undann brauch se eh **schon** ma zwei Jahre, un auch zwei Jahre
32 s muß ja / darf / ich mein, der kann **schon** mal rausspringen, der darf aber ni
33 ule? Ich mein, sicher, ich hab auch **schon** ma öfter ma abends lang gearbeitet,

89 cf. König *et al.* 1990: 201ff.
90 The use of the particle combination SCHON MAL EBEN in this context seems highly idiosyncratic and has not been analysed further.

There is a difference in meaning between those occurrences where SCHON MAL collocates with a verb form indicating past (lines 17, 18, 23, 25, 28, 29, 30, 33) and those where it does not.

In collocation with a verb form indicating past tense, SCHON MAL indicates that the action has happened before; MAL takes on a temporal function as in 'einmal'. Thus, the combination SCHON (EIN)MAL could be literally translated into 'already at one other time', the English translation equivalent being 'before', as shown below:

17 ob ich dir das **schon ma** erzählt hab
[whether I have told you this **before**]
18 Ich hab mir **schon mal** überlegt,
[I have thought about this **before**]
23 Is das einer, der **schon ma** hier war?
[Is that someone who has been here **before**?]
25 Ich hatte **schon ma** angerufen
[I have called **before**]
28 sie war ja **schon ma** vorher da,
[she has been here **before**, you know]
29 da ham wir das **schon ma** zusammengelegt
[we have celebrated together **before**]
30 Klar, das wurd auch **schon ma** später
[Of course, it also got late sometimes **before**]
33 hab auch **schon ma** öfter ma abends lang gearbeitet,
[I have also worked late a number of times **before**]

With the exception of line 24 (and possibly line 21), which constitutes a formulaic expression, the combination SCHON MAL in collocation with verb forms indicating present or future indicates a starting point. It can be translated into English by the phrase 'to start with'.

19 un da bisde natürlich **schon** mal . en bißchen gehemm!
[and naturally you are a little inhibited **to start with**]
20 auf jeden Fall gebrauchsde **schon** ma das Wort "werden" nich
[in any case you don't use the word "werden" **to start with**]

```
21      aber so ab un zu kommt es schon mal[91]
22      undann schon ma sons bißchen was vorbereiten,
        [and then to prepare a few things to start with]
24      Das kommt schon ma vor,
        [It sometimes happens]
26      das is also schon mal ne qanze Menqe
        [that's quite a lot to start with]
27      Dann wer ich mir das schon ma merken!
        [Then I'll remember that to start with!]
31      undann brauch se eh schon ma zwei Jahre
        [ an then she needs two years to start with]
```

Focus particle

In nine instances, SCHON acts as a focus particle without having a temporal function.

```
1  Hm B: Ja, . aber die waren . also . schon zu kritisch . und deswegen  is die
2 e die andern an, und das sieht alles schon so  unheimlich elegant aus, ne, ich
3 rauch! A: (lacht) Ja! B:  Da bin ich schon ganz froh drüber! ((4s)) Naja! Mein
4 ein. Das bringt ne schwächere Wanze  schon um. A:  Ne stärkere nich? B:  Ja, i
5 nen englischen Leistungskurs, das is schon schwerer   nu !
6 nen was  machen B:  ja, das war also schon nich mehr normal, wie der aussah! A
7 Y fährt, der fährt  abends nit gern. Schon gar net nach Köln! A: Jo! Dann müßt
8 er aufmachen B:  ja A:  jedenfalls . schon gar nich zun Hauptverkehrszeiten B:
9 erhungern? B:  Och ja, 59 bin i auch schon mit zufrieden! Dat reicht  eigentli
```

In those occurrences, SCHON indicates a stage on an assumed scale of properties. SCHON indicates that the value is at the lower end of the scale, i.e. there is scope for higher values (cf. König et al. 1990), as the following translations show:

```
1       aber die waren also schon zu kritisch
        [but even that amount of criticism was too much]
        (and it was not much of a criticism)
2       und das sieht alles schon so unheimlich elegant
        aus,
        [and that looks so terribly elegant to start with]
```

91 This occurrence is an incomplete utterance; the speaker is interrupted by the interlocutor and does not continue the utterance in the next move. The occurrence could therefore not be analysed with any certainty. It might follow the same pattern as line 24: 'es kommt schon mal vor'.

(that I expect things to be really high-class in general)

3 Da bin ich **schon** ganz froh drüber!
[I am quite happy with that to start with]
(but there might be more)

4 Das bringt ne schwächere Wanze **schon** um
[a weaker bed bug is killed by that]
(I don't know about a stronger specimen)

5 nen englischen Leistungskurs, das is **schon** schwerer
[an accelerated English unit, that's already harder]
(but there are even more difficult ones)

6 das war also **schon** nich mehr normal, wie der aussah!
[that was not normal any more, the way he looked]
(of all the possible ways to look, the way he looked was sub-standard)

9 bin i auch **schon** mit zufrieden!
[I am happy with as little as that]
(but there might be more)

There is no one translation equivalent, as the exact meaning is highly context dependent.[92] A particular meaning arises when SCHON in this function collocates with 'gar nicht' as in lines 7 and 8. Here, the meaning can be translated into English by the phrase 'least of all':

7 **Schon gar net** nach Köln!
[**Least of all** to Cologne]

8 **schon gar nicht** zun Hauptverkehrszeiten
[**least of all** in the rush hour]

Answering Particle

There is one occurrence of SCHON in answering function in the BRO data.

1 n interessiert seid. A: Jaja, doch, **schon**. Wenn hier . en bißchen besseres We

92 König *et al.* (1990: 204) suggest: "*even, the very/mere,alone, if only (because (of), if only for the reason that, as little.*"

This type of occurrence is categorised in various ways in the literature on modal particles. Bublitz (1977) categorises such instances as 'Modalwort', which can be used in equivalence with a whole clause, Thurmair (1989) classifies it as 'Affirmationsadverb', which is similar to JA, NEIN, DOCH but not equivalent to a clause to the same degree as those. Gornik-Gerhardt (1981) classifies such types of occurrences as 'modal particle function', whereas the term 'answering particle' can be found in Franck (1980).

In the one occurrence in the BRO data, SCHON collocates with the answering particles JA and DOCH. Speakers A and B are both female and close relatives. They talk about the fact that A and her husband are looking to buy a property.

A:	Ja, gibt's hier auch. Also, ja, doch, diese eine zu 80.000. [Yes, there are some around here, too. Well, yes, yes, the one for 80.000.]
B:	Also, ich meine, es muß natürlich auch wat sein, aber . wart da ma auf ne günstige Gelegenheit, es muß nich die erstbeste sein, wir finden schon was. Eventuell machen wer /machen wer son Zweifamilienhäuschen oder so was. Wenn ihr dadran interessiert seid. [Well, I mean, it has to be something decent . you'd better wait for a good deal, it doesn't have to be the first one that comes along, we'll find something, don't worry. Perhaps we'll do/ we'll do a duplex or something like that. If you're interested]
A:	Jaja, doch, **schon**. Wenn hier . en bißchen besseres Wetter is, es gibt so allerlei, aber alles weiter, in Siegburg un Troisdorf un so, da in der Gegend [Yes, yes, we <u>ARE</u>. If here . the weather is a little better, there is this that and the other, but everything further away, in S. and T. and around there, in that area]
B:	Nee, ich würd nich noch weiter von Köln weggehn, dann

lieber in / in die andere Richtung.
[No, I would move any further away from Cologne, then better into the other direction]

A: Ja, das sind alles so fiese Vororte /
[Yes, there all quite nasty suburbs/]

(BRO 29BD.56T)

A's answer to B's proposal to buy something together "Jaja, doch, SCHON" is an affirmation in principle. Although no concessions are mentioned explicitly, the series of answering particles (JA – positive polarity, DOCH – answering positively to a preceding utterance with negative polarity, followed by SCHON) implies that there are possible objections to B's proposal. A does not state those, but rather moves on to another subtopic: the position of the prospective property. The meaning of SCHON in this instance can be rendered in English by an intonation pattern indicating emphasis (see underlined): "Yes, yes, we ARE."

Modal Particle

In the following 33 occurrences SCHON functions as modal particle:

1 gedacht A: och, is ja/ B: aber, is **schon** ne schwierige Angelegenheit. Natürl
2 Großbetrieb zu leiten, das war also **schon** ne Aufgabe, er wär froh, daß er da
3 rworren, so. B: Jaja, manchma is et **schon** janz schön schwierig! A: Hm. ((3s)
4 ... Naja! . Auf jeden Fall, das is **schon** schwierig. ((3s)) 36 B: Gut, daß
5 u machen. B: (lacht) A: Ja, das is **schon** verworren, so. B: Jaja, manchma is
6 t aus? 61 A: Ja, das kann **schon** sein. Sehr sportlich wirkte er
7 t schlecht aus, naja, doch, dat kann **schon** sein, ich find, elf Kilo is wirkli
8 Und dick werden. B: Doch, dagegen **schon**. C: Nee, aber jetz wirklich/ also
9 a immer weiter voraus sein, man muß **schon** bißchen Űberblick haben, wenn man a
10 ch viel im Fernsehen los, wir gucken **schon** von einem Programm ins andere, abe
11 e schreibe, dann überlegik natürlich **schon** jenauer A: hm B: aber so beim Erz
12 f. B: Ja.. Ja. A: Ja, das würd mich **schon** sehr interessieren. Wann k/ B: Die
13 immer wie ne Pinte ( ) Also, das war **schon** irgendwie zuviel, ne. Die krichten
14 mand, der konnte arbeiten, ne, also **schon**, ne/ B: Ja, (ja auch) A: (
15 , šh, sie mit ihrem Bekannten dann. **schon** B: hm A: auf die Bekanntgabe der
16 das war ne gute Investition, muß ich **schon** sagen funktioniert immer. A: Ja.
17 rliteratur über den, und ich glaub **schon**, daß ich das ganz gut hinkriege, da
18 üsiert oder nich? B: Och, ich glaub **schon**. C: Ja? B: Ich mein, kenns ja Y,
19 / du darfs ja nich! B: Nöö, ich mag **schon**, ich darf nich im Augenblick! Zwei
20 ghafen iss . irgendwo . in der Nähe **schon** B: Jaja, irgendwo in der Nähe isse
21 B: Jaja, irgendwo in der Nähe isser **schon**, das is klar, aber ich kann jetzt
22 f einem Termin, sondern / oder oder **schon** in ein Termin, aber et / braucht gl
23 lich auch einige sein, das weiß ich **schon**, aber / A: Oh! Das hasde wieder gan
24 t angewöhnen, das Rauchen. Wenn man **schon** nich mehr essen darf, dann muß man
25 ! B: Hm... Oh, doch, die können das **schon**! A: Ah nee, das is dann auch wiede
26 d Rath auf der Hälfte. Sehn Sie aber **schon**, links das groBe Neubaugebiet. Un
27 einjeguckt, naja A: hm B: ma kommt **schon** irgendwie mit A: ja, sicher! Vor a

28 elleicht widder. B: Och, dat klappt **schon**! C: (lacht) B: Ich hab ja auch ni
29 ersuchen. A: Ja. B: Jaja, er wirds **schon** alleine schaffen. A: Ja, nee.. Ich
30 nich die erstbeste sein, wir finden **schon** was. Eventuell machen wer /machen
31 nnen. A: Jo. Ah, irgendwie wer ichs **schon** finden! B: Sind Se mitgekommen? Ne
32 o an ne Ecke kleben B: Ja, werd ich **schon** machen, gut, A. A: Jo. B: Ja, dan
33 ir ja auch dumm! Aber wo findet man **schon** jemanden, der das macht, du. A: Ja

The function of SCHON as modal particle is to confirm a proposition in principle while pointing to possible adverse or opposing arguments. The proposition in question might have been posed in the interlocutor's previous utterance as in the following example:

Line 4

B: Ich mein, wenn zwei Leute sich scheiden lassen, und beschließen, daß, öh, keinem dadurch Nachteile entstehen sollen, em, da können die doch nich gezwungen werden, trotzdem, öh, da irgendwelche Zahlungen zu leisten.
[I mean, if two people are getting a divorce, and decide, that, er, none of them should be disadvantaged by it, er, then they can't be forced, regardless, er, to make any payments.]

A: Eigenlich ja, ne.
[Not really, can they?]

B: Das glaub ich nich.
[I don't think so.]

A: ((3s)) Ja, vielleicht kann man dann irgendwelche Verzichtserklärungen abgeben oder sowas ... Naja! . Auf jeden Fall, das is **schon** schwierig. ((3s))
[Well, maybe it's possible to put that in writing somehow or something… Oh well! In any case, it **is** difficult, **though**]

(BRD 8 Bd 2/4)

Speaker A agrees in principle with speaker B's proposition, that in case of a divorce, where both partners have agreed not to make any payments to one another, they should not be forced to do so by law. A confirms this position while still expressing doubt [Not really, can they?]. B reconfirms the proposition [I don't think so.]. A then expands on the proposition [maybe it's possible to put that in writing somehow] and closes the topic (her last utterance is followed by a three second pause) with a final evaluation [in any case] containing SCHON. SCHON in this utterance indicates that she is principally in agreement with B's argument, but that they are opposing ones, not mentioned explicitly, that have to be taken into account. In the English translation this meaning of SCHON is rendered by 'though' and a particular intonation pattern (see underlining; underlined word carries the main stress).

SCHON in this function might also refer back to a previous utterance of the speaker him/herself, as in the following example, where B, a female student (24) talks to A, a close male relative (56) of hers:

Line 1

```
B:    und es is ja, man hei/ wir sind ja mit dabei, es
      is ja nich so, daß man alleine heiratet, das
      stimmt ja nicht. Man meint immer, man heiratet als
      Einzelner einen Einzelnen. Nich, die Familie is da
      mit bei
      [and it's, isn't it, one ma/ we are going to be
      there, too, it's not as if one would marry on
      one's own, that's not the way it is. People always
      think, they'd marry as individuals. No, the family
      is there, too]
A:    die Familie jaja,
      [the family, yes yes]
B:    und insofern ises auch ganz gut, wenn man die
      Familie bei
      etwas mitberücksichtigt. Ich hab au noch mal
      drüber nachgedacht
      [and in that regard it's a good thing, too, to
      consider the family a little. I've also thought
      about it again]
A     och, is ja/
              [oh, that's]
B:    aber, is schon ne schwierige Angelegenheit.
      Natürlich fühlen wir uns auch nich ganz wohl mit
      dieser Geschichte. Aber bei der anderen würden wir
      uns noch weniger wohl fühlen.
      [but, it is a difficult matter, though. Of course
      we don't feel all that good about the whole thing.
```

```
But with the other (solution) we'd feel even
worse.]
```

(BRO 1 Bd 1/9)

Here, the speaker develops an argument (that A should consider the whole family when planning her wedding). In B's last move, he takes back part of his argument by conceding 'it is a difficult matter, though' which is then elaborated on with the following sentences. Thus, he puts forward his proposition in principle but concedes that there are other points of view, namely A's, to be taken into account. Here, SCHON works pragmatically as well as discursively. It has a mitigating effect in that it conveys to the interlocutor: I do have my point of view, but I acknowledge yours.

This function of SCHON is particularly salient in those occurrences, where SCHON occurs in an utterance where the speaker makes explicit that s/he is stating a personal opinion:

16 das war ne gute Investition, muß ich **schon** sagen
[that was a good investment, I have to admit that, though]

17 und ich glaub **schon**, daß ich das ganz gut hinkriege,
[and I **do** think, that I'll manage quite well]

18 C: Aber der Y hat sich . an der Uni amüsiert oder nich?
[But Y had fun at uni, didn't he?]
B: Och, ich glaub **schon**.
[Oh, I **do** think so.]
C Ja?
[Yes?]

Here, the speaker explicitly puts forward a personal evaluation, leaving room for differing ones. In occurrences 17 and 18, SCHON has been translated by 'do' which carries the main stress in the English clause, rather than by 'though'.

The concessive meaning of SCHON is especially obvious, when it collocates with ABER[93] (see lines 21, 22, 23), as exemplified in the following excerpt:

Line 21

B: öh, nun weiß ich nicht, ob das nich auch Lärmzone is, nich.
[er, now I don't know, whether that area is noise affected too, do I?]

A: Em ., also, Sie meinen, ja, der Flughafen iss . irgendwo . in der Nähe schon
[erm, so you think, though, the airport is somewhere close by]

B: Jaja, irgendwo in der Nähe isser **schon**, das is klar, **aber** ich kann jetzt von hier aus nicht beurteilen, ob, öh, das Gebiet überhaupt förderungsfähig ist.
[Yesyes, it **certainly** is close by, that's for sure, **but** from where I stand I can't say, whether, er, the area is worth subsidising/supporting.]

(BRO 16 Bd 4/4)

The speaker concedes – in this example particularly clearly by repeating the interlocutor's proposition [the airport is close by] – that he is in agreement with the interlocutor's proposition but at the same time the use of SCHON points to further information that has to be taken into account. This information is introduced by ABER. In English the meaning of SCHON in collocation with ABER can be rendered by 'certainly … but'.

In utterances which refer to the future (see lines 25-32), SCHON has an additional pragmatic function: reassuring the interlocutor that

93 This type of occurrence is categorised in various ways in the research on modal particles.Gornik-Gerhardt (1981) categorises it as modal particle, Thurmair (1989) argues that it is stressed and can't therefore be categorised as modal particle. As it does not differ in its grammatical and discursive function from other modal particle occurrences, it is here discussed as modal particle.

the proposition in question will eventuate to the interlocutor's satisfaction. The following excerpt exemplifies this:

Line 31

(The dialogue takes place between A, a research assistant, female, 24 years old, and B, a head teacher (Oberstudiendirektor), male, 53 years old. A and B do not know one another, A has responded to an offer of employment by B. B explains to A how to get to the place where they agreed to meet.)

B: ja, die bin ich jahrelang gefahren, da . müssen Sie mit einem Stau rechnen. Und dann müßten Sie durch die gesamte .. Innenstadt, das heißt, Sie führen die Nord-Süd-Fahrt, das kennen Sie ja auch?
[yes, I took that route for years, there . you have to be prepared for a lot of traffic. And then you would have {to drive} through all of the .. inner city, that is, you'd take the north-south route, you do know that, don't you?]

A: Jaja.
[Yes,yes.]

B: Nord-Süd-Fahrt, kämen am . Ebert-Platz aus, kenn Se den?
[North-south route, you'd arrive at E.square, you know that?]

A: Ja, sicher.
[Yes, sure.]

B: Gut! Führen ein kleinen Bogen im / auf dem Ebert-Platz herum, biegen in die Neusser-StraSe ein, kreuzen den / die Innere-KanalstraSe, dasis also ziemlich leer da, Innere-Kanalstraße, und biegen dann von der Neusser-Straße ab auf die Merheimer-Straße, hinter der Kanal-Straße geht eine halblinke Abfahrt Abzweig, fahrn die Merheimer-Straße immer weiter durch, bis Sie in die Gegend des Bahnhofes Nippes kommen, da macht die Straße so einen / na son, son / geht so rund über Brücken, das sin ganz neue Brückenbauwerke, un dann kommen Sie am Güter / am, am, / na, nich am Güter / am S-Bahnhof / S-Bahnhof Geldern-Straße aus. Das is der Weg, den Sie über die Severins-Brücke fahrend machen können / nehmen können.
[Good. You'd do a little round along E.square.

```
       turn into N.street, cross the I.-K.street, it's
       pretty empty around there, I.-K.street, and then
       you turn from N.street into M.street, behind
       K.street, there is a turn half left, drive along
       M.street all along, until you come into the area
       of the train station N., there the street sort of
       /sort of /turns over some bridges, they are brand
       new bridges, and then you'll arrive at the
       freight/at,at/well/not the freight/at the train
       station G.street. That is the route, that you
       could make/take if driving across the S.bridge
A:     Ah, irgendwie wer ichs schon finden!
       [Yes. Well, somehow I'm going to find it, don't
       worry!]
```

With her final utterance containing SCHON, A acknowledges what B is not stating directly, but implying by a rather verbose description: that A might have difficulties in finding the way. Thus, the function of SCHON as modal particle described above – confirming a proposition in principle while pointing to possible opposing arguments – is present. Those opposing arguments are not necessarily stated explicitly; here it is implied that A's navigational aptitude is better than B expects.

The pragmatic function of 'reassuring' can also be found with respect to a speaker's own previous proposition, as in the following excerpt:

Line 27

```
B:     Ich wär in Englisch total doof!
       [I'd be hopeless in English!]
A:     Ach, so'n paar Bildergeschichten, das schaffsde do
       auch!
       [Ah, a few stories like that, you'd manage
       that,too, don't you think?]
B:     Ich hab ganz kurz reinjeguckt, naja
       [I had a quick look at it, oh well]
A:     hm
B:     ma kommt schon irgendwie mit
       [one would manage somehow, I suppose]
```

(BRO 22 Bd 15/15)

The translation given for line 21 'don't worry' is not appropriate here, as the reassurance is not directed at the interlocutor, but at the speaker herself. Therefore, rendering SCHON in English by 'I suppose' seems more appropriate.

In occurrences 1-32, SCHON appears in statements, there is only one occurrence of SCHON as modal particle in an interrogative:

Line 33

```
A:    Also, wenn mir jemand anbieten würde, mir mein
      Gehalt so
              zu zahlen, ich würd nich arbeiten gehen!

      [Well, if someone offered to pay my salary just
      like that, I wouldn't work!]
B:    Ja, ich auch nich, Mann! Da wärn wir ja auch dumm!
      Aber
              wo findet man schon jemanden, der das
      macht, du.
      [Yes, me neither {nor would I}, man! We'd be
      stupid if we did. But where do you possibly find
      somebody who does that?]
```

SCHON marks the question as rhetorical. The principal function of SCHON as modal particle – confirming a proposition in principle while pointing to possible opposing arguments – is present here as well. B agrees in principle with A (if one would get a salary without working, one would not work), the interrogative containing SCHON contains the opposing argument (but who would pay?).

Summary of results: schon

Position in clause	**Grammatical co-occurence**	**Lexical collocation**	**Category**	**Meaning**
inital			answering particle	'yes, (but)'
medial	statement		temporal adverb	'already'
medial	question		temporal adverb	'yet'
medial	indication of past	MAL	temporal adverb	'before'
medial	indication of present	MAL	temporal adverb	'to start with'
medial	indication of present or future	temporal phrase	focus particle	'already', 'as early as', 'the very next'
medial	indication of future indication of future question		modal particle	• 'tough' (and intonation for emphasis) • 'do' for emphasis • 'certainly … but' • 'don't worry' (reference to other) • 'I suppose' (reference to self) • 'possibly

As the analysis of SCHON has shown its meaning is very complex and highly dependent on grammatical and lexical collocations. The following sample worksheet only focusses on some of those meanings to introduce the learner to the complexity of SCHON.

Sample Work Sheet: SCHON

1.) The word SCHON may have different meanings depending on its context of use. Please look carefully at the following groups of examples and decide which translation or description best captures the meaning of SCHON in each group.

before	**to start with**	**already/ yet**	**though**	**don't worry**

Group 1 ____________________

Group 2 ____________________

Group 3 ____________________

Group 4 ____________________

Group 5 ____________________

Group 1

B: Mir ham se **schon** das Kindergeld abgezogen. A Ja? B
. dann lag das genau daran, wie ich **schon** vermutet hatte, e, war nämig ein di
du auch garnich, da warst du nämlich **schon** weg. Du bis ja unheimlich früh die
Aber ich glaub, da die ganze Sache **schon** am Laufen war, äh, verjährt das gl
Promotion fertig is, ne. Un er hat **schon** gesacht, also . unter ner eins is
: Wie war's im Übrigen noch, ham Se **schon** den Kaufvertrag abgeschlossen? A:
B: Wann soll das denn sein, hat se **schon** was gesagt? A: Ja, sie denkt an de
(lacht) B: Wie lange fährt se jetz **schon**? A: Ich? B: Na, du fährs ja bald
t solles? A: (lacht) Hatteter euch **schon** dran gewöhnt? B: (lacht) A: Aber i
n von Holland zurück/ A: Hasde auch **schon**? B: Hab ich auch schon, sind auch

Group 2

gedacht A: och, is ja/ B: aber, is **schon** ne schwierige Angelegenheit. Natürl

Großbetrieb zu leiten, das war also **schon** ne Aufgabe, er wär froh, daß er da

rworren, so. B: Jaja, manchma is et **schon** janz schön schwierig! A: Hm. ((3s)

... Naja! . Auf jeden Fall, das is **schon** schwierig. ((3s)) 36 B: Gut, daß

u machen. B: (lacht) A: Ja, das is **schon** verworren, so. B: Jaja, manchma is

f. B: Ja.. Ja. A: Ja, das würd mich **schon** sehr interessieren. Wann k/ B: Die

immer wie ne Pinte ( ) Also, das war **schon** irgendwie zuviel, ne. Die krichten

das war ne gute Investition, muß ich **schon** sagen funktioniert immer. A: Ja.

lich auch einige sein, das weiß ich **schon**, aber / A: Oh! Das hasde wieder gan

ir ja auch dumm! Aber wo findet man **schon** jemanden, der das macht, du. A: Ja

Group 3

hab doch, weiß nich, ob ich dir das **schon ma** erzählt hab, ma für son Lederty

Ja. Ja. B: (lacht) A: Ich hab mir **schon mal** überlegt, bin ich da eigenlich

e im Hintergrund)) Is das einer, der **schon ma** hier war?.. Wie heißt der? ((St

hier is B. A: Tach B! B: Ich hatte **schon ma** angerufen, aber da war keiner da

aber ich glaub, also, sie war ja **schon ma** vorher da, ne, an der Schule, d

nach mir, Geburtstag, da ham wir das **schon ma** zusammengelegt, ne. ob mer dat

ne. A: hmhm B: Klar, das wurd auch **schon ma** später. A: jaja B: wenn ich ir

ule? Ich mein, sicher, ich hab auch **schon ma** öfter ma abends lang gearbeitet,

Group 4

ne B: ja A: un da bisde natürlich **schon mal** . en bißchen gehemmt und so, n

A: Also, auf jeden Fall gebrauchsde **schon ma** das Wort "werden" nich, anschei

den ganzen Scheiß, besorgen, undann **schon ma** sons bißchen was vorbereiten, d

is, un so. Un denn/ Ne, das is also **schon mal** ne qanze Menqe wert. Un dann m

n! B: Ja, Gut! Dann wer ich mir das **schon ma** merken! ((3s)) Bestell dem X ma

n, aber ich glaub, also, sie war ja **schon ma** vorher da, ne, an der Schule, d

nach mir, Geburtstag, da ham wir das **schon ma** zusammengelegt, ne. ob mer dat

ne. A: hmhm B: Klar, das wurd auch **schon ma** später. A: jaja B: wenn ich ir

s muß ja / darf / ich mein, der kann **schon mal** rausspringen, der darf aber ni

Group 5

! B: Hm... Oh, doch, die können das **schon**! A: Ah nee, das is dann auch wiede

d Rath auf der Hälfte. Sehn Sie aber **schon**, links das groBe Neubaugebiet. Un

einjeguckt, naja A: hm B: ma kommt **schon** irgendwie mit A: ja, sicher! Vor a

elleicht widder. B: Och, dat klappt **schon**! C: (lacht) B: Ich hab ja auch ni

ersuchen. A: Ja. B: Jaja, er wirds **schon** alleine schaffen. A: Ja, nee.. Ich

nich die erstbeste sein, wir finden **schon** was. Eventuell machen wer /machen

nnen. A: Jo. Ah, irgendwie wer ichs **schon** finden! B: Sind Se mitgekommen? Ne

o an ne Ecke kleben B: Ja, werd ich **schon** machen, gut, A. A: Jo. B: Ja, dan

2.) Let's have a closer look at groups 3 and 4 now. Which other word collocates with (i.e.appears next to) SCHON in groups 3 and 4?

____

3.) What is the reference to time in those groups?

Group 1 ____________________

Group 2 ____________________

4.) What is the reference to time in Group 5?

Group 5 ____________________

5.6 DOCH

The particle DOCH appears 174 times in 21 texts in BRO. The occurrences belong to two function categories. In addition to modal particle function, DOCH was found to occur in a re-asserting function as an answering particle.

Answering Particle

As an answering particle (30 occurrences) DOCH is easily recognised within the concordance data, as it can be found in the initial position of an utterance. In some instances its representation is capitalised, as an utterance on its own:

```
1  bitte? C:  Du bis doch verrückt! B:  Doch! C:  Hör ma, ich erkenn dich ja dem
2 e denn kein Ei, en hartgekochtes? B:  Doch! En hartgekochtes Ei darfsde auch e
3 kann doch nich sein, kilomäßig ja/ B: Doch! C: un von der Figur her nich! B: J
```

or as the opening of an utterance where it is separate from the following proposition:

```
4 l, dann  schicke ik se eben nich. A:  Doch, schick sie ruhig! Ich bin so wild
5 ssen .  Und das zweite auch noch. B:  Doch, ich ( ) et erste Ehejahr is immer
6 der, öh, da . zu beigetragen, ne. B:  Doch, ich find ooch, wenn irjentwat kapu
7 überhaupt Geld kriegt! B:  Öm . doch! Doch, denn, ö, das einzige, was sich änd
8 ihr könnt nich zu uns kommen, ne? B:  Doch, sicher können wir zu euch kommen,
9 Bier trinken C:  Und dick werden. B:  Doch, dagegen schon. C:  Nee, aber jetz
```

It is sometimes repeated for emphasis:

```
10  na, kommt janich in Frage. A:  Doch, doch. B:  Wie war denn dein Jeburtstag?
11   Ach, na, kommt janich in Frage. A:  Doch, doch. B:  Wie war denn dein Jeburt
12 ch, kann ich mir nich vorstellen. B:  Doch, doch! Ja, aber wir ham dem jetz ab
13 nn ich mir nich vorstellen. B:  Doch, doch! Ja, aber wir ham dem jetz abgeholf
14  gar nich der Z selbst? 142 C:  Doch, doch, er is mir zuvorgekommen, un deshal
15 as war gar nich der Z selbst? 142 C:  Doch, doch, er is mir zuvorgekommen, un
16 end? B:  Ja / D:  Nix mehr? B:  Doch, doch, sicher, abends kann man dann . ric
17 ag, Abend? B:  Ja / D:  Nix mehr? B:  Doch, doch, sicher, abends kann man dann
```

In all these occurrences it serves to counter the polarity of the interlocutor's previous contribution(s), as the following instance exemplifies:

Line 4

B: Also, hör ma, das is ja nu keen ( ), also ik schick dir die hin, un wenn du dik darüber freust, dann freu ik mich ooch.
[Well, listen, that really is no ( ), so I'll send those to you, and if you're happy about that, then I'm happy,too.]

A: Na klar freu ich mich dadrüber!
[Of course I'm happy about that.]

B: Naja, siehsde. Un wenn ich dir die nich schicken will, dann schicke ik se eben nich.
[Well, there you go. And if I don't want to send them, then I simply won't.]

A: **Doch**, schick sie ruhig! Ich bin so wild auf Comics im Augenblick.
[**Yes, do** send them. I'm really mad about comics at the moment.]

(BRO 21 Bd 11/1)

Frequently, DOCH occurs as an answer to a question with negative polarity, as in the following example:

Line 8

A: Ja, X hat nämig auch Urlaub, och, das wär doch schön! .. Könntet ihr denn, ach so, ihr könnt nich zu uns kommen, ne?
[Yes, X is on leave, too, you know, oh, that'd be nice! ..Could you then, ah well, you can't come over, can you?]

B: **Doch**, sicher können wir zu euch kommen, Y hat ja keine Rufbereitschaft, hat ja Urlaub.
[**Yes**, of course we can come over, Y is not on stand-by, you know, he's on leave.]

(BR0 11 Bd 2/6)

DOCH collocates with a second answering particle JA/JAJA ('yes'),

18 Nee, das fändich ja echt prima. B: **Doch**, ja, wenn ik da ma wieder hinkomme,
19 ich hinterher, wo se gewesen sind? B: **doch** ja, klar, wennich se frache erzähle
20 berhaupt abnehmen mußten! 145 B: Ja, **doch** / D: Wie die C mir dat erzählt hat,
21 a nochnich so schlimm, oder? B: Ja, **doch**, neenee, die Tertianer sind die . S

22 a, natürlich, klar. A: Hm. C: Jaja, **doch**, das is also (so ne unheimlich per
23 r wohnen wir selber auch A: Aha! Ja, **doch**, das wär ja interessant. B: Also,
24 dadran interessiert seid. A: Jaja, **doch**, schon. Wenn hier . en bißchen bess

where JA serves to further emphasise the positive polarity, as shown in the following instance:

Line 19

B: Naja, bloß Mensch, also nee, ich weiß nich, die fangen soön richtijet Landstreicherleben an!
[Well yes, it's just that, well no, I don't know, they are starting to lead a real nomad type of life!]
A: Ja, erzählen die denn nich hinterher, wo se gewesen sind?
[Well, don't they tell you then afterwards where they've been?]
B: **doch** ja, klar, wennich se frache erzählen se mir Himmel und Wunda
[**yes, they do**, yes certainly, when I ask them they tell me abcut God and the world]

In collocation with 'naja' ('well', 'yes'), the force of DOCH is downtoned; the contradiction to the negative polarity of the preceding utterance not quite as strong:

25 B: Ja?
A: Hm. 114
B **Naja**, manch / **doch**, naja, kommt imma drauf an!
[**Well yes**, some/**yes**, well, it all depends]
A: ..
26 C: Du sähst schlecht aus, **naja, doch**, dat kann schon sein, ich find, el
[..., **well yes**, **yes**, that is possible]

Similarly, discourse markers like 'öm', 'och' and 'ach' serve as downtoning devices:

27 dann überhaupt Geld kriegt! B: Öm . **doch**!

```
    Doch,denn, ö, das einzige, was si
    [B: Erm, yes! Yes, because…]
28  sowas kein Verständnis hat... B:  Och doch! Aber..
    die war/ die war nich sauer
    [B: Er, yes! But…]
29  st, den man kennt, oder daß / B:  ach doch, Mensch,
    öhm, Sie haben Recht. ö, ö
    [B: ah, yes, boy, erm, you're right]
```

whereas 'oh' lends emphasis to the meaning of DOCH:

```
30  ix mitenander anfangen! B:  Hm... Oh, doch, die
    können das schon! A:  Ah nee,
    [B:Erm..Oh yes, they can do that!]
```

Modal particle[94]

There are 144 occurences of DOCH in modal particle function, mainly in declaratives (134 occurences) but also in imperatives (10 occurrences).

Declaratives

The main function of DOCH in declaratives is to refer to shared knowledge while at the same time expressing the wish to overcome a perceived difference of opinion. (cf. Thurmair 1989, Helbig 1994)[95]. DOCH refers to meta-knowledge about what speaker and hearer share and/or to meta-knowledge about what is generally known (cf. Schiffrin 1987 on discourse markers in English).

In declaratives in the BRO data, DOCH collocates with a very high frequency with the verb 'sein' (to be) (45:134 occurrences, which represents more than 30% of the occurrences). In most of those

94 A full list of DOCH in modal particle function is given in the appendix.

95 Graefen (1999: 112) claims: "Der Sprecher insistiert gegenüber dem Hörer auf einem bestimmten Wissen oder Anspruch, bewußt gegen dessen Infragestellung, Ignorierung oder Kritik."

occurrences, the subject is a deictic element, mainly 'das' ('that'), ellipsed in a large number of instances[96]. In all those occurrences, the deictic element 'das' links the speaker's utterance by means of anaphoric reference to the interlocutor's preceding utterance(s):

```
1  auch bei der Z mal  belegt A:  Das is doch egal, das heißt doch nur, daß du di
2  a", sachich, "und warum?" "Ja, das is doch dat Normale!" A:  Hm (lacht) B:  Jo
3   dann der 31. frei sein. Denn das  is doch en evangelischer Feiertag! B:  Ja,
4  ulkollegium angefordert war.  "Das is doch zusätzliche Arbeit!" Hü, weg! A:  (
5  cht man noch leichter weg! B:  Das is doch Wahnsinn! A:  Nee, man muß dann war
6  h da? A:  Ja B:  - Titel - A:  Das is doch toll! B:  Ja, da kommt dann das Pro
7  h hier nah an der Brücke wärt, is das doch so schlimm nich. Also ich würd mich
8  lig. Ob das ne Wanze  is? Aber das is doch  unwahrscheinlich! C:  Seit wann ha
9  kann man ohnehin . und öh . da is das doch wesentlich einfacher, sich zu tren
10  daß die Spüle verstopft war, das wär doch  einlich interessanter gewesen? B:
11 :  Sin auch drin, ia. B:  Ja, das wär doch auch nich uninteressant, oder / A:
12 : Hm. B:  Aber erstensmal wäre das ja doch eine . ziemliche finanzielle  Einbu
13 X hat nämig auch Urlaub, och, das wär doch schön! ..  Könntet ihr denn, ach so
14 ten von heute auf morgen, ne, das war doch ne  Leistung! B: Ja sicher, auf jed
15  noch? Das  war  aber  schon  dieser  Tage  doch!  A:   ((3s))  Nee,  ich  hatte  sie  beim
(ellipsed:)
16   sich das nennt D:  is doch egal, is doch egal B:  jedenfalls . hat das so un
17 jetz nich, wie  sich das nennt D:  is doch egal, is doch egal B:  jedenfalls .
18  A:  Nö, sehr böse natürlich nich, is doch klar/ B:  Ich hab grade mit X telef
19  tun B:  Ja, die zähl ich mit? A:  Is doch klar! Guck mal, wenn de/ wenn de da
20  B:  Ach, hattest du frei? A:  Ja, is doch Feiertag. Oder? Bei euch nich? B:
21 t, wo der Mann  wohnt. A:  Ja. B:  Is doch en Nachteil, ich habs ja immer gesa
22 A:  Sin vorgestern angekommen! B:  Is doch nich nötig! A:  Sin echt prima! B:
23 du kanns ja nich loslassen!.. Nee! Is doch heller  Wahnsinn! . Bin froh, daß d
24  fahren war, stell dir das ma vor! Is doch Wahnsinn! A:  Ja, sobald (der B:  W
25 mehr, wenn's schneit. A:  Jaa. B:  Is doch was mehr draußen... Hmhm. A:  Ja so
```

In most of those occurrences, DOCH ascribes a value to the proposition referred to by 'das' and it seeks the interlocutor's approval of this value[97], as the following excerpt exemplifies:

Line 7

A: Ja, nee, das is so viel zu fahren für X, dat will er nich. Also, wir haben aber so die Eigentumswohnungen zwischen Köln und Porz, die anzubieten waren, so ziemlich abgeklappert, also Vings ist ein widerliches Kaff, Kalk genauso / [Well, no, that's too much driving for X, he doesn't want that. Well, but we had a look at most

96 Other deictic elements which were found in collocation with DOCH and a verb form of 'sein' were personal pronouns and definite articles functioning as personal pronouns. Only in five instances there was no deictic element present.

97 A number of phrases with the pattern: "DAS + form of SEIN + DOCH + Attribute" can be seen as formulaic, i.e. "das ist doch egal" (lines 1, 16, 17) and "das ist doch klar" (lines 18 & 19).

```
        of the appartments for sale between K. and F., V.
        is a horrible place, K. too/
B:      Nein, nein da kann man nich hinziehn, das is
        unmöglich!
        [no, no you can't move there, that's impossible!]
A:      un, öh, was ham wer noch? Neubrück, also..
        unmöglich!
        [and, erm, what else is there? N., well ...
        impossible!
B:      Och, hör ma, wenn ihr doch hier nah an der Brücke
        wärt, Is das doch so schlimm nich.
        [Oh, listen, how about if you were close to the
        bridge here, that's not so bad, is it?)
```

(BRO 29 Bd 5/6)

The proposition referred to by 'das' ('that') is "if you were living close to the bridge here"; the following clause containing DOCH evaluates and asks for agreement. DOCH marks the proposition "living close to the bridge here is not so bad" as shared knowledge, in this instance knowledge within a social group and it reinforces membership of that group (cf. Luchtenberg 1989). Thus, DOCH functions discursively by creating exophoric reference and pragmatically in that it seeks the interlocutor's agreement.

The agreement the speaker seeks to establish is not generally stated as explicitly as it is in the clause type "DAS +SEIN +SCHON". In the majority of ccurrences in the BRO data, the speaker implies with the use of DOCH that a fact, knowledge shared by the interlocutors, should be considered in the ongoing exchange.

The reference to shared knowledge is particularly obvious in those occurrences where there is some explicit reference to conventions, according to Luchtenberg (1989) knowledge within a society or larger social group about everyday processes which are self-evident within the group (lines 26, 27, 29, 30, 32) or about traditions (28) and cultural experience (31):

```
26      dachte immer/ sons, im Büro, tut man doch immer
        so,  als würd man unheimlich
        […in the office, one always behaves as if.as if
        one would…, doesn't one?]
        […in the office, we always behave as if,as if we
```

would..., **don't we**?]

27 wieso das denn?" "Ja, das macht <u>man</u> **doch** so!" 41
A: Das macht man so! B: "
[...Well, that's the way it's done, **isn't it**?...]

28 wie Arzt is, Doktor Sounso, sagt <u>man</u> **doch** zu sein / seiner Frau auch Frau Do
[if someone is a doctor, Dr Soandso, one also calls his wife "Frau Doktor", **doesn't one**?]
[if someone is a doctor, Dr Soandso, we also call his wife "Frau Doktor", **don't we**?]

29 A: aber . manchmal kriegt <u>man</u> dann **doch** sehr große Schwierigkeiten, wenn .
[but sometimes one gets into great trouble, when... **doesn't one**?]

30 ch ne Geschichte, die <u>einen</u> **doch** etwas ruhiger schlafen läßt. A: Hm
[...plot, which comes you down a bit, **doesn't it**]

31 indesde en offenes Geschäft! Es macht **doch** <u>alles</u> Inventur! B: Och nö, die, e
[...But everyone is taking stock, **aren't they**...]

32 ster feiert, aber meistens macht <u>man</u> **doch** son Riesenspökes! A: Ja, nee, wir
[... but generally, there's so much fussing, **isn't there**?]

In those occurrences the reference to shared knowledge is particularly explicit because of the collocation with indefinite pronouns like 'man/einen' ('one') and 'alles' ('everyone'). The clause containing DOCH is a move within a larger argument, the speaker wants to remind the hearer of this meta-knowledge so that the hearer will take it into account in the continuation of the exchange. The following excerpt provides an example:

Line 32

A: Ja, das war so, e, das is nämig ein / ja / am 24. selbs konnte man auch nich feiern
[Well, it was like, er, that's a/you know/yes/ we also couldn't have the party on the day, the 24th,]

B: nee, sicher nich / Scheißgeburtstag, was?
[no, of course not/ a real nuisance of a

```
        birthday, is it?]
A:      und dann wollten wir das Wochenende danach nehmen!
        Weil wir dachten, Silvester, da steht man ja erst
        gegen abend auf un zieht sich dann fein an und
        geht dann tanzen, da kann man doch am Abend davor
        auch schon was machen.
        [and then we wanted to have it on the following
        weekend! Because we thought, New Years Eve, you
        don't get up until late afternoon and then you get
        dressed and then you go dancing, so it's quite ok
        to have something else on the night before]
B:      Hm, naja, ich weiß nich, wie ihr Silvester feiert,
        aber meistens macht man doch son Riesenspökes!
        [hm, well yes, I don't know how you celebrate New
        Years Eve, but generally there's so much fussing,
        isn't there?]
```

BRO 10 (Band 2/1)

In this exchange, speaker A (female, 25) and speaker B (female, 26), who have been fellow students, talk about the difficulty of celebrating a birthday which falls on the 24th December and discuss the possibility of celebrating on the evening before New Years Eve. Speaker B does not share A's evaluation that "it's quite ok to have something else on the night before", she appeals to what she perceives as shared knowledge "but generally there's so much fussing, isn't there?". Her counter-argument is hedged, however, by conceding "I don't know how you celebrate New Years Eve". With this hedge she leaves speaker A the option of not accepting the reference to shared knowledge as a valid reason to modify her position.

There are six occurrences of DOCH in clauses which have the grammatical structure of declaratives (SUBJECT-VERB, no inversion)[98] but a rising intonation (lines 1, 3, 6) or the addition of a question tag (lines 4-5 "ne", line 2 "wa") gives them the illocutionary force of an interrogative:

98 In Line 38 the subject "das" is ellipsed.

33 ! B: "So denkst du? Das wirst du uns **doch** wohl nich antun!"A: (lacht) Wieso
[...you're not going to do that to us, **are you**?]

34 (lacht) B: ja, aber deine Frau hatte **doch** en VW oder sowat, wa? A: Nein, wir
[yes, but you're wife used to have a VW or something, **didn't she**]

35 iese Kraftfahrzeugverbände, die geben **doch** immer den Tip? Man/ B: Auf jeden
[they always provide this advice, **don't they**?...]

36 immer noch / dann würdich vielleicht **doch** am ma besten anrufen, ne? A: Ja, n
[then it would probably be best to call, **wouldn't it**?..]

37 n, ne. A: Toll, ja! Un das immerhin . **doch** direkt in der Innenstadt, ne? B:
[And that {is} immerhin directly in the city centre, **isn't it**?

38 chreiben? B: Nö!... Oder? . Kann man **doch**? A: Ich mein,ja. Aber ich weiß es
[One /you can {do} that, **can't one/you**?]

In these types of occurrences, the reference to common knowledge is not quite as strong, the speaker offers it as a suggestion, rather than a fact. Therefore, the element of correction, which is often present in utterances containing DOCH, does not exist here.

In summary, it can be said that the function of DOCH as a modal particle in declaratives is to point to meta-knowledge which the speaker wants the hearer to consider in order to overcome a perceived difference of opinion. Thus, DOCH functions discursively as part of the argumentative structure of an exchange. It creates exophoric reference as it relates the proposition in question to the wider context of situation, i.e. knowledge shared by the interlocutors as members of a family, social group or culture. This reference to common knowledge can be seen as an implicit way of expressing subjective attitude. DOCH provides a hedge (for a discussion see Chapter 2.5): rather than stating "This is the way I see it" the speaker tries to establish common ground by referring to common knowledge.

Imperatives

There are ten occurrences of DOCH as a modal particle in imperatives:

1	prima aus. A: Gut! B: Sprechen wer	**doch**	noch mal am Freitag drüber, nich? A
2	das verstehen. 180 B: Versuchen Sie	**doch**	mal ., Frau, öh, öh, A, versuchen S
3	h en doofer Termin! B: Ja, aber sach	**doch**	mal, wann de mal hier vorbeikommen
4	mal ., Frau, öh, öh, A, versuchen Sie	**doch**	mal, ne Parallele zum Schiffsbau z
5	ssen dumm, da dachte ich mir, fragste	**doch**	ma die C, ob die nich mit mir ne R
6	uhr, sagte meine Mutter,"ja, B, komm	**doch**	jetz ma en bißchen öfter nachhause!
7	B: "Nein", sacht meine Mutter, "red	**doch**	nich so'n Quatsch, die ham sich nu
8	htig, mit wem, ne." "Ach so! Ach, red	**doch**	nich son Unsinn!" (lacht) A: (lac
9	den? Is das denn schlimm? Komm, steh	**doch**	wieder auf, was is denn los?" A: (
10	n mir aus, ich würd sagen, kommen Se	**doch**	einfach. aber ich hoffe, daB es dan

In six of those occurrences, DOCH collocates with MAL (lines 1-6). The collocation of those two modal particles in imperatives serves as a downtoning device (cf. Faerch & Kasper 1989, see also Chapters 2&3). Whereas the straight imperative form would have the illocutionary force of a request, the collocation with DOCH MAL indicates the illocutionary force 'suggestion', corresponding with the English formulaic expression 'why don't you', as shown in the following example:

Line 3

B: aber trotzdem muß ich en bißchen was . anpacken!
[but nevertheless I have to help out a little]

A: Naja, sicher, klar! Ja, das is wirklich en doofer Termin!
[Well yes, certainly, sure! Yes, that really is a silly date!]

B: Ja, aber sach **doch mal**, wann de mal hier vorbeikommen
kanns, damit wer das gleich festmachen, sons wird dat ja doch nix! Warte mal, Freitag bin ich dann weg, namittags...
[Yes, but **why don't you** tell me, when you'll be able to come over, so that we fix that, otherwise it's not going to come about, is it? Wait a second, Friday I'm gone, in the afternoon ...]

(BRO 10 Bd 2/1)

In collocation with the negation particle 'nicht' (line 7-8), DOCH emphasises the contrast between the speaker's and the hearer's stance and thus lends emphasis to the request expressed by the imperative:

Line 7

```
B:     Bis du sicher, daß die sich nur verlobt haben,
       oder ham die vielleicht geheiratet?
       [Are you sure, that they only got engaged, or did
       they perhaps get married?]
A:     (lachend) geheiratet?
       [(laughing) married?
B:     "Nein", sacht meine Mutter, "red doch nich so'n
       Quatsch, die ham sich nur verlobt!"
       ["No", my mother said, "don't talk [doch] such
       nonsense, they only got engaged!"]
```

(BRO 8 Bd 2/4)

When DOCH does not collocate with MAL in imperatives, its general function can be described as emphasising a contrast between what the speaker asks the hearer to do, and possible objection or hesitation on the part of the hearer.

Line 9

```
B:     Meine Mutter hatte das nich mitgekriegt, die war
       irgendwie am Lesen, guckt auf einmal hoch und
       sieht mich mit verdrehten Augen nebenem Sessel
       liegen.
       [My mother didn't notice anything, she was reading
       or something, suddenly she looks and sees me lying
       next to the armchair with my eyes rolling]
A:     (lacht)[laughing]
B:     Die hat geschrien, das kannsde dir nich
       vorstellen. "B, was is denn los? Is dir
       schlechtgeworden? Is das denn schlimm?
       Komm, steh doch wieder auf, was is denn los?"
       [She screamed, like you couldn't imagine. "B,
       what's happening? Are you feeling ill? Is it bad
       then? Come, do get up again, what is it then?]
```

(BRO 8 Bd 2/4)

In this excerpt, where B talks to a friend about an incident that happened with her mother, the mother is reported to have uttered “steh doch wieder auf”. DOCH here emphasises the contrast between what she sees – her daughter lying on the floor, not responding to her questions – and her request “**do** get up again”.

Summary of results: DOCH

Position in clause	**Grammatical co-occurence**	**Lexical collocation**	**Category**	**Meaning**
inital			answering particle	‘yes’ (& emphasis)
medial	declaratives		modal particle	seeking hearer’s agreemend → question tag in English
medial	imperatives	MAL	modal particle	why don’t you
medial	imperatives		modal particle	emphasis

Sample Work Sheet: DOCH

You might have encountered the word DOCH as a response to what someone said, as shown in the following concordance:

1	bitte? C: Du bis doch verrückt! B:	**Doch**!	C: Hör ma, ich erkenn dich ja dem
2	e denn kein Ei, en hartgekochtes? B:	**Doch**!	En hartgekochtes Ei darfsde auch e
3	kann doch nich sein, kilomäßig ja/ B:	**Doch**!	C: un von der Figur her nich! B: J
4	l, dann schicke ik se eben nich. A:	**Doch**,	schick sie ruhig! Ich bin so wild
5	ssen . Und das zweite auch noch. B:	**Doch**,	ich ( ) et erste Ehejahr is immer
6	der, öh, da . zu beigetragen, ne. B:	**Doch**,	ich find ooch, wenn irjentwat kapu
7	überhaupt Geld kriegt! B: Öm . doch!	**Doch**,	denn, ö, das einzige, was sich änd
8	ihr könnt nich zu uns kommen, ne? B:	**Doch**,	sicher können wir zu euch kommen,
9	Bier trinken C: Und dick werden. B:	**Doch**,	dagegen schon. C: Nee, aber jetz
10	na, kommt janich in Frage. A: Doch,	**doch**.	B: Wie war denn dein Jeburtstag?
11	Ach, na, kommt janich in Frage. A:	**Doch**,	doch. B: Wie war denn dein Jeburt
12	ch, kann ich mir nich vorstellen. B:	**Doch**,	doch! Ja, aber wir ham dem jetz ab
13	nn ich mir nich vorstellen. B: Doch,	**doch**!	Ja, aber wir ham dem jetz abgeholf
14	end? B: Ja / D: Nix mehr? B: Doch,	**doch**,	sicher, abends kann man dann . ric
15	ag, Abend? B: Ja / D: Nix mehr? B:	**Doch**,	doch, sicher, abends kann man dann

In all these examples DOCH contradicts to some degree what the previous speaker said – a negative is turned into a positive – and DOCH can be translated with 'yes', depending on the context a rather emphatic 'yes', as the following example within a larger stretch of dialogue shows:

Line 4

A: Also, hör ma, das is ja nu keen ( ), also ik schick dir die hin,

un wenn du dik darüber freust, dann freu ik mich ooch.

B: Naja, siehsde. Un wenn ich dir die nich schicken will, dann schicke ik se eben nich.

A: **Doch**, schick sie ruhig! Ich bin so wild auf Comics im Augenblick.

Frequently, DOCH occurs as an answer to a question in the negative, as in the following example:

Line 8

A: Ja, X hat nämig auch Urlaub, och, das wär doch schön! .. Könntet ihr denn, ach so, ihr könnt nich zu uns kommen, ne?

B: **Doch**, sicher können wir zu euch kommen, Y hat ja keine Rufbereitschaft, hat ja Urlaub.

DOCH not only appears at the beginning of someone's contribution to a dialogue, it can also be found within the clause. Here, it has different meanings depending on the context of use. Let's have a look at some of those meanings.

Study the following group of examples and underline the clause containing DOCH:

1 auch bei der Z mal belegt A: Das is **doch** egal, das heißt doch nur, daß du di
2 a", sachich, "und warum?" "Ja, das is **doch** dat Normale!" A: Hm (lacht) B: Jo
3 dann der 31. frei sein. Denn das is **doch** en evangelischer Feiertag! B: Ja,
4 ulkollegium angefordert war. "Das is **doch** zusätzliche Arbeit!" Hü, weg! A: (
5 cht man noch leichter weg! B: Das is **doch** Wahnsinn! A: Nee, man muß dann war
6 h da? A: Ja B: - Titel - A: Das is **doch** toll! B: Ja, da kommt dann das Pro
7 h hier nah an der Brücke wärt, is das **doch** so schlimm nich. Also ich würd mich
8 lig. Ob das ne Wanze is? Aber das is **doch** unwahrscheinlich! C: Seit wann ha
9 kann man ohnehin . und öh . da is das **doch** wesentlich einfacher, sich zu tren
10 daß die Spüle verstopft war, das wär **doch** einlich interessanter gewesen? B:
11 : Sin auch drin, ia. B: Ja, das wär **doch** auch nich uninteressant, oder / A:
12 : Hm. B: Aber erstensmal wäre das ja **doch** eine . ziemliche finanzielle Einbu
13 X hat nämig auch Urlaub, och, das wär **doch** schön! .. Könntet ihr denn, ach so
14 ten von heute auf morgen, ne, das war **doch** ne Leistung! B: Ja sicher, auf jed
15 noch? Das war aber schon dieser Tage **doch**! A: ((3s)) Nee, ich hatte sie beim
16 sich das nennt D: is doch egal, is **doch** egal B: jedenfalls . hat das so un
17 jetz nich, wie sich das nennt D: is **doch** egal, is doch egal B: jedenfalls .
18 A: Nö, sehr böse natürlich nich, is **doch** klar/ B: Ich hab grade mit X telef
19 tun B: Ja, die zähl ich mit? A: Is **doch** klar! Guck mal, wenn de/ wenn de da
20 B: Ach, hattest du frei? A: Ja, is **doch** Feiertag. Oder? Bei euch nich? B:
21 t, wo der Mann wohnt. A: Ja. B: Is **doch** en Nachteil, ich habs ja immer gesa
22 A: Sin vorgestern angekommen! B: Is **doch** nich nötig! A: Sin echt prima! B:
23 du kanns ja nich loslassen!.. Nee! Is **doch** heller Wahnsinn! . Bin froh, daß d
24 fahren war, stell dir das ma vor! Is **doch** Wahnsinn! A: Ja, sobald (der B: W
25 mehr, wenn's schneit. A: Jaa. B: Is **doch** was mehr draußen... Hmhm. A: Ja so

1.) What is the verb used in these clauses?

____

2.) Which other word appears with great frequency at the beginning of the clause containing DOCH?

____

3.) Two clauses appear more than once. Can you identify them?

____

____

In these examples, the speakers seek agreement from the hearer. They state their assessment of what is being discussed: “that is ...”. The use of DOCH indicates that they are asking for agreement: “that is ..., isn’t it?”

DOCH appeals to the hearer to agree with the speaker and at the same time it refers to knowledge which speaker and hearer (supposedly) share. This is particularly obvious when there is some explicit reference to conventions.

Study the following examples and their translations:

26 dachte immer/ sons, im Büro, tut man doch immer so, als würd man unheimlich
[...in the office, we always behave as if,as if we would..., don't we?]

27 wieso das denn?" "Ja, das macht man doch so!" A: Das macht man so! B: "
[...Well, that's the way it's done, isn't it?...]

28 wie Arzt is, Doktor Sounso, sagt man doch zu sein / seiner Frau auch Frau Do
[if someone is a doctor, Dr Soandso, we also call his wife "Frau Doktor",don't we?]

29) A: aber . manchmal kriegt man dann doch sehr große Schwierigkeiten, wenn .
[but sometimes one gets into great trouble, when... doesn't one?]

30 ch ne Geschichte, die einen doch etwas ruhiger schlafen läßt. A: Hm
[... plot, which comes you down a bit, doesn't it]

31 lindesde en offenes Geschäft! Es macht doch alles Inventur! B: Och nö, die,
[...But everyone is taking stock, aren't they...]

32 ster feiert, aber meistens macht man doch son Riesenspökes! A: Ja, nee, wir
[... but generally, there's so much fussing, isn't there?]

4.) What type of shared knowledge does doch refer to in these examples? Please give the line numbers:

conventions of everyday processes	line(s): ________________
traditions	line(s): ________________
cultural experiences	line(s): ________________

5.) In these examples, the reference to shared knowledge is particularly obvious because the speaker uses indefinite pronouns like 'one' and 'everyone'. Can you find the three different forms used in German?

____

____

Let's examine a different meaning of doch now. Study the following examples and underline the clauses doch appears in:

1	prima aus. A: Gut! B: Sprechen wer	**doch**	noch mal am Freitag drüber, nich? A
2	das verstehen. 180 B: Versuchen Sie	**doch**	mal ., Frau, öh, öh, A, versuchen S
3	h en doofer Termin! B: Ja, aber sach	**doch**	mal, wann de mal hier vorbeikommen
4	mal ., Frau, öh, öh, A, versuchen Sie	**doch**	mal, ne Parallele zum Schiffsbau z
5	ssen dumm, da dachte ich mir, fragste	**doch**	ma die C, ob die nich mit mir ne R
6	uhr, sagte meine Mutter,"ja, B, komm	**doch**	jetz ma en bißchen öfter Nachhause!
7	B: "Nein", sacht meine Mutter, "red	**doch**	nich so'n Quatsch, die ham sich nu
8	htig, mit wem, ne." "Ach so! Ach, red	**doch**	nich son Unsinn!" (lacht) A: (lac
9	den? Is das denn schlimm? Komm, steh	**doch**	wieder auf, was is denn los?" A: (
10	n mir aus, ich würd sagen, kommen Se	**doch**	einfach. aber ich hoffe, daß es dan

6.) In what type of clause does DOCH appear in these examples?

____

____

7.) Which other word appears next or close to DOCH lines 1-6?

____

8.) For which of the following groups of examples does the English translation 'why don't you' fit, for which group is the meaning of DOCH best rendered by emphasis?

Group 1

Versuchen Sie **doch** mal

Ja, aber sach **doch** mal

komm **doch** jetz mal öfter ____________________

Group 2

red **doch** nicht so einen Unsinn

red **doch** nicht so einen Quatsch

steh **doch** wieder auf

kommen Sie **doch** einfach ____________________

5.7 MAL

There are 412 occurrences of the forms MA/MAL in 33 texts in the BRO data. 21 of those occurrences do not represent the particle MAL, but are either a short form of the indefinite pronoun MAN ('one') or the noun MAL ('(one) time'). In the remaining 391 occurrences, MAL has either a downtoning function or a temporal function. The analysis of the concordance data has shown that the line between those two functions is not always clearcut. Following earlier research (Bublitz 1977, Franck 1980, Thurmair 1989, König 1990, Helbig 1994), I here describe MAL in downtoning function as a modal particle in requests, which may be encoded as imperatives or declaratives, where MAL collocates with a modal verb, as well as in yes/no questions.

Modal particle Imperatives

In 77 occurrences, MAL collocates with the grammatical structure 'imperative'. In these instances, MAL has a downtoning function:

```
1   denn mal kommen? 90 B:  Oder rufen Se mal die technische Abteilung oben an und
2    geworden! B:  Hui! A:  Stell dir das mal vor! B:  Das sind ja schlechte Aussic
3   schön! B:  nach Silvester A:  ja, laß ma was von dir hören B: un dann machen we
4   Wochen im Vorsprung, wühlen Sie sich  mal was durch!" ( ) Da war der auf einma
5  B:  Ja, müßt ihr ma machen, macht euch ma widder fit! A:  Ja, ich weiß nich, ich
6  hichtwechsel! . Ja, Mensch,  denn grüß ma schoma den X, ne! Dann erholt euch man
7  hnell kommen? B:  Ja, kommen Se morgen mal eben, ja? A:  Is gut. Hm, danke. B:
8  ik-Wettkampf. A:  Ah so, ja dann kommt mal rüber! B:  Und, em, Frau Y. eh, ja, d
9   is 31. März setzen. A:  Ja. Rechnen Se ma aus, ob der dann überhaupt Geld kriegt
10 ma  wieder jemeldet has, und denn grüß ma dein Frauchen schön  sach ihr schöne J
11 ntlich feiern heute, ne, schwingt euch ma auf! A:  Ja, meinsde? B:  Jo. Hasde so
12 rder im Kino? A:  Nee B:  Ach mach das mal so, und guck nochmal nach. Wenn das n
13 s gar nich möglich? B:  … . warten Sie mal . , daß wir / A:  daß wenigstens jema
14 schon ma merken! ((3s))  Bestell dem X ma noch en schönen Gruß, ne! A:  Mach ich
15 t) A:  Was die Zeit rumgeht! Stell dir ma vor, ich könnte ne  achtjährige Tochte
16 türlich auch wat sein, aber . wart  da ma auf ne günstige Gelegenheit  es muß ni
17 uch ausgehen, ne. Am besten  kommen Se mal vorbei und . eh . bringen nen Plan mi
18    . folgende . Fra /- machen Sie grad mal die Tür zu, Herr X? -  folgende Frage
19   meine Mutter,"ja, B,  komm doch jetz ma en bißchen öfter Nachhause!" Hab ich
20   . A:  Ja klar! B:  Aber . öh, rechnet ma am besten nich damit, denn . es hat ja
21  verstehen. 180 B:  Versuchen Sie doch mal ., Frau, öh, öh, A, versuchen Sie doc
22 , Frau, öh, öh, A, versuchen Sie doch  mal, ne Parallele zum Schiffsbau zu ziehe
23  s, sacht man? 179 B:  Jaha, passen Se ma auf, en Schott hat also die Funktion a
```

When collocating with MAL, the imposition brought about by a request is lessened. MAL thus modifies the illocutionary force of a request (cf.

Faerch & Kasper 1989). This modification can be reflected in English by the use of 'just', as the following example shows:

Line 9

B: Richtig. Und dann könntich auf die, ö,
Viertelstelle von Herrn R, ö, noch jemand anders
bis 31. März setzen.
[Right. Und then I could, er, have somone else on
Mr R's quarter of a position, er, until 31 March]
Ja. Rechnen Se **ma** aus, ob der dann überhaupt Geld
kriegt!
[Yes. **Just** work out, whether he'd get any money
then!]

(BRO 4 Bd 9/2)

The use of MAL is highly conventionalised in imperatives, which consist of the verb form only:

24 l Zeug, zweiundzwanzig Pfund, überleg **mal**! B: Hm... Ja, ich weiß. Aber/ 157 C:
25 nich mitgefahren war, stell dir das **ma** vor! Is doch Wahnsinn! A: Ja, sobald
26 one Milchmädchenrechnung, nee, nee laß **ma** (lacht) A: (lacht) Na, falls wer uns
27 hen / 70 B: Is ja gut! Paß **ma** auf, dann kann ich ja ma zwischendurch
28 n, aber "nach Hause gehen', nö! Sieh **mal** nach! A: Ich seh mal nach B: dann s
29 nn ihr dann zurück seid, rufter mich **ma** an, da komm ich dann vorbei. B: Un d
30 Ja, nich so feierlich, rufs **ma** an! Frau A!.. Sind verheiratet? A: J

and can be seen as formulaic in collocation with a number of verbs. In the BRO data, the verb which appears most frequently in its imperative form in collocation with MAL is "hören" ('listen'), (30 occurrences):

31) çut, okay, tschüs. B: ( ) C: **Hör ma**, wo hälsde den Hörer immer hin, ich hö
32 . ((Gruß von A)) B: Hallo, A. A: **Hör ma**, der X hat sich gewundert, weil ihr eb
33 bestimmt/ B: Na, denn . ach . da **hör ma**, dann werdik sämtliche Telefonate str
34 bloß ne Frage der Zeit, ne. C: Ja, **hör ma**, dann würd ich doch so sagen: wenn / w
35 brück, also.. unmöglich! B: Och, **hör ma**, wenn ihr doch hier nah an der Brücke
36 chen! C: Du wars doch wieder weg! **Hör ma**, nachdem ich dich also, öh, kurz und
37 der wie? A: Ich hoffe ja. B: Ja, **hör mal**, gibts denn da nichts Genaues? A: NŠ
38 dir ma jet zuschicken. A: Au ja! **Hör ma**, wie machen wer das überhaupt mit der
39 ert darüber, un auch nich. C: .. **Hör ma**, was is denn das für'n komisches Geräu
40 f der andern Seite / A: Hia. C: **Hör ma**, is der B irgendwie schlecht gelaunt,
41 hat se nix zu tun, wer weiß? B: **Hör ma**, has du denn nich ma Zeit, en Cafe zu
42 ja, man hat nich allzuviel zu tun. **Hör mal**, weißt du eigentlich genau, wie weit
43 ma einrichten? Daß ihr ma kommt. **Hör ma**, wir müssen hier unbedingt no man Käs
44 ma mein Zimmer aufräumen. A: Ja. **Hör mal**, man kann dich doch normalerweise abe
45 n paarmal gefracht worden, . em, "**hör mal**, wieso verlobst du dich denn einlich
46 Nerven, und da sagich so zu ihm: "**Hör ma**, weißde, was wir jetz machen? Wir gehn
47 niger schlimm! B: (lacht) Ja gut! **Hör mal**, läuft das inn Semesterferien nich?
48 wie geht's dir denn? A: Ja . Gut. **Hör mal**, mir brennt grad das Essen an, ich st
49 . A: Tag, B, hier is A. **Hör mal**, ich wollt dich fragen, mußt du denn
50 Ich dacht schon, du wärst sauer, **hör ma**, du warst grad so kurz angebunden! B:

51 53 B: 1000 Kalorien! C: 1000? Ja **hör ma**, was/was ißt du denn dann? . Meine Mut
52 a wieder welche rüba. A: Ja, aber **hör ma**, stürz dich nich in Unkosten! B: Ach,
53 da wird nischt bezahlt! A: Komm, **hör ma**, das kannsde nich machen! Die sin doch
54 dich nich in Unkosten! B: Ach, na **hör ma**, is nich so schlimm! 110 A: Ja, billi
55 die Sprache verschlagen, so isses. **Hör ma**, sach ma C: Bitte? B: Willsde morgen
56 in. B: Was macht dann die Schule, **hör mal**? A: Ach so, da bin ich rausgeflogen!
57 reichen! A: Ach, ja nu! B: Also, **hör ma**, das is ja nu keen ( ), also ik schick
58 t nich dicker! (lacht) Ich hab/ C: **Hör mal**, wenn du sonst überall abnimms, und
59 u bis doch verrückt! B: Doch! C: **Hör ma**, ich erkenn dich ja demnächst nich meh
60 uch ja die Zeitungen immer geben, **hör mal**, mit den Immobiliensachen. B: Das wä

The very high frequency of this formulaic expression can be ascribed to the channel of communication.[99] All dialogues under discussion are carried out via telephone; in this context, the phrase HÖR MAL is used as a discursive device to direct the hearer's attention (cf. Schiffrin 1987 on '*y'know*'). It generally occurs when a new topic or subtopic is introduced by the speaker, often at the beginning of the speaker's turn. Mostly, it precedes the new topic introduced, but occasionally it is used retroactively (see e.g. line 56). The request expressed by the phrase HÖR MAL ('listen!') is thus not meant to be taken literally – the hearer is doing just that anyhow, otherwise no communication via the telephone would take place – rather it serves to direct the hearer's attention to the fact that a new topic or new thought on the topic under discussion is going to be introduced by the speaker.

Other formulaic phrases, consisting of a verb form in the imperative and MAL, which occur with some frequency in the BRO data are:

WARTE MAL (9 occurrences)

61 hm B: die ham zusammenjewohnt, **warte mal**, da war Y en halbes Jahr also seit
62 Montag in acht Tagen! Oder? Ja. **Warde ma**, hier hängt dochen Kalender! (Einatme
63 Ach, soo lange fahr ich no nich, **warte ma**! . Seit . 69, ja 69 fahr ich, sin jet
64 burtstag, wa? A: Am Montag, nö! **Warte ma**, oder? B: Freitag, Sonnabend, Sonntag
65 ei oder vier jetz, ich glaub d / **warde ma**, drei ., ja, ich glaub drei Jahre fŠh
66 hen, sons wird dat ja doch nix! **Warte mal**, Freitag bin ich dann weg namittags.
67 lich. B: Ja, un dann haste also, **warte ma**, fünfhundert, fuffzig, siebenhundertf
68 nau, Frau, öh / A: In Porz. B: **Warte mal**, kann ich noch mal eben sehen? Das is
69 oche Montag? Ach so, der Montag! **Warte ma**! Da arbeite ich waascheinlich auf ner

SAG MAL (6 occurrences)

70 A: Is sehr schnell wieder da, ja! **Sa ma**, du has das nich aufgeräumt deinen S
71   doofer Termin! B: Ja, aber **sach doch mal**, wann de mal hier vorbeikommen
72 Du arbeitest wohl ununterbrochen, **sach ma**? B: Nee, ich hab doch, weiß nich, ob
73 Finnen, nicht ich! A: Ah so! B: **Sach mal**, hast du die Stelle jetzt angetreten?
74 he verschlagen, so isses. Hör ma, **sach ma** C: Bitte? B: Willsde morgen nich mit
75 Ja, fahrt schön weg! A: Nee/ B: **Sach mal**, C, du weiß auch keinen Rat, die A ha

99 For a discussion of the distorting effect of the limited corpus data see Chapter 6: Conclusion.

GUCK MAL (2 occurrences)

76 sein! 59 B: **Guck ma**, wenn ich ne Wohnung unheimig gut find
77 e zähl ich mit? A: Is doch klar! **Guck mal**, wenn de/ wenn de dasselbe Thema von

Whereas WARTE MAL ('wait!') and GUCK MAL ('look!') function like HÖR MAL – they focus the hearer's attention on a speaker's contribution – SAG MAL ('say!') may contain a literal element, asking the hearer for a contribution on the topic under discussion.

Declaratives with modal verbs

There are twelve instances where MAL occurs in declaratives in collocation with a form of the modal verbs 'müssen' ('have to/must'), 'sollen' ('ought to/should') or 'können' ('be able to/can'):

1 14. hab ich schon was! . Aber müßter **ma** sehn, wir machen dann großes Feierpro
2 neues Relais reinjetan. Da müssen Se **mal** irjentwann reinkommen, dat dauert ja
3 ns jetz was hinlegen/ B: Ja, müßt ihr **ma** machen, macht euch ma widder fit! A:
4 / kann jamal versuchen! B: Ja. Mußde **ma** ausprobieren. A: Vielleicht könnt ihr
5eicht wird es auch noch ma was! Mußt es **ma** in Ruhe lassen, das kleine Mäuschen.
6 anz gut! Sollte man unserer Regierung **mal** vorschlagen! A: Ich kann mich nämig
7 einen Arbeitsvertrag, die sollten sich **mal** nich so so beeilen! B: Ja! Da sind
8 n Cognac mitgebracht un den sollten se **mal** probieren, und ich sollt mit rüber,
9 Vielleicht könnt ihr alle am Samstag **mal** kommen un es euch angucken. (lacht)
10 sich da nix. Da könnt ihr mich (dann **mal** /) B: Wie war das denn mit der Schre
11eg zu sein A: Ja dann kannsde ja noch **mal** anrufen, falls ihr kommt. B: Ja. A:
12natürlich auch machen! B: Könnter mich **mal** ganz flach bewundern! C: Ja, also dan

Rather than simply stating facts, those declaratives have the illocutionary force of either a request ('müssen', lines 1-5) or a suggestion ('sollen' & 'können', lines 6-12). Here again, the function of MAL is to downtone this illocutionary force, as the following examples demonstrate:

Line 2

B: Aber der darf jetz nich, wenn Sie bremsen, Jott weiß wie schnell, äh, blinken.
[But it's not supposed to now, when you use the brakes, to flicker like crazy]
A: ((einatmen))[breathing in]
B: Das darf er nich... Wer ham en neues Relais reinjetan. Da **müssen Se mal** irjentwann reinkommen,

dat dauert ja nur fünf Minuten, is et widder / müssen wer nochen neues drauftun.
[It's not supposed to do that… We put in a new relais. **You'll just have to** come in some time, it doesn't take more than five minutes/ it's again/we have to put in a new one.

(BRO 25 Bd 9/11)

Line 6

B: Das sollte man übrigens einführen! Man sollte den Leuten Prämien bezahlen, wenn se nich mehr arbeiten und der Arbeitsplatz für andere Leute frei wird!
[One should introduce that by the way! One should pay a bonus to people when they don't work any more and their place of work becomes available to others!]

A: Ja, ne?
[Yes, shouldn't one?]

B: Find ich auch. Das wär ganz gut! **Sollte** man unserer Regierung **mal** vorschlagen!
[I think so too. That would be really good! One should propose that to the government!]

(BRO 8 Bd 2/4)

Line 9

B: Ja. **Mußde ma** ausprobieren.
[Yes. **You'll just have to** try that.]

A: Vielleicht könnt ihr alle am Samstag **mal** kommen un es euch angucken. (lacht)
[Maybe you **could** all come over on Saturday to have a look at it.(laughing)]

(BRO 27 Bd 5/1)

In all those occurrences, MAL lends a 'matter-of-fact' element to the request/suggestion, thus leaving the hearer the option to decline without any loss of face.

Yes/no interrogatives

In the BRO data, there are eleven occurrences of MAL in yes/no interrogatives which have the illocutionary force of a request or suggestion:

1 eben. B: Das geht nich. Könn Se noch **mal** irjentwann reinkommen? A: Soll ich m
[…could you come in again some time…]

2 In Porz. B: Warte mal, kann ich noch **mal** eben sehen? Das is Porz, ja achthund
[…could I quickly have another look…]

3 , fällt mir grade ein, kannst du mir **mal** eben mit kurzen Worten sagen, wie ma
[…could you quickly tell me in a few words…]

4 en lassen. A: Ja B: Können Sie . das **mal**, öh, im Zusammenhang vorlesen, Schot
[…could you read that out in context…]

5 önnen Sie vielleicht freundlicherweise **mal** eben so durchrufen, wann der Herr U
[would you be so kind to give us a quick call]

6 t fragen) Können Sie an unserem Kadett **mal** die Schaltmanschette so draufmachen,
[…could you fix the gearshift boot to our car…]

7 iß nich. A: Sollmer nächstes Semester **mal** zusammen hin gehen? Vielleicht fühlt
[…let's go there together next semester…]

8 hörma, wollder aber dafür nich lieber **ma** hier bei uns vorbeikommen, da machen
[…how about you coming over to our place]

9 mal, ne. A: Bis dann! B: Rufsde dann **mal** an nächste Woche? Wenn de Zeit has/ A
[…you're gonna call next week then?…]

10 machen mer das so an irgendnem Abend **mal** aus? A: Ja, wir hatten noch eine gan
[…let's organise that some evening…]

11 och / dann würdich vielleicht doch am **ma** besten anrufen, ne? A: Ja, ne. Womögl
[…it's probably best to call then, isn't it…]

In these occurrences, rather than modifying illocutionary force by downtoning, MAL indicates the illocutionary force as request (lines 1, 2, 3, 4, 5, 6, 9) or suggestion (lines 7, 8, 10, 11). This is particularly obvious in those instances where MAL collocates with the modal verbs 'können' (lines 1-6). The addition of MAL here indicates that the interrogative is not asking for information about someone's ability to carry out a certain activity – as the verb 'können' might suggest. The following example demonstrates this:

Line 2

```
B:      Wo wohnen Sie . qenau, Frau, öh /
        [Where exactly do you live, Ms, er/]
A:      In Porz.
        [In P.]
B:      Warte mal, kann ich noch mal eben sehen? Das is
        Porz, ja achthundertzwanzig, jo.
        [Hang on, could I quickly have another look? That
        is P., yes, eighthundredtwenty, yea.]
```

(BRO 32 Bd 10/7)

The translation "could I quickly have another look" reflects the fact, that in English this type of interrogative is a highly conventionalised politeness form and thus understood as a request rather than a question for information (cf. Thomas 1984).

Summary of results: mal

Position in clause	Grammatical co-occurence	Lexical collocation	Category	Meaning
medial	imperative		modal particle	downtoning function 'just'
medial	declarative	modal verbs: 'müssen' 'sollen' 'können'	modal particle	downtoning function 'just'
medial	yes/no interrogative	MAL	modal particle	indication of request

Sample Work Sheet: MAL

Please study the following list of examples and underline the clauses MA(L) occurs in:

Group 1

1	denn mal kommen? 90 B: Oder rufen Se	**mal**	die technische Abteilung oben an und
2	geworden! B: Hui! A: Stell dir das	**mal**	vor! B: Das sind ja schlechte Aussic
3	schön! B: nach Silvester A: ja, laß	**ma**	was von dir hören B: un dann machen we
4	Wochen im Vorsprung, wühlen Sie sich	**mal**	was durch!" ( ) Da war der auf einma
5	B: Ja, müßt ihr ma machen, macht euch	**ma**	widder fit! A: Ja, ich weiß nich, ich
6	hichtwechsel! . Ja, Mensch, denn grüß	**ma**	schoma den X, ne! Dann erholt euch man
7	hnell kommen? B: Ja, kommen Se morgen	**mal**	eben, ja? A: Is gut. Hm, danke. B:
8	ik-Wettkampf. A: Ah so, ja dann kommt	**mal**	rüber! B: Und, em, Frau Y, eh, ja, d
9	is 31. März setzen. A: Ja. Rechnen Se	**ma**	aus, ob der dann überhaupt Geld kriegt
10	ma wieder jemeldet has, und denn grüß	**ma**	dein Frauchen schön sach ihr schöne J
11	ntlich feiern heute, ne, schwingt euch	**ma**	auf! A: Ja, meinsde? B: Jo. Hasde so
12	rder im Kino? A: Nee B: Ach mach das	**mal**	so, und guck nochmal nach. Wenn das n
13	s gar nich möglich? B: … . warten Sie	**mal**	. , daß wir / A: daß wenigstens jema
14	schon ma merken! ((3s)) Bestell dem X	**ma**	noch en schönen Gruß, ne! A: Mach ich
15	t) A: Was die Zeit rumgeht! Stell dir	**ma**	vor, ich könnte ne achtjährige Tochte
16	türlich auch wat sein, aber . wart da	**ma**	auf ne günstige Gelegenheit, es muß ni
17	uch ausgehen, ne. Am besten kommen Se	**mal**	vorbei und . eh . bringen nen Plan mi
18	. folgende . Fra /- machen Sie grad	**mal**	die Tür zu, Herr X? - folgende Frage
19	meine Mutter,"ja, B, komm doch jetz	**ma**	en bißchen öfter Nachhause!" Hab ich
20	. A: Ja klar! B: Aber . öh, rechnet	**ma**	am besten nich damit, denn . es hat ja
21	verstehen. 180 B: Versuchen Sie doch	**mal**	., Frau, öh, öh, A, versuchen Sie doc
22	, Frau, öh, öh, A, versuchen Sie doch	**mal**	, ne Parallele zum Schiffsbau zu ziehe
23	s, sacht man? 179 B: Jaha, passen Se	**ma**	auf, en Schott hat also die Funktion a

1.) In what type of clause does MAL appear in these examples?

____

MAL plays an important role when asking someone to do something, when expressing a request. It makes the speaker's request less direct, more casual, thus imposing less on the hearer. This modification can be reflected in English by the use of 'just', as the following example shows:

B: Richtig. Und dann könnt' ich auf die, ö, Viertelstelle von Herrn R, ö, noch jemand

anders bis 31. März setzen.
[Right. Und then I could, er, have someone else on Mr R's quarter of a position, er, until 31 March]

A: Ja. Rechnen Se ma aus, ob der dann überhaupt Geld kriegt!
[Yes. Just work out, whether he'd get any money then!]

In imperative clauses which consist mainly of the verb, the use of MAL is highly conventionalised and can be seen as a fixed expression with some frequently occuring German verbs.

2.) Study the following concordance to identify some formulaic uses of MAL:

Group 2

l Zeug, zweiundzwanzig Pfund, überleg **mal**! B: Hm... Ja, ich weiß. Aber/ 157 C:
nich mitgefahren war, stell dir das **ma** vor! Is doch Wahnsinn! A: Ja, sobald
one Milchmädchenrechnung, nee, nee laß **ma** (lacht) A: (lacht) Na, falls wer uns
hen / 70 B: Is ja gut! Paß **ma** auf, dann kann ich ja ma zwischendurch
n, aber "nach Hause gehen', nö! Sieh **mal** nach! A: Ich seh mal nach B: dann s
nn ihr dann zurück seid, rufter mich **ma** an, da komm ich dann vorbei. B: Un d
Ja, nich so feierlich, rufs **ma** an! Frau A!.. Sind verheiratet? A: J
n paarmal gefracht worden, . em, "hör **mal**, wieso verlobst du dich denn einlich
Nerven, und da sagich so zu ihm: "Hör **ma**, weißde, was wir jetz machen? Wir gehn
niger schlimm! B: (lacht) Ja gut! Hör **mal**, läuft das inn Semesterferien nich?
wie geht's dir denn? A: Ja . Gut. Hör **mal**, mir brennt grad das Essen an, ich st
. A: Tag, B, hier is A. Hör **mal**, ich wollt dich fragen, mußt du denn
in. B: Was macht dann die Schule, hör **mal**? A: Ach so, da bin ich rausgeflogen!
reichen! A: Ach, ja nu! B: Also, hör **ma**, das is ja nu keen ( ), also ik schick
t nich dicker! (lacht) Ich hab/ C: Hör **mal**, wenn du sonst überall abnimms, und
u bis doch verrückt! B: Doch! C: Hör **ma**, ich erkenn dich ja demnächst nich meh
uch ja die Zeitungen immer geben, hör **mal**, mit den Immobiliensachen. B: Das wä
hm B: die ham zusammenjewohnt, warte **mal**, da war Y en halbes Jahr, also seit
Montag in acht Tagen! Oder? Ja. Warde **ma**, hier hängt dochen Kalender! (Einatme
Ach, soo lange fahr ich no nich, warte **ma**! . Seit . 69, ja 69 fahr ich, sin jet
burtstag, wa? A: Am Montag, nö! Warte **ma**, oder? B: Freitag, Sonnabend, Sonntag
ei oder vier jetz, ich glaub d / warde **ma**, drei ., ja, ich glaub drei Jahre fŠh
hen, sons wird dat ja doch nix! Warte **mal**, Freitag bin ich dann weg, namittags.
lich. B: Ja, un dann haste also, warte **ma**, fünfhundert, fuffzig, siebenhundertf
nau, Frau, öh / A: In Porz. B: Warte **mal**, kann ich noch mal eben sehen? Das is
oche Montag? Ach so, der Montag! Warte **ma**! Da arbeite ich waascheinlich auf ner
A: Is sehr schnell wieder da, ja! Sa **ma**, du has das nich aufgeräumt, deinen S
doofer Termin! B: Ja, aber sach doch **mal**, wann de mal hier vorbeikommen
Du arbeitest wohl ununterbrochen, sach **ma**? B: Nee, ich hab doch, weiß nich, ob
Finnen, nicht ich! A: Ah so! B: Sach **mal**, hast du die Stelle jetzt angetreten?
he verschlagen, so isses. Hör ma, sach **ma** C: Bitte? B: Willsde morgen nich mit
Ja, fahrt schön weg! A: Nee/ B: Sach **mal**, C, du weiß auch keinen Rat, die A ha
sein! 59 B: Guck **ma**, wenn ich ne Wohnung unheimig gut find
e zähl ich mit? A: Is doch klar! Guck **mal**, wenn de/ wenn de dasselbe Thema von

Let's now look at the following examples. Please underline the clauses MA(L) occurs in:

Group 3

1 14. hab ich schon was! . Aber müßter **ma** sehn, wir machen dann großes Feierpro
2 neues Relais reinjetan. Da müssen Se **mal** irjentwann reinkommen, dat dauert ja
3 ns jetz was hinlegen/ B: Ja, müßt ihr **ma** machen, macht euch ma widder fit! A:
4 / kann jamal versuchen! B: Ja. Mußde **ma** ausprobieren. A: Vielleicht könnt ihr
5eicht wird es auch noch ma was! Mußt es **ma** in Ruhe lassen, das kleine Mäuschen.
6 anz gut! Sollte man unserer Regierung **mal** vorschlagen! A: Ich kann mich nämig
7 einen Arbeitsvertrag, die sollten sich **mal** nich so so beeilen! B: Ja! Da sind
8 n Cognac mitgebracht un den sollten se **mal** probieren, und ich sollt mit rüber,
9 Vielleicht könnt ihr alle am Samstag **mal** kommen un es euch angucken. (lacht)
10 sich da nix. Da könnt ihr mich (dann **mal** /) B: Wie war das denn mit der Schre
11eg zu sein A: Ja dann kannsde ja noch **mal** anrufen, falls ihr kommt. B: Ja. A:
12natürlich auch machen! B: Könnter mich **mal** ganz flach bewundern! C: Ja, also dan

3.) What type of clause does MAL appear in here?

____

4.) Which verb occurs in the following clauses?

Lines 1-5 __________________

Lines 6-8 __________________

Lines 9-12 __________________

In the examples of Group 3, the meaning of MAL is the same as in those of Group 1; it can again be translated by English 'just'. Although the grammatical structure of the clauses is different to those of Group 1, the function of 'requesting' is brought about by the use of the modal verbs.

Now let's have a look at yet another group of examples. Please underline the clauses containing MA(L):

Group 4

1 eben. B: Das geht nich. Könn Se noch **mal** irjentwann reinkommen? A: Soll ich m
2 In Porz. B: Warte mal, kann ich noch **mal** eben sehen? Das is Porz, ja achthund
3 , fällt mir grade ein, kannst du mir **mal** eben mit kurzen Worten sagen, wie ma
4 en lassen. A: Ja B: Können Sie . das **mal**, öh, im Zusammenhang vorlesen, Schot
5 Können Sie vielleicht freundlicherweise **mal** eben so durchrufen, wann der Herr U
6 t fragen) Können Sie an unserem Kadett **mal** die Schaltmanschette so draufmachen,

5.) What type of clause does MAL occur in here?

____

6.) Which verb occurs in all of the above clauses?

____

Here, MAL is not so much used to soften the imposition of a request as to indicate that the speaker is requesting something of the hearer. In English, these types of requests would typically be expressed by ‚could you...', 'could I...'.

5.8 ABER

The particle ABER occurs 387 times in 30 texts in BRO. In the vast majority of occurrences in the BRO data, ABER has an adversative function, either as a conjunction or as a conjunctional adverb[100]. In 9 instances ABER occurs as modal particle.

Adversative Function – Conjunction[101]

As a conjunction (309 occurrences), ABER is easily recognised within the concordance data as it appears in clause initial position, as the following examples show:

1	Ausstellung. Da kamen se beide hin,	**aber**	sonst sehn die sich nie! B: Ja
2	Daß man da jetz aufgezeichnet wird.	**Aber**	ich warte nich mehr so lang mit de
3	B: oder zwei A: das is alles Mist!	**Aber**	ich hab auch keine Lust, an die Sch
4	dann kannsde, em, eingesetzt werden,	**aber**	nur ganz minimal. A: Hm B: Un di
5	auf Comics im Augenblick. Lesen ja,	**aber**	nich zeichnen, weißde. B: Ja. A:
6	Sie kommen hier drüber geflogen, ja,	**aber**	bei weitem nich soviel wie in Porz
7	B! B: Ich hatte schon ma angerufen,	**aber**	da war keiner da! A: Ja, das is gu
8	Feierei nich hier is, ne A: hm B:	**aber**,	wir teilen uns die Sache, dasis ni
9	doch im Krankenhaus? B: Ja? (lacht)	**Aber**	da warn wer ja no nich verheiratet.
10	Thema sehr beschäftigt has B: Naja,	**aber**	wenn ich die Stunden zusammenzähle,

In these types of occurrences, ABER expresses a contrast in its immediate context. It can be translated with the English 'but', as exemplified in the following excerpts:

Line 1

A: Gegen das Ehepaar! Ah ja. Ja, das is bei uns gut, also meine Schwiegereltern und meine Eltern, die . ham sich glaubich bisher erst zweimal gesehn
[Against the married couple! Ah well. Yes, that's good in our case, you see, my inlaws and my parents have met only twice so far, I think]

100 This distinction is to be found in Thurmair 1989. Other researchers (e.g. Helbig 1994, König *et al.* 1990) only distinguish between conjunction and modal particle.

101 For a full list of occurrences of ABER as conjunction, see appendix.

```
B:     Hm
A:     einmal bei unserer Hochzeit und das zweite mal bei
       X'seiner Ausstellung. Da kamen se beide hin, aber
       sonst sehn die sich nie!
       [Once at our wedding and the second time at X's
       exhibition. They both {they all} attended that,
       but other than that they never meet]
```

(BRO 8 Bd 2/4)

Here (see also lines 2-7), the contrast expressed by ABER lies within A's utterance. ABER refers back to the first part of A's last sentence and thus creates anaphoric reference.

Line 10

```
A:     Das is doch egal, das heißt doch nur, daß du dich
       mit dem
       Thema sehr beschäftigt has
       [ that does't matter, it only means that you have
       really looked into this topic]
B:     Naja, aber wenn ich die Stunden zusammenzähle,
       dann
       [Oh well, but if I add up the hours then]
A:     Die zählste mit, das hat ja nichts zu tun
       [You count those as well, that doesn't have any
       bearing]
B:     Ja, die zähl ich mit?
       [Yes, I count those as well?]
```

(BRO 3 Bd 1/3)

In this type of occurrence (see also lines 8-9), ABER expresses anaphoric reference as well, but in this case the contrast expressed by ABER does not lie within speaker B's utterance. Rather, speaker B uses ABER to express an objection to speaker A's previous utterance.

In general, ABER expressing contrast as a conjunction creates cohesion on the textual level of the dialogue. It contrasts a proposition with a preceding one and thus fulfills a discursive function.

Adversative Function - Conjunctional Adverb[102]

As a conjunctional adverb (69 occurrences), ABER appears within the clause in medial position:

```
1   immer zu sagen. A:  Ja, du gibs dir aber sons Mühe! B:  Ja, wenn das Ding da
2   Ja. A:  ja, gut! B:  Wahrscheinlich aber dann nich, die werden dann ja  best
3   aber dumm, da  hätt se / A:  Sie hat aber auch nich hier angerufen. B:  Nee?
4   B:  Ja, is klar, ersmal/ A:  Ich hab aber inzwischen gehört, daß das also wir
5   da hatter gesacht, Silvester hätter  aber keine Zeit, und er würd doch so ger
6   Das wäre dann' ne Viertelstelle, die aber offiziell aussieht  wie ne halbe, n
7   Dat hat sie gesagt, ja, dat säh sie  aber wat anderes/ anders, un dann isse a
8   im Stadt-Anzeiger gesehen, ich hatte aber . grad zu der  Zeit eben keine Zeit
9   Regelungen zu fallen, ne. B:  Ja, is aber so. (( 3s )) Wieso, habt ihr den Te !
10  was getan!" "Ja",  sag ich, "glaubst aber nich, daß de mich da noch ma hinkri
```

Like ABER as conjunction, its function is to express contrast within the immediate context of the text, thus creating anaphoric reference, as exemplified by the following excerpts:

Line 6

```
B:    das läßt sich auf keinenFall, ö,ö, für ihn, öm,
      dann ja unterbringen, nich?
      [ that would under no circumstances, er, er, for
      him, er, be possible then, would it?]
A:    Ja.
      [Yes.]
B:    Das wäre dann' ne Viertelstelle, die aber
      offiziell ussieht wie ne halbe, nur daß ers mit
      Ihnen intern verrechnen würde, nich? Am besten is,
      wir besprechens noch mal am / ö, wann sind Sie da,
      am Freitag?
      [It would be a quarter of a position then, but
      officially it would look like half a position,
      only that he would work out the finances with you
      internally, wouldn't he? It's probably  best to
      talk about it again, er, when are you in, on
      Friday?]
```

(BRO 4 Bd 9/2)

Here, the contrast lies within B's utterance, in the immediate context of the sentence.

102 For a full list of occurrences of ABER as conjunctional adverb, see appendix.

Line 9

```
A:    und unter solchen Bedingungen ham wer ja nich
      geheiratet, ich finde, wer nach . anderen
      Bedingungen geheiratet is / hat, der kann doch
      nich einfach gezwungen werden, jetz plötzlich
      unter solche Regelungen zu fallen, ne.
      [And we didn't marry under those conditions, did
      we? I reckon they can't force somebody who has
      married under different conditions to suddenly
      adhere to the new ones now, can they?
B:    Ja, is aber so. (( 3s )) Wieso, habt ihr den
      Termin verpaßt, wollt ihr euch scheiden lassen?
      [Yes, but that's the way it is. (Pause) Why, have
      you missed the deadline, do you want to get a
      divorce?
```

(BRO 22 Bd 15/15)

In this excerpt, speaker B's utterance with ABER contradicts speaker A's evaluation of the topic under discussion.

ABER as conjunction and as conjunctional adverb fulfill the same discursive function – expressing contrast on the textual level while creating cohesion through anaphoric reference – but they differ in their grammatic function, as the conjunction is to be found only clause initial, whereas the conjunctional adverb is to be found in medial position. For a non-native speaker of German, it might therefore be more difficult to distinguish between ABER as conjunctional adverb and ABER as modal particle.

Modal particle

Whereas ABER in its adversative function is used frequently in nearly all the texts of the BRO corpus, it rarely occurs as modal particle (9 occurrences). This pattern seems plausible if one takes into account the specific function of ABER as modal particle. As indicated previously (see Chapter 2), it serves to express 'surprise', 'unexpectedness' (cf. Helbig 1994, Thurmair 1989, Weinrich 1993,

Weydt 1983a) which by its very nature is not a very commonly expressed sentiment in most types of text in the data.[103]

The following instances of ABER as modal particle occurred in the BRO data:

```
1 gemacht für sechs Uhr. B:   Ja, das is aber komisch! Ja, dann wundert mich, daß !
2  nich, wohin um sechs! B:   Ja, das is aber gut! A:  Verflucht! 85 B:  Hatten S
3 o ne irrsinnige Hetze! B:   Ja, das is aber gut! Ich dachte, das wär so ausgema
4 ieben, ja, nehm ich doch an! . Das is aber dumm, da  hätt se / A:  Sie hat abe
5 prochen haben. B:  Tja, sowas, das is aber ganz ei / A:  so zwischen / B:  gan
6 Jaja, das weiß ich! ((3s)) Ja, das is aber blöd jetz! A:  Ich wußte auch gar n
7 h, Freitag muß der wider arbeiten? Is aber blöd! So einen  Tag in der Woche no !
8 um noch en Wort! C:  Mensch, die kann aber auch alles, die Frau, die is prakti !
9 n auch zwei Jahre Ruhe zu. B:  Das is aber sehr schön. A:  Un hinterher kann s
```

Line 1-6 are uttered by the same speaker in a dialogue between a young female academic (speaker A) and the mother of one of her female friends. The following excerpt contains those occurrences.

Lines 1-6

B: isch weiß et natürlich nit.
[I don't know that of course]

A: und jetz hat sie / jetz wartet sie irgendwo auf mich in Bonn?
[and now she has /she's waiting for me somewhere in Bonn?]

B: isch nehm es an / isch / isch hab es so angenommen, ich hab's / sie hat sich ja noch mit jemand getroffen um halb fünf, unda sagtse, "um sechs kommdie A".
[I suppose so/ I/ I supposed so, I had/ she met with someone else, you know, at half past four, and she said " A will be coming at six]

A: Verflucht! . Wissen Sie, das ging so schnell, da zwischen der Prüfung, da hab ich ihr noch gesagt "Ich ruf noch an!"

103 Hentschel (1986: 245): "So steigt zwar, [...], mit zunehmender Intimität auch die Wahrscheinlichkeit dafür, daß eine Partikel wie aber, die dem Ausdruck des Erstaunens dient, benutzt wird; ob sie aber auch wirklich eingesetzt wird, ist davon abhängig, ob im Verlauf des Gesprächs ein Sachverhalt zur Sprache kommt, den einer der Sprecher für erstaunlich hält. Dies wird, wie man leicht einsehen kann, vermutlich eher selten der Fall sein; [...]".

[Damn! You know, it happened so quickly, in between the exam, I said to her "I'll call you later"]

B: ja?
[yes?]

A: Wegen heute abend, unda mußte se dann schon da rein, unda haben wir gar nich ausgemacht, wann un wo.
[Regarding tonight, and then she had to go in, and we didn't at all discuss, when and where]

B: Jetz weiß ich natürlich / da weiß ich jetz eigenlich gar nix, kommt die jetz nach Hause, und, und /
[Now I don't know/ I don't really know anything now, is she coming home and, and]

A: Mist, da is die jetz womöglich ganz sauer! Wir hatten auch gar keinen Ort ausgemacht für sechs Uhr.
[Geez, she is probably really cheesed off now! We hadn't talked about where to meet at six either]

B: **Ja, das is aber komisch!** Ja, dann wundert mich, daß se zu mir nix gesagt hat, ne, daß se nach Hause kommt un daß se Se dann verständigt oder was! Ich hatte das so verstanden
[**Well, that sure is strange!** Yes, then I don't understand that she didn't tell me anything, did she, that she was coming home, and that ahe would let you know or something. I understood that]

A: Wir hatten am Telefon vorn paar Tagen das irgendwie so Ausgemacht
[We agreed on the phone a few days ago somehow]

B: Ja, daß Sie sie um / um sechs Uhr abholen!
[Yes, that you would pick her up at/at six o'clock!]

A: Ja, aber dann haben wir gar nichts mehr fest ausgemacht, un ich wußte ja auch gar nich, wohin um sechs!
[Yes, but then we did not definitely agree on anything any more, and I really didn't know where to go at six, you know]

B: **Ja, das is aber gut!**
[**Well, that really is great!**]

A: Verflucht!
[Damn!]

B: Hatten Sie denn, öh, öh, als Sie dieser Tage mit ihr sprachen, irgenden Ort ausgemacht?
[Did you then, er,er, when you spoke to her recently talk about where to meet?]

A: Ja, für zwei Uhr!
[Yes, for two o'clock!]

B: Für sechs Uhr nicht?
[Not for six?]

A: Nee!
[No!]

B: Ja sowas! Hab ich die denn so mißverstanden?
[Oh, my! Did I get her that wrong then?]

A: Nee, wahrscheinlich hat se das gemeint, das war / wir, wir ham einfach nich dran gedacht, das noch abzureden, sie hatte so wenig Zeit zwischen den beiden Prüfungen, das war so ne irrsinnige Hetze!
[No, she probably meant that, that was/ we, we just didn't think of talking about it, she was in such a hurry between the two exams, that was such a mad rush!

B: **Ja, das is aber gut!** Ich dachte, das wär so ausgemacht, daß das um sechs Uhr, weil die sagte, die sachte noch vorhin nachmittag: "Ich muß jetz gehn"; junge Mann war schon da, "und um sechs, dann kommt die A". Komisch, ne?
[**Well, that really is great!** I thought you had agreed, that that at six o'clock, because she said" I have to go now"; young man was already there "and A is coming at six". Strange, isn't it?]

A: Mensch, son Pech! Jetz wartet die irgendwo, aber ich weiß au nich, wo.
[Boy, what a disaster! Now she's waiting somewhere, but I wouldn't have a clue where.]

B: Ich weiß auch nit, wo. ((5s)) Ja, ich wüßt auch gar nit, was man da machen soll.
[I don't know where, either. Yes, I wouldn't really know what could be done]

A: Ja, wahrscheinlich hat ses inzwischen auch schon gemerkt, ne.
[Well, she'll possibly have found out by now, won't she?]

B: Ja, wie spät es es denn?
[Yes, so what's the time now?]

A: Halb sieben.
[Half past six]

B: Halb sieben, ja, nehm ich doch an! . **Das is aber dumm**, da hätt se /
[half past six, yes, I suppose so! **That really is a nuisance,** she could have/

A: Sie hat aber auch nich hier angerufen.
[But she hasn't called here either.]

B: Nee? . Ja, sonst, könnt ja sein, ne, daß, wenn Se nit kommen, daß se dann bei Ihnen anruft. Ja, vielleicht macht se das noch. Also, ich weiß jetz praktisch überhaupt nix mehr, ich hatte jetz fest damit gerechnet, hab mich drauf eingestellt, daß Sie zusammen kommen.
[Hasn't she. Well, otherwise, it could be, couldn't it, if you're not coming, that she'll call you then. Yes, perhaps she's still going to do that. Well, I really don't know anything any longer, I was counting on it, was reckoning with it, that you would meet.]

A: Son Mist!
[What a nuisance!]

B: Hm.

A: Und ich hatte gedacht, sie wird von demjenigen gebracht, der sie . noch . öh /
[And I thought, she was going to be brought by the one who . still . er]

B: Ja, das is ohne weiteres möglich, der kann se ja mitnehmen!
[Yes, that's quite possible, he can take her, can't he!]

A: Jaja, ich hab auch gedacht, das wär.. dann hinterher so geplant gewesen. Weil wir auch gar nich mehr darüber gesprochen haben.
[Yes, yes, I really thought, that was the way it was meant to be then. Because we didn't talk about it again.]

B: Tja, sowas, **das is aber ganz ei** /
[Well, how about that, **that really is a**

A: so zwischen /
[like between]

B: **ganz ungeheures Mißverständnis!**
[**what a misunderstanding!**]

A: so zwischen so, so zwei . Prüfungen, nich, da kann

man sich au nich vernünftig unterhalten!
[like between like, like two exams, you really can't talk properly!]

B: furchtbar! Ach, die war so fertig
[horrible! Ah, she was so down]

A: ja
[Yes]

B: die / die hat richtig geheult im Cafe, konnt sich gar nimmer halten, weil se se so . praktisch . zwischen den Prüfungen hatte se auch gar keine Zeit, da mußte se mit den Cuverts rumsausen, do, mit den versiegelten, wo die Note drinsteht, mußte se zum Seminar bringen, unddann . hat se zwischen . der öh, öh, Prüfungen au kaum Zeit gehabt,
[she actually cried in the coffe shop, couldn't hold back, because she she practically didn't have time between the exams, she had to run around with the envelopes, with the sealed ones, where the mark is noted, had to bring them to the seminar, andthen she rarely has time between the er, er, Exams]

A: Ja. Jaja.
[Yes. Yesyes.]

B: wor ganz ferdig.
[was really down]

A: ((4s)) Mensch!
[Oh boy!]

B: (Kam) jo praktisch, ich hab seit . zwanzig vor vier hab ich da gesessen un gewartet, so zehn vor hab fünf kam se dann an, un um halb fünf war der junge Mann schon da, ne. Also hab ich auch bloß fünf Minuten mit ihr gesprochen, un da hammer bloß, sie sagte bloß "Ja, sommers dann dabei belassen?" und da hab ich gesagt "Ja, mir isses recht!"
[(came) yea, practiclly, I have been sitting there wating since twenty to four, she arrived around ten to half past four {sic} then,and at half past four the young man was already there, wasn't he? So I only talked to her for five minutes, and we only, she cnly said "Well, shall we leave it at that then?" and I said " Yes, I don't mind!"]

A: Hm.

B: Unda hab ich das so aufgefaßt, ja, um sechs, dann

```
        kommt die A under Y.
        [And so I gathered, yes, at six A and Y will be
        coming.]
A:      Ja, (aber) er hat auch nich gesagt, wohin, ne?
        [Yes, (but) he didn't say where either, did he?
B:      Ja, aber letztens hatte se, hat se nich was vom
        Seminar, und. wie war das noch? Das war aber schon
        dieser Tage doch!
        [Yes, but recently she,didn't she about a seminar
        and what was it all about? But that's a few days
        ago!]
A:      ((3s)) Nee, ich hatte sie beim / im Innenhof von
        der
        Universität abgeholt um zwei Uhr!
        [No, I piscked her up at/ from the courtyard of
        the university at two o'clock!
B:      Jaja, das weiß ich! ((3s)) Ja, das is aber blöd
        jetz!
        [Yes, yes, I know that. Well, that really is messy
        now!]
A:      Ich wußte auch gar nich, wo se um sechs Uhr dann
        sein würde!
        [I really didn't know, where she'd be at six
        o'clock]
```

(BRO 15 Bd 4/2)

In all these occurrences as modal particle ABER expresses 'astonishment/surprise'. The clauses ABER occurs in serve as exclamations and ABER further emphasises the aspect of 'surprise' that is part of the illocutionary force of an exclamation. 'Surprise' may refer to the extent of divergence from what is expected (as in lines 2-6) or it may refer to the fact that there is divergence from expectations at all (as in line 1). The dialogue between speakers A and B revolves around the fact that speaker A failed to meet speaker B's daughter as arranged. In her first utterance containing the modal particle ABER (line 1), speaker B expresses her surprise at the fact that A and her daughter did not meet – her expectation was that they would meet, she is surprised about the divergence from her expectations. In the course of the dialogue B learns details about the failed meeting and her following utterances containing the modal particle ABER express her surprise about the extent of divergence from her expectations. Lines 2 and 3 are uttered ironically; B's evaluation is a negative one, as is obvious in lines 4, 5 and 6:

1	Ja, das is **aber** komisch!	Well, that **sure** is strange!
2	Ja, das is **aber** gut!	Well, that **really** is great!
3	Ja, das is **aber** gut!	Well, that **really** is great!
4	Das is **aber** dumm,	That **really** is a nuisance,
5	Das ist **aber** ganz ei / ganz ungeheures Mißverständnis!	that **really** is a / **what** a misunderstanding!
6	Ja, das is **aber** blöd jetz!	Well, that **really** is messy now!

The element of 'surprise' is particularly salient in the occurrence of ABER in line 7, as the following excerpt shows:

Line 7

B: Wie lange hader denn noch Urlaub?
[How long is he on leave for then?]
A: Bis Donnerstag!
[Till Thursday]
B: Eh, Freitag muß der wider arbeiten? **Is aber blöd!** So einen Tag in der Woche noch!
[Er, he's got to work again on Friday? **How annoying!** That one working day!]

(BRO 8 Bd 2/4)

Speaker B answers speaker A's move, which provides a particular piece of information, with an interrogative that is not asking for information, but is rhetorical in nature, expressing incredulity. The following utterance containing the modal particle ABER emphasises the surprise about the information given by A: the expectation being that people start work again on Mondays after a having had a holiday. Here, it is particularly clear that the utterance containing ABER refers to the wider context of the situation, namely to common knowledge about 'how things are normally done'.

The occurrence of ABER in line 8 is introduced by another element expressing 'surprise':

Line 8

C: Hör ma, was is denn das für'n komisches Geräusch im Hintergrund?
[Listen, what kind of funny sound is that in the background, then?]
B: Ja, ich sag dir, die A näht da in ihrem Zimmer!
[Yes, let me tell you, A is sewing in her room1]
C: Die A näht?
[A is sewing?]
B: Ich versteh kaum noch en Wort!
[I can hardly hear anything now!]
C: Mensch, **die kann aber auch alles**, die Frau, die is praktisch veranlagt/
[Boy, **that woman really knows how to do everything**, she's got practical talent]

(BRO 30 Bd 5/5)

The interjection "Mensch", which precedes the utterance containing ABER indicates surprise in itself which is then specified by the clause containing ABER. Not quite as distinct is the occurrence of ABER in line 9, shown in context in the following excerpt:

Line 9

A: Undie Arbeit macht ihr zwar im Augenblick noch keinen Spaß
[and she doesn't like the work very much yet]
B: hm
A: aber vielleicht kommd's noch, so, vor allen Dingen will sie ja promovieren jetz, undann brauch se eh schon ma zwei Jahre, un auch zwei Jahre Ruhe zu.
[but maybe that'll come later, most of all she wants to get her doctorate now, you know, and then she needs two years to start with, and two years with peace and quiet, that is]
B: **Das is aber sehr schön.**
[That is really excellent]
A: Un hinterher kann se ja weiter sehn, dann
[And later on she'll see then]

(BRO 21 Bd 11/1)

Speaker A (male) is talking to a friend (speaker B, female) about his wife's career plans. It seems to me, that in this occurrence an element of surprise is less obvious at a first glance. However, when taking the wider context of the speech event into account the function of ABER as expressing surprise about the extent of divergence from expectations becomes clear. Preceding the excerpt shown above, B had asked A whether his wife was working as a teacher now – that was the information she had prior to the conversation with B. She then learns that A's wife is now working as a research assistant at a university. B's move containing ABER sums up her surprise about the career developments of A's wife, it does not only refer to A's preceding utterance. Whereas ABER as a conjunction/conjunctional adverb expresses a contrast on the textual level of the dialogue, e.g. by contrasting two adverse propositions as in (see line 1, conjunction):

> Da kamen se beide hin, **aber** sonst sehen die sich nie!
> [They both attended that, **but** other than that they never meet]

ABER in its function as modal particle operates on the interpersonal level of the dialogue, emphasising the subjective evaluation by the speaker. This function is particularly obvious in relational clauses[104], where the main verb is 'sein' ('to be'):

das	is	aber	komisch!
das	is	aber	gut!
das	is	aber	gut!
Das	is	aber	dumm,
Das	ist	aber	ganz ei/ganz ungeheures Mißverständnis
das	is	aber	blöd jetz!
(ellipsed)	Is	aber	blö!
Das	is	aber	sehr schön
Carrier	Process: relational Intensive: attributive		Attribute

104 "relational" is here used as a systemic functional term as coined by Halliday (e.g. 1994).

Subject	Finite/ Predicator	Interpersonal Adjunct Modality: Implicit	Adjunct/ Complement
Mood	Resi-	Mood	due

ABER is part of the *attribute* ascribed to the *carrier*, which in all these occurrences in the BRO data is a deictic, linking the utterance to a preceding stretch of dialogue. ABER is not, however, part of the *adjunct*, the quality ascribed to the *carrier*, rather, it is part of the Mood structure, adding the element of subjective evaluation mentioned above.

What ABER is implying in the above occurrences is:

> "I am surprised how (+attribute)"

In the one occurrence in the BRO data, where it does not appear in a relational clause:

`Mensch, die kann` **`aber`** `auch alles`

it implies:

> "I am surprised that…"

The implication in relational clauses as outlined above: "I am surprised how…" can in general terms be translated by a phrase like "That really is …", where "really" is carrying the main stress. In occurrences, where the implication is "I am surprised that…" translations into English of ABER are context dependent and carried to a large extent by intonational patterns expressing 'surprise'.

In summary, it can be said that ABER as a modal particle links the actual speech event with a wider context – with 'what is expected'; shared knowledge – and serves to enhance the element 'surprise' in an utterance with the illocutionary force 'exclamation'.

Summary of results: ABER

Position in clause	**Grammatical co-occurence**	**Lexical collocation**	**Discursive function**	**Category**	**Meaning**
initial			expressing contrast at text level	conjunction	'but'
medial			expressing contrast at text level	conjunction al adverb	'but'
medial	exclamative deictic (e.g. 'das')	verb 'sein'	expressing contrast to speaker's expectiations	modal particle	expression of surprise "X really is Y"
medial	exclamative		expressing contrast to speaker's expectations	modal particle	expression of surprise

Sample Work Sheet: ABER

1.) The word ABER has different meanings which depend on the context of use. In general terms, it is used to express contrast. Can you find out by looking at the following groups of examples which meaning of ABER they represent?

but	***expression of surprise***

Group 1

```
1   Ausstellung. Da kamen se beide hin, aber sonst sehn die sich  nie!     B:  Ja
2   Daß man da jetz aufgezeichnet wird. Aber ich warte nich  mehr so lang mit de
3  B:  oder zwei A:  das is alles Mist! Aber ich hab auch keine Lust, an die Sch
4  dann kannsde, em, eingesetzt werden, aber nur ganz  minimal. A:  Hm B:  Un di
5  auf Comics im  Augenblick. Lesen ja, aber nich zeichnen, weißde. B:  Ja. A:
6   immer zu sagen. A:  Ja, du gibs dir aber sons Mühe! B:  Ja, wenn das Ding da
7   Ja. A:  ja, gut! B:  Wahrscheinlich aber dann nich, die werden dann ja  best
8  aber dumm, da  hätt se / A:  Sie hat aber auch nich hier angerufen. B:  Nee?
9  B:  Ja, is klar, ersmal/ A:  Ich hab aber inzwischen gehört, daß das also wir
1  da hatter gesacht, Silvester hätter  aber keine Zeit, und er würd doch so ger
```

Group 2

```
1 gemacht für sechs Uhr. B:  Ja, das is aber komisch! Ja, dann wundert mich, daß !
2  nich, wohin um sechs! B:  Ja, das is aber gut! A:  Verflucht! 85 B:  Hatten S
3 o ne irrsinnige Hetze! B:  Ja, das is aber gut! Ich dachte, das wär so ausgema
4 ieben, ja, nehm ich doch an! . Das is aber dumm, da  hätt se / A:  Sie hat abe
5 prochen haben. B:  Tja, sowas, das is aber ganz ei / A:  so zwischen / B:  gan
6 Jaja, das weiß ich! ((3s)) Ja, das is aber blöd jetz! A:  Ich wußte auch gar n
7 h, Freitag muß der wider arbeiten? Is aber blöd! So einen  Tag in der Woche no !
8 um noch en Wort! C:  Mensch, die kann aber auch alles, die Frau, die is prakti !
9 n auch zwei Jahre Ruhe zu. B:  Das is aber sehr schön. A:  Un hinterher kann s
```

Group 1 ____________________

Group 2 ____________________

2.) Which verb appears in most clauses in Group 2? What tense is it in?

____

____

3.) Now study the following two examples of ABER in the context of a dialogue and the explanations for its use given below.

```
B:    Wie lange hat der denn noch Urlaub?
A:    Bis Donnerstag!
B:    Eh, Freitag muß der wieder arbeiten? Is aber
      blöd! So einen Tag in der Woche noch!
```

Speaker B answers speaker A, who provides a particular piece of information ("Bis Donnerstag"), with a question which is not asking for information, but is rhetorical in nature, expressing incredulity. The following expression containing the modal particle ABER emphasises the surprise about the information given by A: the expectation being that people start work again on Mondays after a having had a holiday.

Here, ABER refers to the wider context of the situation, namely to common knowledge about "how things are normally done". ABER here emphasises the subjective evaluation by the speaker. This function of ABER is particularly obvious in clauses, where the main verb is 'sein' ('to be'). What ABER is implying in such occurrences is:

```
"I am surprised how (+ attribute) "
```

which can in general terms be translated by a phrase like “That really is …”, where “really” is carrying the main stress.

4.) Now let’s have a look at another example of ABER in context:

C: .. Hör ma, was is denn das für’n komisches Geräusch im
Hintergrund?

B: Ja, ich sag dir, die A näht da in ihrem Zimmer!

C: Die A näht?

B: Ich versteh kaum noch en Wort!

C: Mensch, die kann aber auch alles, die Frau, die is praktisch
veranlagt/

Here, the clause with ABER is introduced by another element expressing ‘surprise’: The interjection “Mensch” indicates surprise in itself ABER here implies:

“I am surprised that…”

In such occurrences translations of ABER into English are context dependent and would be expressed in English by intonational patterns expressing ‘surprise’.

5.9 AUCH

There are 415 occurrences of AUCH in 27 texts in BRO. AUCH occurs either as modal particle or as focus particle, but the distinction between the two categories is difficult[105], particularly on the basis of written concordance data only, as focus particle and modal particle differ through intonation patterns not visible in the written version of the data.

Focus particle

AUCH can be categorised as focus particle if its scope can be clearly identified to be a noun phrase rather than the clause on the whole. This is the case when AUCH is found to occur in clause initial position, as in the following examples:

1	ei uns hat keiner die Ringe gesegnet.	**Auch**	bei der Hochzeit nicht, wir ham au
2	Schön, ne? A: Ja? Was denn? B: Hm.	**Auch**	als Technischer Zeichner. Also, in
3	a. B: Da kannsde nix mehr sagen, du.	**Auch**	jetz zu dieser Demonstration in Ka

or in clauses where the verb has been ellipsed:

4	s, ich weiß gar nix mehr. A: Ja, ich	**auch**.	B: Ja, da rufen wer noma an, ne.
5	h bin total doof da drin. B: Ja, ich	**auch**.	C: Da is die A ja wirklich . im V
6	kenn den ja. B: Na, ich ja im Grunde	**auch**.	Da ham wer eben/ C: Ja, ich hab d
7	hterlich! A: Ja B: Bekannte von mir	**auch**,	die haben am 27. Scheidungstermin.
8	, is Wahnsinn. Gut. Machs gut! A: Du	**auch**!	B: Bestell viele Grüße! A: Jau!
9	h non schönen Abend, ne? A: Wir euch	**auch**!	Ne? B: Is ja nich viel im Fernseh
10	ankheitskur an! A: Ja? Ihr auch? Wir	**auch**!	Endgültig? B: Ja, nich endgültig,
11	e. B: (lacht) Ja, bei mir vielleicht	**auch**!	C: Naja, wie gesacht, e / B: Ja,
12	A: Joa. B: Jut dann mach's jut! A: Du	**auch**!	B: Hm. A: Tschüs, B! B: Tschüschen
13	n Glückwunsch! 42 B: Danke! Wieso, du	**auch**?	A: Ja, am 24.! B: Nachträglich h
14	t die Schlankheitskur an! A: Ja? Ihr	**auch**?	Wir auch! Endgültig? B: Ja, nich
15	brav, besauft euch nicht/ A: Du dich	**auch**	nicht! B: Ne, was meinsde, was das
16	ich genug Geld bekomme. B: Du, ich	**auch**	absolut nich. Es gibt nämig soo vie
17	d nich arbeiten gehen! 51 B: Ja, ich	**auch**	nich, Mann! Da wärn wir ja auch dum
18	ieben? B: Wahnsinnig viel Literatur,	**auch**	Sekundärliteratur über den, und ic
19	e Kopie meiner Eltern A: (lacht) B:	**auch**	von Aussehn, ne A: Das gibt's gar

105 cf. Thurmair (1989: 155): "Gerade in den Aussagesätzen ist die Unterscheidung zwischen *auch* in Gradpartikel- und Modalpartikel-Funktion oft recht schwierig."; see also Bublitz 1978.

As focus particle, the function of AUCH is to link clausal elements by addition. It can be translated into English in the sense of 'too', 'also', 'as well' as the following excerpts show:

Line 5

```
C:    Ja, ich weiß überhaupt nich, wie man ne
      Nähmaschine bedient, ich bin total doof da drin.
      [Well, I don't have any idea how to use a sewing
      machine, I am really stupid with that kind of
      thing.]
B:    Ja, ich auch.
      [Yes, me too. /Yes, so am I.]
```

(BRO 30 Bd 5/5)

Line 12

```
A:    Joa.
      [Yeah.]
B:    Jut dann mach's jut!
      [Well, all the best to you!]
A:    Du auch!
      [To you, too.]
```

(BRO 21 Bd 11/1)

In clauses with negative polarity AUCH may be translated by 'neither':

Line 17

```
A:    Also, wenn mir jemand anbieten würde, mir mein
      Gehalt so zu zahlen, ich würd nich arbeiten gehen!
      [Well, if someone offered to pay my salary just
      like that, I wouldn't work!]
B:    Ja, ich auch nich, Mann!
      [Yes, me neither, man!]
```

(BRO 8 Bd 2/4)

For most occurrences in the BRO data, it is not possible to interpret the meaning of AUCH on the basis of the concordance data alone. The meaning of AUCH is ambivalent without information about intonation patterns and/or about the linguistic context surrounding the clause containing AUCH. The following concordance line exemplifies this:

ie Nord-Süd-Fahrt, das kennen Sie ja **auch**? A: Jaja. B: Nord-Süd-Fahrt, käme

There are two ways of interpreting the clause: "das kennen Sie ja auch"

4) AUCH = focus particle, expressing addition
→ [you know that too, don't you]
stress would be on 'Sie': "das kennen Sie ja **auch**"

5) AUCH = modal particle, asking for reconfirmation
→ [you do know that, don't you]
stress would be on 'kennen': "das kennen Sie ja **auch**"

Modal particle

When looking at the clause within a larger stretch of discourse the meaning of AUCH is less opaque:

B: ja, die bin ich jahrelang gefahren, da . müssen Sie mit einem Stau rechnen. Und dann müßten Sie durch die gesamte .. Innenstadt, das heißt, Sie führen die Nord-Süd-Fahrt, das kennen Sie ja auch?
[yes, I took that route for years, there. you have to be prepared for a lot of traffic. And then you would have {to drive} through all of the ..inner city, that is, you'd take the north-south-route, you do know that, don't you?]

A: Jaja.
[Yesyes.]

B: Nord-Süd-Fahrt, kämen am . Ebert-Platz aus, . kenn Se den?
[North-south-route, you'd arrive at Ebert square, you know that?]

A: Ja, sicher.
[yes, sure.]

(BRO 32 Bd 10/7)

In the context of the dialogue it is obvious that here the function of AUCH is to ask for reconfirmation. Speaker A responds to speaker B by confirming "yesyes". It is interesting to note that AUCH here collocates with the modal particle JA. Whereas the use of JA implies that a fact is known to both interlocutors (for details see Chapter 5.10), AUCH as modal particle in a yes/no question as discussed above expresses a slight doubt. The combination of both particles thus emphasises the speaker's wish to have the hearer reconfirm the proposition posed in the interrogative, as shown above.

With more than 10% of total occurrences (42 instances), the collocation of AUCH with JA is frequent in the BRO data:

1 die Nord-Süd-Fahrt, das kennen Sie	**ja auch**	? A: Jaja. B: Nord-Süd-Fahrt, kämen
2 . nich irgendwie was Großes, weils	**ja auch**	so viele sin un dann sehr wer zu, d
3 noch! B: Hmhm. A: Ja, das reicht	**ja auch**	, solang das noch bleibt, so B: Ja,
4 / B: So / A: Englisch hab ich	**ja auch**	gar keine Unterrichts / B: Neenee, i
5 Maus-Hefte auf Englisch, ne, gibt's	**ja auch**	jede Menge. B: Ach so, die hab ik a
6 : Ja? B: Ich mein, kenns ja Y, is	**ja auch**	ziemlich schüchtern un zurückhalten
7 n gutes Werk getan, wenn Ihre Frau	**ja auch**	abjenomm / B: Oh, die hat mich ganz
8 n denn sowas hörst!.. Jaa, ich hab	**ja auch**	en sehr . angenehmes Weihnachtsfest
9 erheiratet war. A: Jaja.. Un es is	**ja auch**	so . bei . öh . den / ich mein, bei
10nd so B: ja, mit Musik ham die das	**ja auch**	gemacht, hm, so Märsche und so A:
11ie weiß das. A: Hm. B: Und daß wär	**ja auch**	ne . also, ö, daß so unter der Hand
12n Tag früher aufhörst, dann kannsde	**ja auch**	schließlich en Tag früher gehn, ne
13h Hause, und so weiter! A: Hm.. Is	**ja auch**	nich grade viel! 112 B: Nö, also . v
14in ja hier auch dran. Ich füll das	**ja auch**	aus. B: Ja, müssen mer ma vorbeikom
15B: Hja, gute Lage, die kriecht man	**ja auch**	immer wieder los. A: Naja, aber isj
16h, nee. A: Ja, ich mein, ich hab's	**ja auch**	wieder aufgeschoben, ne. B: Was has
17in. Das gilt für uns alle. Ich hab	**ja auch**	nen weiten Weg. Ne, wir könn alle nu
18wer direkt tanzen gegangen. Du bis	**ja auch**	vielleicht ne Type! B: Och, jetz bi
19e, also schon,ne/ B: Ja, (	**ja auch**	) A: ((gleichzeitig)) ( ) drin
20mere auch noch! B: Ja, den gibt es	**ja auch**	! Wird zwar en bißchen anders geschr
21appt schon! C: (lacht) B: Ich hab	**ja auch**	nichts gegen Feten feiern und Bier t
22war's . ganz ulkig. Aber .kann ich	**ja auch**	, wenn wer da sind, was länger erzähl
23t) A: (lacht) Stark! . Ja, ich bin	**ja auch**	schon fast en alter Ehekrüppel. B:
24ht) B: Naja, so . ja, dann wirders	**ja auch**	verlängern . nur, du mußt dir das w
25 so, an un für sich, da hätt er dir	**ja auch**	einreden können, du hättest se gema
26bald ma verheiratet is, da hat man	**ja auch**	die Pflicht, so schnell wie möglich
27r uns ma wieder ne? A: Ja, das war	**ja auch**	wirklich lange, ne? B: Ja Jaja, gu
28: Ja, wenn's ja nichts frißt, kann	**ja auch**	hinten nix rauskommen! A: Jaja.. A
29mehr fest ausgemacht, un ich wußte	**ja auch**	gar nich, wohin um sechs! B: Ja, da
30e angefangen has? B: Ja, ich kann	**ja auch**	jetz nich fottgehn hier, ne. A: Ja
31 Vermutlich... Naja. 40 A: Wir ham	**ja auch**	so recht plötzlich geheiratet, nich,
32 sicher. 176 B: Ne, das werden Sie	**ja auch**	wohl tun, nich, Frau A? A: jaaa.. B
33man aber oft, du. ((3s)) Ich bin da	**ja auch**	immer skeptisch, wenn ich sowas hör
34f doch nicht! Jaja, sicher, hab ich	**ja auch**	gesacht!... Und?.. Was macht er den
35ser Bestes daran und wir wolln das	**ja auch**	, aber . irgendwann wolln wer auch m
36ht) A: (lacht) Ja, richtig, stimmt	**ja auch**	! (lacht) Ich vergeß das Ding auch s
37 also / B: Och, ich mein, Steak is	**ja auch**	en Schlankheitsessen, ne. A: Ja, ma
38ches Urteil bilden A: dann hörste	**ja auch**	verschiedene Sachen, ne. B: Ach, hi
39n wieder längst vergessen, naja, is	**ja auch**	egal. B: ( ) Ich hab da einige sild
40 es läuft. B: Ja, ne. Es quietscht	**ja auch**	nich. A: Has ja nich umsorst deine
41 (lacht) Ja, die Leute, die spinnen	**ja auch**	so. Sobald ma verheiratet is, da ha
42a, ich auch nich, Mann! Da wärn wir	**ja auch**	dumm! Aber wo findet man schon jema

With the exception of line 1, which has been discussed above, the clauses containing the collocation JA AUCH are declaratives or exclamatives. In these instances – if both JA and AUCH are not stressed – the combination of both particles functions discursively in that the utterance is linked to the preceding text. JA points to shared knowledge between speaker and hearer (for a detailed analysis see Chapter 5.10), whereas AUCH implicitly acknowledges the preceding proposition – the combined force of both particles is then to imply that there is nothing surprising about the proposition(s) put forth in the preceding text, as the following example shows:

Line 15

```
B:    Wieviel Quadratmeter warn das denn?
      [How many square metres did it have then?]
A:    Achtzig, also 160.000 Mark wollten die haben.
      [Eighty, so they wanted 160,000 marks for it.]
B:    Hja, gute Lage, die kriecht man ja auch immer
      wieder los.
      [Well, a good position, you can always sell that
      again]
A:    Naja, aber isja schon alt, ne.
      [yes, but then it's old, isn't it?]
```

(BRO 29 Bd 5/6)

This stretch of dialogue is an excerpt from a conversation between a female (speaker A) and an older close relative (speaker B), who is also female, about A's plans for buying an apartment or a house. B' s turn containing the utterance "die kriecht man JA AUCH immer wieder los" is supporting the proposition put forth in A's preceding turn "160.000 Mark wollten die haben". The addition of the two particles JA and AUCH links B's utterance to this proposition and marks agreement with it while implicitly expressing causality: 160, 000 marks are not too much money for the apartment because it is in a good position and can therefore be easily resold.

As I implied earlier, the above explanation only refers to occurrences of JA AUCH where the intonation pattern is such that both particles do not carry stress. If AUCH is stressed in these collocations with JA, it functions in an additive manner, as described under 'focus particle'.

Summary of results: AUCH

Position in clause	Grammatical co-occurence	Lexical collocation	Category	Meaning
initial			focus particle	'also', 'too', 'as well'
initial	negative polarity		focus particle	'neither'
medial/final	ellipsis of verb		focus particle	'also', 'too', 'as well'
medial/final	ellipsis of verb negative polarity		focus particle	'neither'
medial/final	no stress yes/no interrogative	JA	modal particle	asking for information
medial/final	no stress declarative exclamative	JA	modal particle	acknowledging and providing explanation

As I have outlined above, the findings of a concordance-based analysis of AUCH are restricted in that they cannot take into account the intonation patterns of occurrences of AUCH and thus cannot provide a proper disambiguation of the different functions of AUCH. The sample work sheet below is therefore to be seen as an introduction to focusing on the meaning of the particle AUCH and would need to be complemented by audiorecorded data which reflect different intonational patterns and their impact on the meaning of auch.

Sample Work Sheet: AUCH

1.) The word AUCH may have different meanings depending on its context of use. Please look carefully at the following groups of examples and decide which translation or description (in italics) best captures the meaning of AUCH in each group.

also/ too/ as well	neither	acknowledgement/ explanation

Group 1 ____________________

Group 2 ____________________

Group 3 ____________________

Group 1

ei uns hat keiner die Ringe gesegnet. **Auch** bei der Hochzeit nicht, wir ham au
brav, besauft euch nicht/ A: Du dich **auch** nicht! B: Ne, was meinsde, was das
ich genug Geld bekomme. B: Du, ich **auch** absolut nich. Es gibt nämig soo vie
d nich arbeiten gehen! 51 B: Ja, ich **auch** nich, Mann! Da wärn wir ja auch dum

Group 2

Schön, ne? A: Ja? Was denn? B: Hm. **Auch** als Technischer Zeichner. Also, in
B: Da kannsde nix mehr sagen, du. **Auch** jetz zu dieser Demonstration in Ka
s, ich weiß gar nix mehr. A: Ja, ich **auch**. B: Ja, da rufen wer noma an, ne.
h bin total doof da drin. B: Ja, ich **auch**. C: Da is die A ja wirklich . im V
kenn den ja. B: Na, ich ja im Grunde **auch**. Da ham wer eben/ C: Ja, ich hab d
hterlich! A: Ja B: Bekannte von mir **auch**, die haben am 27. Scheidungstermin.
, is Wahnsinn. Gut. Machs gut! A: Du **auch**! B: Bestell viele Grüße! A: Jau!
h non schönen Abend, ne? A: Wir euch **auch**! Ne? B: Is ja nich viel im Fernseh
ankheitskur an! A: Ja? Ihr auch? Wir **auch**! Endgültig? B: Ja, nich endgültig,
e. B: (lacht) Ja, bei mir vielleicht **auch**! C: Naja, wie gesacht, e / B: Ja,

Group 3

```
ich irgendwie was Großes, weils ja auch so  viele sin un dann sehn wer zu, d
noch!  B:  Hmhm. A:  Ja, das reicht ja auch, solang das noch bleibt, so B:  Ja,
 /      B: So / A: Englisch hab ich ja auch gar keine Unterrichts / B: Neenee, i
Maus-Hefte auf Englisch, ne, gibt's ja auch jede Menge. B:  Ach so, die hab ik a
:  Ja? B:  Ich mein, kenns ja Y, is ja auch ziemlich schüchtern un  zurückhalten
n gutes Werk  getan, wenn Ihre Frau ja auch abjenomm / B:  Oh, die hat mich ganz
n denn sowas hörst!.. Jaa, ich  hab ja auch en sehr . angenehmes Weihnachtsfest
erheiratet war. A:  Jaja.. Un es is ja auch so . bei . öh . den / ich mein, bei
nd so B:  ja, mit Musik ham die das ja auch gemacht, hm, so Märsche  und so A:.
ie weiß das. A:  Hm. B: Und das wär ja auch ne . also, ö, daß so unter der Hand
```

2.) Now look at the following stretch of dialogue. Here you will find an example of AUCH in context. The example, which is representative of the meaning of AUCH in Group 3, shows how AUCH can be used by a speaker (here B) to ask for acknowledgement:

B: ja, die bin ich jahrelang gefahren, da . müssen Sie mit einem Stau rechnen. Und dann müßten Sie durch die gesamte .. Innenstadt, das heißt, Sie führen die Nord-Süd-Fahrt, das kennen Sie ja auch?
[yes, I took that route for years, there. you have to be prepared for alot of traffic. And then you would have {to drive} through all of the ..inner city, that is, you'd take the north-south-route, you do know that, don't you?]

A: Jaja.
[Yesyes.]

B: Nord-Süd-Fahrt, kämen am . Ebert-Platz aus, . kenn Se den?
[North-south-route, you'd arrive at Ebert square, you know that?]

A: Ja, sicher.
[Yes, sure.]

In the example above, neither JA nor AUCH would be stressed. The emphasis in the question asked by B "das kennen Sie ja auch?" would be on 'kennen'.

5.10 JA

There are 1481 occurrences of JA in 35 texts in BRO. In the majority of cases by far (868 occurrences), JA is to be found turn-initial, either on its own or in collocation with other particles (e.g. DOCH) or interjections (e.g. 'ach so'). In these instances it functions discursively as a response signal (cf. Schiffrin 1987 on WELL) and its high frequency can be ascribed to the nature of the data – telephone dialogues – where the speakers are limited to signal response verbally without recourse to non-verbal response signals (e.g. facial expressions and gestures).

Discursive function: turn-initial[106]

Earlier on, I discussed EBEN (see 5.2), SCHON (see 5.5) and DOCH (see 5.6) in their functions as answering particle. JA in turn-initial position may also serve as an answering particle but its discursive function is wider than that of EBEN, SCHON and DOCH, as outlined further below.

In turn-initial position, JA may signal agreement with the interlocutor's previous utterance:

1 Öh, das is auf der linken Seite? B: **Ja**, links, ja. Rechts is ja unbebaut, d
2 Ebert-Platz aus, . kenn Se den? A: **Ja**, sicher. B: Gut! Führen ein kleinen
3 Ah, Sie haben eine Fußgängerzone? B: **Ja** A: Hm B: Ja, in der wohnen wir sel
4 Fete/ B: Jo, is das der Y, jetz? A: **Ja**! B: Ach prima, has du mit dem gespr
5 B: Könnwer ja essen gehn! A: **Ja**. B: In der Quelle. Steak. A: Wie a
6 . soviel / kann jamal versuchen! B: **Ja**. Mußde ma ausprobieren. A: Vielleic
7 Sons hattesdu ja noch viel mehr! B: **Ja**! Aber ganz groß wirdes nich, viele s
8 / brauch ja nich lange denn sein! A:**Ja**. B: Weil ja / wenns mitten in der W
9 . wieder mal die Eßbremse ziehen. D: **Ja**, eben, kann ich verstehn, dat kann i
10 angerufen, aber da war keiner da! A:**Ja**, das is gut möglich B: Nee, ich war

The agreement expressed by JA may be in response to an interrogative[107] (lines 1-4) or in response to a declarative (lines 5-10).

106 I have not provided a full list of occurrences of JA in turn initial position, as the examples given in the text outline its major functions and a full list would have been very extensive without contributing additional information.

107 Lines 1&3 are structurally declaratives, i.e. there is no inversion, their interrogative force is brought about by rising intonation, here indicated by the question mark.

In such instances, JA is functioning as an answering particle and translates into English as ‘yes’, as the following example shows:

Line 1

A: Öh, das is auf der linken Seite?
[Err, is that to the left?]
B: **Ja**, links, ja. Rechts is ja unbebaut, da is das
[**Yes**, left, yes. The right side is not built up, there is]

(BRO 28 Bd 5/2)

JA does not only signal agreement on the textual level, i.e. agreement with the interlocutor’s proposition, but it also has an interactive function by contributing to the turn-taking system. Thus, it marks the speaker’s turn-taking, it introduces his/her following utterance. This may happen either in response to the interlocutor, as in the following occurrences:

11 jetz nimmer angerufen. A: Klar! B: **Ja**, ich war au zwischendurch mal in Wer
12 Wie geht’s Ihnen? A: Guut, joa. B:**Ja**... öh, Sie ham mir hier en paar Frag
13 hm A: aber das dürfte mir blühen B: **ja**, das wird in der nachsten Zeit wahrs
14 auch nur mit eim aus unserm Haus. A: **Ja**, Öh / B: So / A: Englisch hab i
15 bloß noch Quark un sowas! C: (lacht). **Ja**, nee, das müssen wer aber unbedingt

where JA can be translated by the English response marker ‘well’ (cf. Schiffrin 1987):

Line 12

B: Wie geht’s Ihnen?
[How are you?]
A: Guut, joa.
[Good, yes.]
B: **Ja**... öh, Sie ham mir hier en paar Fragen gestellt
[**Well**,...err, you asked me a few questions here]

(BRO 33 Bd 17/3)

In other instances, JA is used when the speaker interrupts his/her interlocutor’s turn:

16 aber noch mal anrufen, und zwar/ B: **Ja**, dann rufsde aber so/wenns geht so m
17 weißde, von dem ich dir dieses / B: **Ja**, ich weiß! . Taschenbuch, oder? A:
18 das sind alles so fiese Vororte / B: **Ja**, geht doch linksrheinisch! 138 A: J

In these instances, the function of JA can be seen as twofold: on the one hand it serves to acknowledge the interlocutor's proposition, on the other hand it marks the beginning of the speaker's utterance, so that a translation into English with 'yes' seems appropriate[108]:

Line 18

A: ...das sind alles so fiese Vororte /
[.. they are all such horrible suburbs/]
B: Ja, geht doch linksrheinisch!
[Yes, why don't you look on the left bank of the Rhine!]

(BRO 29 Bd 5/6)

In turn-initial position, JA occurs also on its own:

19	Nee, dat reicht ja nun noch, ne! A:	**Ja**? B:	Ich hab so ne große Liste un so
20	damit wer schön einschlafen, ne. B:	**Ja**? A:	Unda hab ich da den Rotwein von
21	a guck ich auch noch ma n bißchen B:	**ja**? A:	da bei denen, dann deck ich mic
22	so daß also das nur bis zum 1.4. B:	**ja** A:	liefe mit dieser Regelung. B: J
23	furchtbar! Ach, die war so fertig A:	**ja** B:	die / die hat richtig geheult im
24	Stadtbücherei, öh, die Geschäfte A:	**ja** B:	un Schulen, und, em, na, Büchere

In such instances, it can be interpreted as backchanelling (e.g. Brown & Yule 1983): JA here serves to provide feedback to the interlocutor by letting him/her know, that s/he has the listener's attention and by encouraging him/her to continue talking. Again, the translation into English is 'yes'.

Line 19

B: Nee, dat reicht ja nun noch, ne!
[No, that's still enough now, isn't it?]
A: **Ja**?
[**Yes**?]
B: Ich hab so ne große Liste un so
[I have such a long list and so]

(BRO 9 Bd 2/2)

108 An alternative translation would be 'you're right', which expresses the acknowledgement of the interlocutor's previous utterance even more explicitly.

Discursive function: medial and final position in a turn

In addition to the large number of occurrences of JA in utterance-initial position, where it appears on its own or separate from the following proposition, JA as a discourse marker also occurs within a speaker's turn, but separate from the preceding or subsequent proposition (204 occurrences).

When followed by a proposition, it introduces this proposition and connects it to the preceding text, as in the following examples:

25 krichten wir so interessante Briefe: **Ja,** das wär ja schön, so schnell verhe
26 das A: Ach so, ohne Lohnsteuerkarte. **Ja,** dann geht es B: so schlecht is das
27 das, was wir uns nich leisten können. **Ja,** so zweihundertsechzig bis dreihund
28 im Lande, das is ja schon viel wert. **Ja,** mach ich gleich en Kreuzchen, hier
29 Is auch die gleiche Nummer dann noch! **Ja,** mit abends erreichen is en bißchen

JA in these types of occurrences may be translated into English with 'well', as the following example shows:

Line 26

B: ne, ohne Lohnsteuerkarte und so, da lohnt sich das
[no, without a tax file number and so on, then it's worth it]
A: Ach so, ohne Lohnsteuerkarte. **Ja,** dann geht es
[ah, I see without a tax file number. **Well,** then it's possible]

(BRO 8 Bd 2/4)

When JA is tagged onto a proposition, it may be used to ask for confirmation as in the following occurrences, where JA would have been uttered with a rising tone[109]:

109 The question mark used in the data transcription has been taken as a way of indicating rising tone. This is, of course, not as reliable an indication as working with the original spoken text could be.

30 recht. Ich beschreibs Ihnen ma kurz, **ja**? Also, Sie kommen die Frankfurter St
31 en? B: Ja, kommen Se morgen mal eben, **ja**? A: Is gut. Hm, danke. B: Ne? Bidd
32 sehr lange. B: Mit einjen Nachwehen, **ja**? A: Hm, so ungefähr kann man's nenn
33 : Jaja... Warte, ich gebn dir no mal, **ja**? C: Ja, is gut! B: ((4s)) Na? C:
34 ch trage Sie dann schon für 9 Uhr ein, **ja**? A: Ja . das wär gut. B: Un Sie wi

Here, JA would typically be translated into English by the use of a question tag, as exemplified below:

Line 31

B: Ja, kommen Se morgen mal eben, **ja**?
[Well, come over here quickly tomorrow, **won't you**?]
A: Is gut. Hm, danke.
[OK. Hm, thanks.]

(BRO 24 Bd 10/16)

In other instances, exemplified by the following occurrences, JA is not so much asking for confirmation of the preceding proposition by the interlocutor as it is reconfirming the speaker's proposition and at the same time indicating the end of the speaker's turn. Here, JA would be uttered with a falling rather than a rising tone:

35 ntuell noch mal! A: Ja, das wär fein, **ja**! B: Jedenfalls schön, daß du angeru
36 und jetz off eenma sind se ausenander, **ja** . A: Wann? ((4s)) Wann sind die aus
37 s umsonst? B: Die machen das umsonst, **ja**. A: Ich bin nämlich zur Stadt gegan
38 r direkt zugeschlagen! B: Sehr schön, **ja**. A: Un der fährt noch, ne, die Frau
39 o B: das wird aus der Kasse genommen, **ja**. A: Ja. B: Da zahlt man also r

JA in these occurrences could again be rendered in English by **"yes"**, as the example shows:

Line 37

A: Zum Pfarramt! Die machen das umsonst?
[To the priest's office! They do it for free?]
B: Die machen das umsonst, **ja**.
[They do it for free, **yes**.]

(BRO 3 Bd 1/3)

Modal Particle[110]

There are 402 occurrences of JA as a modal particle in the BRO data, mainly in declaratives (373 occurrences) but also in exclamatives (29 occurrences.)[111]

Declaratives

In declaratives, JA marks the proposition it occurs in as 'known' to both interlocutors (e.g. Helbig 1994, König et al. 1990, Thurmair 1989, Franck 1980, Bublitz 1978) and in this respect its function is similar to that of DOCH (see Chapter 5.6).

1	B: sons atmesde das	**ja**	ein. Das bringt ne schwächere Wanze
2	21 A: Nee, die / Sie wollten ihn	**ja**	für Herrn R un Herrn S gleichsei/ z
3	((lacht)) Ja. Ja, ja. A: Die tu ich	**ja**	sowieso, so/ also . das mach ich man
4	Ach, ja nu! B: Also, hör ma, das is	**ja**	nu keen ( ), also ik schick dir die
5	der W wirds allein schaffen, der muß	**ja**	da / der hat ja als 122 freier Mitar
6	irgendwann ma mit dem / naja, du has	**ja**	keine Zeit / ah, der W wirds allein
7	Is ja gut! Paß ma auf, dann kann ich	**ja**	ma zwischendurch anrufen, sons komm
8	Ja, ich auch nich, Mann! Da wärn wir	**ja**	auch dumm! Aber wo findet man schon
9	Ne, die Frankfurter Straße verbindet	**ja**	Porz mit Köln A: Jaa B: Ne? . KHD-
10	((lacht)) A: Aber solang is die Post	**ja**	nich unterwegs. B: Ja.. Das is glau
11	25 bis 30 Minuten. 88 B: Och, das is	**ja**	kein Problem. Da kamma ja immer noch
12	A: Ah so. B: Nich, dann könnde mans	**ja**	so machen A: Dann . ja, dann würd i
13	A: Ja, ich weiß nich, ich hätte mich	**ja**	eigenlich was früher melden müssen!
14	A: Jaja! Aber solche Sachen wird man	**ja**	immer gefragt. B: Hm... Vermutlich.
15	alles aus B: mal alles aus, weil wer	**ja**	eben wissen müssen, was wer noch ka
16	an zu nähen! C: (lacht) Nee, ich bin	**ja**	sowieso da, ich muß die ganzen Büche
17	anderes mehr leisten. Un dann sin wer	**ja**	noch auf Wohnungssuche! B: (
18	angenommen, ich hab's / sie hat sich	**ja**	noch mit jemand getroffen um halb f
19	ankommen. Wenn des überweist, kommt's	**ja**	sowieso nachm Termin an. Un, öh/ we
20	B: Doch! C: Hör ma, ich erkenn dich	**ja**	demnächst nich mehr. B: (lacht) Ich
21	B: Eh, nein, diesmal nicht, weil ich	**ja**	nicht wieder zum Flughafen zurückko
22	B: Ja, is Klasse, der unterhält dich	**ja**	köstlich, und du wirst dafür auch n
23	bei Z diese Fete, da brauch man sich	**ja**	heute noch gar nich drüber aufregen!
24	Bus, da kannsde ja nich /da kanns du	**ja**	nich fahren. A: Neenee! B: Naja, w
25	dann laß es sein! B: Nö, da könn wer	**ja**	ers mal hören! Ich werd mich ers mal
26	das/ dases nich geklappt hat, das lag	**ja**	dann wohl an der Schule und an der
27	daß man alleine heiratet, das stimmt	**ja**	nicht. Man meint immer, man heirate
28	Dat weiß ich nich.. Aber ich mein, is	**ja**	eigenlich Quatsch, die Vereinbarung
29	denn da nichts Genaues? A: Nä! B: s	**ja**	doof, ne. Und der X läßt sich da au
30	denn der Freund bestanden? B: Der is	**ja**	noch nich fertig. A: Der is noch ni

Like DOCH, JA refers to shared knowledge about what speaker and hearer share and/or to meta-knowledge about what is generally known

110 A full list of JA occuring as modal particle is given in the appendix.

111 In the remaining 7 occurrences out of the total of 1481, JA appears in a stressed form in a concessive function in contrast with aber: JA...ABER ('yes...but'). Due to the very small number of occurrences and the straightforward translation into English I do not discuss these occurrences in more detail.

(cf. Schiffrin 1987 on discourse markers in English). The following excerpt provides an example of JA referring to metaknowledge of a general kind:

Line 9

B:	Wenn Sie die Frankfurter Straße runterkommen, und biegen in die Rösrather Straße ein [When you come along Frankfurter Straße and turn into Rösrather Straße]
A:	Frankfurter Straße
B:	Ne, die Frankfurter Straße verbindet **ja** Porz mit Köln [Well, Frankfurter Straße is the connection between Porz and Cologne, **isn't it**]
A:	Jaa [Yes]

(BRO 28 Bd 5/2)

Through the addition of JA, the proposition "Frankfurter Straße is the connection between Porz and Köln" is introduced as shared knowledge which needs to be taken into account by both interlocutors in the context of the dialogue. Whereas DOCH (see Chapter 5.6) also refers to a perceived difference of opinion, this element is not present in the use of JA. Without pointing to differing assumptions which are to be reconciled in the course of the exchange, JA marks a proposition as a premise which the speaker expects the hearer to share. Like DOCH as a modal particle, JA can be translated into English by a question tag in these types of occurrences.[112]

The type of knowledge JA refers to may be of a specific rather than a general nature, as the following example shows:

112 An alternative translation would be the phrase 'as you know': '...is the connection between Porz and Cologne, as you know." It seems to me, though, that the use of this phrase in English places slightly more emphasis on the reference to common knowledge than JA does in the German version of the text. It might also have a patronising ring to it in the context of a rather informal telephone conversation.

Line 30

A: Guten Tag, hier ist A. Ist die X da?
    [Hello, this is A speaking. Is X there?]
B: Nee, die is nich da, die is im Moment, ich glaub in Hilden oder so, bei ihrem Freund.
    [No, she is not here, she is at the moment, I think in Hilden or somewhere, with her boyfriend.]
A: Ah so...
    [I see...]
B: Die wird also in den nächsten 2,3 Wochen kaum hier auftauchen.
    [So she won't be around much in the next 2 to 3 weeks.]
A: Ah so! Ehm, was is denn/ hat denn der Freund bestanden?
    [I see. Err, what is then/ has her boyfriend passed the exam then?]
B: Der is **ja** noch nich fertig.
    [He hasn't finished yet, **has he**?]
A: Der is noch nich fertig?
    [He hasn't finished?]
B: Nee, ich glaub, der hat die mündlichen Prüfungen noch vor
    sich!
    [No, I think he's still got to do the oral examinations.]

(BRO 5 Bd 1/8)

Here, in addition to marking the proposition "he has not finished" as known, JA implies causality: X's boyfriend has not passed his exams because he has not completed all examinations (not because he failed).

Exclamations

In 29 instances JA occurs in clauses with the illocutionary force 'exclamation':

1 Troisdorf? B: (lacht) Ja. A: Das is **ja** irre! Da wolln wir ja hin ziehen! B:
2 as klappt! A: Ja? B: Das isja / datis **ja** tierisch! A: .. Och, das is echt ne
3 e. Zweienhalb Jahre. B: Ah so, das is **ja** schnell! A: Zweienhalb oder drei B:
4 is jedes Mal dran, ne. A: Och, das is **ja** schlimm! B: Neulich hat se mir erzä
5 s Thema steht jetz fest A: Ja, das is **ja** gut B: ( ) A: Naja, und jetz liest
6 zelabmachung treffen. A: Hoch, das is **ja** ärgerlich! B: Ja, das is sehr ärger
7 Type! B: Och, jetz bin ich's! (Das is **ja**!) C: Du bis alles schuld! B: (lach

8	25 geworden am 24. Dezember. B: Dass	**ja**	passend! Warum denn nich am 25. Deze
9	31. feiern, abends. B: Ja, eben. dass	**ja**	wirklich Klasse! A: Hm. Ja, hoffent
10	! B: (hoffen, vielleicht) Is	**ja**	bald! Kanns vielleicht aber irgendw
11	en un anzuziehen / 70 B: Is	**ja**	gut! Paß ma auf, dann kann ich ja ma
12	ensuppe zu Butterbroten. B: Hmhm, is	**ja**	. reichhaltig! A: Spaghetti is auch
13	lls isses 110 Quadratmeter A: 110! Is	**ja**	irre! Wir ham nur 90! B: In nem gep
14	schon solange her? A: Ja! B: Poh! Is	**ja**	Wahnsinn! ((3s)) A: Ich würd's nich
15	tzt für 3 Tage 400 Mark A: Bo! B: is	**ja**	echtes Geld! Meine Schwester macht a
16	urück, oder wie? C: Ja, genau! B: Is	**ja**	praktisch!.. Schade, ich wär ma gern
17	k einen Sinn, ne. A: Ja, sicher. Is	**ja**	klar! B: Denn . allmählich ermüdet
18	((Anfang fehlt auf Band)) A: der is	**ja**	noch ganz neu (lacht) B: ja, aber d
19	e Viertel. B: nur ne Viertel! Das wär	**ja**	ne Möglichkeit! A: Und dann hätte e
20	B: ((lacht)) A: Aber der Termin war	**ja**	rum! Den hab ich am zehnten bekomme
21	wo versteckt haben. 189 A: Das gibt's	**ja**	gar nich! B: Hm. ((3s)) A: Naja. B:
22	m. Denk ich auch, Mensch, das gibt es	**ja**	nich, die müssen ja knapp vor der S
23	men, und es sich angucken, das klingt	**ja**	sehr gut! (lacht) Öh, is es so/ ach
24	) Ja. A: Das is ja irre! Da wolln wir	**ja**	hin ziehen! B: Jaa. Is das sicher?
25	ch nee, du magst das ja nich/ du darfs	**ja**	nich! B: Nöö, ich mag schon, ich da
26	der so. B: Ja, Mensch, das häuft sich	**ja**!	. Woma sehn, wie wir über die Rund
27	lacht) ja. B: Hm... Nee, das find ich	**ja**	lustig! . Aber ich glaub, das kann
28	ster noch ma? A: Ja! B: Ach, du has	**ja**	Geburtstag! A: Die Tatsache, daB ic
29	nn fürchterlich aussehn, dann wirk der	**ja**	noch dicker! B: Nein, der wirkt nich

In the majority of occurrences (20:29), JA collocates with a form of the verb 'sein'[113] and in nearly all occurrences (with the exception of lines 21&29) it collocates with a deictic ('das', 'der', 'da'; see underlining). The most common deictic is 'das' which JA collocates with in 25 out of the 29 occurrences[114]. The most common pattern by far (17 occurrences) is:

das + ist + JA + Attribute

This pattern in relational clauses is identical to the one for ABER in modal particle function as described earlier in this chapter (see 5.8):

1	Das	is	**ja**	irre!
2	dat	is	**ja**	tierisch!
3	das	is	**ja**	schnell!
4	das	is	**ja**	schlimm!
5	das	is	**ja**	gut
6	das	is	**ja**	ärgerlich
7	das	is	**ja**	*(interrupted)*
8	Das	s	**ja**	passend!
9	Das	s	**ja**	wirklich Klasse!
10	das	Is	**ja**	bald!
11		I	**ja**	gut!

113 ellipsed in lines 8-9 "dass" = das is = das ist

114 "das" is ellipsed in lines 10-18.

12	is	**ja**	reichhaltig!
13	Is	**ja**	irr!
14	Is	**ja**	Wahnsinn!
15	is	**ja**	echtes Geld!
16	Is	**ja**	praktisch!
17	Is	**ja**	klar!

Carrier	Process: relational Intensive: attributive	Attribute

Subject	Finite/ Predicator	Interpersonal Adjunct Modality: Implicit	Adjunct/ Complement
Mood	Resi-	Mood	due

As described for ABER earlier, JA is here part of the *attribute* ascribed to the *carrier*, which in these occurrences is the deictic 'das', linking the utterance to a preceding stretch of dialogue. JA is not, however, part of the *adjunct*, the quality ascribed to the *carrier*, rather, it is part of the Mood structure. It operates on the interpersonal level of the dialogue, emphasising the subjective evaluation by the speaker. In the above occurrences JA is implying:

I am surprised that x is (+attribute)

The following excerpt exemplifies this:

Line 6

B: Also, die stellen sich wirklich an, ja, das wäre schwierig, dann müßte man ja für jede / Hilfskraft extra Abrechnung führen und . die werden ja pauschal bezahlt, da gibt es sonst keinerlei . em . individuelle . Vergütung und ä, das wird eben dadurch erleichtert, daß es nur halbe und ganze Stellen haben, es gibt insgesamt vierzehnhundert und sie könn nich für jeden ne Einzelabmachung treffen.
[Now, they really make a fuss, yes, it would be

difficult, then they would have to keep a separate account for each research assistant and they are being paid a flat rate , aren't they, there is no other inidividual way of payment and err, that is made easier precisely by the fact that there are only half positions and full positions, there are fourteenhundred in total and they can't have some sort of special agreement for each and every one of them.]

A: Hoch, das is **ja** ärgerlich!
[ahh, that is annoying!/that is annoying!]

(BRO 4 Bd 9/2)

In such instances JA is not translated into English by lexical means but rather by an intonation pattern which emphasises the attribute (see underlining). This way of translating JA into English may be applied to all occurrences of JA in exclamatives in the BRO data, though it is not always an attribute which is emphasised (see lines 23-29).

18 der is **ja** noch ganz neu
[he/it is still very new]

19 Das wär **ja** ne Möglichkeit!
[that would be an option]

20 Aber der Termin war **ja** rum!
[but it was past the deadline]

21 Das gibt's **ja** gar nich!
[that's not possible]

22 Mensch, das gibt es **ja** nich,
[boy, that's not possible]

23 das klingt **ja** sehr gut!
[that sounds very good/ that sounds very good]

24 Da wolln wir **ja** hin ziehen!
[that is where we want to move]

25 du magst das **ja** nich/ du darfs **ja** nich!
[you don't like it/you're not allowed to]

26 Ja, Mensch, das häuft sich **ja**!
[yes, boy, it's getting more and more]

27 Hm... Nee, das find ich **ja** lustig!
[well...no,that I find funny]

28 Ach, du has **ja** Geburtstag!
[ah, it's your birthday]

29 dann wirk der **ja** noch dicker!
[then he'll seem even <u>bigger</u>]

The main difference between JA as modal particle in exclamatives and in declaratives lies in the negotiation of agreement between speaker and hearer. Whereas the use of JA in a declarative indicates that the speaker is trying to establish 'common ground' by marking a proposition as known to the hearer, thus inviting him/her to either accept the proposition as premise for the following exchange or to ask for clarification, the use of JA in an exclamative marks the proposition as a subjective appraisal by the speaker. This appraisal contains an element of surprise, as outlined above.

Summary of results: JA

Position in clause	**Grammatical co-occurence**	**Lexical collocation**	**Category**	**Meaning**
inital			answering particle response marker backchannelling	'yes' 'well'/'yes'
final (following proposition)	rising tone		discourse marker	question tag
final (following proposition)	falling tone			'yes'
medial	declarative			question tag
medial	exclamative deictic (e.g. 'das')	verb 'sein'		*expression of surprise* 'X is <u>Y</u>'

Sample Work Sheet: JA

1.) You will already be familiar with the word JA expressing agreement, 'yes' in English. Although JA is frequently used in response to a question this is not always the case as the following examples show:

Group 1

```
1  Öh, das is auf der linken Seite?  B:  Ja, links, ja. Rechts is ja unbebaut, d
2  Ebert-Platz aus, . kenn Se den?   A:  Ja, sicher. B:  Gut! Führen ein kleinen
3  Ah, Sie haben eine Fußgängerzone? B:  Ja A:  Hm B:  Ja, in der wohnen wir sel
4  Fete/ B:  Jo, is das der Y, jetz? A:  Ja! B:  Ach prima, has du mit dem gespr
5          B:  Könnwer ja essen gehn! A: Ja. B:  In der Quelle. Steak. A:  Wie a
6   . soviel / kann jamal  versuchen! B: Ja. Mußde ma ausprobieren. A:  Vielleic
7    Sons hattesdu ja noch viel mehr! B: Ja! Aber ganz groß wirdes nich, viele s
8   / brauch ja nich lange denn  sein! A:Ja. B:  Weil ja / wenns mitten in der W
9   . wieder mal die Eßbremse ziehen. D: Ja, eben, kann ich verstehn, dat kann i
10   angerufen, aber da war keiner da! A:Ja, das is gut möglich B:  Nee, ich war
11  aber noch mal anrufen, und zwar/ B:  Ja, dann rufsde aber so/wenns geht so m
12  weißde, von dem ich dir dieses / B:  Ja, ich weiß! . Taschenbuch, oder? A:
13  das sind alles so fiese Vororte / B: Ja, geht doch linksrheinisch! 138 A:  J
14ntuell noch mal! A:  Ja, das wär fein, ja! B:  Jedenfalls schön, daß du angeru
15und jetz off eenma sind se ausenander, ja . A:  Wann? ((4s)) Wann sind die aus
16s umsonst? B:  Die machen das umsonst, ja. A:  Ich bin nämlich zur Stadt gegan
17r direkt zugeschlagen! B:  Sehr schön, ja. A:  Un der fährt noch, ne, die Frau
18o B:  das wird aus der Kasse genommen, ja. A:  Ja. B:  Da zahlt man also r
```

JA may also be used in response to a statement or a suggestion (see lines 5-10), it may be used when interrupting the person one is talking to (see lines 11-13) or to reconfirm one's own position (see lines 14-18).

2.) In some instances we use JA not so much to express or emphasise agreement, but rather as a more general response signal to the person we are talking to. In those instances JA may be translated by either 'well' or 'yes':

Group 2: 'well'

```
    jetz nimmer angerufen. A:  Klar! B:  Ja, ich war au zwischendurch mal in Wer
      Wie geht's Ihnen? A: Guut, joa. B:Ja... öh, Sie ham mir hier en paar Frag
   hm A: aber das dürfte mir blühen B:  ja, das wird in der nachsten Zeit wahrs
  auch nur mit eim aus unserm Haus. A:  Ja, Öh /      B: So / A: Englisch hab i
  bloß noch Quark un sowas! C: (lacht). Ja, nee, das müssen wer aber unbedingt
```

Group 3: 'yes'

```
    Nee, dat reicht ja nun noch, ne! A:  Ja? B:  Ich hab so ne große Liste un so
  damit wer  schön einschlafen, ne. B:  Ja? A:  Unda hab ich da den Rotwein von
a guck ich auch noch  ma n bißchen B:  ja? A:  da bei denen, dann deck ich mic
  so daß also das nur bis zum 1.4. B:  ja A:  liefe mit dieser Regelung. B:  J
 furchtbar! Ach, die war so fertig A:  ja B:  die / die hat richtig geheult im
 Stadtbücherei, öh, die  Geschäfte A:  ja B:  un Schulen, und, em, na, Büchere
```

3.) In JA may also be used to ask for agreement as in the following group of:

Group 4

```
 recht. Ich beschreibs Ihnen ma  kurz, ja? Also, Sie kommen die Frankfurter St
en? B:  Ja, kommen Se morgen mal eben, ja? A:  Is gut. Hm, danke. B:  Ne? Bidd
 sehr lange. B:  Mit einjen Nachwehen, ja? A:  Hm, so ungefähr kann man's nenn
:  Jaja... Warte, ich gebn dir no mal, ja? C:  Ja, is gut! B:  ((4s )) Na? C:
ch trage Sie dann schon für 9 Uhr ein, ja? A:  Ja . das wär gut. B:  Un Sie wi
```

In such instances it may be translated into English by a question tag, as the following excerpt from a telephone conversation shows:

A: Ja, kommen Se morgen mal eben, **ja**?
[Well, come over here quickly tomorrow, **won't you**?]

B: Is gut. Hm, danke.
[OK. Hm, thanks.]

4.) Have a look at the above groups of examples again. In which positions does JA occur in these examples?

Group 2 ____________________

Group 3 ____________________

Group 4 ____________________

5.) Now let's have a look at JA in a different setting. Please underline the clauses containing JA. What is the position of JA in the following group of examples?

____

Group 5

1	B: scns atmesde das	**ja**	ein. Das bringt ne schwächere Wanze
2	21 A: Nee, die / Sie wollten ihn	**ja**	für Herrn R un Herrn S gleichsei/ z
3	((lacht)) Ja. Ja, ja. A: Die tu ich	**ja**	sowieso, so/ also . das mach ich man
4	Ach, ja nu! B: Also, hör ma, das is	**ja**	nu keen ( ), also ik schick dir die
5	der W wirds allein schaffen, der muß	**ja**	da / der hat ja als 122 freier Mitar
6	irgendwann ma mit dem / naja, du has	**ja**	keine Zeit / ah, der W wirds allein
7	Is ja gut! Paß ma auf, dann kann ich	**ja**	ma zwischendurch anrufen, sons komm
8	Ja, ich auch nich, Mann! Da wärn wir	**ja**	auch dumm! Aber wo findet man schon
9	Ne, die Frankfurter Straße verbindet	**ja**	Porz mit Köln A: Jaa B: Ne? . KHD-
10	((lacht)) A: Aber solang is die Post	**ja**	nich unterwegs. B: Ja.. Das is glau
11	25 bis 30 Minuten. 88 B: Och, das is	**ja**	kein Problem. Da kamma ja immer noch
12	A: Ah so. B: Nich, dann könnde mans	**ja**	so machen A: Dann . ja, dann würd i
13	A: Ja, ich weiß nich, ich hätte mich	**ja**	eigenlich was früher melden müssen!
14	A: Jaja! Aber solche Sachen wird man	**ja**	immer gefragt. B: Hm... Vermutlich.
15	alles aus B: mal alles aus, weil wer	**ja**	eben wissen müssen, was wer noch ka
16	an zu nähen! C: (lacht) Nee, ich bin	**ja**	sowieso da, ich muß die ganzen Büche
17	anderes mehr leisten. Un dann sin wer	**ja**	noch auf Wohnungssuche! B: (
18	angenommen, ich hab's / sie hat sich	**ja**	noch mit jemand getroffen um halb f
19	ankommen. Wenn des überweist, kommt's	**ja**	sowieso nachm Termin an. Un, öh/ we
20	B: Doch! C: Hör ma, ich erkenn dich	**ja**	demnächst nich mehr. B: (lacht) Ich
21	B: Eh, nein, diesmal nicht, weil ich	**ja**	nicht wieder zum Flughafen zurückko
22	B: Ja, is Klasse, der unterhält dich	**ja**	köstlich, und du wirst dafür auch n
23	bei Z diese Fete, da brauch man sich	**ja**	heute noch gar nich drüber aufregen!
24	Bus, da kannsde ja nich /da kanns du	**ja**	nich fahren. A: Neenee! B: Naja, w
25	dann laß es sein! B: Nö, da könn wer	**ja**	ers mal hören! Ich werd mich ers mal
26	das/ dases nich geklappt hat, das lag	**ja**	dann wohl an der Schule und an der
27	daß man alleine heiratet, das stimmt	**ja**	nicht. Man meint immer, man heirate
28	Dat weiß ich nich.. Aber ich mein, is	**ja**	eigenlich Quatsch, die Vereinbarung
29	denn da nichts Genaues? A: Nä! B: s	**ja**	doof, ne. Und der X läßt sich da au
30	denn der Freund bestanden? B: Der is	**ja**	noch nich fertig. A: Der is noch ni

Here again, the use of JA is about agreement between speaker and hearer, but in these instances the speaker is not asking the hearer, rather s/he is implying that there is agreement between the two, as the following excerpt from a telephone conversation shows:

A: Wenn Sie die Frankfurter Straße runterkommen,

und biegen
in die Rösrather Straße ein
[When you come along Frankfurter Straße and turn into Rösrather Straße]

B: Frankfurter Straße

A: Ne, die Frankfurter Straße verbindet ja Porz mit Köln
[Well, Frankfurter Straße is the connection between Porz and Cologne, isn't it]

B: Jaa [Yes]

6.) How would you translate the clauses containing JA in the following lines from Group 5, following the example given in the excerpt above for line 9?

Lines 6 ____________________

Lines 7 ____________________

Lines 8 ____________________

Lines 10 ____________________

Lines 11 ____________________

7.) Now look at the following group of examples and underline the clauses containing JA. Then answer the questions below:

Group 6

```
 1 Troisdorf? B:  (lacht) Ja. A:  Das is ja irre! Da wolln wir ja hin ziehen! B:
 2 as klappt! A: Ja? B:  Das isja / datis ja tierisch! A:  .. Och, das is echt ne
 3 e. Zweienhalb Jahre. B:  Ah so, das is ja schnell! A:  Zweienhalb oder drei B:
 4 is jedes Mal dran, ne. A:  Och, das is ja schlimm! B:  Neulich hat se mir erzä
 5 s Thema steht jetz fest A:  Ja, das is ja gut B:  ( ) A:  Naja, und jetz liest
 6 zelabmachung treffen. A:  Hoch, das is ja ärgerlich! B:  Ja, das is sehr ärger
 7 Type! B:  Och, jetz bin ich's! (Das is ja!) C:  Du bis alles schuld! B:  (lach
 8 25 geworden  am 24. Dezember. B:  Dass ja passend! Warum denn nich am 25. Deze
 9 31. feiern, abends. B:  Ja, eben. dass ja wirklich Klasse! A:  Hm. Ja, hoffent
10 ! B:  (          hoffen, vielleicht) Is ja bald! Kanns vielleicht aber  irgendw
11 en un anzuziehen /               70 B:  Is ja gut! Paß ma auf, dann kann ich ja ma
12 ensuppe zu  Butterbroten. B:  Hmhm, is ja . reichhaltig! A:  Spaghetti is auch
```

```
13 lls isses 110 Quadratmeter A:  110! Is ja irre! Wir ham nur 90! B:  In nem gep
14 schon solange her? A:  Ja! B:  Poh! Is ja Wahnsinn! ((3s)) A:  Ich würd's nich
15 tzt für 3 Tage 400 Mark A:  Bo! B:  is ja echtes Geld! Meine Schwester macht a
16 urück, oder wie? C:  Ja, genau! B:  Is ja praktisch!.. Schade, ich wär ma gern
17   k einen Sinn, ne. A:  Ja, sicher. Is ja klar! B:  Denn . allmählich ermüdet
18 (( Anfang fehlt auf Band )) A:  der is ja noch ganz neu (lacht) B:  ja, aber d
19 e Viertel. B:  nur ne Viertel! Das wär ja ne Möglichkeit! A:  Und dann hätte e
20  B:  ((lacht)) A:  Aber der Termin war ja rum! Den hab ich am zehnten  bekomme
21 wo versteckt haben. 189 A:  Das gibt's ja gar nich! B:  Hm. ((3s)) A: Naja. B:
22 m. Denk ich auch,  Mensch, das gibt es ja nich, die müssen ja knapp vor der  S
23 men, und es sich angucken, das klingt  ja sehr gut! (lacht) Öh, is es so/ ach
24 ) Ja. A:  Das is ja irre! Da wolln wir ja hin ziehen! B: Jaa. Is das sicher?
25 ch nee, du magst das ja nich/ du darfs ja nich! B:  Nöö, ich mag schon, ich da
26 der so. B:  Ja, Mensch, das häuft sich ja! . Woma sehn, wie wir über die  Rund
27 lacht) ja. B:  Hm... Nee, das find ich ja lustig! . Aber ich glaub, das kann
28 ster noch  ma? A:  Ja! B:  Ach, du has ja Geburtstag! A:  Die Tatsache, daB ic
29 nn fürchterlich aussehn, dann wirk der ja noch dicker! B: Nein, der wirkt nich
```

a) In what type of clauses does JA occur in this group of examples?

____

b) What is the position of JA in the clauses in these examples?

____

c) Which verb does JA collocate with in most lines?

____

d) Which deictics does JA collocate with?

____

e) Could you complete the pattern below – which underlies most of the examples in Group 6 - based on the information which you have collected in c) and d)?

_________ + ___________ + JA + Attribute

In these examples there is no lexical translation for JA, it has to be translated into English by an intonation pattern which emphasises the attribute, as the following excerpt from a telephone conversation shows (underlining indicates emphasis):

B: Also, die stellen sich wirklich an, ja, das wäre schwierig, dann müßte man ja für jede / Hilfskraft extra Abrechnung führen und . die werden ja pauschal bezahlt, da gibt es sonst keinerlei . em . individuelle . Vergütung und ä, das wird eben dadurch erleichtert, daß es nur halbe und ganze Stellen haben, es gibt insgesamt vierzehnhundert und sie könn nich für jeden ne Einzelabmachung treffen.
[Now, they really make a fuss, yes, it would be difficult, then they would have to keep a separate account for each research assistant and they are being paid a flat rate, aren't they, there is no other individual way of payment and err, that is made easier precisely by the fact that there are only half positions and full positions, there are fourteenhundred in total and they can't have some sort of special agreement for each and every one of them.]

A: Hoch, das is **ja** ärgerlich!
[ahh, that is <u>annoying</u>!/ahh, that is annoying!]

5.11 The procedure in action

I have presented detailed analyses of the particles EBEN, NUR, DENN, SCHON, DOCH, MAL, ABER, AUCH and JA. Their meanings in modal particle function were differentiated from meanings in other functions, namely as conjunction, answering particle, focus particle, discourse particle (JA) and as adverb of time. The analysis of real-language data unveiled structures, patterns and predictable features relating to the various usages of the particles and their collocations and formed the basis for sample worksheets for learners of German. These provide an example as to how the results of the corpus-based analysis might be used in teaching. As I outlined at the beginning of this chapter, the materials are created to facilitate comprehension, they do not aim at the production of modal particles by learners of German. It will depend to a large degree on the learners' proficiency, learning styles, etc. how these teaching materials might be incorporated into a teaching context and what type of activities they will encourage. The sample worksheets presented here illustrate only one option as to how the data analysis might be exploited for teaching.

A first evaluation of the explorative approach proposed here showed learners' reactions to be positive. One of the sample worksheets – the material on EBEN – was trialled with a group of 19 learners at upper intermediate to advanced level, who were third-year students of German at Macquarie University in Sydney. Most students were at a level of proficiency in German where they were either preparing for the "Zentrale Mittelstufenprüfung"[115] conducted by the Goethe-Institut or had passed this particular examination six months earlier. The students were asked to engage with the worksheet and to then briefly comment in writing on the kind of work presented to them. Immediately afterwards, a group discussion took place on the corpus-based teaching approach exemplified by the worksheet. This discussion was taped and qualitatively evaluated by the researcher.

115 This examination aims at testing German language proficiency in all four skills (listening/speaking, reading/writing) at upper intermediate level.

With the exception of one student, who was concurrently enrolled in linguistics courses, the students had never been presented with concordances or corpus data in general and therefore found the presentation of language data in this particular form slightly overwhelming, as the following excerpts from students' written comments and contributions to the discussion on the nature of the data show:

> "The sentences in the boxes are difficult to understand, because the excerpts are relatively short and the words are not complete and there are letters in between."

> "The sample text lines were difficult to understand at first because they were very colloquial and we didn't see the whole sentence."

> "Some of the sentences were difficult to understand because they were incomplete and included slang."

> "I found this exercise quite hard, mostly I think because of the examples – not complete sentences/words."

> "It was hard to read the data at first – words were cut in half."

The student familiar with concordance data expressed the following view:

> "I found it in no way difficult to understand, although those inexperienced at reading corpora may."

The difficulty of being confronted with concordance data, which students commented on as being "hard to read", was addressed in the discussion which followed the work on the tasks. It was agreed that this problem could be faced by an introduction to concordance data in general, in particular data based on spoken German. As a preamble to the worksheets, students should be given a brief explanation of the features of such data and be introduced to a reading of concordance lines.

On the whole, however, the students' written comments show a favourable response to the approach presented to them, as the following excerpts from their evaluations indicate:

> "The questions asking us to write the verbs and tenses was good. For me, it is easier to remember a rule if I "discover" it myself."

> "It is difficult to distinguish these "EBEN" without any knowledge. If we have a table like the one above [i.e.in the worksheet] in our heads it's easier."

> "This exercise was different to anything I've really done before – I've never really thought about how/when modal particles (like eben) are used. 'Eben' has been a particularly difficult modal particle for me in terms of translation in the past – therefore I found it useful. It was interesting – it made me think. I'd like to do it for other modal particles as well."

> "It is a good way for German language learners to acquaint themselves with the modal particles. The multiple examples of the same usage of the modal particle and the analysis in steps all are of great help."

> "It is good to identify the meaning yourself. This is better because it is the same process as listening to somebody speaking. It is better than being given the rules."

> "Overall the worksheet works much better in identifying how to use 'eben' than the way most textbooks give multiple translations and different contexts. Here I identified the meanings myself."

> "I found it very effective, particularly to choose the best meaning from an initial reading and then to see how the tense of the verb form helps to emphasise this. I think it's a fabulous way of looking at difficult expressions in a language."

The students' comments indicate how much they valued the explorative nature of the task, which allowed them to discover rather than being told about the patterns of use determining the meaning of the particle EBEN.

When evaluating the students' performance in the tasks presented in the worksheet, the following pattern emerges:

	No. students with **appropriate solutions**	No. students with **inappropriate/no solutions**
Task 1	16	3
Task 2	16	3
Task 3	13 & 5*	1
Task 4	16	3
Task 5	15	4
Task 6	12 & 3 (mostly appropriate)	4

The results indicate that the majority of students was able to engage successfully with the tasks presented in the sample worksheet. In Task 3, where students were asked to identify the verb forms and their tenses in specified concordance lines, some students (see*) were not quite clear about the instructions and presented either the actual verb form or the tense only. One student commented as follows

> "I wasn't sure what type of tense should be indicated – ie. past/present – or was more detail needed, e.g. Präsens, Plusquamperfekt, Perfekt, etc.? I wasn't sure exactly what 'verb form' meant – was I to put the infinitive or was I to copy it straight from the text?"

To further clarify Task 3, an example was added to a modified version of the sample worksheet on EBEN.

Three students performed significantly worse on all tasks than the majority of the group. These students also performed consistently worse on all other tasks presented to the students in the course of the semester, in fact two of the three did not pass the German course they were enrolled for. This seems to indicate that the tasks in their present form are appropriate for learners of German whose proficiency meets the standards of upper intermediate to advanced level.

Overall, the students' performance in the tasks as well as their evaluation of the approach presented in the worksheet can be seen as positive and encouraging. In particular, students appreciated the explorative nature of the tasks presented to them, which allows them to discover patterns and regularities for themselves. Their positive response to the explorative learning tasks indicates that there is much scope for data-driven learning (e.g. Johns and King 1991) in a university foreign language curriculum.

6. Conclusion

It is the contention of this study, that the analyses given can be seen to represent the use of particles in everyday spoken German, but the findings described in Chapter 5 need to be considered with a degree of caution in regard to their validity. With the corpus-based approach outlined in Chapter 4 and applied in Chapter 5, it is possible to come to conclusions about the use of the analysed particles within the particular corpus under investigation, but a generalisation of the findings is problematic as the BRO corpus is both extremely small and very specific, in that it consists of telephone conversations only. I have shown, for example, that the high frequency of use of the particle JA can be ascribed to the nature of the data – telephone dialogues – where the speakers are limited to signalling responses verbally without recourse to non-verbal response signals, e.g. facial expressions and gestures.

Nevertheless, the analyses of particle occurrence presented here reflect the natural use of those particles in a subset of everyday situations – telephone conversations – and can thus be used to provide language learners with authentic examples of use. As the particles considered here occur frequently in the data, it was possible to detect patterns of use which can be relayed to language learners in order to provide them with tools for the decoding of particle meaning (cf. Tribble 1997). This is not to say that all possibilities of particle occurrences have been covered by the analyses. There will be a large number of possible combinations of context, co-text and particle use which have not occurred in the particular corpus under analysis, but which are quite probable and might occur frequently in different speech situations. The implications of this gap between what is possible and what is documented by corpus data have been discussed, rather heatedly, by scholars in the field of applied linguistics (see e.g. Widdowson 2000, 2001, Stubbs 2001).

With regards to German modal particles, there are comprehensive teaching materials which describe 'what is possible', i.e. which list German particles and account for possible meanings (see Weydt et al. 1983, Helbig 1994, Helbig & Helbig 1995). The materials proposed in the present study – based on authentic dialogue data – aim at engaging the language learner with the meanings of particles in context. Rather than being given an explanation of a list of different particle meanings, learners are encouraged to explore these meanings and – with guidance – to recognise categories of meaning and the accompanying grammatical and lexical collocations.

This explorative approach is not only in keeping with the trend towards viewing teaching as mediated learning rather than an imparting of knowledge which is discussed in particular with regard to the university context (Laurillard 1993), it is also in keeping with the current view of language as communication and of language learning as a process, where the classroom is viewed as an interactive site of engagement (Candlin 2000). Underlying the approach presented here is a view of teaching as an instructing, mentoring and facilitating process (van Lier 1996) and as such, it harmonises with the principles underlying a communicative curriculum as proposed by Breen and Candlin (1980).

The tasks presented in the sample worksheets in this study are designed to enable learners to construct their knowledge of language structures and functions, so that they will attain both a high degree of linguistic competence and become aware of the social meanings and potential communicative functions of particles in different situations. Such worksheets could represent a first step in the process of acquiring modal particles, which could be followed by focussing on specific modal particles in the context of larger stretches of dialogue where speaker roles and speech situations could be analysed in more detail (see Weinrich 1993: 842-3). In a next step learners might work with recordings of spoken German to identify the intonation patterns accompanying the different usages of particles.

In their present form, the worksheets are based on data provided by the teacher so that teacher input is fairly high. The data could be amended in the way suggested by one of the students who trialled the worksheets:

> It may also be useful for students (if possible in a foreign country) to collect and analyse their own data and compare it with that in the corpora.

It would be highly interesting to evaluate how such learner involvement affects the learner's accomplishment of the task (cf. Candlin 2000: 240). What can definitely be said is that such learner engagement would make for truly student-centred learning and would be a valuable extension to the approach proposed in this study.

Appendix

I. *Total occurrences of* SCHON *in temporal function*

B: Mir ham se schon das Kindergeld abgezogen. A: Ja? B
57 B: Jao, ne. Ich dachte schon, der wäre, jetz so nachm Examen un
20 A: Ja. B: Nun . hab ich schon gedacht, vielleicht wäre eine Mögli
Aber ich glaub, da die ganze Sache schon am Laufen war, šh, verjährt das gl
an. B: Ja, aber wenn die schon namittachs sacht, daß et ihr nich g
Hasde auch schon? B: Hab ich auch schon, sind auch wunderbar geworden, mit
nich gedacht! B: Nee? (lacht) Bin schon alter Ehekrüppel! (lacht) A: (lach
Promotion fertig is, ne. Un er hat schon gesacht, also . unter ner eins is
un um halb fünf war der junge Mann schon da, ne. Also hab ich auch bloß fün
"Ich muß jetz gehn"; junge Mann war schon da, "und um sechs, dann kommt die
(lacht) B: Wie lange fährt se jetz schon? A: Ich? B: Na, du fährs ja bald
A: Ja, ich meine, dasss/ hilft uns schon enorm weiter, sie verdient also fa
auf jeden Fall im Lande, das is ja schon viel wert. Ja, mach ich gleich en K
B: Wann soll das denn sein, hat se schon was gesagt? A: Ja, sie denkt an de
bisde drei Monate dabei, da sollsde schon en Thema überlegt haben? B: Jaja,
das / schließlich is se unterdessen schon unterwegs nachhause, ne. A: Ich w
erkältet! A: Nööö. Warn wer vorher schon. B: Hm, hm. B: Ja, ich wollt ma f
machen. B: Hm? A: Die wissen alle schon so klar, was se machen, fangen ganz
noch ganz gut! A: Findsde? B: Bin schon 26! A: Oh, siehst aber noch aus wi
Referendarbezüge is? . Da wird doch schon lange was gequakt, is das eigenlic
schon alt, ne. B: Dreiunsechzig is schon dreizehn Jahre. Da zeigen sich scho
schön wärs! B: (lacht) A: Ich harre schon der Dinge, die da kommen. B Ja? A:
Seinen Chef? B: jaja, der eine lag schon bei ihm oben im Bett, ne A: toll B
siehts aus? A: Och, Kater! B: Ja? Schon? A: Ja, wir warn dummerweise geste
unten A: Ja B: und war/ A: War's schon abgekühlt B: war schon zuviel kalt
Y ist acht und X is sechs. A: Acht schon, mein Gott! B: (lacht) A: Was die
zu viel auf einmal, denn die feiern schon . nächste Woche Weihnachten, weil
(lacht) Jaja .. Einer, seid ihr auch schon sicher? B: Neeneenee, eine . Eine
(lacht) Stark! . Ja, ich bin ja auch schon fast en alter Ehekrüppel. B: Ja,
, datihr euch da / A: Nee, wir gehn schon um halb sieben B: in Porz oder wie
. dann lag das genau daran, wie ich schon vermutet hatte, e, war nämig ein di
. Wahrscheinlich war das... war das schon zu weit unten A: Ja B: und war/ A
: Hm 34 A: Also jetz bereu ich das schon, das is / ((?s)) B: Nee, ich hab
: Jo, dat geht aber, das Gröbste is schon hinter mir, das is immer so ne Gel
: nee, das/das fand ich ich sowieso schon so sch/ ich hab das ja ma gemacht,
: Wie war's im Űbrigen noch, ham Se schon den Kaufvertrag abgeschlossen? A:
? . Meine Mutter hat dich zwar eben schon den ganzen Quark gefragt, aber . i
87 A: Ah so.. Mensch, die sind alle schon so fest. Ganz klar wissense, was s
a ruf ich nochma an! B: 14. hab ich schon was! . Aber müßter ma sehn, wir mac
a sachte der, "ja, das wolltich auch schon grade sagen, aber wie kommwer hier
achdem der Y Job aus hat, fahrn wir schon nach Hilden, ne, un übernachten da
ch 25 geworden bin! B: Geworden bin schon? A: Ja, am 24. Dezember! B: Hm, h
ch keins. B: (lacht) Mensch, is das schon solange her? A: Ja! B: Poh! Is ja
ch! ... Na, sicher . ((3s)) Aber das schon so alt is, hättich nich gedacht! B
chwiegermutter hat mir am Wochenende schon gesacht, ich säh schlecht aus. C:
da kann man doch am Abend davor auch schon was machen. B: Hm, naja, ich weiß
derstag ginge auch, . em / B: wären schon vier Stunden A: un freitag ginge a
du auch garnich, da warst du nämlich schon weg. Du bis ja unheimlich früh die
e hätte die ganze Zeit in der Messe schon so ne Unruhe gehabt, sie hätte sic
e nichts gefressen, ich hatte nämig schon Salat für das Schwein geholt undas
e, nicht... Weil die Sache ja einmal schon ans Laufen gekommen is, ne. A: Hm
echend en bißchen ein, verhält sich schon ganz anders B: hm A: un, öh, jetz

egen heute abend, unda mußte se dann	schon	da rein, unda haben wir gar nich a
eht aber sehr langsam die 71 hattich	schon	am Samstag nach dem Ball da gehabt
eicht hatte se das von / dieser Tage	schon,	als . e, perfekt angesehn A: ja
el, ich weiß nich, ob ich dir davon	schon	erzählt hatte, A: nee B: da hab i
Frau A? A: jaaa.. B: ne, A: wo Se	schon	. sehen, wie ich damit zurecht komm
geklatscht, das sachte er mir vorher	schon	"Wenn wer da jetz reinkommen, da s
gen "Ja, grade verlobt, un da isser	schon	mit ner anderen Frau in der Kneipe!
h! (lacht) Ich vergeß das Ding auch	schon	völlig. Dat läuft hier einfach so s
hat ganz wenig Kalorien. C: Hm, hab	schon	verstanden. B: Ich glaub 0,7 hat d
hier gefahren war, da war der selber	schon	so bedient, daß er gesacht hat: "D
Hm, das wäre, dann / dann würde mir	schon	die Lust vergehen, wenn ich zu nem
hr viel Zeit A: Ja B: Morgen is ja	schon	der letzte Tach/ für die Anmelderei
hrscheinlich hat ses inzwischen auch	schon	gemerkt, ne. B: Ja, wie spät es e
ht wurde, ohne daß ich . mich sch /	schon	seit . Rosenmontag nich mehr gemeld
ich seh gar nich ein, ich meine, is	schon	lange her, als ich Sie eben Sie ge
ich öh Mädchen, die machen dat jetz	schon	ungefähr drei Jahre, ne A: hm B:
ich! A: Ja, legen wir ganz bestimmt	schon	in den nächsten Tagen dann fest. B
ig! A: Och! C: Ja, ich hab mir das	schon	gedacht, ne, der is mir also zuvor
ion gewesen sein.. Die ham dem, öh,	schon	zu Anfang gesagt, sie müßten im .
is gut! B: ((4s)) Na? C: Ich dacht	schon,	du wärst sauer, hör ma, du warst g
Ja! Der is ganz dünn, aber der liegt	schon	ganz hoch! B: Ah so, dann habt ihr
jut! Die sind janz schön selbständig	schon,	muß ich sagen! A: Ja? B: Die kom
lacht) Em, ( ) aber mein Chef kommt	schon	am 31. / am 30. wieder / B: ah so
leben, aber / B: Ich überleg mir ja	schon,	ob ich das jemals en erstes Mal tu
loß dann sind die immer ziemlich alt	schon.	A: Ja? . Och! ... Na, sicher . ((
meckern, ne. A: Hm B: das ging mir	schon	auf die Nerven, und da sagich so zu
mmer wieder los. A: Naja, aber isja	schon	alt, ne. B: Dreiunsechzig is schon
n vcn Holland zurück/ A: Hasde auch	schon?	B: Hab ich auch schon, sind auch
n, ess'ne Idee! C: Ja, nee, ich bin	schon	morgen abend eingeladen. Geht schl
n? A: Ich? B: Na, du fährs ja bald	schon	zehn Jahre, wa! A: Ach, soo lange
nders, un, öh. naja, aber man sieht	schon,	der Verkäufer wird allmählich wei
nee, die Geschäfte ham doch sowieso	schon	zu! B: Nee, das mach ich hier unte
nö, das hab ieh ja es letzte Ma auch	schon	gemacht, das is harmlos. Also es
Panz is noch gar nich da, un wir ham	schon	die Schränke voll Zeug! A: (lacht
r / jaja, ham die nix von/ "Ich bin	schon	bei Stück 43!" (lacht) B: Nee, als
r ich essen abends mit dem V, hatte	schon	nen Tisch bestellt, sons wär ich ge
r/ A: War's schon abgekühlt B: war	schon	zuviel kaltes Wasser drauf. (hustet
riegt ihr dann ers die Negative oder	schon/	A: Nee, die Photos B: Ah, so
s geht, ja B: Jetz hab ich noch die	schon	von Holland zurück/ A: Hasde auch
samen Umweg zu fahren (das is also	schon	gut) A: hja C: (nich in Riehl) vo
schon dreizehn Jahre. Da zeigen sich	schon	gewisse Schäden... Wenn für uns wa
sätzliche Arbeit!", un dann war das	schon	gleich gestorben A: Ah so! B: und
ster auf. Jaja, das hat se	schon!	A: Müßte man doch eigentlich find
t solles? A: (lacht) Hatteter euch	schon	dran gewöhnt? B: (lacht) A: Aber i
te, ne. A: (lacht) B: Da . war sie	schon	also leicht freudig überrascht, wei
und. wie war das noch? Das war aber	schon	dieser Tage doch! A: ((3s)) Nee, i
Uni kann. B: Ja, ich trage Sie dann	schon	für 9 Uhr ein, ja? A: Ja . das wär
ute, die sich scheiden lassen, oder	schon	geschieden sind. Das is ganz fürcht
wahrscheinlich heute abend um sechs	schon	das große S leuchten. A: Bis Stüss
wirdes nich, viele sin verreist, ham	schon	wat anderes, das ham wer ja en biß
woch vorbeikomme/ A: dann hamer uns	schon	ausgequatscht! B: Ja, ne? (Lachen)
zuschlagen. A: (lacht) Sie hat auch	schon	irgendwelches Babyzeug für euch ge
nich A: hm B: Ich mein, wenn der	schon	mal eben . dieses Knöllchen da aus
hab doch, weiß nich, ob ich dir das	schon	ma erzählt hab, ma für son Lederty
Ja. Ja. B: (lacht) A: Ich hab mir	schon	mal überlegt, bin ich da eigenlich
ne B: ja A: un da bisde natürlich	schon	mal . en bißchen gehemmt und so, n
A: Also, auf jeden Fall gebrauchsde	schon	ma das Wort "werden" nich, anschei
A: hm B: aber so ab un zu kommt es	schon	mal A: ja klar! ... B: Samma, wan
den ganzen Scheiß, besorgen, undann	schon	ma sons bißchen was vorbereiten, d
e im Hintergrund)) Is das einer, der	schon	ma hier war?.. Wie heißt der? ((St
er nochen neues drauftun. Das kommt	schon	ma vor, daß die neuen auch ni mehr
hier is B. A: Tach B! B: Ich hatte	schon	ma angerufen, aber da war keiner da
is, un so. Un denn/ Ne, das is also	schon	mal ne qanze Menqe wert. Un dann m
n! B: Ja, Gut! Dann wer ich mir das	schon	ma merken! ((3s)) Bestell dem X ma
n, aber ich glaub, also, sie war ja	schon	ma vorher da, ne, an der Schule, d

nach mir, Geburtstag, da ham wir das schon ma zusammengelegt, ne. ob mer dat
ne. A: hmhm B: Klar, das wurd auch schon ma später. A: jaja B: wenn ich ir
romovieren jetz, undann brauch se eh schon ma zwei Jahre, un auch zwei Jahre
s muß ja / darf / ich mein, der kann schon mal rausspringen, der darf aber ni
ule? Ich mein, sicher, ich hab auch schon ma öfter ma abends lang gearbeitet,
B: ja? A: die is seit einer Woche schon wieder draußen. B: Schon wieder ra
gar nich, wat da drauf is, hab ich schon wieder längst vergessen, naja, is j
eingladen, da hat der Geburtstag. Is schon wiedder Mist, . könnte sein, daß i
ganz gut. . Du, ich glaube, ich muß schon wieder Schluß machen, ich muß mir n
h, öh, hat, unnsofern hebt sich das schon wieder auf. Kanns also zig hartgek
iner Woche schon wieder draußen. B: Schon wieder raus? Ham wer die damals neu
n wolltse sich wieder melden. Is die schon wieder zurück? A: Jaja. B: Ahso
Wochen noch, ne, un dann müßtich ja schon wieder neue kaufen. C: Och, sach d

II. *Total occurrences of* DOCH *in modal particle function*

15 A: Un dann / ich hab doch zwei auch in Holland gemacht, könn
/ B: Nönö, ach D: dann, da stimmt doch wat nich! B: (lacht) Die könnt man
B: "Ja, wieso das denn? Die ham dir doch nie was getan!" "Ja", sag ich, "gl
gesagt, ne, falls . wider Erwarten . doch klappt, dann ruf ich vorher noch k
gleich festmachen, sons wird dat ja doch nix! Warte mal, Freitag bin ich dan
hätter aber keine Zeit, und er würd doch so gerne die Ringe segnen. "Ja", h
nich verdient habe, ham / hat der X doch wesentlich weniger Steuern bezahlt
soll! 104 A: Ja, paß auf, die macht doch irgendwelche Arbeiten über . Futur
, wieso dat denn? B: Jaja, ich hatt doch unheimlich was zugenommen im letzte
. A: Ja, gibt's hier auch. Also, ja, doch, diese eine zu 80.000. B: Also, ic
: Auf jeden Fall lächerlich, ich hab doch bei der ( ) mein Teil getan, ne. B
: Ja, ne. Womöglich kommt se nämlich doch erst ganz spät nachhause, weil / B
A: hm B: un dann, weil jede Familie doch unterschiedlich heizt unverbraucht
alles so fiese Vororte / B: Ja, geht doch linksrheinisch! 138 A: Ja, nee, da
ang du allein gelebt has, dann hasde doch so einige . Gewohnheiten angenomme
Brügge und Gent. A: Hm B: Da saßen doch verschiedene Leute permanent aufm K
ch allzuviel abnehme . dann nehm ich doch nich da ab, wo ich sollte, ne. B:
dann / wieso, nee, die Geschäfte ham doch sowieso schon zu! B: Nee, das mach
du das nich? A: Nee. 183 B: Die hat doch ., ich weiß nich,. ((ausatmen)) ich
ein!" B: Umm! A: Ja, jetz . hab ich doch nen andern Studenten als Kollegen,
eit, ne. C: Ja, hör ma, dann würd ich doch so sagen: wenn / wenn ihr dann zur
elegt A: Das is doch egal, das heißt doch nur, daß du dich mit dem Thema seh
ensch, anderthalb Stunden, das reicht doch wohl! B: Ja, ich weiß nich, wie di
h tun! B: Hm A: sons nehm ich nämig doch nur an den falschen Stellen ab B:
im Grunde den andern und stellt sich doch dementsprechend en bißchen ein, ver
irgenwas aus, ne. Vielleicht hasdann doch was an der Uni zu tun oder sonst wa
jegeben oder in der/ A: Nee, ich war doch seit Jahren nich mehr schwimmen B:
lar! B: Denn . allmählich ermüdet se doch . relativ schnell. A: Ja. Ja klar
n eigenen Körper berühren, da würdse doch lieba, öh, Binden nehmen." A: Jao.
n is 65 B: furchbar da ham doch die Schüler nichts von! A: die fin
n Schnäppchen drinstehn sondern, öh, doch Sachen, die an sich so leicht nich
neunzig Prozent der Fälle, sagen die doch. B: Ich glaube nich, wenn die Sach
ng der Referendarbezüge is? . Da wird doch schon lange was gequakt, is das ei
s auch in Deutsch nich verstehe, aber doch dann in Franz/ B: Ach, in Französ
s, eine Viertelstelle bliebe ja dann doch übrig. 20 A: Ja. B: Nun
sen. Weil die sich sagen, wir spinnen doch nich. Wenn wir verheiratet sinn, k
sich, ja, bloß, es is eben, . daß ich doch son bißchen / also, meine Tätigkei
sieben. B: Halb sieben, ja, nehm ich doch an! . Das is aber dumm, da hätt se
stellen, und sagen wieso, Ich hätt's doch überwiesen?. Ich kann ja die Belege
terbrochen, sach ma? B: Nee, ich hab doch, weiß nich, ob ich dir das schon ma
u Y wieder zurück, die scheint also doch nich endgültig weg zu sein A: Ja d
uf Band)) A: oh, ich nehm doch an, daß se was zu trinken haben dür
unheimig gut finde, dann/ da geh ich doch das Risiko nich ein, daß der die Wo
v begrüßt hatte, ja hab ich von euch doch rein nichts mehr gesehen. B: Ja, ic
dachte immer/ sons, im Büro, tut man doch immer so, als würd man unheimlich

wieso das denn?" "Ja, das macht man doch so!" 41 A: Das macht man so! B: "
) A: aber . manchmal kriegt man dann doch sehr große Schwierigkeiten, wenn .
ch ne Geschichte, die einen doch etwas ruhiger schlafen läßt. A: Hm
indesde en offenes Geschäft! Es macht doch alles Inventur! B: Och nö, die, e
ster feiert, aber meistens macht man doch son Riesenspökes! A: Ja, nee, wir
wie Arzt is, Doktor Sounso, sagt man doch zu sein / seiner Frau auch Frau Do
sich das nennt D: is doch egal, is doch egal B: jedenfalls . hat das so un
A: Nö, sehr böse natürlich nich, is doch klar/ B: Ich hab grade mit X telef
B: Ach, hattest du frei? A: Ja, is doch Feiertag. Oder? Bei euch nich? B:
dann der 31. frei sein. Denn das is doch en evangelischer Feiertag! B: Ja,
ma, das kannsde nich machen! Die sin doch bestimmt/ B: Na, denn . ach . da
nur, eh, um neunzehn Uhr dreißig is doch so ein interessanter Leichtathleti
tun B: Ja, die zähl ich mit? A: Is doch klar! Guck mal, wenn de/ wenn de da
. A: Ah so.. Ja, aber meistens isses doch so, daß . nich nur einer allein sc
? B: Jaja. D: Wie bitte? C: Du bis doch verrückt! B: Doch! C: Hör ma, ich
a", sachich, "und warum?" "Ja, das is doch dat Normale!" A: Hm (lacht) B: Jo
A: Sin vorgestern angekommen! B: Is doch nich nötig! A: Sin echt prima! B:
abt? A: Nee. ((3s)) Vielleicht is es doch was anderes! B: Jaja. In der Wäsch
auch bei der Z mal belegt A: Das is doch egal, das heißt doch nur, daß du di
cht man noch leichter weg! B: Das is doch Wahnsinn! A: Nee, man muß dann war
cktheit und so. Aber das Eine is eben doch ne Geschichte, die einen
du kanns ja nich loslassen!.. Nee! Is doch heller Wahnsinn! . Bin froh, daß d
fahren war, stell dir das ma vor! Is doch Wahnsinn! A: Ja, sobald (der B: W
h da? A: Ja B: - Titel - A: Das is doch toll! B: Ja, da kommt dann das Pro
h hier nah an der Brücke wärt, isdas doch so schlimm nich. Also ich würd mich
hab nich angerufen da . 2.000 Mark is doch toll! B: Ja. A: Happig, ne? 134 B
hönes Wetter, weil es im Augenblick doch sehr schön is/ A: Ja, in der Schwe
hr traurig, ne? B: Wieso? Ach 25, is doch noch ganz gut! A: Findsde? B: Bin
jetz nich, wie sich das nennt D: is doch egal, is doch egal B: jedenfalls .
kann man ohnehin . und öh . da is das doch wesentlich einfacher, sich zu tren
lig. Ob das ne Wanze is? Aber das is doch unwahrscheinlich! C: Seit wann ha
mehr, wenn's schneit. A: Jaa. B: Is doch was mehr draußen... Hmhm. A: Ja so
men hätte! D: Eben, ich denk, die is doch gar ni mehr da, dann! B: Neenee. D
r könnja nachmittags!) B: Ja, die is doch sowieso in der Uni! C: Ja, ich mein
rer auch gesagt, "ja, wieso, Sie sind doch für die Ausfallstunden da!" Nem. D
rwald versunken, aber dann isser ja . doch wohl wieder da. A: Ja, er kommt d
sser in der Spüle nich ab, und da is doch oben in dem Sieb so ne Schraube, di
t dann da? A: Ah so, nee, dann is es doch noch ganz unten auf der Seite! Die
t, wo der Mann wohnt. A: Ja. B: Is doch en Nachteil, ich habs ja immer gesa
ulkollegium angefordert war. "Das is doch zusätzliche Arbeit!" Hü, weg! A: (
daß die Spüle verstopft war, das wär doch einlich interessanter gewesen? B:
: Sin auch drin, ia. B: Ja, das wär doch auch nich uninteressant, oder / A:
: Hm. B: Aber erstensmal wäre das ja doch eine . ziemliche finanzielle Einbu
arks- Häuser / B: Ja, vielleicht wär doch mim Zweifamilienhaus was zu machen
unmöglich! B: Och, hör ma, wenn ihr doch hier nah an der Brücke wärt, isdas
X hat nämig auch Urlaub, och, das wär doch schön! .. Könntet ihr denn, ach so
Nee? Nee. Siebenunsiebzig war die Y doch im Krankenhaus? B: Ja? (lacht) Abe
noch? Das war aber schon dieser Tage doch! A: ((3s)) Nee, ich hatte sie beim
ten von heute auf morgen, ne, das war doch ne Leistung! B: Ja sicher, auf jed
ter... B: Ach nee? Auf der Karte war doch ... Schnee Ihr wartetet auf einwan
warsde nich zu erreichen! C: Du wars doch wieder weg! Hör ma, nachdem ich dic
entstehen sollen, em, da können die doch nich gezwungen werden, trotzdem, ö
paar Platten mit, ich mein, kannsde doch durchaus / . ich mein, ess'ne Idee!
A: aber so ein großes Vieh kann sich doch nich unbemerkt mit mir einschleppe
an und geht dann tanzen, da kann man doch am Abend davor auch schon was mache
äumen. A: Ja. Hör mal, man kann dich doch normalerweise abends erreichen, wi
chreiben? B: Nö!... Oder? . Kann man doch? A: Ich mein,ja. Aber ich weiß es
e einzige Möglichkeit, aber das kann doch nich / B: daß da irgendeiner gepe
gungen geheiratet is / hat, der kann doch nich einfach gezwungen werden, jetz
h glaub, das kann einem mit der Zeit doch ganz schön auf die Nerven gehen, n
hörst, dann B: Ja, dann kann ich mir doch viel besser ein kritisches Urteil
ibt's gar nich! B: Jaa... Die könnten doch schließlich, öh, die geschiedenen
ix machen! B: Ja, aber du kanns dich doch wieder um'nen Schuljob bemühen! A:
r, dat darf / dat kann die sich aber doch nit erlauben! B: Och, so zwei, dre
t mir einschleppen B: Ihr könnt das doch nich aus / aus S mitgebracht haben,

timeter kleiner geworden. C: Das kann doch nich sein, kilomäßig ja/ B: Doch! C
A: Wie Heftzwecken, ja die müßte man doch finden! B: Wie heißen die nochma i
b ich am zehnten bekommen, der hätte doch vor dem sechsten da sein müssen, o
ck! A: Weil wer meinen, da müßte man doch gegen angehn, ne! Aber wenn da nun
er nich? Aber heißes Wasser müßte den doch auflösen? B: Das hab ich ja versu
h oder richtig?... He? A: Ja. , müßte doch eigentlich auch möglich sein! Aber
jährt is.. Aber ich muß mich ja jetz doch noch mit ner Sache rumschlagen, die
Jaja, das hat se schon! A: Müßte man doch eigentlich finden, son Biest! Ja, w
rifft beim Notar oder so, die müßten doch einlich gültig sein, ne. A: ((3s
uch sind weg! C: Hörma, B, dann mußde doch jetz älter aussehn! B: Ja, ich seh
, zu heiraten!" "Ja, B, aber du wills doch ma Kinder haben!" - "Och nee", sag
del von der Allergie sein, wir wolln doch ma ers etwas vorsichtig sein mit d
eier." "Ja, ich weiß, die wollt sich doch erst Silvester verlobe " "Ja", sagt
keine Zeit." - "Ja, aber du wolltest doch kommen!" "Ja", sagich, "wolltich, d
öhnt? B: (lacht) A: Aber ihr wolltet doch das zweite adoptieren? B: Ach, ja.
ön, an sich. Die Z wollte mit dem Boy doch heute tatsächlich auf diesem . Mop
! B: Gottes Willen! A: Dann soll se doch lieber in en Büro gehen! B: Vielle
ich gar nich/ B: Jaja! C: Cola soll doch soviel haben, ne? B: Tja, keine Ah
m Hintergrund)) Jaja... Ja, das darf doch nicht! Jaja, sicher, hab ich ja auc
! B: "So denkst du? Das wirst du uns doch wohl nich antun!" A: (lacht) Wieso
(lacht) B: ja, aber deine Frau hatte doch en VW oder sowat, wa? A: Nein, wir
iese Kraftfahrzeugverbände, die geben doch immer den Tip? Man/ B: Auf jeden
immer noch / dann würdich vielleicht doch am ma besten anrufen, ne? A: Ja, n
n, ne. A: Toll, ja! Un das immerhin . doch direkt in der Innenstadt, ne? B:
prima aus. A: Gut! B: Sprechen wer doch noch mal am Freitag drüber, nich? A
das verstehen. 180 B: Versuchen Sie doch mal ., Frau, öh, öh, A, versuchen S
h en doofer Termin! B: Ja, aber sach doch mal, wann de mal hier vorbeikommen
mal ., Frau, öh, öh, A, versuchen Sie doch mal, ne Parallele zum Schiffsbau z
ssen dumm, da dachte ich mir, fragste doch ma die C, ob die nich mit mir ne R
uhr, sagte meine Mutter,"ja, B, komm doch jetz ma en bißchen öfter Nachhause!
B: "Nein", sacht meine Mutter, "red doch nich so'n Quatsch, die ham sich nu
htig, mit wem, ne." "Ach so! Ach, red doch nich son Unsinn!" (lacht) A: (lac
den? Is das denn schlimm? Komm, steh doch wieder auf, was is denn los?" A: (
n mir aus, ich würd sagen, kommen Se doch einfach. aber ich hoffe, daß es dan

III.a) Total Occurrences of ABER as Conjunction

B: Jah, also, ich müßte das sehn, aber Quaddeln, das machen Wanzen. Flöhe
abgeschlossen? A: Nein, noch nich, aber / B: Und das is Ersterwerb, ja? A:
Ausstellung. Da kamen se beide hin, aber sonst sehn die sich nie! 38 B: Ja
Daß man da jetz aufgezeichnet wird. Aber ich warte nich mehr so lang mit de
Feierei nich hier is, ne A: hm B: aber, wir teilen uns die Sache. dasis ni
kannsdes ja machen. A: Tja. ((2s)) Aber . ich weiß nich, ob man . soviel /
oweh, Marschmusik! (lacht) B: Nee, aber diese Bewegungsübungen, die sind ve
versuchen, obs klappt, klappt nich, aber manchmal / Un dann komm dazu die H
überleg mal! B: Hm... Ja, ich weiß. Aber/ 157 C: Hörma, nee, ich kann mir g
( ) einfach nix (mehr drin) ((2s)). Aber, wie gesacht, man / man is mir als
. aber . kann ma nix machen! B: Ja, aber du kanns dich doch wieder um'nen Sc
. Sorge braun Se also nich zu haben. Aber . wir hätten ganz gern ein / ich s
A: hm... Na, ich stell mir das / B: aber / A: ganz interessant vor B: Ja, k
auch nich gesagt, wohin, ne? B: Ja, aber letztens hatte se, hat se nich was
auch noch ein Fest, wahrscheinlich, aber man / es is so schwierig, die Leute
auf Comics im Augenblick. Lesen ja, aber nich zeichnen, weißde. B: Ja. A:
B! B: Ich hatte schon ma angerufen, aber da war keiner da! A: Ja, das is gu
B: in vollem Jacket un so, also ( ) aber die ham nix mehr gemerkt, die hätt
B: is für die W fach A: Hm, ja B: aber das vergessen die sofort, mit dem,
B: Ja, das is auch schrecklich, ne? Aber das geht ja schnell wieder! A: Is
B: oder zwei A: das is alles Mist! Aber ich hab auch keine Lust, an die Sch
da müßte man doch gegen angehn, ne! Aber wenn da nun jetz fast alle nich kön
dann kannsde, em, eingesetzt werden, aber nur ganz minimal. A: Hm B: Un di
Der Bauch is zwar no nich ganz weg, aber en bißchen wenigstens! D: Ja, un /

die fand's sehr schön. A: Hjo! B: Aber könn mer ja alles ma sehn, ne? A:
doch im Krankenhaus? B: Ja? (lacht) Aber da warn wer ja no nich verheiratet.
eben schon den ganzen Quark gefragt, aber . ich habe das nich mitgekriegt! B
einzige Möglichkeit, die sie sieht, aber die möchtich Ihnen auf keinen Fall
ers mal erkundigen, ne. A: Ja. B: Aber wie es heißt, weißt du nich? A: Ne
es uns genehmigt. A: Ah so, ja! B: Aber sie war nicht besonders begeistert.
Franzšsisch erzählen B: (lacht) A: aber . er lernt dabei nix. B: Ja, is Kl
ganz gut überstanden, ne. A: hm B: aber so ab un zu kommt es schon mal A:
gemacht! B: un gefragt, wo du bist, aber die wußtes auch nich. C: Ich war d
geworden. A: Das verträgt der nich? Aber heißes Wasser müßte den doch auflö
guten Gegenden drinstehn B: ja? A: aber das is ja genau das, was wir uns ni
hab ich no nich viel Ahnung! ((3s)) Aber es sind ja kleine, die sind ja noch
haben? A: Nee, die muß man bis Mai, aber danach komm ich nich mehr dazu, we
hinterher ganz schön fertig... Naja, aber trotzdem, war gut. A: Muß man ja
Hm... Nee, das find ich ja lustig! . Aber ich glaub, das kann einem mit der
ich will mich da nich gegen sperren, aber, ö, gibts da nich irgendwie ne Mög
ich's auch in Deutsch nich verstehe, aber doch dann in Franz/ B: Ach, in Fr
im Hause? A: Nee, die is grade weg. Aber die bleibt nich lange. B: Ja? Isch
is es noch viel dicker geworden. B: Aber des blutet nich? A: Nee? 140 B: U
jetz auf eenma iss . aus. A: hm B: Aber, ich weeß nich, vielleicht . finden
jetz, ne, Freitag kommt noch keiner, aber das is en bißchen ei/ plötzlich je
mit . Pfeffer un Salz ange/ C: Ja, aber grad ne Salatgurke is so unattrakti
natürlich en bißchen danach stinken, aber das kann man wohl nich ändern. B:
nich vorstellen. B: Doch, doch! Ja, aber wir ham dem jetz abgeholfen, wir ha
nich, jedenfalls war's . ganz ulkig. Aber .kann ich ja auch, wenn wer da sin
nichts zusätzlich, das hieß immer:" Aber das is ja zusätzliche Arbeit!", un
oder sowas ((lacht)) A: Hm B: Ja, . aber die waren . also . schon zu kritisc
schön. Das Haus so gefällt mir gut, aber ich bin noch nich drin gewesen. Y w
Sie kommen hier drüber geflogen, ja, aber bei weitem nich soviel wie in Porz
Thema sehr beschäftigt has B: Naja, aber wenn ich die Stunden zusammenzähle,
unmöglichsten Typen rum, ne. A: Ja, aber ich war gar nich an dem Tag in der
V auch wär die einzige Möglichkeit, aber das kann doch nich / B: daß da ir
viel Arbeit, die auf einmal! B: Ja, aber ein oder zwei is sowieso scheißegal
vielleicht auch mit! B: Ja, ja. Ja, aber die sin dann auf jeden Fall im Land
W, un da war zimlich viel Gedränge, aber ich bin also auch nich mit der Bah
was ich mir wünsche zum Geburtstag! Aber ich weiß nichts Grandioses! B: Ja
was das in Finnland kostet! A: Jaja, aber diese Feste in Finnland, von denen
weiß nich, wie ihr Silvester feiert, aber meistens macht man doch son Riesen
weiß zwar nich, wann die das machen, aber/ A: jaa, wahrscheinlich nach Feier
weiß zwar nimmer genau, wat dat war, aber . war ganz amüsant... Ja, und . da
Weißt du, das Einzige, was ich wei§, aber da hab ich überhaupt keine Ahnung,
Weihnachten un Neujahr kommter mal, aber danach hat er wieder soooooo viel
weil für den die Sache verjährt is.. Aber ich muß mich ja jetz doch noch mit
wer gedacht, wer gehn früh ins Bett, aber wer gehn vorher noch ein trinken,
wir wissen zwar no nich genau, wann, aber wir wollnirgendwann mal ne Fete ge
wäre eine Möglichkeit . vielleicht. Aber das . das kommt mirn bißchen krumm
würd sagen, kommen Se doch einfach. aber ich hoffe, daß es dann da is. daß s
überhaupt nich an. B: Ja, aber wenn die schon namittachs sacht, da
ziemlich kompliziert die Sache hier, aber . ich mein, ich helf ihr, soweit's
Z-Weg B: Stüssgen ist bereits Z-Weg, aber Sie müssen sich links von Stüssgen
! B: Un der hat ne Menge zu tun. A: Aber danach könnder ja mal vorbeikommen.
((Räuspern)) A: Sicher. ((Einatmen)) Aber . was somer machen? Millionär her
(lacht) A: Ja, is natürlich drollig! Aber wenn deine Schwester für sowas kei
, möchtich auch nich länger bleiben, aber . sowas gab's nich. Unterhalb der
, bis et spät wird, 113 A: Jaja. B: aber die haun immer gleichab denn. A: W
, dann kommt die A under Y. A: Ja, (aber) er hat auch nich gesagt, wohin, ne
, er wollt ja sowieso an die Schule, aber an der Uni wär er damit wohl nichts
, ich weiß es nicht, ne. A: hmhm B: Aber wo Sie sagen Porz-Lind, da is das R
, nur inner Schule immer! A: Hm B: Aber die Geschäfte und so is allet offen
, son Pech! Jetz wartet die irgendwo, aber ich weiß au nich, wo. B: Ich weiß
, um eins wolltest du zur Uni kommen, aber das brauchsde ja nich, dann. C: J
. Ich könntdie auch heute abgeben B: aber? A: aber dann kämich nich mehr daz
... Bracht die also kurz vorbei, (war aber) gut, okay, tschüs. B: ( ) C:
/öh, Ei essen, das hat über achtzig, aber das verbraucht beim Verdauen mehr a
: (lacht) Nein, d/ das weiß ich, ne. Aber das is mir zuviel, das immer zu sa

: Der hatte mich nämig auch gefragt, aber ich weiß nichmehr, da war irgendwa
: Ja? . Och! ... Na, sicher . ((3s)) Aber das schon so alt is, hättich nich
? Hatte man das angenommen? B: Jaja! Aber seit gestern is es sicher! A: Ja,
ß de dich en bißchen ablenken kanns. Aber quält ihm kein Essen rein! A: Neen
ß nich, war der Hase auch ma / der is aber wieder gesund geworden? Oder was?
ßchen. Ja, nicht so direkt aufs Bett, aber so übers Bett, am Bett natürlich
a nicht zu sagen, ne. A: Ja? Hm. B: Aber der darf jetz nich, wenn Sie bremse
a, das da würd ich mich drüber freun, aber wie gesagt, ich hab keine Ahnung,
a, ich hab auch etwas . es geht zwar, aber / ich merk es sofort, hab dann dic
acht) War richtig köstlich! A: Jaja! Aber solche Sachen wird man ja immer gef
alles im Wörterbuch B: ((lacht)) A: aber . manchmal kriegt man dann doch seh
alles schuld! B: (lacht) Na gut. C: Aber der Y hat sich . vh an der Uni amüs
als Steuerklasse eins, ne B: Hm A: Aber jetz fang ich an zu verdienen, unje
an sich müßt ich Sie beglückwünschen, aber ich seh gar nich ein, ich meine, i
anchmal vergess ichs! (lacht) Em, ( ) aber mein Chef kommt schon am 31. / am
anruf loslassen, ne. A: Ja klar! B: Aber . öh, rechnet ma am besten nich dam
arbeit gebrauchen würde? B: Hm, nee, aber ik kann mir ja nich vorstellen, wie
as hätte sie ja noch keinem erzählt. Aber wär ja einlich Quatsch, warum sollt
as mach ich hier unten in der Kneipe, aber sons isses nachher zu voll undann
as war schön, das war wirklich schön. Aber danach war kein schöner Tag mehr
asse auch nich üblich, ne. B: Hm A: Aber die / die standen zum Beispiel auf,
auf / wann se streiken. B: Aha 81 A: Aber da muß man natürlich Sätze bauen, w
aupt kein Lust, zu heiraten!" "Ja, B, aber du wills doch ma Kinder haben!" -
bbencocktails oder so wat A: Hm! B: aber trotzdem muß ich en bißchen was . a
bei heißtet immer, es wär das siebte, aber dat stimmt glaubich garnich. B: N
ber nich zusammen leben. A: Naja B: Aber sind wahnsinnig gute Freunde, ne A:
bißchen Bier un so weiter hinterher . aber jedenfalls war ich no einer von de
ch / ich / es tut mir furchtbar leid, aber ich bin da völlig ratlos, ich weiß
ch en evangelischer Feiertag! B: Ja, aber das hatten wer eigenlich ooch nie,
ch glaub, dann wär's Unsinn gewesen. Aber ich glaub, da die ganze Sache schon
ch hinten nix rauskommen! A: Jaja.. Aber . es bläht sich so auf, es is hinte
ch schon dran gewöhnt? B: (lacht) A: Aber ihr wolltet doch das zweite adoptie
ch, daß Se damit auch das Z kriegen, aber das is schomal ne Antragsfrist. A:
chluckt natürlich auch welche runter, aber das is gar nich schlimm, die schm
chma an! B: 14. hab ich schon was! . Aber müßter ma sehn, wir machen dann gr
cht Stunden. A: Hm, ja. B: Insgesamt. Aber das könn sich natürlich denken, un
cht) B: a, es gibt nur einige Worte, aber, na, die gebrauchste ja selten. A:
chten in Ruhe lassen," he. A: Hm B: Aber . ham sich wohl nich dran gehalten.
da bin ich immerhin noch stolz drauf, aber wenn ich mir vorstelle, wie ich, ä
da sowieso nich drum! A: Jaja.. Nee, aber ich find das ganz gut. . Du, ich gl
dann haben Sen Rechtsanspruch drauf. Aber bis dahin vergeht noch einige Zeit,
das ganze Bettzeug abgezogen und so, aber/ Ich weiß nich, die/ die verstecke
das wolltich auch schon grade sagen, aber wie kommwer hier bloß raus?" (lacht
das/du wirst nich mehr! 32 B: Hm A: Aber irgendwie vertragen se sich wohl tr
de ja'n Scheibenwischer. A: Jaja B: Aber hier, da schneit dir das auf die .
deswegen sind wir so plötzlich frei. aber die wolln heute nachmittag kommen.
Die ham se auf zwei Stunden gesetzt, aber die dauerte ewig. Da bin ich spät n
die hat ihr Examen mit eins gemacht, aber i/ die halt ich für ne also ziemisc
die Kinder is et bestimmt ooch schön, aber ich würd's besser finden, wenn se
die nördlichen, Richtung . Neuß die, aber gute / A: Welche sind denn das? B:
dieses Wochenende keine Zeit." - "Ja, aber du wolltest doch kommen!" "Ja",
due hab ich noch nich gemacht. B: .. Aber du bis ja vielleicht ne Type, du. C
e hat als als an uns, ne A: ah so B: aber wir sind ziemlich ( ), weil A: naj
e vertragen se sich wohl trotzdem B: Aber das findet man aber oft, du. ((3s))
e von da nach hier schleppen! A: Ja. Aber das is ihm, glaubich, nicht mehr au
e, unter Umständen ausfallen lassen, aber sehr ungern. (lacht) B: Ja, so bli
e. Alles scheußliche Tapeten und so, aber sauber, ne, nich irgendwie in nem
e. So ne richtig schöne Bettlektüre. Aber a propos Lektüre, ne, fällt mir gr
e/ da kennen die nix! A: Ja nee, dann aber das klappt bestimmt! Bloß ich ärger
edlung". A: weißes Hinweisschild B: Aber nich/ nicht bis Rath durchfahren, j
Ei darfsde auch essen! Zum Beispiel. Aber es muß hartgekocht sein. C: Un die
eißt du ja gar nich B: ehen 107 A: aber, wenn / wenn irgendwas genau festst
eicht kommt es noch mal irgendwann! . Aber . grad auf solchen Festen laß ich
eine, es muß natürlich auch wat sein, aber . wart da ma auf ne günstige Geleg
eit gehabt, was zu lesen. B: Hm A: Aber ich nehme an, die ganzen öh, Aktion

eit, meine Doktorarbeit zu schreiben, aber . vielleicht, wenn ich mich jetz e
eit. So ises ne Verrücktheit und so. Aber das Eine is eben doch ne
eiter! A: Tut mir ja furchtbar leid, aber ich nehm an, in Bonn find ich se
elegt! In ne andere Wohnung im Haus. Aber is kein Problem, da kannsde auch a
elle für ne halbe . em, ö, übernimmt, aber nur offiziell, und inoffiziell, ö,
emerkt, die hättste klauen können ( ) Aber war ganz nett, der Abend. A: Jo.
en wir uns noch mal. A: Gut! B: Ja, aber macht unsertwegen/ bleibt unsertweg
en, die se gerne als Lehrerin haben, aber, öh, eben nich als / als Referendar
en. B: Doch, dagegen schon. C: Nee, aber jetz wirklich/ also nur mit der fün
er allerdings selber renovieren, ne, aber sie is nich in nem scheußlichen Zu
er gewesen sein! B: Ach so, der. A: Aber das war jemand, der konnte arbeiten
er, als ich Sie eben Sie gesehn hab, aber . daß Sie überhaupt abnehmen mußten
er, so ganz A: Ja! Der is ganz dünn, aber der liegt schon ganz hoch! B: Ah s
er? . Kann man doch? A: Ich mein,ja. Aber ich weiß es nich. B: Nö! A: Werd
eres Wetter is, es gibt so allerlei, aber alles weiter, in Siegburg un Troisd
ern / oder oder schon in ein Termin, aber et / braucht glaubich ziemlich lan
ern den Z angestellt B: hm . hm A: aber auf ne / auf ne richtige Stelle und
ers mittendrin eingeschaltet, un so, aber wenn du dagegen bis, ich lösch es
eute nich? B: Ach, ich mag die Leute, aber ich bin eso fremd, da is halt bess
euzchen, hier auf der Liste! A: Ja, aber die kommen, wie gesagt, nur mal kur
f jeden Fall mal hin, weil ich / öh, aber bis jetz hab ich no nichts getan, i
fiziell wie ne halbe Stelle aussieht, aber er verrechnets mit Ihnen intern, n
ften oder / keine Ahnung! B: So! A: Aber es soll gut sein! (lacht) B: Na gu
ganz schön. Nich unheimlich viel, ne, aber. macht was aus, wenn de die Tomate
ge eine Wahnsinnshetzerei. B: Hm A: Aber danach geht's mir wohl besser. B:
geit. B: Das darf allerdings nicht . Aber dieses . etwas anschlagen, ja? Wen
genblick noch keinen Spaß B: hm A: aber vielleicht kommd's noch, so, vor al
gieren lassen, ne. A: (lacht) Nee... Aber ich werd dir das mal zeigen / es gi
h dir ma wieder welche rüba. A: Ja, aber hör ma, stürz dich nich in Unkosten
h überhaupt nich, wat dat heißt! Ne, aber ich hab ein Fachwörterbuch, un das
h bin/ ich bin fotografiert worden ., aber die könn auf dem Foto nur erkennen
h ham wer nix dagegen, warum nich B: aber andererseits, wenn ich Mittwoch vor
h hätt gern mit dir ne Runde gedreht, aber/ B: Ich hab die X mal getroffen
h selbst zu tragen hat, andererseit. aber auch gegen Umstürzen, bei nem Bran
h, das wird ne Schnake gewesen sein, aber erstensma is keine Schnake im Zimm
h, es is kein . großer Fortschritt . aber . kann ma nix machen! B: Ja, aber
haben, vor allem eine ziemlich lange, aber/ hilft wohl nichts. B: Wie lang h
hlankheitsessen gemacht! B: Aha! A: Aber heut abend gehts dann wieder los, a
ht) Voriges Jahr hat es gepaßt!... Ja aber/ weil man an diesem Tag selbst kei
ich hab ja noch / nee, ich hatte 710, aber ich hab ja jetz noch en Viertel me
ich wollte da immer ma hin B: hm A: aber zu der Zeit, wo ich . Zeit habe, da
ich? B: Wenn in einem Raum, dann ... Aber man muß das mal gerochen haben, so
icht antue. B: Ja. A: Ja. B: Naja, aber da hätteter dabeisein müssen, mein
ichtiges is. Ich glaub, ich hatte da aber nix Großartiges! . Das is immer so
ie alte Weise da rein kommt B: hm A: aber das dürfte mir blühen B: ja, das w
ie um / um sechs Uhr abholen! A: Ja, aber dann haben wir gar nichts mehr fest
ielleicht gar nich ungünstig gewesen, aber, nuja, wat solles? A: (lacht) Hat
ielleicht mit jemanden zusammenleben, aber / B: Ich überleg mir ja schon, ob
ienzwanzig Mark 191 B: ((lacht)) A: Aber der Termin war ja rum! Den hab ich
iertel Wissenschaftliche. B: Hm A: - aber . man stellt niemanden ein mit nur
ik natürlich schon jenauer A: hm B: aber so beim Erzählen, ah . sowieso die
il sie en andern hat. A: Ah so.. Ja, aber meistens isses doch so, daß . nich
in der Nähe isser schon, das is klar, aber ich kann jetzt von hier aus nicht
in Lindenthal, Baujahr dreiunsechzig, aber da kostete der Quadratmeter 2.000
in, also, es gibt auf jeden Fall was, aber ich weiß nich, was. B: Okay! A: D
ine halbe Stelle abtreten. A: Hm. B: Aber erstensmal wäre das ja doch eine .
instellplätze nehmen! B: Ja, leider. Aber wir warn damals laut Vertrag an den
ir gehn zwar aus essen, in Burscheid, aber feiern danach in Hochtal undda wom
irgendwie drei Jahre getrennt leben. Aber dat geht auch mit einem Jahr! Unter
is denn da groß zu kochen? ja Moment, aber, dat darf / dat kann die sich aber
is mir, ich meine in etwa'n Begriff, aber . wat 1000 Kalorien sin, weiß ich
is wirklich en doofer Termin! B: Ja, aber sach doch mal, wann de mal hier vor
it einem Schlag davon befreien kanns, aber wenn das dann auch nich geht, dann
ix mehr! B: Dass vernünftig! A: Ja, aber / B: Ja, und wie sieht das mit Don
ja, denn / denn wir gehn Steak essen, aber . wir sind um acht da fertig! B:

Ja, ich wär ja mitgekommen, morgen!.. Aber um eins, da muß ich noch arbeiten!
Jaja, hätte er, hm. (lacht) Aber ich hätte alles geglaubt, weißdu, a
kein Verständnis hat... B: Och doch! Aber.. die war/ die war nich sauer, die
Kreisrund und leuchtend rot? Nee! B: Aber ringsum kann sich natürlich dann du
könnten Sie jetz nichts mehr machen. Aber wir könn nich so rumfahrn, das mach
l ich gedacht hab, das neutralisiert, aber das hat nix genutzt. Naja,.. Wahrs
lacht) A: Selbst ganz überrascht! .. Aber es wird immer besser, glaubich. B:
Lage, ja. A: Hm.. Ja, wir ham keine, aber (lacht) äh, also, es liegt aber tr
legen. B: Ja, dat mach ich auch, ne, aber . eh A: Nee, ne kein liniertes Bla
lich auch die Severinsbrücke fahren, aber / A: da is voll, ne7 1
Lieb von dir, daß du an uns denkst! - Aber was anderes: Was macht ihr heute
ls wissenschaftliche Hilfskraft nich, aber als Assistent. B: Ach so! Dann nut
machen, obwohl ich den X nett finde, aber das is so ein Quatsch zu heiraten.
Magen gehalten, mir war so schlecht, aber ich konnte auch nich kotzen. Das wa
mal wieder sehr lustig. ((3s)) A: Aber, ich/ ich hab jetz / den letzten Ta
me, dann holik ma wieder welche. A: Aber überstürz dich damit nich, ne, das
mecken nach nichts. A: ((lacht)) B: Aber versuch das mit dem Spray, vor alle
Morgen wird's regnen", ne, B: ja A: aber du wirs nich sagen "Morgen regnet's
mäßig hab ich ganz schön abgenommen, aber so vonner Figur her kaum was, der
n fünften datiert. B: ((lacht)) A: Aber solang is die Post ja nich unterweg
n ich gucke mal hier mal sehn, ne. . Aber ich würd sagen, wer machen dat näc
n ja auch immer wieder los. A: Naja, aber isja schon alt, ne. B: Dreiunsechz
n können Sie zwar das Objekt kaufen, aber es kann nicht gefördert werden. A:
n ma öfter ma abends lang gearbeitet, aber einfach deshalb, weil ich erst um
n man sich das nich anrechnen lassen? Aber nich als Lehrer, ne? A: Nee, wahr
n sechs spätestens zurück C: hm B: aber so kann's natürlich länger dauern.
n un Monate sein. A: Ja. Also, aber / aber jetz nich en Jahr oder so, also, so
n Wochen un Monate sein. A: Ja. Also, aber / aber jetz nich en Jahr oder so, a
Nee, ich bin mal bei der VHS gewesen. Aber da bin ich nur drei oder vier mal
ngsum quaddelig. Ob das ne Wanze is? Aber das is doch unwahrscheinlich! C:
nich die Zeit aussuchen. B: Hm. A: Aber is ja immerhin noch besser als . so
nich ganz wohl mit dieser Geschichte. Aber bei der anderen würden wir uns no
nich, Mann! Da wärn wir ja auch dumm! Aber wo findet man schon jemanden, der
nie wissen. B: (lacht) Eben! C: Ja, aber hättsde das direkt gesagt, wärn wer
nn irgendwann Mitte Januar B: Hm A: aber da ruf ich nochma an! B: 14. hab i
normale Cola hat mehr als, als Bier, aber es gibt ne ganz spezielle, die heiß
ntlich nämlich dann! A: Ja klar! B: Aber ich wollte auch mal 55 Kilo wiegen,
nun wieder auch nich, ne. B: Hm. A: Aber . es war natürlich erstmal . ein ar
nzen gezogen worden im letzten Jahr, aber ob das jetzt, öh, für Sie zutrifft,
nzig Mark die Stunde gebe B: hm A: aber der kommt jetz/ zwischen Weihnachte
ob sich dat alles lohnt, du. A: Ja, aber was wills/ has dun Examer, mit dem
olut nichts passiert, ne. A: Hm. B: Aber, also, weiß nich, die/die Polizei,
ons, ich wär gern (lacht) (was raus), aber / B: jo A: is schlecht. B: Viell
onär heiraten wär gut, nech? B: Ja, aber weißde, die gibt's so selten A:
owieso nich bekehren, ne, B: Hm A: aber so sonst so Sachen, zum Beispiel, d
r adoptieren was Schlimmes? B: Nein. Aber es gehört sich nicht. Weiß auch nic
r dafür bezahlt, um es zu bauen, ne, aber es liegt an so ner miesen Straße. U
r ich ja so'n nettes Mädchen gewesen. aber heute wär überhaupt nix mehr mit m
r is ja noch ganz neu (lacht) B: ja, aber deine Frau hatte doch en VW oder so
r letzte Tach/ für die Anmelderei... Aber mit X bin ich gut voran gekommen,
r nichts. Ich hab alles durchgeguckt, aber es war eine Sache in Lindenthal, B
r no nich zugenommen. So Weihnachten. Aber R natürlich! B: Ja, ich hab auch
r nur offiziell, und inoffiziell, ö, aber nicht bei mir arbeitet und Ihnen da
r Schule hatten mer auch am 31. frei, aber.. jetz . im Berufsleben nich mehr.
r soviel zugenommen hattn A: ja B: aber is trotzdem ne ganz schöne Portion,
r, was passiert wär). 137 A: hm B: Aber sowas versuchen die all, ne. Wenn's
reckigen Unterkünften schläft ((2s)) aber das tut ihr ja nich A: So dreckig
reut is, dann kann man wieder fahrn, aber.. die brauchen ja'n Tach, bis se a
rher noch gesehn mit irgend jemadem, aber da wollt ich dann au nich stören (1
richtigen Schock gekriegt!... Naja... Aber ich war am Montag nachmittag so fe
rreden, mit mir Gymnastik zu machen, aber da denkt der ja nicht dran! B: Ja,
s gültig, ne, B: Dat weiß ich nich.. Aber ich mein, is ja eigenlich Quatsch,
s hattesdu ja noch viel mehr! B: Ja! Aber ganz groß wirdes nich, viele sin ve
s kann / das kann natürlich sein, ne, aber/ wenn wer Glück haben, kommt se au
s wie 25! 68 B: Genau, ne. Aber warum feierder denn an son ungünsti

s/ ich glaube nicht/ 9 A:	aber	so ein großes Vieh kann sich doch n
's? B: Ich hab's noch nich gefunden,	aber	ich ruf gleich noch ma zurück! . D
sch . fast gar nich möchlich! A: Ja,	aber	wat machemer denn da? B: Müssemer
schlank, hem, 29 A: hm B:	aber	was danach kam, du! A: (lacht) B:
Schlitten? A: Nee, wir ham hier nix.	Aber	((3s)) vielleicht... io. Bis morgen
schon von einem Programm ins andere,	aber	es is nix drin, ne. A: Nee, also w
Se vielleicht vorher drannehmen, ne.	Aber	je nach dem, wie das is. A: Hm. Da
seither noch nich mit ihr gesprochen,	aber	ich glaub, also, sie war ja schon
sen aufm Tisch. A: Ah, so jo. B: Ja	aber	mit dem Lebenslauf, also wie gesagt
sgemacht? A: Das war son vager Plan,	aber	ich mein, das hätten wer hinterher
sinnige da vor mich hinhacken werde,	aber	heute tu ich trotzdem nix mehr! B:
so nich bis in alle Ewigkeit machen,	aber	ich mein, wenn de Lust hast, Y kom
t A: Das is auch auf der Seite fünf,	aber	. weiter unten. B: Ringanker! Verb
t geht, sons muß se wieder arbeiten,	aber	dat sin ja nur noch 4 Wochen, glau
t mich ja am Samstag gesehen! C: Ja,	aber,	wie gesagt, da/ B: Da hattich en
tdie auch heute abgeben B: aber? A:	aber	dann kämich nich mehr dazu, die dur
te also auch mal geistig abschalten,	aber	ich hab mich totgelacht, nee nee n
te doch eigentlich auch möglich sein!	Aber	an un für sich findet man es unsch
ten. Das machen die zwar freiwillig,	aber	mit dem, wo sie in der Klasse sin,
ter nomal?/ im Westerwald versunken,	aber	dann isser ja . doch wohl wieder d
tes daran und wir wolln das ja auch,	aber	. irgendwann wolln wer auch mal un
trinkt ja auch nicht. B: Die wissen	aber	in dem Fall besser selbst, was ihne
t's nich so besonders, un, öh. naja,	aber	man sieht schon, der Verkäufer wird
u. B: Das wollt ich ers an sich, ne.	Aber	das hab ich dann do nich ausgehalt
uch einige sein, das weiß ich schon,	aber	/ A: Oh! Das hasde wieder ganz fein
un das mußde dann ausfüllen. B: Ja,	aber	der will so viel absetzen, weil der
und das sieht man dann auch. ((3s))	Aber	. öm . am Samstag abend, da habiche
us, eh, so kurz vor der Reise, nich,	aber	em, ich würde auch gerne sehn, ich
weg, das wird z/zusammengeschrieben,	aber	"nach Hause gehen', nö! Sieh mal na
werds mir überlegen, ob ich was esse,	aber	wenn ich verhungeren sollte bei eu
wieder . nix zu tun, ne. A: jaja B:	aber	jeden Abend is Quatsch! A: Jeden A
wollteh bestimmtes Haus gern kaufen,	aber,	öh, das kann nur C: Kaufen? Ein H
über nachgedacht A: och, is ja/ B:	aber,	is schon ne schwierige Angelegenhe
z, ja achthundertzwanzig, jo. 172 A:	Aber	montags geht eben / B: Ja, Augenbli
zu motzen, als ich ihr das verbot! .	Aber	der Junge is dann, als der ankam, d
zwar wieder en Blötsch reingefahren,	aber	gewöhnt sich dran! B: Jo, würd mir
die ham zwar . 84 Kalorien so rum, .	aber	. die verbrauchen beim Verdauen me

III.b) Total Occurrences of ABER *as conjunctional adverb*

immer zu sagen. A: Ja, du gibs dir	aber	sons Mühe! B: Ja, wenn das Ding da
Ja. A: ja, gut! B: Wahrscheinlich	aber	dann nich, die werden dann ja best
aber dumm, da hätt se / A: Sie hat	aber	auch nich hier angerufen. B: Nee?
B: Ja, is klar, ersmal/ A: Ich hab	aber	inzwischen gehört, daß das also wir
da hatter gesacht, Silvester hätter	aber	keine Zeit, und er würd doch so ger
Das wäre dann' ne Viertelstelle, die	aber	offiziell aussieht wie ne halbe, n
Dat hat sie gesagt, ja, dat säh sie	aber	wat anderes/ anders, un dann isse a
im Stadt-Anzeiger gesehen, ich hatte	aber	. grad zu der Zeit eben keine Zeit
Regelungen zu fallen, ne. B: Ja, is	aber	so. ((3s)) Wieso, habt ihr den Te
was getan!" "Ja", sag ich, "glaubst	aber	nich, daß de mich da noch ma hinkri
wiegen, ne, D: aha B: wenn ich das	aber	bloß, äh, auf 75 runtergehe, un ess
zu seiner Großmutter gefahrn, wollte	aber	nachher wiederkommen und mit ihr t
! C: (lacht). Ja, nee, das müssen wer	aber	unbedingt ma machen. B: Ja sicher.
, aber, dat darf / dat kann die sich	aber	doch nit erlauben! B: Och, so zwei
, wobei ich bei diesen beiden Posten	aber	gleich sagen muß, daB wir in den l
ande. Nee, also (son Scheiß) kann mir	aber	keiner erzählen. Gottes Willen! 6
ann schon mal rausspringen, der darf	aber	nit alle 8 Tage da . losjehn, ne. A
ch. Dann müßtich aber / dann würdich	aber	noch mal anrufen, und zwar/ B: Ja,
d dann noch en anderer, ne. Die warn	aber	beide ziemich kritisch und bestimm
dem gesprochen? A: Hm, und er . käme	aber	mal so ne halbe Stunde rein, um eu
e Ihrer Stelle übernimmt, inoffiziell	aber	nur ein Viertel und Ihnen die Diff

ei wollnmer sowieso nich. A: Ja, is aber viel Arbeit, die auf einmal! B: Ja
eine, aber (lacht) äh, also, es liegt aber trotzdem relativ ruhig? Oder? 127
einige Bücher lesen, und die hab ich aber no nich angeguckt, da komm ich eh!
eltern vertragen, ne... Ja, das kann aber auch blöd werden, wenn die sich zu
em (...) un so is, ja, hörma, wollder aber dafür nich lieber ma hier bei uns
enn man anfängt.. Dafür hat man dann aber anschließend wieder . nix zu tun, n
gar nich! B: Hm, und . da . ham sich aber die ganzen, öh, öh, Eltern wahnsin
gs aufgeräumt. A: Oh, das hätte mich aber nich davon abgehalten B: Ja! Ich m
h hab keine genaue Ahnung, ich glaube aber, das Gesetz is noch nich raus, daß
h kam, du! A: (lacht) B: da bin ich aber fast zusammengebrochen. Das war all
hen. A: Du Ärmster! B: Jo, dat geht aber, das Gröbste is schon hinter mir, d
hengekommen." "Ja", sachtse, "du mußt aber kommen das Wochenende!" "Naja, wie
idung stehen, ne. A: Hm B: Ich kenn aber au unheimlich viele Leute, die sich
im und Rath auf der Hälfte. Sehn Sie aber schon, links das groBe Neubaugebie
inar, und. wie war das noch? Das war aber schon dieser Tage doch! A: ((3s))
Ja, das ginge wohl auch. Dann müßtich aber / dann würdich aber noch mal anruf
lig, ne, spricht für Wanzen. Es gibt aber ungezählte andere/ A: Sind die gr
lleicht) Is ja bald! Kanns vielleicht aber irgendwann ma mit dem / naja, du h
meine, ja, wenns euch paßt, wir könns aber auch verschieben, wir könns auch m
mmen!" "Ja", sagich, "wolltich, da is aber was zwischengekommen." "Ja", sacht
n hšr ich auf. C: Mann! B: Das geht aber sehr langsam die 71 hattich schon a
nrufen, und zwar/ B: Ja, dann rufsde aber so/wenns geht so mittags an, eben,
nteressantes mal dabei is, könnter's aber auch immer sagen, ne. A: Hio. B:
on biBchen schmuddelig aus, ich weiß aber nich mehr, wie die heißt. Und die h
phantastisch, ne. A: Hm B: Die könn aber nich zusammen leben. A: Naja B: A
r W fuhr A: hm B: und da ham X un Y aber gesagt, sie ständen im Examen, un
r wei/ in der Fußgängerzone, blicken aber zum Königsforst raus. Vorne, also
rgendeiner gepennt hat. In S habt ihr aber keine Stiche gehabt? A: Nee. ((3s
rr V! V: Ja, das war's! B: Da müßte aber da noch eine / A: Eins, zwei, drei
rs geschrieben/ A: (lacht) jaja, is aber nich gemeint B: (lacht) A: nich d
sde? B: Bin schon 26! A: Oh, siehst aber noch aus wie 25! 68 B: G
ssen? 82 A: Ja! B: Ja? A: Ich weiß aber noch nich, was. Vielleicht Butterbr
t B: Ja A: Em . da konnte er sich aber dann nich die Zeit aussuchen. B:
tzungen alle erfüllen. Inwieweit das aber möglich is, das können wir nich be
wohl trotzdem B: Aber das findet man aber oft, du. ((3s)) Ich bin da ja auch
X, dat will er nich. Also, wir haben aber so die Eigentumswohnungen zwischen

IV. Total occurrences of JA in modal particle function

3 B: sons atmesde das ja ein. Das bringt ne schwächere Wanze
21 A: Nee, die / Sie wollten ihn ja für Herrn R un Herrn S gleichsei/ z
((lacht)) Ja. Ja, ja. A: Die tu ich ja sowieso, so/ also . das mach ich man
Ach, ja nu! B: Also, hör ma, das is ja nu keen ( ), also ik schick dir die
der W wirds allein schaffen, der muß ja da / der hat ja als 122 freier Mitar
irgendwann ma mit dem / naja, du has ja keine Zeit / ah, der W wirds allein
Is ja gut! Paß ma auf, dann kann ich ja ma zwischendurch anrufen. sons komm
Ja, ich auch nich, Mann! Da wärn wir ja auch dumm! Aber wo findet man schon
Ne, die Frankfurter Straße verbindet ja Porz mit Köln A: Jaa B: Ne? . KHD-
((lacht)) A: Aber solang is die Post ja nich unterwegs. B: Ja.. Das is glau
25 bis 30 Minuten. 88 B: Och, das is ja kein Problem. Da kamma ja immer noch
A: Ah so. B: Nich, dann könnde mans ja so machen A: Dann . ja, dann würd i
A: Ja, ich weiß nich, ich hätte mich ja eigenlich was früher melden müssen!
A: Jaja! Aber solche Sachen wird man ja immer gefragt. B: Hm... Vermutlich.
alles aus B: mal alles aus, weil wer ja eben wissen müssen, was wer noch ka
an zu nähen! C: (lacht) Nee, ich bin ja sowieso da, ich muß die ganzen Büche
anderes mehr leisten. Un dann sin wer ja noch auf Wohnungssuche! B: (
angenommen, ich hab's / sie hat sich ja noch mit jemand getroffen um halb f
ankommen. Wenn des überweist, kommt's ja sowieso nachm Termin an. Un, öh/ we
B: Doch! C: Hör ma, ich erkenn dich ja demnächst nich mehr. B: (lacht) Ich
B: Eh, nein, diesmal nicht, weil ich ja nicht wieder zum Flughafen zurückko
B: Ja, is Klasse, der unterhält dich ja köstlich, und du wirst dafür auch n

bei Z diese Fete, da brauch man sich ja heute noch gar nich drüber aufregen!
Bus, da kannsde ja nich /da kanns du ja nich fahren. A: Neenee! B: Naja, w
dann laß es sein! B: Nö, da könn wer ja ers mal hören! Ich werd mich ers mal
das/ dases nich geklappt hat, das lag ja dann wohl an der Schule und an der
daß man alleine heiratet, das stimmt ja nicht. Man meint immer, man heirate
Dat weiß ich nich.. Aber ich mein, is ja eigenlich Quatsch, die Vereinbarung
denn da nichts Genaues? A: Nä! B: s ja doof, ne. Und der X läßt sich da au
denn der Freund bestanden? B: Der is ja noch nich fertig. A: Der is noch ni
Denn, immer Käse, ich mein, das wird ja auf die Dauer auch langweilig, ne. B
die Schreibmaschine, man könnte sich ja vielleicht so ma . ne Stunde zusamm
erzählt hatte, A: nee B: da hab ich ja jetz am Montag auch Gerichtstermin.
essen darf! C: Ach nee, du magst das ja nich/ du darfs ja nich! B: Nöö, ich
hammer noch gar nix vor B: Da könner ja dann mal gucken. Bis dann, ne. A: B
heut nachmittag nochma runter. Es hat ja jetzt da oben auch zu kalt, im Grun
Ich . weiß es nich! B: Ja, das müßte ja eigenlich die gleiche Form sein, wie
ich ja was von ihm gewollt, ich hätt ja hinfahren (sollen). B: Hm. C: Un da
ja nu Moment, die, die die A, die is ja ni mehr da, ich seh nur Ihre Frau n
Ja, eben. (lacht) A: (lacht) B: Bis ja noch da anner Uni, ne. 165 A: So sc
Ja, ich weiß es nich, damals gabs dat ja noch nich. A: ( ) Wie kann man denn
Ja, so ne Kleine, ne? B: Hm. Die hat ja nach Frankreich geheiratet. A: Ja?
Ja. B: Is doch en Nachteil, ich habs ja immer gesagt. A: Ja, und wir wollten
Jaja, eben. So lange dauert die Fahrt ja nich. B: Wie lange fahrn Se denn? A
jetz schon? A: Ich? B: Na, du fährs ja bald schon zehn Jahre, wa! A: Ach,
klappt schon! C: (lacht) B: Ich hab ja auch nichts gegen Feten feiern und B
Knöllchen-Bußgeldbescheid is, ich hab ja gleich en primär Bußgeldbescheid be
könn wer die auch angucken, ich weiß ja gar nich, wat da drauf is, hab ich
Ich hätt's doch überwiesen?. Ich kann ja die Belege beifügen. B: . Dass nat
mal irjentwann reinkommen, dat dauert ja nur fünf Minuten, is et widder / mü
man hei/ wir sind ja mit dabei, es is ja nich so, daß man alleine heiratet,
Menge zu tun. A: Aber danach könnder ja mal vorbeikommen. B: Ja, gerne. A:
Moped, oder wat dat is, ich kann die ja nich ausenanderhalten A: hm B: nac
muß se wieder arbeiten, aber dat sin ja nur noch 4 Wochen, glaubich. . Dann
nämig grad was warmmachen, . Essen is ja . zur Zeit nich mehr drin bei unsre
neuen Scheidungsrecht. Ja, da wirsde ja die Verpflichtungen, die de / die di
nich aufmachen, ne.. Das is für mich ja besonders schlimm, du. Da . ich wei
nich lästig? B: Nö - nö, das hab ieh ja es letzte Ma auch schon gemacht, das
noch nich gemacht. B: .. Aber du bis ja vielleicht ne Type, du. C: Wieso? B
ö zweitens, eine Viertelstelle bliebe ja dann doch übrig.   20 A: J
Och, das is ja kein Problem. Da kamma ja immer noch / dann würdich vielleich
Öh /   B: So / A: Englisch hab ich ja auch gar keine Unterrichts / B: Neen
Sache verjährt is.. Aber ich muß mich ja jetz doch noch mit ner Sache rumsch
sachte sie "Ja, öh, weißt du, ich geh ja jetz arbeiten." Ja, dann hat se mir
sagen "Morgen regnet's", das weißt du ja gar nich B: ehen 107 A: aber, wen
Schwiegermutter. 123 B: Ja, kann man ja ma versuchen. A: Ja. B: Jaja, er w
sein. Das gilt für uns alle. Ich hab ja auch nen weiten Weg. Ne, wir könn al
sich wider Erwarten fühlt, können wer ja noch kurzfristig en Telefonanruf lo
sie ja noch keinem erzählt. Aber wär ja einlich Quatsch, warum sollte man da
sie möche! (lacht) 47 B: Das fänd se ja soo ekelhaft! A: (Ach so, em) wie w
Sobald ma verheiratet is, da hat man ja auch die Pflicht, so schnell wie mö
soll ma dat nich ausnutzen? A: (Könn ja später nochma fahren!) B: Wat sachs
sons irgendwie erfahrn, ich hatte das ja einfach heitshalber da einfach an d
und unter solchen Bedingungen ham wer ja nich geheiratet, ich finde, wer nac
unser Bestes daran und wir wolln das ja auch, aber . irgendwann wolln wer a
V en paar schöne Grüße, wir sehn uns ja dann sicher nächste Woche mal oder s
viel essen also, ich glaube, es gibt ja wohl kein, der auf der einen Seite,
vielleicht nen Tanzpartner, kann man ja nicht wissen! Ne? Dann is das sogar
wahrhaftig nit, du. A: (lacht). Soll ja eine ideale Grundlage für eine Ehe s
wer uns ma wieder ne? A: Ja, das war ja auch wirklich lange, ne? B: Ja. Jaj
Westerwald versunken, aber dann isser ja . doch wohl wieder da. A: Ja, er k
wörtlich übernehmen. A: Ja, ich kann ja nochma gucken, ob ich's in der Uni i
Z zusammengewesen, ich mein, wir tun ja unser Bestes daran und wir wolln da
zu wünschen! B: Prima, dann weiß ich ja da auch Bescheid. Den kann man nämi
! B: Ja, wenn's ja nichts frißt, kann ja auch hinten nix rauskommen! A: Jaj
! Ich ich gratulier' in jedem Fall, is ja von Erfolg gekrönt. B: (lacht) D:
(3s)) Aber es sind ja kleine, die sind ja nochnich so schlimm, oder? B: Ja,

) en Tag früher aufhörst, dann kannsde ja auch schließlich en Tag früher geh
, . sicher. 176 B: Ne, das werden Sie ja auch wohl tun, nich, Frau A? A: jaa
, aber trotzdem, war gut. A: Muß man ja mal was für sich tun! B: Hm A: son
, ach, is nich schlimm, ne? A: Jo, is ja ejal, ne. B: Ja, eben. lacht) A:
, alle zwei Stunden en Bus, da kannsde ja nich /da kanns du ja nich fahren. A
, B, wenn du Examen hast, dann mußt du ja noch ungefähr en Jahr auf nen Refer
, dann sei nich mehr so traurig, hilft ja nix. Ne, mein Kleines. Kommter zu u
, das is ja en anderes werden, das is ja kein Futur-werden. B: Jaja. A: Immer
, die weiß das. A: Hm. B: Und daß wär ja auch ne . also, ö, daß sc unter der
, ja. ... Ja, meine Mutter erzählt mir ja immer, seitdem ich hier in Köln wär
, was is Freitag? A: Ah, nee, das is ja nächsten Freitag bei Z diese Fete, d
, weißde. B: Ja. A: Nee, das fändich ja echt prima. B: Doch, ja, wenn ik da
, wennden auf 100.000 krist, kannsdes ja machen. A: Tja. ((2s)) Aber . ich w
, Y hat ja keine Rufbereitschaft, hat ja Urlaub. A: Ach so, ja, denn / denn
. 22 A: Ja. Ja, dann funktioniert das ja. B: Ja. A: Gut. B: Richtig. Und d
. B: Theoretisch nicht. A: Kann mich ja niemand zwingen,meine/ meine Anlagen
. C: Ja? B: Ich mein, kenns ja Y, is ja auch ziemlich schüchtern un zurückh
. C: Ob mit oder ohne Knubbel, wir ham ja jetz einmal erlebt, es klappt. Oder
. das kostet 5 Mark, nich, das kann ma ja tragen. 1 A: ((lacht)) Joa! Jo, wie
. Ich fürchte, nicht... Weil die Sache ja einmal schon ans Laufen gekommen is
. verheiratet war. A: Jaja.. Un es is ja auch so . bei . öh . den / ich mein,
... Vermutlich... Naja. 40 A: Wir ham ja auch so recht plötzlich geheiratet,
/ B: Nee, das glaub ich nich, die war ja so ferdig. Das wird vielleicht am b
: Ah so, dann habt ihr mehr! Ihr habt ja glaubich meistens mehr, wenn's schn
: Bißchen woll / naja, also da ham Se ja noch'n gutes Werk getan, wenn Ihre
: Das is das Normale... Dann weißt du ja, was du zu tun hast. B: Jo, weiß ic
: hm A: und jetz am Telefon merkt es ja keiner. B: Ja, eben! A: Und dann k
: Ja . das wär gut. B: Un Sie wissen ja, falls was dazwischen kommen sollte,
: Ja, dat is klar. Ich mein, da hasde ja überhaupt keine Zeit zu, da muß ers
: Ja? A: hoffe ich B: Naja, kann ich ja ma gucken, ob es da sowas gibt. Ja?
: Stell dir das mal vor! B: Das sind ja schlechte Aussichten! Denn ne eins m
: "Nein, also . Tampons, die würde sie ja nich nehmen, denn da müßte man ja,
: jugendlichen Leichtsinn kann man ihm ja wohl nicht unterstellen, ne, der wu
? B: Ja, sicher, dass klar, die mußde ja sowieso schreiben. A: ((Einatmen))
? B: Ja. Jaja, gut. Im Moment sin wer ja gleichaltrig, ne? Denk ich grad! A:
a, 600, oder was? A: Jaja, un ich hab ja noch / nee, ich hatte 710, aber ich
a, das kann ma ja nich, also, du kanns ja diese Assistentenzeit oder diese Ze
a, das wäre schwierig, dann müßte man ja für jede / Hilfskraft extra Abrechnu
a, wenner nich klar kommt, kanner mich ja anrufen. Dann würdich ma vorbeikomm
A: Hoch! B: Viel Betreuung haben Sie ja nich von uns zu erwarten. A: Ja, .
A: Ja. B: Jo, is gut, dann kanner Se ja ma anrufen, wenner Se braucht, ne.
aben Recht. ö, ö, natürlich, das wäre ja am allereinfachsten, daß ich auf die
aben? B: Jaja, sicher. A: Ja, dat is ja Grunde nur noch so ne Fortführung de
acht) A: (lacht) Stark! . Ja, ich bin ja auch schon fast en alter Ehekrüppel
acht, unda meinte der X, naja, es wär ja nich so schlimm bei ihm, er wollt ja
Ah so. B: Nich, ich werd ja, ich fahr ja mit dem Z zurück. A: Z? B: Das ist
Ah, so, an un für sich, da hätt er dir ja auch einreden können, du hättest se
al bei ihr vorbeigehn un dann könnwer ja überlegen, wies Beste is. B: Jaja,
ammenleben, aber / B: Ich überleg mir ja schon, ob ich das jemals en erstes M
angerufen. B: Nee? . Ja, sonst, könnt ja sein, ne, daß, wenn Se nit kommen,
ann euch das ma kurz erklären, ich bin ja hier auch dran. Ich füll das ja auc
ann ja bestimmt auch sehen, der U is ja sportinteressiert. A: Ah so, jo!
ann mach's jut, wa? A: Hm. .. Ich kann ja schlecht sagen, grüß die Familie! B:
ar ganz amüsant... Ja, und . dat ging ja ziemlich plötzlich mit der Verlobun
as daalles drin is, ne. A: Ja, das is ja zu verstehen, ja. Öh, ich würd's mir
as Thema noch erweitern / denn der is ja jetz ers mal weg bis zum 25., er me
aß er dann mal eben so tickt, das hat ja nicht zu sagen, ne. A: Ja? Hm. B:
aß ik später komme . und denn könn se ja meintwejen abflitzen ja meinetwegen
aub schon. C: Ja? B: Ich mein, kenns ja Y, is ja auch ziemlich schüchtern un
auch man ja nich einzuladen, die kommt ja von selbst! B: Ja, das kann /
auf keinenFall, ö,ö, für ihn, öm, dann ja unterbringen, nich? A: Ja. B: Das
B: (lacht) Ja, die Leute, die spinnen ja auch so. Sobald ma verheiratet is,
B: Wollmer hoffen, ne. A: (lacht) Is ja erst zwei Tage drin! B: Ja.. Ja, ve
ben auch nich! B: Meistens sitzen die ja im Bett, nich, oder in der Wand. A:
ben? Auf das T (=Zeitungsname) bin ich ja unheimich sauer. A: Ja? B: Die ham

besser. B: Naja, och, an sich hat set ja alles ganz gut überstanden, ne. A:
bis ik komme A: hm B: es handelt sich ja höchstens ma um ne Viertelstunde, da
C: Jaja, ich kenn den ja. B: Na, ich ja im Grunde auch. Da ham wer eben/ C:
ch mal drüber nachgedacht A: och, is ja/ B: aber, is schon ne schwierige An
chalthebel reintun. A: Hm. B: Es muß ja / darf / ich mein, der kann schon ma
ch'n gutes Werk getan, wenn Ihre Frau ja auch abjenomm / B: Oh, die hat mich
chon wieder längst vergessen, naja, is ja auch egal. B: ( ) Ich hab da einige
chst du morgen?" und so, und dann heiß ja, "ja, ich mache morgen das un das!"
chtig sein mit der Diagnose. Es kann ja sein/ en Flohstich is kreisrund und
ckkomme. A: Ah so. B: Nich, ich werd ja, ich fahr ja mit dem Z zurück. A: Z
d und so B: ja, mit Musik ham die das ja auch gemacht, hm, so Märsche und so
da rein, auch zwölf, ne. Ja, wir wolln ja da keine irre / nich irre irgendwie
da warst du nämlich schon weg. Du bis ja unheimlich früh diesmal gegangen", s
da, ne, an der Schule, das schien ihr ja ganz gut zu gefallen da. A: Jo, dan
darf doch nicht! Jaja, sicher, hab ich ja auch gesacht!... Und?.. Was macht e
de / , ich mein, schließlich . hab ich ja was von ihm gewollt, ich hätt ja hi
de ja nich, dann. C: Ja, nee, ich muß ja um ülf die ganzen Bücher abgeben. Da
der Schule, und dachte, das schaffsde ja nich beides, das is zuviel auf einma
der, oder so, ja. A: Ja, das hat man ja oft, ne, daß man dann mal, wenn man
dicht damit besprühen, nich, das geht ja dann weg, und dann das Zimmer, so r
du zur Uni kommen, aber das brauchsde ja nich, dann. C: Ja, nee, ich muß ja
e haben immer so viele / ich kann euch ja die Zeitungen immer geben, hör mal,
e Möglichkeit. A: .... Das brauch ich ja noch gar nich über/ bemerkt zu haben
e Zeit aussuchen. B: Hm. A: Aber is ja immerhin noch besser als . so um die
eben, genau! Vor allen Dingen, es geht ja gar nich um das Hochdeutsch reden!
edingungen. Ich weiß etau nich, dat is ja alles so kompliziert geworden, du.
ehabt un drittensmal, ja, jucken die ja nich so schrecklich. B: Ja. Das spr
ehydrate. A: Hm. ((3s)) Ja, euers hat ja wenigstens mehr Bewegung! B: Ja, ic
eider jetz och nit weiter! A: Tut mir ja furchtbar leid, aber ich nehm an, in
ein Bauch, ganz schmal/ B: Ja, ich wär ja mitgekommen, morgen!.. Aber um eins,
ellung der Semester A: Ja B: Das is ja vielleicht ein/ 13
en . einfach ma nur so vorbei / brauch ja nich lange denn sein! A: Ja. B: We
en die Nord-Süd-Fahrt, das kennen Sie ja auch? A: Jaja. B: Nord-Süd-Fahrt,
en Seite? B: Ja, links, ja. Rechts is ja unbebaut, da is das/ A: Ah so! B:
end, ne? A: Wir euch auch! Ne? B: Is ja nich viel im Fernsehen los, wir guck
ensch, das gibt es ja nich, die müssen ja knapp vor der Scheidung stehen, ne.
er melden müssen! B: Nee, dat reicht ja nun noch, ne! A: Ja? B: Ich hab so
er der will so viel absetzen, weil der ja als freier Mitarbeiter . gearbeitet
er hat man son Blähbauch! A: Kann man ja wieder rausschmeißen, die Zwiebeln,
er sagte, ach, Mann, in Finnland gibts ja viele Mücken, und die fliegen so d
er un dann... ah nee, dat Paßbild muß ja noch irgendwo hin A: Dat kannsde ja
er verrückt machen! B: Ach, ich kann ja keinen verrückt machen, ich mach das
erden auch einige sein!" . Nee, das is ja en anderes werden, das is ja kein F
es geglaubt, weißdu, an dem Abend war ja sowieso wieder leicht, na, wie nennt
esehen, lieber Gott nochmal! Da kriste ja graue Haare drüber, bis das klappt!
eso nimehr da, nehm ich an, die bleibt ja niet ne Stunde da stehn. Ja, was ma
Essen machen, so viel Arbeit wird das ja wohl nich geben, da machen wern paar
et man aber oft, du. ((3s)) Ich bin da ja auch immer skeptisch, wenn ich sowa
et, und so jung noch,und das/"da würde ja bald ein Kindchen auch nicht auf si
eu . Brück A: Ja B: Öh. Wenn Sie das ja nich wissen, wo das liegt, deswegen
findich gut! B: Joja. Neue kaufen hat ja keinen Sinn, denn irgendwann bin ic
ften schläft ((2s)) aber das tut ihr ja nich A: So dreckig is es bei uns ja
ganz davon abgesehen, nem. Ich seh das ja auch bei unheimlich vielen Bekannte
gültig weg zu sein A: Ja dann kannsde ja noch mal anrufen, falls ihr kommt. B
h mehr viel Zeit A: Ja B: Morgen is ja schon der letzte Tach/ für die Anmel
h bei der S un beim T, ne. Die hatten ja in ( ) gemacht, den Polterabend. Da
h bin ja hier auch dran. Ich füll das ja auch aus. B: Ja, müssen mer ma vorb
h in der Uni, ne. 159 C: Ja, ich kann ja auf jeden Fall mal bei ihr vorbeigeh
h mal en andermal machen, ich weiß es ja nich. Y hat jetz nur grade noch son
h so recht. B: (lacht) Ja, da muß man ja viele Sachen bei bedenken! A: Isch
h weiß nich, die/ die verstecken sich ja dann wahrscheinlich irgendwo! B: Ja
h, ersten Weihnachstag is meine Mutter ja fast gestorben, ne. Der Verlobte vo
h, höchstens verdursten, ne. Es trinkt ja auch nicht. B: Die wissen aber in
hasde weenstens freie Sicht, da hasde ja'n Scheibenwischer. A: Jaja B: Aber
haus? B: Ja? (lacht) Aber da warn wer ja no nich verheiratet. A: Ach so. Ja.

he Ansichten gekriegt, früher wär ich ja so'n nettes Mädchen gewesen. aber he
heschließung ( ). Ich mein, könnt ihr ja mal versuchen. Reise zu schwer erkra
hle, dann A: Die zählste mit, das hat ja nichts zu tun B: Ja, die zähl ich m
hm. B: für diese Klasse. A: Ja, das is ja leicht. B: Un die Zehn hat das auch
hon gesacht, also . unter ner eins is ja auf ne Assistentenstelle heutzutag n
ht, un hat gedacht "Ach, dann is der Z ja versorgt, wenn die A den ne Viertel
ianer sind die . Schwierigsten.. Sind ja Tertianer, Klasse neun und Klasse ze
ibung un so/ B: Nö, ich mein, das geht ja jetz . nich unbedingt mit um die Sc
ich angefaBt hat! B: Nee, so sah sie ja au nich aus! A: (lacht) Naja! B: N
ich hab die Fahrt bezahlt und es wäre ja nun schade, wenn es nich klappte. A
ich mal irgendwann ändert, kannsde das ja alles nachholen, dann kommen auf ei
ich normal. En andren Sinn hat die Ehe ja nich, ne. A: Ahja... Is ja en tota
ich so aus? A: Ja, also, er wird mich ja wohl nich grade dann nich verlänger
ich sowieso schon so sch/ ich hab das ja ma gemacht, nem A: Ja? B: und, öh,
ich, B. B: Ja, ich mein, du hast mich ja am Samstag gesehen! C: Ja, aber, wi
icher können wir zu euch kommen, Y hat ja keine Rufbereitschaft, hat ja Urlau
iegen, ö, in Französisch, nu weiß ich ja nit, ob Sie dat übersetzen müssen, o
iehungsweise einen Tag danach hab ich ja wieder zwei Familien verärgert, ne.
in Richtung Mühlheim, dann kommen Sie ja zunächst durch Ostheim, in Ostheim
in Berlin treffen, dann kann ich mich ja revanchieren. B: Ach, na, kommt jan
in der Universität, weißde, da laufen ja die unmöglichsten Typen rum, ne. A:
inige Worte, aber, na, die gebrauchste ja selten. A: Ja. Heute wußtich ma wi
inlich aber dann nich, die werden dann ja bestimmt auch sehen, der U is ja s
ion in Kalkar, ne. A: Hm. B: Da sind ja solche Sauereien geschrieben worden,
ir so interessante Briefe: Ja, das wär ja schön, so schnell verheiratet, und
irgendwie durchkommen, ich mein, sind ja so viele Kontrollen im Augenblick,
is furchbar. B: Ja, da is der Effekt ja oh ni mehr da! A: Ja, eben, genau!
is auch schrecklich, ne? Aber das geht ja schnell wieder! A: Is sehr schnell
it machen. A: Jaja, klar. B: Das is ja eben dat Doofe. ((Räuspern)) A: Sic
it, wo ich da angefangen hab, ich hab ja am ersten neunten ers angefangen, h
iwillig? B: (lacht) Ja, ich weeß immer ja nich, wo die sind. A: (lacht) B: Als
ja B: und es is ja, man hei/ wir sind ja mit dabei, es is ja nich so, daß ma
ja, da/ B: Der / der Richter, der muß ja heute / heutzutage alles machen, er
Ja, es läuft. B: Ja, ne. Es quietscht ja auch nich. A: Has ja nich umsonst d
Jahre! B: Fünf Jahre? Ach! . Naja, is ja gar nich so schlimm! A: Ich hätte n
l angefangen hab, ne, wo ich/ man muß ja immer weiter voraus sein, man muß s
l wir dachten, Silvester, da steht man ja erst gegen abend auf un zieht sich
lacht) A: (lacht) Ja, richtig, stimmt ja auch! (lacht) Ich vergeß das Ding a
lacht) B: Naja, so . ja, dann wirders ja auch verlängern . nur, du mußt dir
le Kontrollen im Augenblick, man weiß ja nie, ne B: ja A: ham wer vor, nach
le mere auch noch! B: Ja, den gibt es ja auch! Wird zwar en bißchen anders g
le, ne. A: hm B: Und / und, du kanns ja nich loslassen!.. Nee! Is doch helle
lein schaffen, der muß ja da / der hat ja als 122 freier Mitarbeiter gearbeite
lich Geld verdient, ne. Vorher das is ja au nich so besonders als Referendar.
llte man das keinem erzählen, das wär ja nichts Schlimmes! A: Ja, ne? B: Eb
ls war's . ganz ulkig. Aber .kann ich ja auch, wenn wer da sind, was länger e
lso/ B: is möglich A: Der./ der wird ja dann immer der Sündenbock bei allen
lt zu setzen, ne. A: Jaja. B: Das is ja schließlich normal. En andren Sinn h
m Automätchen, ne. Bis morgen hab ich ja sons nich mehr viel Zeit A: Ja B:
m Mittwoch. B: Mittwoch, ne, Sie sinn ja Montag, Dienstag nit da. A: Ja. B:
m wer noch vier Monate Zeit, wir hams ja Gott sei Dank früh genug gemerkt!"
m. Hab mich wahnsinnig gefreut. B: Is ja schön. Ja, wenn ik ma wieder vorbeik
m/ ja, in der Ausbildungsordnung steht ja, ein Monat hasde Schonfrist, brauch
ma am besten nich damit, denn . es hat ja auch keinen Sinn, ne. A: Ja, siche
man wieder fahrn, aber.. die brauchen ja'n Tach, bis se kapiert ham, daß se
mig . nich irgendwie was Großes, weils ja auch so viele sin un dann sehn wer
mit mir sprechen. C: Ja, nee, du weiß ja, worum's ging, ne. A: Jaja... Warte
mmert sich vielleicht, oder der U hat ja immer den Mann, der von S da ist, da
n dann auf jeden Fall im Lande, das is ja schon viel wert. Ja, mach ich gleic
n de angefangen has? B: Ja, ich kann ja auch jetz nich fottgehn hier, ne. A:
n macht das! B: Ja, ich mein, du siehs ja dann wahrscheinlich morgen die A no
n meinte se: "Ja, B, eins will ich dir ja sagen, es wird für dich jetz auch g
n wollte. A: Nich? Also eigenlich muß ja die ältere Schwester vor der jünger
n würde? B: Hm, nee, aber ik kann mir ja nich vorstellen, wie se dat verwend
n. A: Hm. B: Aber erstensmal wäre das ja doch eine . ziemliche finanzielle E

n. B: Hja, gute Lage, die kriecht man ja auch immer wieder los. A: Naja, abe
nach Hause, und so weiter! A: Hm.. Is ja auch nich grade viel! 112 B: Nö, als
nden drinstehn B: ja? A: aber das is ja genau das, was wir uns nich leisten
ne. Es quietscht ja auch nich. A: Has ja nich umsonst deine vielen werden von
ner A: (lacht) jaja. B: Bis jetz war ja noch nich sicher, ob's eine oder zwe
nerstag. A: Ja, oder . davor kann ich ja mittwochs auch noch. Und samstags o
nich lange denn sein! A: Ja. B: Weil ja / wenns mitten in der Woche is A: d
nich viel Ahnung! ((3s)) Aber es sind ja kleine, die sind ja nochnich so sch
nich weg, das, das/ C: Ach, B! Das muß ja dann fürchterlich aussehn, dann wirk
nich, nee. A: Ja, ich mein, ich hab's ja auch wieder aufgeschoben, ne. B: Wa
nlich nisch! B: Hm, naja, das kann ma ja nich, also, du kanns ja diese Assis
nner widder nich. B: Hm. Ja, undas is ja wahrscheinlich nich mehr, als du als
noch das Rauchen ein . stellt, das is ja ne, ne St / , dat is anne Folter. :
o B: (lacht) A: Doktor med, dat geht ja noch! B: (lacht).. Und was macht de
och . einlade! A: Ja, die brauch man ja nich einzuladen, die kommt ja von s
och / nee, ich hatte 710, aber ich hab ja jetz noch en Viertel meiner Stelle
och! B: Ja, ich weiB es nich, das war ja nur ne Frage, ne. Freitag, was is F
ohl nicht unterstellen, ne, der wußte ja, was er schrieb. Ja, und dann noch
ön sach ihr schöne Jrüße, wa, kann se ja allet selber nachher hörn. (lacht)
on nich mehr essen darf, dann muß man ja irgenwas anderes / D: Ach, ohne all
ons alles normal. A: Ja, du kanns dir ja unten drunt:er en Linienblatt legen.
orbei un würds ihm übersetzen, weiler ja sonst es nich mehr kriegt bis Mittwo
os, also / B: Och, ich mein, Steak is ja auch en Schlankheitsessen, ne. A: J
paar Wochen noch, ne, un dann müßtich ja schon wieder neue kaufen. C: Och, s
r sich! A: Ah, so! Na, dann kann man ja noch nichts sagen. Weiß du, wie's i
r das gleich festmachen, sons wird dat ja doch nix! Warte mal, Freitag bin ic
r findet au noch was Besseres, es muß ja nich von heute auf morgen sein. Ich
r ja nich A: So dreckig is es bei uns ja nun wieder auch nich B: Nee, eben (
r ja nich so schlimm bei ihm, er wollt ja sowieso an die Schule, aber an der
r normal, wie der aussah! A: Ich will ja den X immer überreden, mit mir Gymna
r sehr schön. A: Un hinterher kann se ja weiter sehn, dann B: Mann, Frau Dok
r Welt schaffen könn wer die Flugzeuge ja nich A: Neenee, irgendwas hat man i
ra Abrechnung führen und . die werden ja pauschal bezahlt, da gibt es sonst
rd hinten immer dicker! B: Ja, wenn's ja nichts frißt, kann ja hinten ni
rde A: Au! B: und, öh, aus mir würde ja nie was, wenn ich nen eigenen Haush
rholt haben, mittlerweile, die kriegt ja bloß noch Quark un sowas! C: (lacht)
rig sein B: (lacht) Ja nun, wird sich ja wohl nich vermeiden lassen, ne. Irg
rin. B: Ja, ich auch. C: Da is die A ja wirklich . im Vorteil. B: Ja, vor a
rlin nich. A: Deshalb trifft sich das ja so gut! Ich kann immer direkt am 31
rn is es sicher! A: Ja, also, das wär ja schlimm! B: Ach nee, wär mir auch n
rn wer direkt tanzen gegangen. Du bis ja auch vielleicht ne Type! B: Och, je
rochen, aber ich glaub, also, sie war ja schon ma vorher da, ne, an der Schul
rückhaltend,ne. C: Jaja, ich kenn den ja. B: Na, ich ja im Grunde auch. Da h
s kann immer wat passieren und es muß ja morgen glatt gehen, weißde, ich hab
's noch, so, vor allen Dingen will sie ja promovieren jetz, undann brauch se
s! B: Nö? A: Nö! B: Könnwer ja essen gehn! A: Ja. B: In der Quell
s, B: (lacht) A: man selbst kann das ja nich so beurteilen B: hm 111 A: Naj
sätzlich, das hieß immer:" Aber das is ja zusätzliche Arbeit!", un dann war d
se auch nich verkaufen, ne. A: Ja. Is ja unverschämt, was die für Einstellplä
segnen. "Ja", hamse gesacht, könnt er ja machen. Undda hat er das auch gemac
sehr schön. A: Hjo! B: Aber könn mer ja alles ma sehn, ne? A: Ja. B: Ja, A
selber auch A: Aha! Ja, doch, das wär ja interessant. B: Also, für, öh, Fami
sie ja nich nehmen, denn da müßte man ja, em . seinen eigenen Körper berühre
so kalorienarm kocht. D: So, ja,ja is ja klar, wat is denn da groß / B: So d
so mit den Flohstichen, das krieg ich ja nun leider nich mehr mit, wies weit
so un rechts dann das Paßbild, das muß ja oh noch drauf A: Ja, B: Ah, ich ha
ß ja noch irgendwo hin A: Dat kannsde ja irgendwo an ne Ecke kleben B: Ja, w
ste noch! B: Hmhm. A: Ja, das reicht ja auch, solang das noch bleibt, so B:
ster verlobe!" "Ja", sagtse "du weißt ja, der Onkel von ihm, der is . öh . Pa
strationen, ne. B: Naja, in Kalkar is ja absolut nichts passiert, ne. A: Hm.
streut, daß man rumfahren kann. B: Is ja sehr schön, an sich. Die Z wollte mi
t die Ehe ja nich, ne. A: Ahja... Is ja en totaler Quatsch, nur um Steuern z
t nich zurück." A: Ah so! B: Bin ich ja froh, daß das Kind nich mitgefahren
t! Da muß ich mal da anrufen! Ich kann ja immer . als Hausgespräch anrufen, d
t, ham schon wat anderes, das ham wer ja en bißchen kurzfristig gemacht, ne.

te den doch auflösen? B: Das hab ich ja versucht! Ich hab da heißes Wasser r
tisches Urteil bilden A: dann hörste ja auch verschiedene Sachen, ne. B: Ac
ts mehr fest ausgemacht, un ich wußte ja auch gar nich, wohin um sechs! B: J
tterbrote! B: (lacht) Ja, nu, ich muß ja wissen, ob ich nun was essen soll v
ttich en Flatterhemd an! C: das liegt ja klar an meinem Zustand, daß ich das
u das? A: ((3s)) Ja.. ja... Ich hatte ja damals das mit der Schule, und dach
überhaupt denn schwierig, ne. Der hat ja denn Angst, du könns ihm ürgendwie s
uch günstig nach Gummersbach, ne. Muß ja ab 1.2. nach Gummersbach. A: Ja. Fr
uch nich, wo / und außerdem, sie wird ja nich da wie angenagelt gestanden /
ück? A: Jaja. B: Ahso .. Jo, wir sin ja jetz . einigermaßen eingerichtet, al
ukünftijet jetz / A: Ja, jetz weißdes ja, jetz is eh zu spät! B: Ja, isch kö
un am Bauch auch abgenommen, ich sach ja, acht Zentimeter Bauch sind weg! C:
Und dann meinte sie, ja, das hätte sie ja noch keinem erzählt. Aber wär ja ei
ung sacht, vielleicht wär das was, is ja ganz schön. Das Haus so gefällt mir
ung? B: Mit der Bezahlung? Na, du bis ja lustik, da wird nischt bezahlt! A:
upt, das wird lange dauern, der kommt ja dann nich mehr raus, aus dPm Keller
ür uns aus. A: Hm, jaja B: und es is ja, man hei/ wir sind ja mit dabei, es
ur! B: Ja, nur, ne! A: Sons hattesdu ja noch viel mehr! B: Ja! Aber ganz gr
war jetz längere Zeit nich da, ich war ja . sechs Wochen in Urlaub' A: Toll,
wenn denn sowas hörst!.. Jaa, ich hab ja auch en sehr . angenehmes Weihnachts
werden! B: Es is so mit dem Z, der is ja an der Anlage, an der Eisenbahnanla
Woche irsendwann mal sagen? Ihr könnt ja denn auch zu uns kommen, A. Ihr könn
Woche, ja 108 A: ja, ia B: ach so, is ja noch ne janze Woche Zeit! A: Ja, sch
X einladen will, ja un von mir is das ja nich viel, ich glaube nich, daß ich
y Maus-Hefte auf Englisch, ne, gibt's ja auch jede Menge. B: Ach so, die hab
ymnastik zu machen, aber da denkt der ja nicht dran! B: Ja, dat will ich auch
zu mir kommen, wo ich wohne, weiß sie ja. A: Is gut. B: Ich bin zuhause, ja?
B: ((lacht)) A: Aber der Termin war ja rum! Den hab ich am zehnten bekomme
Troisdorf? B: (lacht) Ja. A: Das is ja irre! Da wolln wir ja hin ziehen! B:
! B: (hoffen, vielleicht) Is ja bald! Kanns vielleicht aber irgendw
((Anfang fehlt auf Band)) A: der is ja noch ganz neu (lacht) B: ja, aber d
) Ja. A: Das is ja irre! Da wolln wir ja hin ziehen! B: Jaa. Is das sicher?
31. feiern, abends. B: Ja, eben. dass ja wirklich Klasse! A: Hm. Ja, hoffent
as klappt! A: Ja? B: Das isja / datis ja tierisch! A: .. Och, das is echt ne
ch keinen Sinn, ne. A: Ja, sicher. Is ja klar! B: Denn . allmählich ermüdet
ch nee, du magst das ja nich/ du darfs ja nich! B: Nöö, ich mag schon, ich da
der so. B: Ja, Mensch, das häuft sich ja! . Woma sehn, wie wir über die Rund
e Viertel. B: nur ne Viertel! Das wär ja ne Möglichkeit! A: Und dann hätte e
e. Zweienhalb Jahre. B: Ah so, das is ja schnell! A: Zweienhalb oder drei B:
en un anzuziehen / 70 B: Is ja gut! Paß ma auf, dann kann ich ja ma
ensuppe zu Butterbroten. B: Hmhm, is ja . reichhaltig! A: Spaghetti is auch
is jedes Mal dran, ne. A: Och, das is ja schlimm! B: Neulich hat se mir erzä
lacht) ja. B: Hm... Nee, das find ich ja lustig! . Aber ich glaub, das kann
lls isses 110 Quadratmeter A: 110! Is ja irre! Wir ham nur 90! B: In nem gep
m. Denk ich auch, Mensch, das gibt es ja nich, die müssen ja knapp vor der S
men, und es sich angucken, das klingt ja sehr gut! (lacht) Öh, is es so/ ach
nn fürchterlich aussehn, dann wirkder ja noch dicker! B: Nein, der wirkt nich
s Thema steht jetz fest A: Ja, das is ja gut B: ( ) A: Naja, und jetz liest
schon solange her? A: Ja! B: Poh! Is ja Wahnsinn! ((3s)) A: Ich würd's nich
ster noch ma? A: Ja! B: Ach, du has ja Geburtstag! A: Die Tatsache, daB ic
Type! B: Och, jetz bin ich's! (Das is ja!) C: Du bis alles schuld! B: (lach
tzt für 3 Tage 400 Mark A: Bo! B: is ja echtes Geld! Meine Schwester macht a
urück, oder wie? C: Ja, genau! B: Is ja praktisch!.. Schade, ich wär ma gern
wo versteckt haben. 189 A: Das gibt's ja gar nich! B: Hm. ((3s)) A: Naja. B:
zelabmachung treffen. A: Hoch, das is ja ärgerlich! B: Ja, das is sehr ärger

V. Total occurrences

	DSK		**FKO**		**PFE**		**BRO**	
	occ	**txts**	**occ**	**txts**	**occ**	**txts**	**occ**	**tx ts**
ABER	1198	70	3399	220	2489	386	387	30
AUCH	1618	70	4899	218	7284	386	415	27
BLOSS	23	16	78	38	138	74	28	10
DENN	333	64	993	181	2403	350	160	27
DOCH	593	58	1671	184	1790	347	174	21
EBEN	469	58	1214	171	1597	308	88	20
EH	9	7	5	5	15	8	18	8
EIGENTLICH	317	47	549	149	1007	290	13	10
EINFACH	164	39	424	126	266	142	27	11
ERST	123	37	348	127	591	251	22	16
ETWA	109	29	489	127	349	142	6	3
HALT	99	26	105	58	307	92	8	8
JA	3955	70	9348	205	7077	386	1481	35
MAL	674	64	1279	164	2020	332	412	33
NUR	513	65	1795	199	1637	366	109	26
RUHIG	26	11	41	27	39	34	7	4
SCHON	486	69	1385	202	2346	384	174	27
SOWIESO	33	23	51	35	47	39	36	15
ÜBERHAUPT	140	46	456	135	524	247	46	17
VIELLEICHT	335	58	981	179	817	281	72	20
WOHL	94	39	297	119	593	219	57	18

Bibliography

Aarts, Jan M. G. / Meijs, Willem 1984. *Corpus linguistics: recent developments in the use of computer corpora in English language research*. Amsterdam: Rodopi.

Abraham, Werner (ed.) 1991. Special Issue: Discourse particles across languages. *Multilingua*. 10, 1/2.

Abraham, Werner 1991a. Discourse Particles in German: how does their illocutionary force come about? In Werner Abraham (ed.), *Discourse Particles*. Amsterdam; Philadelphia: John Benjamins, 203-252.

Abraham, Werner 1991b. Modal particle research. The state of the art. *Multilingua* 10, 1/2, 9-15.

Aijmer, Karin 1997. I think - an English modal particle. In Swan and Westvik (eds.), 1-47.

Aijmer, Karin / Altenberg, Bengt (eds.) 1991. *English corpu linguistics: studies in honour of Jan Svartvik*. London; New York: Longman.

Al-Wadi, Doris 1994. *COSMAS - Ein Computersystem für den Zugriff auf Textkorpora. Version R.1.3-1*. Mannheim: Institut für deutsche Sprache.

Asbach-Schnitker, Brigitte 1977. Die Satzpartikel *wohl*. Eine Untersuchung ihrer Verwendungsbedingungen im Deutschen und ihrer Wiedergabemöglichkeiten im Englischen. In Weydt (ed.), 38-61.

Bakhtin, Mikhail 1986. *The dialogic imagination*. Trans. C. Emerson and M. Holquist. (M. Holquist, ed.) Austin: University of Texas Press.

Beerbom, Christiane 1991. *Modalpartikeln als Übersetzungsproblem. Eine kontrastive Studie zum Sprachenpaar Deutsch - Spanisch*. (Heidelberger Beiträge zur Romanistik 26) Frankfurt a.M.; Bern; New York: Peter Lang.

Berglund, Ylva 1999. Exploiting a large corpus: an end-user's way to the BNC. *International Journal of Corpus Linguistics* 4/1, 29-52.
Bialystok, Ellen 1993. Symbolic representation and attentional control in pragmatic competence. In Kasper *et al.* (eds), 43-59.
Biber, Douglas 1988. *Variation across speech and writing*. Cambridge: Cambridge University Press.
Biber, Douglas / Conrad, Susan / Finegan, Edward, *et al.* 1999. *Longman grammar of spoken and written English*. London; New York: Longman.
Biber, Douglas / Conrad, Susan / Reppen, Randi 1994. Corpus-based approaches to issues in applied linguistics. *Applied Linguistics* 15/2, 169-189.
Biber, Douglas / Conrad, Susan / Reppen, Randi 1998. *Corpus linguistics. Investigating language structure and use*. Cambridge: Cambridge University Press.
Billmyer, Kristine 1990. "I really like your lifestyle": ESL learners learning how to complement. *Pennsylvania Working Papers in Educational Linguistics* 6/2, 31-48.
Blum-Kulka, Shoshana / House, Juliane / Kasper, Gabriele (eds.) 1989. *Cross-Cultural Pragmatics: Requests and Apologies*. Norwood, N.J.: Ablex.
Blum-Kulka, Shoshana / Olshtain, Elite 1984. A cross-cultural study of speech act realization patterns (CCSARP). *Applied Linguistics* 5/3, 196-213.
Borst, Dieter 1985. *Die affirmativen Modalpartikeln* doch, ja *und* schon. *Ihre Bedeutung, Funktion, Stellung und ihr Vorkommen*. Tübingen: Niemeyer.
Bouton, L. F. 1994. Conversational implicature in a second language: learned slowly when not deliberately taught. *Journal of Pragmatics* 22, 157-167.
Breen, Michael P. / Candlin, Christopher N. 1980. The essentials of a communicative curriculum for language teaching. *Applied Linguistics* 1/2, 89-112.
Brettschneider, Gunter / Lehmann, Christian (eds.) 1980. *Wege zur Universalienforschung: sprachwissenschaftliche Beiträge zum 60. Geburtstag von Hansjakob Seiler*. Tübingen: Narr.

Brindley, Geoff 1987. Verb tenses and TESOL. In Nunan (ed.), 173-204.

Brons-Albert, Ruth 1984. *Gesprochenes Standarddeutsch: Telefondialoge*. Tübingen: Günter Narr.

Brown, Gillian / Yule, George 1983. *Discourse analysis*. Cambridge; New York: Cambridge University Press.

Brown, Penelope / Levinson, Stephen C. 1987. *Politeness: some universals in language usage*. Cambridge; New York: Cambridge University Press.

Bublitz, Wolfram G. 1977. Deutsch "aber" als Konjunktion and als Modalpartikel. In Sprengel *et al.* (eds.), 199-209.

Bublitz, Wolfram G. 1978. *Ausdrucksweisen der Sprechereinstellung*. Tübingen: Niemeyer.

Burkhardt, Armin 1989. Partikelsemantik. In Weydt (ed.), 354-369.

Busse, Dietrich 1992. Partikeln im Unterricht Deutsch als Fremdsprache. *Muttersprache* 102/1, 37-59.

Bußmann, Hadumod 1990. *Lexikon der Sprachwissenschaft*. Stuttgart: Kröner.

Butt, David / Fahey, Rhondda / Feez, Susan, *et al.* 1995. *Using Functional Grammar*. Sydney: NCELTR.

Butt, David / Fahey, Rhondda / Feez, Susan, *et al.* 2000. *Using Functional Grammar*. Sydney: NCELTR.

Bygate, Martin / Skehan, Peter / Swain, Merrill 2001. *Researching pedagogic tasks: second language learning, teaching, and testing*. Harlow, England; New York: Longman.

Candlin, Christopher N. 1987. Beyond description to explanation in cross-cultural discourse. In Smith (ed.), 22-35.

Candlin, Christopher N. 2001. Afterword: Taking the curriculum to task. In Bygate *et al.* (eds.), 229-242.

Carter, Ronald / McCarthy, Michael 1997. *Exploring spoken English*. Cambridge; New York: Cambridge University Press.

Cheon-Kostrzewa, Bok-Ja / Kostrzewa, Frank 1997a. Der Erwerb der deutschen Modalpartikeln. Ergebnisse aus einer Longitudinalstudie (I). *Deutsch als Fremdsprache* Heft 2, 86-92.

Cheon-Kostrzewa, Bok-Ja / Kostrzewa, Frank 1997b. Der Erwerb der deutschen Modalpartikeln. Ergebnisse aus einer Longitudinalstudie (II). *Deutsch als Fremdsprache* Heft 3, 150-155.

Conrad, Susan 2000. Will corpus linguistics revolutionize grammar teaching in the 21 century? *TESOL Quarterly* 34, 548-560.

Coseriu, Eugenio 1980. Partikeln und Sprachtypus. Zur strukturell-funktionellen Fragestellung in der Sprachtypologie. In Brettschneider *et al.* (eds.), 199-206.

Coulmas, Florian 1981. *Conversational routine: explorations in standardized communication situations and prepatterned speech*. The Hague; New York: Mouton de Gruyter.

Coulmas, Florian 1981. Introduction: Conversational routine. In Coulmas (ed.), 1-17.

Coulthard, Malcolm 1985. *An introduction to discourse analysis*. Harlow, England; New York: Longman.

Dallapiazza, Rosa-Maria / Jan, Eduard von / Schönherr, Til 1998. *Tangram. Deutsch als Fremdsprache. Kursbuch 1*. Ismaning: Hueber.

Dalmas, Martine 1990. Partikelforschung 'konkret'. *Deutsch als Fremdsprache* 27/5, 285-289.

Dalmas, Martine 1992. Bewertung durch Partikeln. *Deutsch als Fremdsprache* 29/2, 90-95.

Dardano, Maurizio / Dressler, Wolfgang U. / Held, Gudrun 1983. *Parallela: Akten des 2. Österreichisch-Italienischen Linguistentreffens 1982*. Tübingen: Gunter Narr.

De Vriendt, Sera / Vandeweghe, Willy / Van de Craen, Piet 1991. Combinatorial aspects of modal particles in Dutch. *Multilingua* 10 1/2, 43-59.

Diewald, Gabriele 1997. *Grammatikalisierung. Eine Einführung in Sein und Werden grammatischer Formen*. Tübingen: Niemeyer.

Dodd, Bill 1997. Exploiting a corpus of written German for advanced language learning. In Wichmann *et al.* (eds.), 131-145.

Dodd, Bill (ed.) 2000. *Working with German corpora*. Birmingham: Birmingham University Press.

Eggins, Suzanne 1994. *An introduction to systemic functional linguistics*. London: Pinter Publishers.

Færch, Claus / Kasper, Gabriele 1983. *Strategies in interlanguage communication*. London; New York: Longman.

Færch, Claus / Kasper, Gabriele 1989. Interlanguage request modification. In Blum-Kulka *et al.* (eds.), 221-247.

Fairclough, Norman 1995. *Critical discourse analysis: the critical study of language*. London; New York: Longman.

Feyrer, Cornelia 1998. *Modalität im Kontrast: Ein Beitrag zur übersetzungsorientierten Modalparttikelforschung anhand des Deutschen und des Französischen*. Frankfurt a.M.; Bern; New York: Peter Lang.

Fligelstone, Steven 1993. Some reflections on the question of teaching, from a corpus linguistics perspective. *ICAME Journal* 17, 97-109.

Foolen, Ad 1983. Zur Semantik und Pragmatik der restriktiven Gradpartikeln: *only*, *nur* und *maar/alleen*. In Weydt *et al.* (eds.), 188-202.

Franck, Dorothea 1979. Abtönungspartikel und Interaktionsmanagement. Tendenziöse Fragen. In Weydt (ed.), 3-13.

Franck, Dorothea 1980. *Grammatik und Konversation*. Königsstein/ Ts.: Scriptor.

Freundenberg-Findeisen, Renate (ed.) 1999. *Ausdruckgrammatik versus Inhaltsgrammatik: lingusitische und didaktische Aspekte der Grammatik*. München: Iudicium.

Gardner, Robert C. / Lambert, Wallace E. 1972. *Attitudes and motivation in second-language learning*. Rowley, Mass.,: Newbury House Publishers.

Gornik-Gerhardt, Hildegard 1981. *Zu den Funktionen der Modalpartikel "schon" und einiger ihrer Substituentia*. Tübingen: Gunter Narr.

Götze, Lutz 1993. Modalpartikeln aus der Sicht der Sprachlehr- und Sprachlernforschung. *Deutsch als Fremdsprache* 30/4, 227-232.

Götze, Lutz / Hess-Lüttich, Ernst WB 1989. *Grammatik der deutschen Sprache. Sprachsystem und Sprachgebrauch*. München: Lexikographisches Institut.

Graefen, Gabriele 1999. Eine streitbare Partikel: DOCH. In Freundenberg-Findeisen (ed.), 111-128.

Grice, H.P. 1968. Utterer's meaning, sentence-meaning and word-meaning. *Foundations of Language* 4, 1-18.

Halliday, M. A. K. 1978. *Language as social semiotic: the social interpretation of language and meaning*. London: Edward Arnold.
Halliday, M. A. K. 1985. *An introduction to functional grammar*. London; New York: Edward Arnold.
Halliday, M. A. K. 1994. *An introduction to functional grammar*. 2nd ed. London; New York: Edward Arnold.
Halliday, M. A. K. / Hasan, Ruqaiya 1976. *Cohesion in English*. London; New York: Longman.
Halliday, M. A. K. / Hasan, Ruqaiya 1985. *Language, context and text: aspects of language in a social-semiotic perspective*. Waurn Ponds, Vic: Deakin University Press.
Harden, Theo / Rösler, Dietmar 1981. Partikeln und Emotionen - zwei vernachlässigte Aspekte des gesteuerten Fremdsprachenerwerbs. In Weydt (ed.), 67-80.
Hartmann, Dietrich 1977. Aussagesätze, Behauptungshandlungen und die kommunikativen Funktionen der Satzpartikeln *ja*, *nämlich* und *einfach*. In Weydt (ed.), 101-114.
Hartmann, Dietrich 1979. Syntaktische Funktionen der Partikeln *eben*, *eigentlich*, *einfach*, *nämlich*, *ruhig*, *vielleicht* und *wohl*. Zur Grundlegung einer diachronischen Untersuchung von Satzpartikeln im Deutschen. In Weydt (ed.), 121-138.
Helbig, Gerhard 1977. Partikeln als illokutive Indikatoren im Dialog. *Deutsch als Fremdsprache* 14/1, 30-43.
Helbig, Gerhard 1988. *Lexikon deutscher Partikeln*. Leipzig: Verlag Enzyklopädie.
Helbig, Gerhard 1989. Die Partikeln - keine Wortklasse, eine Wortklasse oder mehrere Wortklassen? *Germanistisches Jahrbuch DDR-UVR* 8/194-209.
Helbig, Gerhard 1994. *Lexikon deutscher Partikeln*. 2nd. ed. Leipzig; Berlin; München: Langenscheidt.
Helbig, Gerhard / Helbig, Agnes 1995. *Deutsche Partikeln - richtig gebraucht?* Leipzig; Berlin; München: Langenscheidt.
Held, Gudrun 1983. "Kommen Sie *doch*" oder "Venga *pure*". Bemerkungen zu den pragmatischen Partikeln im Deutschen und Italienischen am Beispiel auffordernder Sprechakte. In Dardano *et al.* (eds.), 316-336.

Hentschel, Elke 1986. *Funktion und Geschichte deutscher Partikeln : ja, doch, halt und eben*. Tübingen: Niemeyer.

Hentschel, Elke / Weydt, Harald 1989. Wortartenprobleme bei Partikeln. In Weydt (ed.), 3-18.

House, Juliane 1989. Politeness in English and German: The functions of *please* and *bitte*. In Blum-Kulka *et al.* (ed.), 96-122.

House, Juliane 1996. Developing pragmatic fluency in English as a foreign language: Routines and metapragmatic awareness. *Studies in Second Language Acquisition* 18/2, 225-252.

House, Juliane / Kasper, Gabriele 1981. Politeness markers in English and German. In Coulmas (ed.), 157-186.

Husso, Aila 1981. Zum Gebrauch von Abtönungspartikeln bei Ausländern. In Weydt (ed.), 81-99.

Jacobs, Joachim 1986. Abtoenungsmittel als Illokutionstypsmodifikatoren. *Groninger Arbeiten zur Linguistik* 27, 100-111.

Jiang, Minhua 1994. *Deutsche Modalpartikeln als Lehr- und Lernproblem im Fach Deutsch als Fremdsprache für Ausländer mit didaktischen Überlegungen*. Frankfurt a.M.; Bern; New York: Peter Lang.

Johns, Tim / King, Philip (eds.) 1991. *Classroom Concordancing*. English Language Research Journal. Birmingham: Birmingham University Press.

Jones, Randall L. 1997. Creating and using a corpus of spoken German. In Wichmann *et al.* (eds.), 146-156.

Kasper, Gabriele 1981. *Pragmatische Aspekte in der Interimsprache*. Tübingen: Gunter Narr.

Kasper, Gabriele 1984. Pragmatic comprehension in learner-native speaker discourse. *Language Learning* 34/4, 1-20.

Kasper, Gabriele 1996. Introduction: Interlanguage Pragmatics in SLA. *Studies in Second Language Acquisition* 18/2, 145-148.

Kasper, Gabriele 2000. *Four perspectives on L2 pragmatic development*. (Revised version of a plenary given at the annual AAAL conference; March 2000) Vancouver.

Kasper, Gabriele 2001. Four perspectives on L2 pragmatic development. *Applied Linguistics* 22/4, 502-530.

Kasper, Gabriele / Blum-Kulka, Shoshana (eds.) 1993. *Interlanguage pragmatics*. New York: Oxford University Press.

Kasper, Gabriele / Dahl, Merete 1991. Research methods in interlanguage pragmatics. *Studies in Second Language Acquisition* 13/2.

Kasper, Gabriele / Rose, Kenneth R. 1999. Pragmatics and SLA. *Annual Review of Applied Linguistics* 19, 81-104.

Kasper, Gabriele / Rose, Kennneth R. 2001. Introduction. Pragmatics in language teaching. In Kasper *et al.* (eds.), 1-9.

Kasper, Gabriele / Schmidt, Richard 1996. Developmental issues in interlanguage pragmatics. *Studies in Second Language Acquisition* 18/2, 149-170.

Kemme, Hans-Martin 1979. "Ja", "denn", "doch" usw. Die Modalpartikeln im Deutschen. Erklärungen und Übungen für den Unterricht an Ausländer. In, *Projekt Lehrschwierigkeiten im Fach 'Deutsch als Fremdsprache'*. München: Goethe Institut, Arbeitsstelle für wissenschafliche Didaktik.

Kennedy, Graeme D. 1998. *An introduction to corpus linguistics*. London; New York: Longman.

Klein, Eberhard / Pouradier Duteil, Françoise / Wagner, Karl Heinz (eds.) 1991. *Betriebslinguistik und Linguistikbetrieb*. Akten des 24. Linguistischen Kolloquiums, Universitèat Bremen, 4.-6. September 1989. 2 vols. Tübingen: Niemeyer.

König, Ekkehard 1977. Modalpartikeln in Fragesätzen. In Weydt (ed.), 115-130.

König, Ekkehard / Requardt, Susanne 1991. A relevance-theoretic approach to the analysis of modal particles in German. *Multilingua* 10 1/2, 63-77.

König, Ekkehard / Requardt, Susanne / Stark, Detlef 1990. *Adverbien und Partikeln. Ein deutsch-englisches Wörterbuch*. Heidelberg: Julius Groos Verlag.

König, Ekkehard / Stark, Detlef 1987. Function words in a bilingual German-English dictionary: A new approach. *Lexicographica* 3, 158-177.

Kosaka, Koichi 1989. Abtönungspartikel *denn* und Satznominalisiserung. In Weydt (ed.), 160-170.

Kriwonossow, Alexej 1977a. *Die modalen Partikeln in der deutschen Gegenwartssprache*. Göppingen: Kümmerle.

Kriwonossow, Alexej 1977b. Deutsche Modalpartikeln im System der unflektierten Wortklassen. In Weydt (ed.), 176-216.

Kriwonossow, Alexej 1989. Zum Problem der Klassifizierung der deutschen Partikeln. In Weydt (ed.), 30-38.

Kummer, Manfred 1984. *Modalpartikeln*. Bonn: Internationes.

Kutsch, Stefan 1985. Zur Entwicklung des deutschen Partikelsystems im ungesteuerten Zweitspracherwerb ausländischer Kinder. *Deutsche Sprache* 3, 230-257.

Lakoff, George / Johnson, Mark 1990. *Metaphors we live by*. Chicago: University of Chicago Press.

Laurillard, Diana 1993. *Rethinking university teaching: a framework for the effective use of educational technology*. London; New York: Routledge.

Leech, Geoffrey 1991. The state of the art in corpus linguistics. In Aijmer *et al.* (eds.), 8-29.

Leech, Geoffrey 1997. Teaching and language corpora - a convergence. In Wichmann *et al.* (eds.), 1-23.

Leech, Geoffrey N. 1983. *Principles of pragmatics*. London; New York: Longman.

Levinson, Stephen C. 1983. *Pragmatics*. Cambridge; New York: Cambridge University Press.

Liedke, Martina 1994. *Die Mikro-Organisation von Verständigung. Diskursuntersuchungen zu deutschen und griechischen Partikeln*. Frankfurt a.M.; Bern; New York: Peter Lang.

Lightbown, Patsy 1983. Exploring relationships between developmental and instructional sequences in L2 acquisition. In Seliger *et al.* (eds.), 217-245.

Luchtenberg, Sigrid 1987. “Mein Vater war vielleicht wütend”. Zur Partikel vielleicht und ihrer Vermittlung an ausländische Deutschlerner(innen). *Deutsche Sprache* 15, 1-24.

Luchtenberg, Sigrid 1989. Partikeln und Alltagswissen. In Weydt (ed.), 661-672.

Lütten, Jutta 1979. Die Rolle der Partikeln doch, eben und ja als Konsensus-Konstitutiva in gesprochener Sprache. In Weydt (ed.), 30-38.

Macheiner, Judith 1991. *Das grammatische Varieté*. Frankfurt a.M.: Eichborn.

Martin, Jim R. / Matthiessen, Christian / Painter, Clare 1997. *Working with Functional Grammar*. London; New York: Arnold.

Masi, Stefania 1996. *Deutsche Modalpartikeln und ihre Entsprechungen im Italienischen*. Frankfurt a.M.; Bern; New York: Peter Lang.

May, Corinna 2000. *Die Deutschen Modalpartikeln. Wie übersetzt man sie (dargestellt am Beispiel von eigentlich, denn und überhaupt),wie lehrt man sie?* Frankfurt a.M.; Bern; New York: Peter Lang.

McCarthy, Michael / Carter, Ronald 1994. *Language as discourse: perspectives for language teaching*. London; New York: Longman.

McCarthy, Michael J. 1993. Spoken Discourse Markers in Written Text. In Sinclair *et al.* (eds.), 170-182.

McEnery, Tony / Wilson, Andrew 2001. *Corpus linguistics*. Edinburgh: Edinburgh University Press.

Meibauer, Jörg 1994. *Modaler Kontrast und konzeptuelle Verschiebung*. Tübingen: Niemeyer.

Mey, Jacob 1993. *Pragmatics: an introduction*. Oxford, UK: Blackwell.

Möllering, Martina / Nunan, David 1995. Pragmatics in Interlanguage: German Modal Particles. *Applied Language Learning* 6/1&2, 41-64.

Molnár, Anna 2002. *Die Grammatikalisierung deutscher Modalpartikeln*. Frankfurt a.M.; Bern; New York: Peter Lang.

Morris, Pam (ed.) 1994. *The Bakhtin reader: selected writings of Bakhtin, Medvedev, and Voloshinov*. London; New York: Arnold.

Muhr, Rudolf 1989. Zur Didaktik der Modalpartikel im Unterricht Deutsch als Fremdsprache. In Weydt (ed.), 645-660.

Nehls, Dietrich 1989. German modal particles rendered by English auxiliary verbs. In Weydt (ed.), 282-292.

Nekula, Marek 1996. *System der Partikeln im Deutschen und Tschechischen. Unter besonderer Berücksichtigung der Abtönungspartikeln*. Tübingen: Niemeyer.

Nunan, David (ed.) 1987. *Applying second language acquisition research*. Adelaide: National Curriculum Resource Centre.

Nunan, David 1989. *Understanding language classrooms: a guide for teacher-initiated action*. London: Prentice-Hall.

Nunan, David 1991. Methods in second language classroom-oriented research. A critical review. *Studies in Second Language Acquisition* 13, 249-274.

Nunan, David 1992. *Research methods in language learning*. Cambridge: Cambridge University Press.

Nunan, David 1995. Closing the gap between learning and instruction. *TESOL Quarterly* 29/1, 133-158.

Orth-Chambah, Jutta / Perlmann-Balme, Michaela / Schwalb, Susanne 1999. *em. Abschlusskurs. Deutsch als Fremdsprache für die Mittelstufe*. (Arbeitsbuch) Ismaning: Hueber.

Palmer, F. R. 1986. *Mood and modality*. Cambridge: Cambridge University Press.

Paneth, E. 1981. Partikeln im Unterricht - Erfahrungen mit englischen Studenten. In Weydt (ed.), 101-110.

Pérennec, Marcel 1989. *Nur*: funktionale Vielfalt und semantische Einheit. In Weydt (ed.), 451-463.

Perlmann-Balme, Michaela / Schwalb, Susanne / Weers, Dörte 2000. *em. Abschlusskurs. Deutsch als Fremdsprache für die Mittelstufe*. Ismaning: Hueber.

Pica, Teresa 1985. The selective impact of classroom instruction on second language acquisition. *Applied Linguistics* 6/3, 214-222.

Rall, Marlene 1981. ¿Se puede ensenar la necesidad de emplear particulas intencionales? Ein Experiment mit spanischen Studenten. In Weydt (ed.), 123-136.

Rehbein, Jochen 1979. Sprechhandlungsaugmente. Zur Organisation der Hörersteuerung. In Weydt (ed.), 58-74.

Richards, Jack C. / Platt, John Talbot / Weber, Heidi 1985. *Longman dictionary of applied linguistics*. Harlow, England; New York: Longman.

Rose, Kenneth R. 2000. An Exploratory Cross-Sectional Study of Interlanguage Pragmatic Development. *Studies in Second Language Acquisition* 22/1, 27-68.

Rose, Kenneth R. / Kasper, Gabriele 2001. *Pragmatics in language teaching*. New York: Cambridge University Press.

Rösler, Dietmar 1982. Teaching German Modal Particles. *International Review of Applied Linguistics* 20/1, 33-38.
Rösler, Dietmar 1983. Der Erwerb der Abtönungspartikeln im institutionalisierten Lernprozeß Deutsch als Fremdsprache. In Weydt *et al.* (eds.), 291-300.
Rudolph, Elisabeth 1989. Partikeln in der Textorganisation. In Weydt (ed.), 498-510.
Rudolph, Elisabeth 1991. Relationships between particle occurrence and text types. *Multilingua* 10 1/2, 203-223.
Rüschoff, Bernd / Wolff, Dieter 1999. *Fremdsprachenlernen in der Wissensgesellschaft. Zum Einsatz der neuen Technologien in Schule und Unterricht*. Ismaning: Hueber.
Rutherford, William E. 1987. *Second language grammar: learning and teaching*. London; New York: Longman.
Sacks, Harvey / Schegloff, Emanuel A. / Jefferson, Gail 1974. A simplest systematics for the organisation of turn-taking for conversation. *Language* 50/4, 696-735.
Schiffrin, Deborah 1987. *Discourse markers*. Cambridge: Cambridge University Press.
Schiffrin, Deborah 1994. *Approaches to discourse*. Oxford, UK: Blackwell.
Schneider, Ulrike 1996. Die Thema-Rhema-Gliederung im Deutschen und ihre Bedeutung für den Unterricht des Deutschen als Fremdsprache. *Deutsch als Fremdsprache* 33/2, 78–85.
Scollon, Ronald / Scollon, Suzanne B. K. 1981. *Narrative, literacy, and face in interethnic communication*. Norwood, N.J.: Ablex.
Scott, Mike / Johns, Tim 1993. *MicroConcord*. Oxford: Oxford University Press.
Searle, John R. 1969. *Speech acts: an essay in the philosophy of language*. Cambridge: Cambridge University Press.
Seliger, Herbert W. / Long, Michael H. 1983. *Classroom oriented research in second language acquisition*. Rowley, MA: Newbury House.
Sigley, Robert 1997. Text categories and where you can stick them: a crude formality index. *International Journal of Corpus Linguistics* 2/3, 199-237.

Sinclair, John 1991. *Corpus, Concordance, Collocation*. Oxford: Oxford University Press.

Sinclair, John 1997. Corpus evidence in language description. In Wichmann *et al.* (eds.), 27-39.

Sinclair, John / Hoey, Michael / Fox, Gywneth, *et al.* (eds.) 1993. *Techniques of description: spoken and written discourse. A festschrift for Malcolm Coulthard*. London; New York: Routledge.

Smith, Larry E. 1987. *Discourse across cultures: strategies in world Englishes*. New York: Prentice-Hall.

Sprengel, Konrad / Bald, Wolf-Dietrich / Viethen, Heinz Werner 1977. *Semantik und Pragmatik*. Tübingen: Niemeyer.

Steinmüller, Ulrich 1981. Akzeptabilität und Verständlichkeit - Zum Partikelgebrauch von Ausländern. In Weydt (ed.), 137-148.

Stubbs, Michael 2001. Texts, corpora, and problems of interpretation: a response to Widdowson. *Applied Linguistics* 22/2, 149-172.

Svartvik, Jan 1992. *Directions in corpus linguistics*. (Proceedings of Nobel Symposium 82, Stockholm, 4-8 August 1991) Berlin; New York: Mouton de Gruyter.

Swan, Toril / Westvik, Olaf Jansen 1996. *Modality in Germanic languages: historical and comparative perspectives*. Berlin; New York: Mouton de Gruyter.

Tannen, Deborah 1984. The pragmatics of cross-cultural communication. *Applied Linguistics* 5/3, 189-195.

Tarone, Elaine / Yule, George 1989. *Focus on the language learner: approaches to identifying and meeting the needs of second language learners*. Oxford: Oxford University Press.

Thomas, Jenny 1983. Cross-cultural pragmatic failure. *Applied Linguistics* 4/2, 91-112.

Thomas, Jenny 1984. Cross-cultural discourse as 'unequal encounter': towards a pragmatic analysis. *Applied Linguistics* 5/3, 226-235.

Thomas, Jenny / Short, Mick 1996. *Using corpora for language research: studies in honour of Geoffrey Leech*. London; New York: Longman.

Thurmair, Maria 1989. *Modalpartikeln und ihre Kombinationen*. Tübingen: Niemeyer.

Thurmair, Maria 1991a. Zum Gebrauch der Modalpartikel "denn" in Fragesätzen. Eine korpusbasierte Untersuchung. In Klein *et al.* (eds.), 377-387.

Thurmair, Maria 1991b. 'Kombinieren Sie doch nur ruhig auch mal Modalpartikeln!': Combinatorial regularities for modal particles and their use as an instrument of analysis. *Multilingua* 10 1/2, 19-42.

Thurstun, Jennifer / Candlin, Christopher N. 1997. *Exploring academic English: a workbook for student essay writing.* Sydney: National Centre for English Language Teaching and Research.

Tribble, Chris / Jones, Glyn 1990. *Concordances in the classroom.* Harlow, England; New York: Longman.

Trömel-Plötz, Senta 1979. "Männer sind eben so": Eine linguistische Beschreibung von Modalpartikeln aufgezeigt an der Analyse von dt. *eben* und engl. *just*. In Weydt (ed.), 318-334.

Van Lier, Leo 1996. *Interaction in the language curriculum: awareness, autonomy, and authenticity.* London; New York: Longman.

Voloshinov, Valentin. N. 1973. *Marxism and the philosophy of language.* Trans. L. & I.R.Titunik Matejka. New York: Seminar Press.

Vorderwülbecke, Klaus 1981. Progression, Semantisierung und Übungsformen der Abtönungspartikeln im Unterricht Deutsch als Fremdsprache. In Weydt (ed.), 149-160.

Vorderwülbecke, Klaus / Vorderwülbecke, Anne 1995. *Stufen International 1. Lehr- und Arbeitsbuch.* München: Klett.

Weinrich, Harald / Thurmair, Maria / Breindl, Eva, *et al.* (eds.) 1993. *Textgrammatik der deutschen Sprache.* Mannheim: Dudenverlag.

Weiss, Walter E. / Wiegand, Herbert E. / Reis, Marga (eds.) 1986. *Textlinguistik contra Stilistik? Wortschatz und Wörterbuch. Grammatische oder pragmatische Organisation von Rede.* Tübingen: Niemeyer.

Westheide 1991. Dutch maar and North German man - on their use as downtoning particles in related speech economies. *Multilingua* 10 1/2/123-138.

Weydt, Harald 1969. *Abtönungspartikel. Die deutschen Modalwörter und ihre französischen Entsprechungen*. Bad Homburg: Gehlen.

Weydt, Harald (ed.) 1977. *Aspekte der Modalpartikel. Studien zur deutschen Abtönung*. Tübingen: Niemeyer.

Weydt, Harald 1977a. Ungelöst und strittig. In Weydt (ed.), 217-225.

Weydt, Harald 1979. *Die Partikeln der deutschen Sprache*. Berlin; New York: Mouton de Gruyter.

Weydt, Harald 1981. *Partikeln und Deutschunterricht: Abtönungspartikeln für Lerner des Deutschen*. Heidelberg: Julius Groos Verlag.

Weydt, Harald 1981a. Partikeln im Rollenspiel von Deutschen und Ausländern. In Weydt (ed.), 161-166.

Weydt, Harald (ed.) 1983. *Partikeln und Interaktion*. Tübingen: Niemeyer.

Weydt, Harald 1983a. *Aber*, *mais* und *but*. 148-159.

Weydt, Harald 1986. Betonungsdubletten bei deutschen Partikeln. In Weiss *et al.* (eds.), 391-403.

Weydt, Harald (ed.) 1989. *Sprechen mit Partikeln*. Berlin; New York: Mouton de Gruyter.

Weydt, Harald 1989a. Partikelfunktionen und Gestalterkennen. In Weydt (ed.), 330-345.

Weydt, Harald / Ehlers, Klaas-Hinrich 1987. *Partikelbibliographie. Internationale Sprachenforschung zu Partikeln und Interjektionen*. Frankfurt a.M.; Bern; New York: Peter Lang.

Weydt, Harald / Harden, Theo / Hentschel, Elke, *et al.* 1983. *Kleine deutsche Partikellehre*. Stuttgart: Klett.

Weydt, Harald / Hentschel, Elke 1983. "Kleines Abtönungswörterbuch". In Weydt *et al.* (ed.), 3-24.

Wichmann, Anne / Fligelstone, Steven / McEnery, Tony, *et al.* (eds.) 1997. *Teaching and language corpora*. London; New York: Longman.

Widdowson, H.G. 2000. On the limitations of linguistics applied. *Applied Linguistics* 21/1, 3-25.

Widdowson, H.G. 2001. Interpretations and correlations: a reply to Stubbs. *Applied Linguistics* 22/4, 531-538.

Wierzbicka, Anna 1985. Different cultures, different languages, different speech acts. Polish vs English. *Journal of Pragmatics* 9/2-3, 145-178.
Wierzbicka, Anna 1986. Introduction (Special Issue on Particles ed. by A. Wierzbicka). *Journal of Pragmatics* 10, 519-534.
Wierzbicka, Anna 1991. *Cross-Cultural Pragmatics. The semantics of human interaction*. Berlin; New York: Mouton de Gruyter.
Wildner-Bassett, Mary E. 1984. *Improving pragmatic aspects of learners' interlanguage: a comparison of methodological approaches for teaching gambits to advanced adult learners of English in industry*. Tübingen: Gunter Narr.
Willing, Ken 1992. *Talking it through*. Sydney: National Centre for English Learning, Teaching and Research.
Wolski, Werner 1989. Modalpartikeln als einstellungsregulierende lexikalische Ausdrucksmittel. In Weydt (ed.), 346-353.
Zifonun, Gisela / Hoffmann, Ludger / Strecker, Bruno 1997. *Grammatik der deutschen Sprache Bd. 2*. (Schriften des Instituts für deutsche Sprache, Bd.7.2) Berlin; New York: Walter de Gruyter.
Zimmermann, Klaus 1981. Warum sind die Modalpartikeln ein Lernproblem? In Weydt (ed.), 111-122.

Index

Linguistic Insights

Studies in Language and Communication

This series aims to promote specialist language studies, both in the fields of linguistic theory and applied linguistics, by publishing volumes that focus on specific aspects of language use in one or several languages and provide valuable insights into language and communication research. A cross-disciplinary approach is favoured and most European languages are accepted.

The series includes two types of books:

- **Monographs** – featuring in-depth studies on special aspects of language theory, language analysis or language teaching.
- **Collected papers** – assembling papers from workshops, conferences or symposia.

Vol. 1 Maurizio Gotti & Marina Dossena (eds.)
Modality in Specialized Texts. Selected Papers of the 1st CERLIS Conference. 421 pp. 2001.
ISBN 3-906767-10-8. US-ISBN 0-8204-5340-4

Vol. 2 Giuseppina Cortese & Philip Riley (eds.)
Domain-specific English. Textual Practices across Communities and Classrooms.
420 pp. 2002.
ISBN 3-906768-98-8. US-ISBN 0-8204-5884-8

Vol. 3 Maurizio Gotti, Dorothee Heller & Marina Dossena (eds.)
Conflict and Negotiation in Specialized Texts. Selected Papers of the 2nd CERLIS Conference. 470 pp. 2002.
ISBN 3-906769-12-7. US-ISBN 0-8204-5887-2

Vol. 4 Maurizio Gotti, Marina Dossena, Richard Dury, Roberta Facchinetti & Maria Lima
Variation in Central Modals. A Repertoire of Forms and Types of Usage in Middle English and Early Modern English.
364 pp. 2002.
ISBN 3-906769-84-4. US-ISBN 0-8204-5898-8

Vol. 5 Stefania Nuccorini (ed.)
Phrases and Phraseology. Data and Descriptions.
187 pp. 2002.
ISBN 3-906770-08-7. US-ISBN 0-8204-5933-X

Vol. 6 Vijay Bhatia, Christopher N. Candlin & Maurizio Gotti (eds.)
Legal Discourse in Multilingual and Multicultural Contexts. Arbitration Texts in Europe.
385 pp. 2003.
ISBN 3-906770-85-0. US-ISBN 0-8204-6254-3

Vol. 7 Marina Dossena & Charles Jones (eds.)
Insights into Late Modern English.
378 pp. 2003.
ISBN 3-906770-97-4. US-ISBN 0-8204-6258-6

Vol. 8 Maurizio Gotti
Specialized Discourse. Linguistic Features and Changing Conventions.
351 pp. 2003.
ISBN 3-03910-027-0. US-ISBN 0-8204-6263-2

Vol. 9 Alan Partington, John Morley & Louann Haarman (eds.)
Corpora and Discourse.
420 pp. 2004.
ISBN 3-03910-026-2. US-ISBN 0-8204-6262-4

Vol. 10 Martina Möllering
The Acquisition of German Modal Particles. A Corpus-Based Approach
290 pp. 2004.
ISBN 3-03910-043-2. US-ISBN 0-8204-6273-X

Vol. 11 David Hart (ed.)
English Modality in Context. Diachronic Perspectives.
261 pp. 2003.
ISBN 3-03910-046-7. US-ISBN 0-8204-6852-5

Vol. 12 Wendy Swanson
Modes of Co-reference as an Indicator of Genre.
430 pp. 2003.
ISBN 3-03910-052-1. US-ISBN 0-8204-6855-X

Vol. 13 Gina Poncini
Discursive Strategies in Multicultural Business Meetings.
338 pp. 2004.
ISBN 3-03910-222-2. US-ISBN 0-8204-7003-1

Editorial address:

Prof. Maurizio Gotti Università di Bergamo, Facoltà di Lingue e Letterature Straniere,
Via Salvecchio 19, 24129 Bergamo, Italy
Fax: 0039 035 235136, E-Mail: m.gotti@unibg.it